Alpha Nu Society
purchased
Dec 21. 1853

ORATIONS AND SPEECHES.

BY

CHARLES SUMNER.

VENIET FORTASSE ALIUD TEMPUS, DIGNIUS NOSTRO, QUO, DEBELLATIS ODIIS, VERITAS TRIUMPHABIT. HOC MECUM OPTA, LECTOR, ET VALE.

Leibnitz.

IN TWO VOLUMES.

VOL. II.

BOSTON:
TICKNOR, REED, AND FIELDS.
M DCCC L.

BOSTON:
THURSTON, TORRY & COMPANY, PRINTERS,
DEVONSHIRE STREET.

CONTENTS.

VOL. II.

THREE TRIBUTES OF FRIENDSHIP.

THE WAR SYSTEM OF THE COMMONWEALTH OF NATIONS. AN ADDRESS BEFORE THE AMERICAN PEACE SOCIETY, AT ITS ANNIVERSARY IN BOSTON, MAY 28, 1849.

That it may please Thee to give to all nations unity, peace, and concord. — The Litany.

What angel shall descend, to reconcile
The Christian States, and end their guilty toil? — Waller.

"I look upon the way of *treaties*, as a retiring from fighting like beasts, to arguing like men, whose strength should be more in their understandings than in their limbs."— CHARLES I. *Eikon Basilike*.

"We daily make great improvements in natural — there is one I wish to see in moral — philosophy; the discovery of a plan that would induce and oblige nations to settle their disputes without first cutting one another's throats. When will human reason be sufficiently improved to see the advantage of this?" — FRANKLIN.

"La même politique qui lie, pour leur bonheur, toutes les familles d'une nation les unes avec les autres, doit lier entre elles toutes les nations, qui sont des familles du genre humain. Tous les hommes se communiquent, même sans s'en douter, leurs maux et leurs biens, d'un bout de la terre à l'autre."— BERNARDIN DE ST. PIERRE.

"Only the toughest, harshest barbarism of past ages — War — remains yet to be vanquished by our innate anti-barbarism. There is a growing insight of its unlawfulness."— JEAN PAUL.

"War is on its last legs; and a universal peace is as sure as is the prevalence of civilization over barbarism, of liberal governments over feudal forms. The question for us is only, *How soon?*" — EMERSON.

EXTRACT FROM THE SOCIETY'S RECORDS.

"*Voted*, That the thanks of this Society be given to Mr. Sumner, for his able and eloquent Address; that a copy be requested for the press, and that efforts be made to give it the widest circulation possible."

A true copy.

Attest, WM. C. BROWN, *Rec. Sec.*

THE WAR SYSTEM

OF THE COMMMONWEALTH OF NATIONS.

Mr. President and Gentlemen, — We are now assembled in what may be called the Holy Week of our community; not occupied by the pomps of a complex ceremonial, swelling in tides of music, beneath time-honored arches; but set apart, according to the severe simplicity of early custom, to the Anniversary meetings of the various associations of charity and piety, from whose good works our country derives such true honor. Each association is distinct. Within the folds of each are gathered its own peculiar members, devoted to its own peculiar objects; and yet all are harmonious together; for all are inspired by one sentiment, the welfare of the united Human Family. Each has its own distinct orbit, a pathway of light, while all together constitute a system which moves in a still grander orbit.

Of all these associations, there cannot be one so comprehensive as ours. The prisoner in his cell, the slave in his chains, the sailor on his ocean wanderings, the Pagan on his distant continent or island, and the ignorant here at home, will all be commended to you by eloquent voices. I need not tell you to listen to these voices, and to answer to their appeal. But, while mindful of all these interests, justly claiming your care, it is my special and most grateful duty to-night, to commend to you that other cause — the great cause of Peace — which, in its Christian embrace, enfolds the prisoner, the slave, the sailor, the ignorant, all mankind; which, to each of these charities, is the source of strength and light, I may say of life itself, as the sun in the heavens.

Peace is the grand Christian charity, the fountain and parent of all other charities. Let Peace be removed, and all other charities sicken and die. Let Peace exert her gladsome sway, and all other charities quicken into celestial life. Peace is a distinctive promise and possession of Christianity. So much is this the case, that, where Peace is not, Christianity cannot be. There is nothing elevated which is not exalted by Peace. There is nothing valuable which does not contribute to Peace. Of wisdom herself it has been said, that all her ways are pleasantness, and all her paths are Peace. Peace has ever been the longing and aspiration of the noblest souls — whether for themselves or for their country. In the bitterness of exile, away from the Florence which he has immortalized by his Divine Poem, pacing the cloisters of a convent, in response to the inquiry of the monk, — "What do you seek?" Dante said, in words distilled from his heart, *Peace, peace.* In the memorable English struggles, while King and Parliament were rending the land, a gallant supporter of the monarchy, the chivalrous Falkland, touched by the intolerable woes of war, cried in words which consecrate his memory more than any feat of arms, *Peace*, *peace*, *peace*. Not in aspiration only, but in benediction is this word uttered. As the apostle went forth on his errand, as the son left his father's roof, the choicest blessing was, *Peace be with you*. As the Saviour was born, angels from Heaven, amidst quiring melodies, let fall that supreme benediction, never before vouchsafed to the children of the Human Family, *Peace on earth and good will towards men*.

To maintain this charity, to promote these aspirations, to welcome these benedictions, is the object of our Society. To fill men in private life with all those sentiments, which make for Peace; to animate men in public life to the recognition of those paramount principles, which are the safeguards of Peace; above all, to teach the True Grandeur of Peace, and to unfold the folly and wickedness of the INSTITUTION of War and of the whole WAR SYSTEM, now recognized and established by the COMMONWEALTH OF NATIONS, as the mode of determining *international* controversies; — such is the object of our Society.

There are persons, who sometimes allow themselves to speak of associations like ours, if not with disapprobation, at least with levity and distrust. A writer, so humane and genial as Robert Southey, has left on record a gibe at the "Society for the Abolition of War," saying, that "it had not obtained sufficient notice even to be in disrepute." It is not uncommon to hear our aims characterized as visionary, impracticable, Utopian. It is sometimes hastily said that they are contrary to the nature of man; that they require for their success a complete reconstruction of his character; and that they necessarily assume in him qualities, capacities, and virtues, which do not belong to his existing nature. This mistaken idea was once strongly expressed by the remark, that "an Anti-War Society seemed as little practicable as an anti-thunder-and-lightning society."

It cannot be doubted that these objections, striking at the heart of our cause, have exerted great influence over the public mind. They proceed often from persons of unquestioned sincerity and goodness, who would rejoice to see the truth as we see it. But plausible as they may appear to those who have not properly meditated this subject, I cannot but regard them — I believe, that all who will candidly listen to me to-night will hereafter regard them — as prejudices, without foundation in reason or religion, which must yield to a plain and careful examination of the precise objects of our society, and of the movement which it represents.

Let me not content myself, in response to these critics, by the easy answer, that, if our aims are visionary, impracticable, Utopian, then the unfulfilled promises of the prophecies are vain; then the Lord's Prayer, in which we ask that God's kingdom shall come on earth, is a mockery; then Christianity is a Utopia. Let me not content myself by reminding you, that all the great reforms, by which mankind have been advanced, have encountered similar objections; that the abolition of the punishment of death for theft was first suggested in the Utopia of Sir Thomas More; that the efforts to abolish the crime of the slave trade were opposed almost in our day, as impracticable and visionary; in short, that all the endeavors for human improvement, for knowledge, for freedom, for virtue, that all the great causes which dignify human history,—which save it from being a mere protracted War Bulletin, a common sewer, a *Cloaca Maxima*, flooded with perpetual uncleanness — have been pronounced Utopian, while, in spite of distrust, of prejudice, of enmity, all these causes have gradually found acceptance, as they gradually became understood, and the Utopias of one age have become the realities of the next.

Satisfactory to many minds as such an answer might be, I cannot content myself on this occasion with leaving our cause on such grounds. I desire to meet directly the objections which have been made, and by a careful exposition of our precise objects, to show that these objects are in no respect visionary; that the cause of Peace does not depend for its success upon any reconstruction of the human character, or upon holding in check the general laws of man's nature; but that it deals with man as he exists, according to the experience of history; and above all, that the immediate and particular aim of our Society, the abolition by the Commonwealth of Nations of the Institution of War, and of the whole War System, as an *established* Arbiter of Right, is as practicable, as it would be beneficent.

And I begin by carefully putting aside several questions, which have often occupied much attention, but which an accurate analysis of our position shows to be independent of the true issue. Their introduction has heretofore perplexed the discussion, by transferring to the great cause of International Peace the doubts by which they have been encompassed.

One of these is the alleged right, appertaining to each individual, to take the life of an assailant in order to save his own life — compendiously called the *right of self-defence*, usually recognized by philosophers and publicists as founded in nature, and in the instincts of men. The exercise of this right is carefully restrained to cases where life itself is placed in actual jeopardy. No defence of property, no vindication of what is called *personal honor*, justifies this extreme resort. Nor does this right imply the right of attack; for instead of attacking one another for injuries past or impending, men need only have recourse to the proper tribunals of justice. There are, however, many most respectable persons, particularly of the denomination of Friends — some of whom I may now have the honor of addressing — who believe that the exercise of this right, even thus limited, is in direct contravention of high Christian precepts. Their views find faithful utterance in the writings of Jonathan Dymond, of which at least this may be said, that they strengthen and elevate, even if they do not always satisfy the understanding. "I shall be asked," says Dymond, — "suppose a ruffian breaks into your house, and rushes into your room with his arm lifted to murder you, do you not believe that Christianity allows you to kill him? This is the last resort of the cause. My answer to it is explicit — *I do not believe it.*" But while thus candidly and openly avowing this extreme sentiment of non-resistance, he is careful to remind the reader, that the case of the ruffian does not practically illustrate the true character of war, unless it appears that war is undertaken simply for the preservation of life, when no other alternative remains to a people than to kill or to be killed.

But according to this view, the robber on land, who places his pistol at the breast of the traveller, the pirate who threatens life on the high seas, and the riotous disturber of the public peace, who puts life in jeopardy at home, cannot be opposed by the sacrifice of life. Of course, all who subscribe to this renunciation of the privilege of self-defence, must join with us in efforts to abolish the Arbitrament of War. But our appeal is addressed to the larger number, who make no such application of the Christian precepts, who recognize the right of self-defence as belonging to each individual, and who believe in the necessity at times of sorrowfully exercising this right, whether against a robber, a pirate, or a mob.

Another question, closely connected with that of self-defence, is the alleged *right of revolt, or of revolution.* Shall a people endure political oppression or the denial of Freedom, without resistance? The answer to this question will necessarily affect the rights of three millions of fellow-men, held in slavery in our country. If such a right unqualifiedly exists — and sympathy with our fathers, and with the struggles for Freedom now agitating Europe, must make us hesitate to question its existence — then these three millions of fellow-men, into whose souls we thrust the iron of the deadliest bondage the world has yet witnessed, would be justified in resisting to death the power that holds them in fetters. A popular writer on Ethics, Dr. Paley, has said: "It may be as much a duty, at one time, to resist government, as it is at another, to obey it, to wit, whenever more advantage will, in our opinion, accrue to the community from resistance, than mischief. The lawfulness of resistance, or the lawfulness of a revolt, does not depend alone upon the grievance which is sustained or feared, but also upon the probable expense and event of the cause." * This view distinctly recognizes the right of resistance, but limits it by the chances of success, founding it on no higher ground than expediency. A right, thus vaguely defined and bounded, must be invoked at any time with reluctance and distrust. The lover of Peace, while admitting, that, in the present state of the world, an exigency may unhappily arise for its exercise, must confess the inherent barbarism of such an agency, and admire, even if he cannot entirely adopt, the sentiment of Daniel O'Connell: "Remember that no political change is worth a single crime, or above all, a single drop of human blood."

But these questions I put aside; not as unimportant, not as unworthy of the most careful consideration; but as unessential to the establishment of the great cause which I have so much at heart. If I am asked — as the advocates of Peace are often asked — whether a robber, a pirate, a mob may be resisted by the sacrifice of life, I answer that they may be so resisted — mournfully, necessarily. If I am asked, if I sympathize with the efforts for freedom now finding vent in rebellion

* Principles of Moral and Political Philosophy, Book VI. cap. 4.

and revolution, I cannot hesitate to say, that, wherever Freedom struggles, wherever Right is, there my sympathies must be. And I believe I may speak, not only for myself, but for our Society, when I add, that, while it is our constant aim to diffuse those sentiments which promote good will in all the relations of life; which exhibit the beauty of Peace everywhere, in the *internal* concerns, as well as in the *international* relations, of States; and while we especially recognize that grand central truth, the Brotherhood of Mankind, in the clear light of whose far-darting beams all violence among men becomes dismal and abhorred, as among brothers; it is nevertheless no part of our purpose to question the right to take life in honest self-defence, or when the public necessity distinctly requires it, nor to question the justifiableness of resistance to urgent outrage and oppression. On these several points there are individual diversities of opinion among the friends of Peace, which our Society, confining itself to efforts for the overthrow of War, is not necessarily called upon to determine.

Waiving, then, these matters, which have often thrown perplexity and difficulty over our cause, making many hesitate, I come now to the precise object which we hope to accomplish, *the Abolition of the Institution of War, and of the whole War System as an established Arbiter of Justice in the Commonwealth of Nations.* In the accurate statement of our aims, you will at once perceive the strength of our position. Much is always gained by a clear understanding of the question in issue; and the cause of Peace unquestionably suffers often, because it is misrepresented, or not fully comprehended. In the hope of removing this difficulty, I shall *first* unfold the true character of War and of the War System, involving the question of Preparations for War, and the question of a Militia. The way will then be open, in the *second* branch of this Address, for a consideration of the means by which this system can be overthrown. And here I shall pass in review the tendencies and examples of nations, and the efforts of individuals, constituting the Peace Movement, with the auguries of its triumph, briefly touching, at the close, on our duties to this great cause, and on the vanity of Military Glory.

I. And, first of War and the War System in the Commonwealth of Nations. By the Commonwealth of Nations I understand the Fraternity of Christian States, recognizing a Common Law to regulate their relations with each other, usually called the Law of Nations. This law being established by the consent of nations is not necessarily the law of all nations, but only of such as recognize it. The Europeans and the Orientals often differ with regard to its provisions; nor would it be proper to say that the Ottomans, or the Mahomedans in general, or the Chinese, had ever become parties to it. The substantial elements of this law are drawn from the law of nature, from the truths of Christianity, from the usages of nations, and from the written texts or enactments of treaties. Thus, in its origin and growth, it is not unlike the various systems of municipal jurisprudence, all of which may be referred to kindred sources.

It is often said, by way of excuse for the allowance of war, that nations are independent, and acknowledge no *common superior*. It is true, indeed, that they are politically independent, and acknowledge no common political sovereign. But they acknowledge a common superior of unquestioned influence and authority, whose rules they cannot disobey. This acknowledged common superior is the Law of Nations. It were superfluous to dwell at length upon the opinions of publicists and jurists in confirmation of this view. "The Law of Nations," says Vattel,* a classic in this department, "is not less *obligatory* with respect to states, or to men united in political society, than to individuals." An eminent English authority, Lord Stowell,† says, "The *Conventional Law of Mankind*, which is evidenced in their practice, *allows* some and *prohibits* other modes of destruction." A recent German jurist ‡ says, "A nation associating itself with the general society of nations, *thereby recognizes a law common to all nations*, by which its international relations are to be regulated." Lastly, a popular English moralist, whom I have already quoted, and to whom I refer because his name is so familiar, Dr. Paley,§ says, that the principal part of what is called the Law of Nations derives its obligatory character "*simply from the fact of its being established, and the general duty of conforming to established rules* upon questions, and between parties, where nothing but *positive regulations* can prevent

---

* Law of Nations, Preface.

† Robinson's Rep. Vol. I. p. 140.

‡ Heffler, quoted in Wheaton's Elements, Part I. cap. 1, § 7.

§ Philosophy, Book VI. cap. 12.

difficulties, and where disputes are followed by such destructive consequences."

The Law of Nations is, then, the Supreme Law of the Commonwealth of Christian States, governing their relations with each other, determining their reciprocal rights, and sanctioning the remedies for the violation of these rights. To the Commonwealth of Nations, this Law is what the Constitution and Municipal Law of Massachusetts are to the associate towns and counties, composing this State, or rather, by an apter illustration, what the Federal Constitution of our Union is to the thirty sovereign States, which now recognize it as the supreme law.

But the Law of Nations — and I now come to a point of great importance in the clear understanding of the subject — while anticipating and providing for controversies between nations, recognizes and establishes War as the final Arbiter of these controversies. It distinctly says to the nations, "If you cannot agree together, then stake your cause upon the *Trial by Battle*." And it proceeds to define, at no inconsiderable length, under the name of Laws of War, the rules and regulations of this combat. "The Laws of War," says Dr. Paley, "are part of the Law of Nations, and founded, as to their authority, upon the same principle with the rest of that code, namely, upon the fact of their being *established*, no matter when or by whom."

It is not uncommon to speak of the *practice* of War, or the *custom* of War, a term adopted by that devoted friend of our cause, the late Noah Worcester. Its apologists and expounders have called it "a judicial trial," — "one of the highest trials of right" — "a process of justice" — "a prosecution of our rights by force" — "a mode of condign punishment" — "an appeal for justice" — "a mode of obtaining rights." I prefer to characterize it as an INSTITUTION, established by the Commonwealth of Nations, as an Arbiter of Justice. As slavery is an Institution, growing out of local custom, sanctioned, defined, and established by the municipal law, so War is an Institution, growing out of general custom, sanctioned, defined, and established by the Law of Nations.

It is only when we contemplate War in this light, that we are fully able to perceive its combined folly and wickedness. Let me bring this still further home to your minds. Boston and Cambridge are adjoining towns, separated by the river Charles. In the event of controversies between these different jurisdictions, the municipal law has established a judicial tribunal, and not War, as the Arbiter. And, ascending in the scale, in the event of controversies between two different counties, as between Essex and Middlesex, the same municipal law has established a judicial tribunal, and not War as the Arbiter. And, ascending yet higher in the scale, in the event of controversies between two different sovereign States of our Union, the Federal Constitution has established a judicial tribunal, the Supreme Court of the United States, and not War, as the Arbiter. It is, however, at the next stage that the Arbiter is changed. In the event of controversies between two different States of the Commonwealth of Nations, the Supreme Law has established, not a judicial tribunal, but War, as the Arbiter. War is the

Institution *established* for the determination of justice between the nations.

But the provisions of the municipal law of Massachusetts, and of the Federal Constitution, are not vain words. It is well known to all familiar with our courts, that suits between towns, and also between counties, are often entertained and satisfactorily adjudicated. The records of the Supreme Court of the United States show also that Sovereign States habitually refer important controversies to this tribunal. There is now pending before this high court, an action of the State of Missouri *against* the State of Iowa, arising out of a question of boundary, wherein the former State claims a section of territory — larger than many German principalities — extending the whole length of the Northern border of Missouri, and several miles in breadth, and containing upwards of two thousand square miles. And within a short period, this same tribunal has decided a similar question, between our own State of Massachusetts and our neighbor Rhode Island; the latter State pertinaciously claiming a section of territory, about three miles broad, on a portion of our Southern frontier.

Suppose that in these different cases between towns, counties, States, War had been *established* by the supreme law as the Arbiter; imagine the disastrous consequences which must have ensued; picture the imperfect justice which must have been the end and fruit of such a contest; and while rejoicing that we are happily relieved, in these cases, from an alternative so dismal and deplorable, do not forget, that, on a larger theatre, where grander interests are staked, in the relations between nations, under the solemn sanction of the Law of Nations, War is *established* as the Arbiter of Justice. Do not forget that a complex and subtle code — the Laws of War — has been established to regulate the resort to this Arbiter.

Recognizing the irrational and unchristian character of War, as an established Arbiter between towns, counties, and States, in our happy land, we may learn to condemn it as an established Arbiter between nations. But history furnishes a parallel, by which we may form a yet clearer idea of its true nature. I refer to the system of *Private Wars*, or, more properly, of *Petty Wars*, and to the *Trial by Battle*, which darkened the dark ages. Both of these, though differing in some respects, concurred in recognizing the sword as the Arbiter of Justice. The *right to wage war* (*le droit de guerroyer*) was accorded by the early municipal law of European States, particularly of the Continent, to all independent chiefs, however petty, but not to their vassals; precisely as the *right to wage war* is now accorded by international law to all independent states and principalities, however petty, but not to their subjects. Nay; it was often mentioned expressly among the "liberties" to which independent chiefs were entitled; as it is still recognized by international law among the "liberties" of independent states. But in proportion as the sovereignty of these chiefs was absorbed in some larger lordship, this offensive *right* or "liberty" gradually disappeared. It continued to prevail extensively in France, till at last king John, by an ordinance dated 1361, expressly forbade Petty Wars throughout his kingdom, saying, "We order that all challenges, and wars, and acts of violence against all persons, in any part whatever of our kingdom, shall in future cease, and also all assemblies, convocations, and cavalcades of men at arms or archers, and also all pillages, seizures of goods and persons without right, *vengeances and counter-vengeances*—all these things we wish to forbid, under pain of incurring our indignation, and of being reputed and held disobedient and rebel."* It was reserved for Louis XI., as late as 1451, to make still another effort in the same direction, by expressly abrogating one of the "liberties" of Dauphiny, which secured to the inhabitants of this province the *right of war*. From these royal ordinances the Commonwealth of Nations might borrow appropriate words, in abrogating forever the Public Wars, or, more properly, the Grand Wars, with their *vengeances and counter-vengeances*, which are yet sanctioned by international law among the "liberties" of Christian States.

At a later day, effective efforts were made in Germany against the same prevailing evil. Contests here were not always confined to feudal chiefs. Associations of tradesmen and of domestics sent defiances to each other, and even to whole cities, on pretences trivial as those which have sometimes been the occasions of the Grand Wars of Nations. There still remain to us *Declarations of War* by a lord of Prauenstein against the free city of Frankfort, because a young lady of the city refused to dance with his uncle; by the baker and other domestics of the Margrave of Baden, against

* Cauchy, du Duel considéré dans ses Origines, Tom. I. ch. v. p. 91.

Eslingen, Reutlingen, and other imperial cities; by the baker of the Count Palatine Louis against the cities of Augsburg, Ulm, and Rothwell; by the shoeblacks of the University of Leipzig against the provost and other members; and, in **1477**, by the cook of Eppenstein, with his scullions, dairy-maids, and dishwashers, against Otho, Count of Solms. Finally, at the Diet of Worms, one of the most memorable in German annals, the Emperor Maximilian sanctioned an ordinance, which proclaimed a permanent Peace throughout Germany, abolished the *right* or "liberty" of Private War, and instituted a Supreme Tribunal, under the ancient name of the Imperial Chamber, to which recourse might be had, even by nobles, princes, and states, for the determination of their disputes, without appeal to the sword.*

But the *Trial by Battle*, or judicial combat, furnishes the most vivid picture of the Arbitrament of War. At one period, particularly in France, this was the universal umpire in disputes between private individuals. All causes, civil and criminal, with all the questions incident thereto, were referred to this Arbitrament. Neither bodily infirmity, nor old age, could exempt a litigant from the hazards of the Battle, even to determine matters of the most trivial character. Substitutes were at last allowed, and, as in War, bravos or champions were hired for wages to enter the lists. The proceedings were conducted gravely, according to prescribed forms, which were digested into a system of peculiar subtlety and minuteness; as War in our day

* Cox's History of the House of Austria, cap. 19 & 21.

has its established code, the Laws of War. Thus do violence, lawlessness, and absurdity, shelter themselves beneath the Rule of Law! Religion also lent her sacred sanctions. The priest, with prayer and encouragement, cheered the insensate combatant, and, like the military chaplain of our day, appealed for aid to Jesus Christ, the Prince of Peace.

To the honor of the Church, however, let me say, it early perceived the wickedness of this system. By the voices of pious bishops, by the ordinances of solemn councils, by the anathemas of Popes, it condemned * whomsoever should slay another in a battle, so impious and inimical to Christian peace, as "a most wicked homicide and bloody robber;" while it regarded the unhappy victim as a volunteer, guilty of his own death, and therefore decreed his remains to an unhonored burial without psalm or prayer. With sacerdotal supplications it vainly sought from rulers, and especially from successive emperors, to withdraw their countenance from this great evil, and with the civil power to confirm the ecclesiastical censures. Let praise and gratitude be offered to these just efforts! But alas! authentic history and the forms, still on record in the ancient missals, attest the unhappy countenance which the Trial by Battle succeeded in obtaining too often even at the hands of the Church — as in our day the Liturgy of the

---

* Statuimus juxta antiquum ecclesiasticæ observationis morem, ut quicumque tam impia et Christianæ paci inimica pugna alterum occiderit seu vulneribus debilem reddiderit, *velut homicida nequissimus et latro cruentus*, ab Ecclesiæ et omnium fidelium cœtu reddatur separatus, etc. (Canon. 13 Concil. Valent.) Cauchy, du Duel, Tom. I. ch. iii. p. 43.

English Church, and the conduct of Christian ministers in all countries, attest the unhappy countenance which the Institution of War yet receives. But the admonitions of the Church, and the efforts of good men slowly prevailed. Proofs by witnesses and by titles were gradually adopted, though opposed by the selfishness of the servants of the camp, of the subaltern officers, and of the lords, greedy of the fees, or wages of the combat. In England, Trial by Battle was attacked by Henry II., striving to substitute the trial by jury. In France, it was expressly forbidden, in an immortal ordinance, by that illustrious monarch, St. Louis. At last, this system, so wasteful of life, so barbarous in character, so vain and inefficient as an Arbiter of Justice, yielded to the establishment of judicial tribunals.

An early king of the Lombards, in formal decree, condemned the Trial by Battle as "impious;" Montesquieu at a later time branded it as "monstrous;" and Sir William Blackstone, a writer of authority on the English law, characterized it as "clearly an unchristian, as well as most uncertain method of trial." In the light of our day all unite in this condemnation. No man hesitates. No man undertakes its apology; nor does any man count as "glory" the feats of arms which it prompted and displayed. But the laws of morals are general and not special. They apply to communities and to nations as well as to individuals; nor is it possible, by any cunning of logic, by any device of human wit, to distinguish between that domestic Institution, the Trial by Battle, *established* by municipal law as the Arbitor between individuals, and that international Institution, the grander Trial by Battle, *established* by the

Christian Commonwealth as the Arbiter between nations. If the judicial combat was impious, monstrous and unchristian, then is War impious, monstrous and unchristian. And so it is regarded by our Society.

Let us look further at the true character of the Institution of War. It has been pointedly said in England, that the whole object of King, Lords, and Commons, and of the complex British Constitution, is "to get twelve men into a jury-box;" and Mr. Hume repeats the idea when he declares that the *administration of justice* is the grand aim of government. If this be true of individual nations in their municipal affairs, it is equally true of the Commonwealth of Nations. The whole complex System of the Law of Nations, overarching all the Christian States, has but one distinct object, *the administration of justice* between nations. Would that with pen or tongue I could adequately expose the enormity of this system, involving, as it does, a violation of the precepts of religion, of the dictates of common sense, of the suggestions of economy, and of the most precious sympathies of humanity! Would that, to all who hear me, I could impart something of the strength of my own convictions!

I need not dwell on the waste and cruelty thus authorized. These stare us wildly in the face, wherever we turn, as we travel the page of history. We see the desolation and death, that pursue War's demoniac footsteps. We look upon sacked towns, upon ravaged territories, upon violated homes; we behold all the sweet charities of life changed to wormwood and gall. Our soul is penetrated by the sharp moan of mothers, sisters and daughters —

of fathers, brothers and sons, who, in the bitterness of bereavement, refuse to be comforted. Our eyes rest at last upon one of those fair fields, where nature, in her abundance, spreads her cloth of gold, spacious and apt for the entertainment of mighty multitudes — or, perhaps, from the curious subtlety of its position, like the carpet in the Arabian tale, seeming to contract so as to be covered by a few only, or to dilate so as to receive an innumerable host. Here, under a bright sun, such as shone at Austerlitz or Buena Vista — amidst the peaceful harmonies of nature — on the Sabbath of Peace — we behold bands of brothers, children of a common Father, heirs to a common happiness, struggling together in the deadly fight; with the madness of fallen spirits seeking with murderous weapons the lives of brothers who have never injured them or their kindred. The havoc rages. The ground is soaked with their commingling blood. The air is rent by their commingling cries. Horse and rider are stretched together on the earth. More revolting than the mangled victims, than the gashed limbs, than the lifeless trunks, than the spattering brains, are the lawless passions which sweep, tempest-like, through the fiendish tumult.

Nearer comes the storm and nearer, rolling fast and frightful on.
Speak, Ximena, speak and tell us, who has lost, and who has won?
"Alas! alas! I know not; friend and foe together fall,
O'er the dying rush the living; pray, my sister, for them all!"

Horror-struck, we ask, wherefore this hateful contest? The melancholy, but truthful, answer comes, that this is the *established* method of determining justice between nations!

The scene changes. Far away on the distant pathway of the ocean two ships approach each other, with white canvas broadly spread to receive the flying gales. They are proudly built. All of human art has been lavished in their graceful proportions, and in their well-compacted sides, while they look in dimensions like floating happy islands of the sea. A numerous crew, with costly appliances of comfort, hives in their secure shelter. Surely these two travellers shall meet in joy and friendship; the flag at the mast-head shall give the signal of fellowship; the delighted sailors shall cluster in the rigging, and even on the yard-arms, to look each other in the face, while the exhilarating voices of both crews shall mingle in accents of gladness uncontrollable. It is not so. Not as brothers, not as friends, not as way-farers of the common ocean, do they come together; but as enemies. The gentle vessels now bristle fiercely with death-dealing instruments. On their spacious decks, aloft on all their masts, flashes the deadly musketry. From their sides spout cataracts of flame, amidst the pealing thunders of a fatal artillery. They, who had escaped "the dreadful touch of merchant-marring rocks;" who on their long and solitary way had sped unharmed by wind or wave; whom the hurricane had spared; in whose favor storms and seas had intermitted their immitigable war; now at last fall by the hand of each other. The same spectacle of horror greets us from both ships. On their decks, reddened with blood, the murders of St. Bartholomew and of the Sicilian Vespers, with the fires of Smithfield, seem to break forth anew, and to concentrate their rage. Each has now become a swimming Golgotha. At length these vessels — such pageants of the sea — once so stately —

so proudly built — but now rudely shattered by cannon-balls — with shivered masts and ragged sails — exist only as unmanageable wrecks, weltering on the uncertain waves, whose temporary lull of peace is their only safety. In amazement at this strange, unnatural contest — away from country and home — where there is no country or home to defend — we ask again, wherefore this dismal duel? Again the melancholy, but truthful, answer promptly comes, that this is the *established* method of determining justice between nations.

Yes! the barbarous brutal relations which once prevailed between individuals, which prevailed still longer between the communities, principalities and provinces composing nations, are not yet banished from the great Christian Commonwealth. Religion, reason, humanity, first penetrate the individual, next small communities, and, widening in their influence, slowly leaven the nations. Thus while we condemn the bloody contests of individuals, of towns, of counties, of provinces, of principalities, and deny to them the *right of waging war*, or of appeal to the *Trial by Battle*, we continue to uphold an atrocious System of folly and crime, which is to nations, what the System of Petty Wars was to principalities and provinces, what the Duel was to individuals; for *War is the Duel of Nations.** As from Pluto's throne flowed those terrible rivers, Styx, Acheron, Cocy-

---

* Plautus speaks, in the Epidicus, of one who had obtained great riches by the *duelling art*, meaning the art of War:

——— *Arte duellicâ*
Divitias magnas adeptum.

And Horace, in his Odes (Lib. iv. 15) hails the age of Augustus,

tus and Phlegethon, with their lamenting waters and currents of flame, so from this established System flow the direful currents of War. "Ours is a damnable profession," is the recent confession of a veteran British general. "War is a trade of barbarians," exclaimed Napoleon, in a moment of truthful remorse, prompted by his bloodiest field. "Give them Hell," was the language written on a slate by a speechless dying American officer. Alas! these words are not too strong. The business of War cannot be other than a damnable profession — a trade of barbarians; and War itself is certainly Hell on earth. But consider well — do not forget — let the idea sink deep into your souls, animating you to constant endeavors — that this damnable profession, that this trade of barbarians, is a part of the War System, which is sanctioned by International Law, and that War itself is Hell, recognized, legalized, established, organized by the Commonwealth of Nations!

"Put together," says Voltaire, "all the vices of all the ages and places, and they will not come up to the mischiefs of one campaign." This is a strong speech. Another of surer truth might be made. Put together all the ills and calamities from the visitations of God, from convulsions of nature, from pestilence and famine, and they shall not equal the ills and calamities inflicted by man upon his brother-man, through the visitation of

---

as at peace or *free from Duels,* and with the temple of Janus closed:

> . . . Tua, Cæsar, ætas
> . . . . . . vacuum *duellis*
> Jovem Quirini clausit.

War — while alas! the sufferings of War are without the alleviation of those gentle virtues which ever attend the involuntary misfortunes of the race. Where the horse of Attila had been, a blade of grass would not grow; but in the footprints of pestilence, of famine, and the earthquake, the kindly charities have sprung into life.

The last hundred years have witnessed three peculiar visitations of God; first, the earthquake at Lisbon; next, the Asiatic Cholera, as it moved slow and ghastly, with its scythe of death, from the Delta of the Ganges, over Bengal, Persia, Arabia, Syria, Russia, till Europe and America shuddered before the spectral reaper; and, lastly, the recent famine in Ireland, consuming, with remorseless rage, the population of that ill-fated land. It is impossible to estimate precisely the deadly work of the Cholera or of the famine, or to picture the miseries which they caused. But the single brief event of the earthquake can be portrayed in authentic colors.

Lisbon, whose ancient origin was referred by fable to the wanderings of Ulysses, was one of the fairest cities of Europe. From the summit of seven hills, it looked down upon the sea, and the bay studded with cheerful villages — upon the broad Tagus, expanding into a harbor ample for all the navies of Europe, and upon a country of rare beauty, smiling with the olive and the orange, amidst the grateful shadows of the cypress and the elm. A climate, which offered flowers in winter, enhanced these peculiar advantages of position; and a numerous population thronged its narrow and irregular streets. Its forty churches, its palaces, its public edifices, its warehouses, its convents, its fortresses, its citadel, had become a boast. Not by War, not by the hand of man, were these solid structures levelled, and all these delights changed to desolation.

Lisbon, on the morning of November 1st, 1755, was taken and sacked by an earthquake. The spacious warehouses were destroyed; the lordly edifices, the massive convents, the impregnable fortresses, with the lofty citadel, were toppled to the ground; and as the affrighted people sought shelter in the churches, they were crushed beneath the falling mass. Twenty thousand persons perished in this catastrophe. Fire and robbery mingled with the earthquake, and this beautiful city seemed to be obliterated. The powers of Europe were touched by this great misfortune, and succor from all sides was soon offered to repair the loss. Within three months English vessels appeared in the Tagus loaded with generous contributions — £20,000 in gold — a similar sum in silver — six thousand barrels of salt meat, four thousand barrels of butter, one thousand bags of biscuit, twelve hundred barrels of rice, ten thousand quintals of corn, besides hats, stockings and shoes.

Such was the desolation, and such the charity sown by the earthquake at Lisbon — an event, which, after the lapse of nearly a century, still stands without a parallel. But War shakes from its terrible folds all this desolation, without its attendant charity. Nay, more; the Commonwealth of Nations *voluntarily agrees, each with the other*, under the grave sanctions of International Law, to invoke this desolation, in the settlement of controversies among its members, while it expressly enjoins upon all its members, not already parties to the controversy, to abstain from rendering succor to the unhappy victim. High tribunals are established, whose special duty it is to uphold this Arbitrament, and, with unrelenting severity, to enforce these barbarous injunctions, to the end that no aid, no charity, shall come to revive the sufferer or to alleviate the calamity. Vera Cruz has been bombarded and wasted by the American arms. Its citadel, its churches, its houses have been shattered, and peaceful families at their firesides have been torn in mutilated fragments by the murderous bursting shell; but the universal, the English charities, which helped restore Lisbon, were not offered to the ruined Mexican city. They could not have been offered, without a violation of the *Laws of War!*

It is because men have thus far seen War chiefly in the light of their prejudices, regarding it only as an agency of attack or defence, or as a desperate sally of wickedness, that it becomes difficult to recognize it as a form of judgment, sanctioned and *legalized* by Public Authority. Let us learn to regard it in its true character, as an *establishment* of the Commonwealth of Nations, and one of the "liberties" of independent states; and it will no longer seem merely an expression of the lawless passions of men; no longer a necessary incident of imperfect human nature; no longer an unavoidable, uncontrollable volcanic eruption of rage, of *vengeances and counter-vengeances*, knowing no bounds; but it will be recognized as a monstrous and gigantic Institution for the adjudication of international rights, — as if it was established that an earthquake, with its uncounted woes, and without its attendant charities, might be legally invoked as the Arbiter of Justice.

All must unite in condemning the Arbitrament of War. Does any one hesitate? He who runs may read and comprehend its enormity. But if War be thus odious; if it be the Duel of Nations; if it be the yet surviving Trial by Battle; then it must affect with its barbarism all its incidents, all its enginery and machinery, all who sanction it, all who have any part or lot in it; in fine, the whole vast system by which it is upheld. It is impossible, by any discrimination, to separate the component parts of this system. We must regard it as a whole, in its entirety. But half our work would be done, if we confined ourselves to a condemnation of this Institution merely. We condemn also all its instruments and agencies, all its adjuncts and accessaries, all its furniture and equipage, all its armaments and operations; the whole apparatus of forts, of navies, of armies, of military display, of military chaplains, and of military sermons; all together constituting, in connection with the Institution of War, what may be called the WAR SYSTEM. It is this which we seek to abolish; believing that religion, humanity, and policy all require the establishment of some peaceful means for the administration of international justice, and that they still further require *the general disarming of the Christian nations*, to the end that the enormous expenditures now lavished upon the War System may be applied to purposes of usefulness and beneficence, and that the *business* of the soldier may finally cease.

While earnestly professing this object, let me disclaim again all idea of questioning the right of strict self-defence, or the duty of upholding government, and of maintaining the supremacy of the law, whether on the land, or on the sea. Reluctantly admitting the necessity of Force, even for such purposes, *Christianity revolts at Force as a substitute for a judicial tribunal.* The example of the great Teacher, the practice of the early disciples, the injunctions of self-denial, of love, of non-resistance to evil — which are sometimes supposed to forbid the resort to Force in any exigency, even of self-defence, — all these must apply with unquestionable certainty to the established System of War. *Here at least, there can be no doubt.* If, sorrowfully, necessarily, cautiously — in a yet barbarous age — the sword, in the hand of an assaulted individual, may become the instrument of sincere self-defence; if, under the sanctions of a judicial tribunal, it may become the instrument of Justice also; *surely it can never be the Arbiter of Justice.* Here is a distinction vital to our cause, and never to be forgotten in presenting its Christian claims. The sword of the magistrate is unlike — oh! how unlike — the flaming sword of War.

Let us now look briefly in detail, at some of the component parts of the War System. All of these may be resolved into PREPARATIONS FOR WAR, as court-house, jail, judges, sheriffs, constables and *posse comitatus* are *preparations* for the administration of municipal justice. If justice were not to be administered, these would not exist. If War were not sanctioned by the Commonwealth of Nations, as the means of determining international controversies, then forts, navies, armies, military display, military chaplains and military sermons, would not exist. They would be as useless and irrational — except for the rare occasions of a police — as similar preparations would now be in Boston for defence against its neighbor Cambridge; or in the County of Essex for defence against its neighbor County of Middlesex; or in the State of Massachusetts for defence against its neighbors, Rhode Island and New York. It is only recently that men have learned to question the propriety and righteousness of these preparations; for it is only recently that men have begun to open their eyes to the true character of the System, in which they are a part. *It will yet be seen, that sustaining these we sustain the System.* Still further, it will yet be seen, that, sustaining these, we offend by wicked waste against the demands of economy, and violate also the most precious sentiments of Human Brotherhood; taking counsel of distrust instead of love, and provoking to rivalry and enmity, instead of association and peace.

Time would fail me now to discuss adequately the nature of these preparations; and I am the more willing to abridge what I am tempted to say, because on another occasion I have treated this part of the subject. I should do wrong, however, not to expose their downright inconsistency with the spirit of Christianity. It is from a clear comprehension of the unchristian character of the War System, that we shall perceive the unchristian character of the preparations which it encourages and requires. I might exhibit this character by an examination of the Laws of War, drawn originally from no celestial founts, but from a dark profound of Heathenism. This is unnecessary. The Constitution of our own country furnishes an illustration so remarkable as to be a touchstone of the whole System. No town, county or State has the "liberty" to "declare War." The exercise of any proper self-defence, arising from actual necessity, requires no such "liberty." But unhappily Congress is expressly authorized to "declare War" — that is, to appeal to the Arbitrament of arms. And the Constitution proceeds to state that all, "giving aid and comfort to the enemy," shall be deemed "traitors." Mark now, what the Gospel has said: *Love your enemies; if thine enemy hunger, feed him; if he thirst, give him drink.* Thus shall obedience to this positive injunction of Christianity, expose a person, under the War System, to the penalty of the highest crime known to the law. Can this be a Christian system?

But the true character of these preparations is distinctly, though unconsciously, attested by the names of the vessels in the British Navy. I select the following offensive catalogue from the latest official List. Most of these are steam-ships of recent construction. They may be considered, therefore, to represent the spirit of the British Navy in our day — nay, of those War Preparations, of which they are a most effective part: — Acheron, Adder, Alecto, Avenger, Basilisk, Blood-hound, Bull-dog, Crocodile, Erebus, Firebrand, Fury, Gladiator, Goliah, Gorgon, Harpy, Hecate, Hound, Jackal, Mastiff, Pluto, Rattlesnake, Revenge, Salamander, Savage, Scorpion, Scourge, Serpent, Spider, Spiteful, Spitfire, Styx, Sulphur, Tartar, Tartarus, Teazer, Terrible, Terror, Vengeance, Viper, Vixen, Virago, Volcano, Vulture, Warspite, Wildfire, Wolf, Wolverine!

Such is the Christian array of Victoria, Defender of the Faith! It may remind us of the Pagan swarm of savage warriors upon our own continent, led by Black Hawk, Man-Killer, and the Wild Bear; or of the companions of King John, in wicked depredations upon his subjects, at another period of English history, "Falco without Bowels," "Maclean the Bloody," "Walter Buch, the Murderer," "Sottim, the Merciless," and "Godeschal, the Iron-Hearted." Or it might seem to be

> —— all the grisly legions that troop
> Under the sooty flag of Acheron.

As a man is known by the company he keeps — as a tree is known by its fruits, so shall the War System be fully and unequivocally known by these its chosen ministers, and by all the accursed fruits of War. Employing such representatives, sustained by such agencies, animated by such Furies — and producing such fruits of tears and bitterness, it must be hateful to all good men. Tell me not that it is sanctioned by the religion of Christ; do not enroll the Saviour and his disciples in its Satanic squadron; do not invoke the Gospel of Peace, in profane vindication of an Institution, which, by its own too palpable confession, exists in defiance of all the most cherished Christian sentiments; do not dishonor the Divine Spirit of gentleness, of forbearance, of love, by supposing that it can ever enter into this System, except to change its whole nature and name, to cast out the devils which possess it, and fill its gigantic energies with the holy inspiration of Beneficence.

I need say little of military chaplains, or military sermons. Like the steamships of the navy, they come under the head of Preparations for War. They are unquestionably a part of the War System. They belong to the same school with the priests of former times, who held the picture of the Prince of Peace before the barbarous champion of the Duel, saying, "Sir Knight, behold here the remembrance of our Lord and Redeemer, Jesus Christ, who willingly gave his most precious body to death in order to save us. Now, ask of him mercy, and pray that on this day he may be willing to aid you, if you have right, for he is the sovereign judge."* They belong to the same school with the English prelates of our day, who, in the name of the Prince of Peace, consecrate banners to be used in remote East Indian wars, saying, "Be thou in the midst of our hosts, as thou wast in the plains of India, and in the field of Waterloo, and may these banners, which we bless and consecrate this day, lead thee ever on to glorious victory." In thus consenting to degrade the "blessedness" of the Gospel to the "blasphemy" of the War System, they follow long established custom, doubtless often without considering the true character of the System, whose ministers they become. Their apology will be, that "they know not what they do."

And here the important practical question occurs, Is the *Militia* obnoxious to the same unequivocal condemnation? So far as the militia constitutes a part of the War System, it is impossible to distinguish it from the rest of the System. It is a portion of the apparatus provided for the administration of interna-

* Cauchy, Du Duel, Tom. I. cap. III. p. 74.

tional justice. From this character it borrows the unwholesome attractions of War, while, like a North American Indian, it disports itself in finery and parade. Of the latter feature I will only incidentally speak. If War be a Christian Institution, let those, who act as its ministers, shroud themselves in colors congenial with their dreadful trade. Let them, with sorrow and solemnity, not with gladness and pomp, proceed to their melancholy office. The Jew, Shylock, speaking through the wisdom of Shakspeare, exposes the mockery of the street-shows of Venice in words which sometimes find an echo here :

> ————————When you hear the drum,
> And the vile squeaking of the wry-necked fife,
> Clamber not up to the casements then,
> Nor thrust your head into the public street,
> To gaze on Christian fools with varnished faces ;
> But stop my house's ears, I mean my casements;
> Let not the sound of shallow foppery enter
> My sober house.

Not as a part of the War System, but only as an agent for preserving domestic peace, and for sustaining the law, can the militia be entitled to support. And here arises the important practical question — interesting to the opponents of the War System and to the lovers of order — whether the same object may not be accomplished by an agent, less expensive, less cumbersome, and less tardy, forming no part of the War System, and, therefore, in no respect liable to the objections encountered by the militia. Even the supporters of the militia do not disguise its growing unpopularity. The eminent Military Commissioners of Massachusetts, to whom, in 1847, was referred the duty of arranging a system for its organization and discipline, confess that there is "either a defect of power in the State government for an efficient and salutary militia organization, or *the absence of a public sentiment in its favor*, and a consequent unwillingness to submit to the requirements of service, which alone can sustain it;" and they add, that "they have been met, in the performance of their task, with information from all quarters, of its general neglect, and of the certain and rapid declension of the militia in numbers and efficiency." And the Adjutant General of Massachusetts, after alluding to the different systems which have been vainly tried, and have fallen into disuse, remarks, that "the fate of each system is indicative of public sentiment, and until public sentiment changes, *no military system whatever can be sustained in the state.*" Nor is this condition of public sentiment for the first time noticed. It was also recognized by the Commissioners, who, as long ago as 1839, were charged by the legislature with this subject. In their report they say, "It is enough to know that all attempts hitherto to uphold the system in its orignal design of organization, discipline and subordination, *are at last brought to an unsuccessful issue.*"

None, who are familiar with public opinion in our country, and particularly in Massachusetts, will question the accuracy of these official statements. It is true, that there is an indisposition on the part of citizens to assume the burthens of the militia. Still further, its offices and dignities have ceased to be an object of general regard. This certainly must be founded in a conviction, that it is no longer necessary or useful; for it is not customary with the people of Massachusetts to decline occasions of service, necessary or useful to the community. The interest which once attended military celebrations has decayed. Nor should the fact be concealed, that there are large numbers, whose sentiments on this subject are not of mere indifference; who regard with aversion the fanfaronade of a militia muster; who question not a little the influence which it exercises over those who take part in it, or even behold it, and who look with regret upon the expenditure of money and time which the service requires.

If such be the condition of the public mind, it is wrong for the Government not to recognize it — that our legislation may be accommodated thereto. The soul of all effective laws is an animating public sentiment. This gives vitality to what else would be a dead letter. In vain do we enact what is not inspired by this spirit. No skill in the device of the system; no penalties; no bounties even; can uphold it. But happily we are not without remedy. If the State Legislatures should deem it proper to provide a substitute for this questionable or offensive agency, as a conservator of domestic quiet, it is entirely within their competency. Let the general voice demand the *substitute.*

Among the powers, recognized as reserved to the States, under the Federal Constitution, is the power of *Internal Police.* Within its territorial limits a State is sovereign. Its municipal arrangements depend entirely upon its own will. In the exercise of this will, let it establish a system, congenial with the sentiment of the age, which shall supply the place of the militia, as a guardian of municipal quiet. This system may consist of unpaid volunteers or special constables, like the fire companies in the country, or of hired men, enrolled for this particular purpose, and always within call, like the fire companies in Boston. It would not be thought desirable, in all probability, that they should be clad in showy costume, or subjected to all the peculiarities of the military drill. I cannot doubt that a system so simple, practical, efficient, unostentatious, and cheap, especially as compared with the militia, would be in entire harmony with the existing sentiment, while it could not fail to remedy those evils which are feared from the present neglect of the militia. Many unsuccessful attempts have been made to reform the militia. *It remains that a proper effort should be made to provide a substitute for it.*

An eminent English jurist, of the last century — renowned as a scholar also — Sir William Jones, in a learned and ingenious tract, entitled "An Inquiry into the Legal Mode of suppressing Riots, with a Constitutional Plan of Future Defence,"* after developing the obligations of the citizen, under the common law, as a part of the Power of the County, has presented a system of organization which is to act independently of the military. It is not probable that this would be acceptable, in all its details, to the people of our community; but there is one of his recommendations, which seems to harmonize with the existing state of sentiment. "Let the companies," he says, "be taught in the most private and orderly manner, for two or three hours

* Jones's Works, Vol. VI. p. 685.

early every morning, until they are completely skilled in the use of their arms; *let them not unnecessarily march through the streets or high roads, nor make any the least military parade, but consider themselves entirely as part of the civil State.*"

But, while divorcing the Police from the unchristian and barbarous War System, I would never fail to inculcate the vital importance of maintaining law and order. Life and property should be guarded. Peace must be preserved in our streets. And it is the duty of the Government to provide such means as shall be most expedient for this purpose, if those already established are found in any respect inadequate, or uncongenial with the Spirit of the Age.

I cannot close this exposition of the War System without a brief endeavor to display the inordinate expenditure by which it is sustained. And here figures appear to lose their functions. They seem to pant, as they toil vainly to represent the enormous sums consumed in this unparalleled waste. Our own experience, measured by the concerns of common life, does not allow us adequately to conceive these sums. Like the periods of geological time, or the distances of the fixed stars, they baffle the imagination. Look, for instance, at the cost of this System to the United States. Without making any allowance for the loss sustained by the withdrawal of active men from productive industry, we shall find that, from the adoption of the Federal Constitution down to 1848, there has been paid directly from the National Treasury —

For the Army and fortifications,	$366,713,209
For the Navy and its operations,	209,994,428
	$576,707,687

This amount of itself is immense. But this is not all. Regarding the militia as a part of the War System, we must add a moderate estimate for its cost during this period, which, according to the calculations of an able and accurate economist, may be placed at $1,500,000,000. The whole presents an inconceivable sum-total of *more than two thousand millions* of dollars, which have been dedicated by our Government to the support of the War System — more than *seven* times as much as was set apart by the Government, during the same period, to all other purposes whatsoever!

Look now at the Commonwealth of European States. I do not intend to speak of the War Debts, under whose accumulated weight these States are now pressed to the earth. These are the terrible legacy of the Past. I refer directly to the existing War System, the establishment of the Present. According to recent calculations, its annual cost is not less than a *thousand millions* of dollars. Endeavor for a moment, by a comparison with other interests, to grapple with this sum.

It is larger than the entire profit of all the commerce and manufactures of the world.

It is larger than all the expenditure for agricultural labor, for the production of food for man, upon the whole face of the globe.

It is larger, by a hundred millions, than the amount of all the exports of all the nations of the earth.

It is larger, by more than five hundred millions, than the value of all the shipping of the civilized world.

It is larger, by nine hundred and ninety-seven millions, than the annual combined charities of Europe and America for preaching the Gospel to the Heathen.

Yes! the Commonwealth of Christian States, including our own country, appropriates, without hesitation, as a matter of course, upwards of a thousand millions of dollars annually to the maintenance of the War System, and vaunts its two millions of dollars, laboriously collected, for diffusing the light of the Gospel in foreign lands! With untold prodigality of cost it perpetuates the worst Heathenism of War, while, by charities insignificant in comparison, it doles to the Heathen the message of Peace. At home it breeds and fattens a cloud of eagles and vultures, trained to swoop upon the land; to all the gentiles across the sea it dismisses a solitary dove.

Still further; every ship of war that floats costs more than a well endowed college.

Every sloop of war that floats costs more than the largest public library in our country.

But it is sometimes said, by persons yet in the leading-strings of inherited prejudice, and with little appreciation of the true safety of the principles of Peace, that all these comprehensive preparations are needed for the protection of the country against enemies from abroad. Wishing to present our cause, without raising any superfluous question as to what have been called "defensive wars," on which there are varieties of opinion among the opponents of War, let me say in reply — *and here all can unite* — that if these preparations should be so needed at any time, according to the aggressive martial interpretation of the right of self-defence, there is much reason to believe it would be, because the unchristian spirit in which they have their birth, and which lowers and scowls in the very names of the ships, had provoked the danger ; as the presence of a bravo in our houses might challenge the attack he was hired to resist. Frederick of Prussia, sometimes called the Great — with an honesty or impudence unparalleled in the history of warriors — has left on record, most instructively prominent among the real reasons which urged him to make war upon Maria Theresa, *that he had troops always ready to act.* Thus did these *preparations* for War become, as they have too often shown themselves, the *incentives* to War. A careful consideration of human nature, as manifest in the conduct of individuals or of communities, will show that the fatal War Spirit derives much of its aliment from these preparations. Indeed they sow the seeds of the evil, which, it is sometimes vainly supposed, that they help to avert. Let it never be forgotten — let it be treasured as a solemn warning of history — that it was the possession of *troops always ready to act*, that served to inspire that succession of bloody wars, which, first pouncing upon Silesia, at last mingled with the strifes of England and France, and, even in the distant colonies across the Atlantic, ranged the savages of the forest under hostile European banners.

But I deny, distinctly, that these preparations are needed for any just self-defence. In the first place, it is difficult, if not impossible, to suppose any such occasion, in the Fraternity of Christian States, if War should cease to be an established Arbitrament, or if any State should be so truly great as to decline its umpirage. There is no such occasion among the towns, or counties, or states, of our extended country. There is no such occasion among the counties of Great Britain, or among the provinces of France. But the same sentiments of good will and fellowship, the same ties of commerce which unite towns, counties, states and provinces, are fast drawing into similar communion the whole Commonwealth of Nations. France and England, so long regarded as natural enemies, are now better known to each other, than, only a short time ago, were different provinces of the former kingdom. And at the present moment, there is a closer intimacy in business and social intercourse, between Great Britain and our own country, than there was, at the beginning of the present century, between Massachusetts and Virginia.

But admitting that an enemy might approach our shores, with purposes of piracy, or plunder, or conquest, who can doubt that the surest protection would be found — not in the insane waste of previous preparations — not in the idle fortresses along our coasts, built at a cost far surpassing all our light-houses, and all our colleges — but in the intelligence, union, and pacific repose of good men, with the unbounded resources derived from an uninterrupted devotion to productive industry? I think it may be assumed as beyond question, in the present light of political economy, that the people who have spent most sparingly in preparations for War — all other things being equal — must possess the most enduring means of actual self-defence at home, on their own soil, before their own hearths — if any such melancholy alternative should occur. Consider the prodigious sums, exceeding in all two thousand millions of dollars, squandered by the United States, since the adoption of the Federal Constitution, in support of the War System. Surely, if these means had been devoted to railroads and canals, to schools and colleges, our country would possess, at the present moment, an accumulated material power grander far than any she now boasts. But there is another power of more unfailing temper, which would also be hers. Overflowing with intelligence, with charity, with civilization, with all that constitutes a generous state, she would be able to win peaceful triumphs transcending all she has yet achieved — surrounding the land with an invincible self-defensive might, and, in their unfading brightness, rendering all glory from War impossible. Well does the poet say, with most persuasive truth,

> What constitutes a State?
> *Not high-raised battlement or labored mound,*
> *Thick wall or moated gate;*
> Not cities proud with spires and turrets crowned;
> Not bays and broad-armed ports,
> *Where, laughing at the storm, rich navies ride;*
> But MEN, high-minded MEN.

Such men will possess a Christian greatness, rendering them unable to do an injury to a neighbor; while their character, instinct with all the guardian virtues, must render their neighbors unable to do an injury to them; and there shall be none to molest them or make them afraid.

The injunction, "In time of Peace prepare for War," is of Heathen origin. As a rule of international conduct, it is unworthy of an age of Christian light. It can be vindicated only on two grounds. First, by assuming that the Arbitrament of War is the proper agency for deciding controversies between nations, and that the War System is, therefore, to be maintained and strengthened, — as the essential means of international justice. Or, secondly, by assuming the rejected dogma of an Atheist philosopher, Hobbes, that war is the natural state of man. Whatever may be the infirmities of our passions, all must perceive that the natural state of individuals, in which they have the highest happiness, and to which they tend by an irresistible heavenly attraction, is Peace. And this is true of communities and of nations, as well as of individuals. The proper rule should be, "In time of Peace cultivate the arts of Peace." So doing, you will render the country truly strong and truly great; not by arousing the passions of War; not by nursing men to the business of blood; not by converting the land into a flaming arsenal, a magazine of gunpowder, or an "infernal machine," all ready to explode; but by dedicating its whole energies to productive and beneficent works.

The incongruity of this System of Armed Peace may be illustrated by an example. Look into the life of that illustrious philosopher, John Locke, and you will find that, in the journal of his tour through France, describing the arches of the amphitheatre at Nismes, he says, "there is a stone laid about twenty inches or two feet square, and about six times the length *of my sword, which was about a philosophic yard long.*" Who is not struck with the incongruity and unseemliness of the exhibition, as he sees the author of the Essay on the Human Understanding, travelling with a sword by his side? But in this he only followed the barbarous custom of his time. Individuals then lived in the same relations towards each other, which now characterize nations. The War System had not yet entirely retreated from municipal law and custom, to find its last citadel and temple in the laws and customs of nations. Do not forget, that, at the present moment, our own country, the great Author, among the nations, of a new Essay on the Human Understanding, not only travels with a sword by its side, but lives encased in complete armor, burthensome to its limbs and costly to its treasury.

In condemning the War System, as a barbarous and most wasteful agency, the token and relic of a state of society alien to Christian civilization, we may except the navy, so far as it is necessary in the arrest of pirates, of traffickers in human flesh, and generally in preserving the police of the sea. But after the present survey, it will be difficult for the unprejudiced mind to regard the array of fortifications and of standing armies, otherwise than as obnoxious to the condemnation which attaches to the War System. The fortifications are the instruments, and the armies are the hired champions, of the great Duel of Nations.

But here I quit this part of the subject. Sufficient has been said to expose the true character of the War System of the Commonwealth of Christian Nations. It stands before us as a colossal image of International Justice, *with the sword, but without the scales;* like a hideous Mexican idol, besmeared with human blood, and surrounded by the sickening stench of human sacrifice. But this image, which seems to span the continents, while it rears aloft its flashing form of brass and of gold, and far in the clouds hides "the top and round of sovereignty" which it wears upon its head, can yet be laid low; for its feet are of clay. Every thing which exists in violation of right and reason, of religion and humanity, is weak and brittle. And such is the condition of the War System. It stands on wrong and folly, on impiety and inhumanity. Surely its feet are of clay.

II. And now I come, in the second branch of this Address, to the more grateful consideration of the means by which the War System can be overthrown. Here I shall unfold the tendencies and examples of nations, and the sacred efforts of individuals, constituting the Peace Movement, now ready to triumph, and shall offer some practical suggestions on our duties to this great cause, with a concluding glance at the barbarism of Military Glory. In this review I shall not be able to avoid the details incident to a multiplicity of topics; but I shall try to introduce nothing that does not bear directly on the subject.

Civilization now writhes in great travail and torment, and asks for liberation from the oppressive sway of the War System. Like a slave, under a weary weight of chains, its raises its exhausted arms, and pleads for the angel Deliverer. And lo! the beneficent angel comes; not like the Grecian God of Day, with vengeful arrow to slay the destructive Python; not like the Archangel Michael, with potent spear to transfix Satan to the earth; but with words of gentleness and Christian cheer, saying to all nations, and to all children of men, "Ye are all brothers, of *one* flesh, of *one* fold, of *one* shepherd, children of *one* Father, heirs to *one* happiness. By your own energies, by united fraternal endeavors, in the name of Christ, shall the tyranny of War be overthrown, and its Juggernaut be crushed to the earth."

In this spirit, and with this encouragement, we should labor for that grand and final object, the watchword of all ages, the Unity of the Human Family. Not in benevolence, but in selfishness, has this been sought in times past; not to promote the happiness of all, but to establish the dominion of one. It was the mad lust for power which carried Alexander from conquest to conquest, till he boasted that the whole world was one empire, of which the Macedonian phalanx was the citadel. Again, the same passion animated Rome; till, at last, while Christ lay in his manger, this city swayed broader lands than had been ruled by Alexander. The Gospel, in its simple narrative, says, "And it came to pass about these times, that a decree went out from Cæsar Augustus, that *all the world* should be taxed." History points to the exile of Ovid, who, falling under the displeasure of the same Emperor, was condemned to close his days in vain longings for Rome, far away in Pontus, beyond the Euxine Sea. With singular significance, these two contemporaneous incidents reveal the universality of Roman dominion, stretching from Britain to Parthia. But this empire crumbled, to be re-constructed for a brief moment, in part by Charlemagne, in part by Tamerlane. In our own age, Napoleon made a last effort for Unity, founded on Force. And now, from his utterances at St. Helena, the expressed wisdom of his unparalleled experience, comes the remarkable confession, worthy of constant memory: "The more I study the world, the more am I convinced of the inability of brute force to create any thing durable." From the sepulchre of Napoleon, now sleeping on the banks of the Seine, surrounded by the vain trophies of battle; nay more, from the sepulchres of all these broken empires seem to proceed the words, "They that take the sword shall perish by the sword."

Unity is the longing and tendency of Humanity; not the enforced Unity of military power; not the Unity of might triumphant over right; not the Unity of Inequality; not the Unity which occupied the soul of Dante, when, in his treatise *De Monarchia*, the earliest political work of modern times, he strove to show that all the world ought to be governed by one man, the successor of the Roman Emperor. Not these; but the blessed voluntary Unity of the various people of the earth in fraternal labors; — the Unity promised, when it was said, "there is neither Jew nor Greek, there is neither bond nor free, there is neither male nor female, for ye are all one in Christ Jesus;" — the Unity which has filled the delighted vision of good men, of prophets, of sages, and poets, in times past; — the Unity which, in our own age, prompted Beranger, the incomparable lyric of France, in an immortal ode, to salute the Holy Alliance of the peoples, summoning them in all lands, and by whatever names they may be called, French, English, Belgian, German, Russian, to give each other the hand, to the end that the useless thunderbolts of War shall all be quenched, and Peace shall sow the earth with gold, with flowers, and with corn ; — the Unity which prompted an early American statesman and poet to anticipate the time when all the nations shall meet in Congress ;

> To give each realm its limits and its laws,
> Bid the last breath of dire contention cease,
> And bind all regions in the leagues of Peace,
> Bid one great empire, with extensive sway,
> Spread with the sun, and bound the walks of day,
> One centered system, one all-ruling soul
> Live through the parts, and regulate the whole ;

the Unity, which has inspired the contemporary British poet, of exquisite beauty, Alfred Tennyson, to hail the certain day,

> When the drums shall throb no longer,
> And the battle-flags be furled,
> In the Parliament of man,
> The Federation of the World.

Such is Unity in the bonds of Peace. The common good and mutual consent are its adamantine base ; Justice and Love its animating soul. These alone can give permanence to any combinations of men, whether in states or in confederacies. In these is the vital elixir of nations — the true philosopher's stone of divine efficacy, potent to keep alive the civilization of mankind. So far as these are neglected or forgotten, will the people, though under one apparent head, cease to be in reality united. So far as these are regarded, will the people within the sphere of their influence constitute one body, and be inspired by one spirit. And just in proportion as these sentiments find recognition from individuals, and from nations, will all War be impossible.

But not in vision, nor in promises, only is this Unity discerned. History reveals constant efforts for it in the voluntary associations, confederacies, leagues, coalitions and Congresses of Nations, which, though fugitive and limited in their influence, all attest the unsatisfied desires of men, solicitous for union, and show the means by which it may yet be permanently accomplished. Let me briefly enumerate some of these. 1. The *Amphictyonic Council*, embracing, at first, twelve, and finally thirty-one states or cities, was established in the year 497 before Christ. Each city sent two deputies, and had two votes in the Council, *which had full power to consider all differences* that might arise between the associate cities. 2. Next comes the *Achæan League*, founded at a very early period, and renewed in the year 284 before Christ. Each member of the League was independent, and yet all together constituted one body. So great was the fame of their justice and probity, that the Greek cities of Italy were glad to refer disputes to their peaceful arbitration. 3. Passing over other confederacies of antiquity, I come to the *Hanseatic League*, begun in the twelfth century, completed near the middle of the thirteenth, and comprising at one time nearly eighty cities. A system of International Law was adopted in their general assemblies, and *courts of arbitration were established to determine controversies among the cities.* The decrees of these courts were enforced by placing the condemned city under what was called the ban, a sentence equivalent to the excommunication of the ecclesiastical law. But this League was not alone. 4. In the twelfth and thirteenth centuries, various other cities and nobles of Germany, entered into alliances and associations for mutual protection, under various names, as the *League of the Rhine* and *the League of Suabia.* 5. To these I may add the combination of the *Armed Neutrality* in 1780, uniting, in declared support of certain principles, a large cluster of nations — Russia, France, Spain, Holland, Sweden, Denmark, Prussia, and the United States. 6. And still further, I may refer to various Congresses, whether at Utrecht, at Westphalia, at Cambray, at Aix la Chapelle, or at Vienna, whose professed object has been, after the wasteful struggles of War, to arrange the terms of Peace and to arbitrate between nations.

These examples, which belong to the Past, reveal the tendencies and capacities of nations. There are other instances, however, which come with the effect of living authority, while they afford a practical illustration of the means by which the War System of the Commonwealth of Christian States may be overthrown. There is, *first*, the Swiss Republic, or *Helvetic Union*, which began as long ago as 1308, and has preserved Peace among its members during the greater part of five centuries. In speaking of this Union, Vattel says, in the early part of the last century,* "The Swiss have had the precaution, in all their alliances among themselves, and even with the neighboring powers, *to agree beforehand on the manner in which their disputes were to be submitted to arbitrators, in case they could not adjust them in an amicable manner.* This wise precaution has not a little contributed to maintain the

* Law of Nations, Book II. chap. 10, § 329.

Helvetic Republic in that flourishing state, which secures its liberty, and renders it respectable throughout Europe." Since these words were written, there have been many changes in the Swiss Constitution, but its present Federal System, embracing upwards of twenty-four different states, established on the downfall of Napoleon, and again confirmed in 1830, provides that differences among the states shall be referred to "special arbitration." This is an instructive example. But *secondly*, our own happy country furnishes one yet more so. The United States of America are a Federal Union of thirty independent sovereign States, — each having peculiar interests, — in pursuance of a Constitution, established in 1788, which not only provides a high tribunal for the adjudication of controversies between the States, but expressly *disarms* the individual States, declaring that "*no State shall, without consent of Congress, keep troops, or ships of war in time of peace, or engage in any war, unless actually invaded, or in such imminent danger as will not admit of delay.*" (Art. 1, Sec. 9.) A *third* example, not unlike that of our own country, is the *Confederation of Germany*, composed of thirty-eight sovereignties, who, by reciprocal stipulation in their Act of Union, (Sec. 12,) on the 8th June, 1815, deprived each sovereignty of the *right of war* with its confederates. The words of this stipulation, as well as those of the Constitution of the United States, might furnish a model to the Commonwealth of Nations. They are as follows: "*The members further bind themselves under no pretence to declare war against one another, nor to pursue their mutual differences by force of arms, but engage to sub-*

mit them to the Diet. The Diet is in such cases competent to attempt a reconciliation by the appointment of a select committee, and should this not prove successful, to procure a decision from a well-organized Court of Arbitration, *whose sentence is implicitly binding* upon the disputing parties."

Such are some of the authentic well-defined examples of history. But this is not all. It seems in the order of Providence, that individuals, families, tribes, and nations, should tend, by means of association, to a final Unity. A law of mutual attraction, or affinity, first exerting its influence upon smaller bodies, draws them by degrees into well-established fellowship, and then continuing its power, fuses the larger bodies into nations; and nations themselves, stirred by this same sleepless energy, are now moving towards that grand system of combined order, which will complete the general harmony;

> Spiritus intus alit, totamque infusa par artus
> Mens agitat molem, et magno se corpore miscet.

History bears ample testimony to the potency of this attraction. Modern Europe, in its early periods, was filled by petty lordships, or communities, constituting so many distinct units, acknowledging only a vague nationality, and maintaining among their cherished "liberties," the *right of war* with each other. The great states of our day have grown and matured into their present form, by the gradual absorption of these political bodies. Territories, which once possessed an equivocal and turbulent independence, now feel new power and happiness in peaceful association. Spain, composed of races, dissimilar in origin, religion and government, slowly ascended by progressive combinations among its principalities and provinces, till at last, in the fifteenth century, by the crowning union of Castile and Aragon, the whole country, with its various sovereignties, was united under one common rule. Germany once consisted of more than three hundred different principalities, each with the *right of war.* These slowly coalesced, forming larger principalities, till at last the whole complex aggregation of States, embracing bishoprics, abbeys, arch-bishoprics, duchies, counties, bailiwicks, electorates, margraviates, and free imperial cities, was gradually resolved into the present Confederation, wherein each state expressly renounces the *right of war* with its associates. France has passed through similar changes. By a power of assimilation, in no nation so strongly marked, she has absorbed the various races, and sovereignties, which once filled her territories with violence and conflict, and has converted them all to herself. The Roman or Iberian of Provence, the indomitable Celtic race, the German of Alsace, have all become Frenchmen, while the various provinces, once inspired by such hostile passions, Brittany and Normandy, Franche Comté and Bourgoyne, Gascogne and Languedoc, Provence and Dauphiny, are now blended in one powerful united nation. And Great Britain shows the influence of the same law. The many hostile principalities of England were first resolved into the Heptarchy; and these seven kingdoms became *one* under the Saxon Edgar. Wales, which was forcibly attached to England under Edward I., has at last entirely assimilated with her conqueror; Ireland, after a protracted resistance, was finally absorbed under

Edward III., and at a later day, after a series of bitter struggles, was united — I do not say how successfully — under the imperial parliament; Scotland became connected with England by the accession of James I. to the throne of the Tudors, and these two countries, which had so often encountered in battle, at last, under Queen Anne, were joined together by an act of peaceful legislation.

Thus has this tendency to Unity predominated over independent sovereignties and states, slowly conducting the great process of crystallization, which is constantly going on among the nations. But this cannot be arrested here. The next stage must be the peaceful association of the Christian States. In this anticipation we but follow the analogies of the material creation, whether regarded in the illumination of chemical or of geological science. Every where nature is proceeding with her combinations; with occult incalculable power, drawing elements into new relations of harmony; uniting molecule with molecule, atom with atom; and, by progressive changes, in the lapse of time, producing new structural arrangements. Look still closer, and the analogy will still continue. At first we detect only the operation of cohesion, rudely acting upon particles near together. This is followed by subtler influences, slowly imparting regularity of form, while heat, electricity, and potent chemical affinities, all conspire in the work. Yet still we have an incomplete body. *Light* now exerts its mysterious powers, and all assumes an organized form. So it is also with mankind. The rude cohesion of early ages, acting only upon individuals near together, first appears.

Slowly does the work proceed. But time and space, the great obstructions, if not annihilated, are now subdued, giving free scope to the powerful affinities of civilization. At last light—hail! holy light!—in whose glad beams are knowledge, morals and religion, with empyrean sway, shall resolve these separate and distracted elements into one organized system.

Thus much for the examples and tendencies of nations. In harmony with these are the *efforts of individuals* in various ages, strengthening with time, till now at last they swell into a voice that must be heard. A rapid glance at these will show the growth of the cause which we have met to welcome. Far off in the writings of the early Fathers of the Christian Church we learn the duty and importance of Universal Peace. But the rude hoof of War trampled down these sparks of generous truth, destined to flame forth at a later day. In the fifteenth century, the character of the *good Man of Peace* was described in that work of unexampled circulation, which has been translated into all modern tongues, and republished more than a thousand times, the Imitation of Christ, by Thomas à Kempis. At the close of the same century, the cause of Peace found important support from the pen of one of the chief scholars of the age, the gentle and learned Erasmus. At last it obtained a specious advocacy from the throne. Henry IV. of France, with the coöperation of his minister, Sully, conceived the grand scheme of blending the Christian States in one Confederacy, with a high tribunal for the decision of controversies between them. He had drawn into his plan Queen

Elizabeth of England, when all was arrested by the dagger of the assassin. But this gay and gallant monarch was little penetrated by the divine sentiment of Peace; for at his death he was gathering the materials for fresh War; and it is unhappily too evident, that even in his scheme of a European Congress, he was animated by a selfish ambition to humble Austria, rather than by a comprehensive humanity. Still his scheme has performed the important office of holding aloft before Christendom the practical idea of a tribunal for the Commonwealth of Nations.

The cause of Universal Peace was not destined thus early to receive the direct countenance of governments. But the efforts of private persons now began to multiply. Grotius, in his great work on the Law of Nations, while lavishing his learning and genius in illustrating the Arbitrament of War, still bears his testimony in favor of a more rational tribunal for international controversies. "It would be useful, and in some sort necessary," he says, in language which, if carried out practically, would sweep away the whole system of the *Laws of War*, — "to have Congresses of the Christian Powers, where differences might be determined by the judgment of those who were not interested in them, and means might be found to constrain parties to accept peace on just conditions." * To the discredit of his age these moderate words were received with smiles of derision, and the eminent expounder of the Laws of War and Peace was, on this account, condemned as rash, visionary, and impracticable. But the sentiment, in which they

* Lib. II. Cap. 23, § 8.

had their origin, found other forms of utterance. Before the close of the seventeenth century, Nicole, the friend of Pascal, belonging to the fellowship of Port-Royal, and one of the highest names in the Church of France, gave to the world, in his Moral Essays, a brief *Treatise on the means of preserving Peace among men,* (*Traité des Moyens de conserver la Paix avec les Hommes,*) a production which Voltaire, in exaggerated praise, terms "a master-piece to which nothing equal has been left by Antiquity." There next appeared a work, little known in our day, entitled *Nouveau Cyneas* — the name being suggested by the pacific adviser of Pyrrhus, the warrior king of Epirus — wherein the unknown author counselled sovereigns to govern their states in Peace, and to cause their differences to be judged by an established tribunal. And in Germany, as we learn from Leibnitz, who also mentions the last authority, at the close of the seventeenth century, a retired general, who had commanded armies, the Landgrave Ernest of Hesse Reinfels, in a work entitled *The Discreet Catholic,* offered a project for Perpetual Peace, by means of a tribunal established by associate sovereigns. Contemporaneously with these efforts, William Penn, in England, published an "Essay on the present and future Peace of Europe," in which he urged the plan of a general Congress for the settlement of international disputes, and referred with praise to the "great design" of Henry IV. Thus, by his writings, as also by his illustrious example in Pennsylvania, did he show himself the friend of Peace.

These were soon followed by the untiring labors of the good Abbé Saint Pierre, of France, — the most efficient among the early apostles of Peace. He is not to be confounded with the eloquent and eccentric Bernardin de St. Pierre, the author of Paul and Virginia, who, at a later day, beautifully painted the true Fraternity of Nations.* Of a genius less artistic or literary than his, the Abbé consecrated a whole life, crowned by extreme old age, to the improvement of mankind. There was no humane cause which he did not espouse ; but he was especially filled with the idea of Universal Peace, and with the importance of teaching nations, not less than individuals, the duty of doing to others as they would have others do unto them. His views are elaborately presented in a work of three volumes, entitled, *A Project for Perpetual Peace*, wherein he proposes a Diet or Congress of Sovereigns for the adjudication of international controversies without resort to War. Throughout his voluminous writings, he constantly returns to this project, which was the cherished vision of his life. More than once the regret falls from him, that the exalted genius of Newton and Descartes had not been devoted to the study and exposition of the great laws which determine the welfare of men and of nations; believing that they might have succeeded in organizing Peace. He often dwells on the beauty of Christian precepts, as a rule of public conduct, and on the true glory of beneficence, while he exposes the vanity of military renown, and does not hesitate to question that false glory which procured for Louis XIV. from flattering courtiers and a barbarous world, the undeserved title of Great. He enriched the French

* Œuvres de Bernardin de St. Pierre, Tom. X. p. 138. *Harmonies de la Nature;* Tom. II. p. 168. *Vœux d'un Solitaire.*

language with the word *bienfaisance;* and D'Alembert said that it was right he should have invented the word, who practised so largely the virtue which it expresses.

I need hardly add that, though thus of benevolence all-compact, St. Pierre was not the favorite of his age. A profligate minister, Cardinal Dubois — the ecclesiastical companion of a vicious regent in the worst excesses, condemned his ideas in a phrase of satire, as "the dreams of a good man." The pen of La Bruyere wantoned in a petty portrait of the good man's personal peculiarities. Many persons averted from him their countenance. To the scandal of literature and of science, the academy of France, of which he was a member, on the occasion of his death, forbore the eulogy which is its customary tribute to a departed academician. But an incomparable genius in Germany — an authority not to be questioned on any subject upon which he ventured to speak — Leibnitz, bears his testimony to the Project of Perpetual Peace, and in so doing, enrolls his own mighty name in the sacred catalogue of our cause. In some observations on this Project, communicated to its author, under date of Feb. 7, 1715,* after declaring, that it touches a matter which interests the whole human race, and is not foreign to his studies, as from his youth he had occupied himself with law, and particularly with the Law of Nations, Leibnitz says: "*I have read it with attention, and am persuaded that such a Project on the whole is feasible, and that its execution would be one of the most useful things in the world.* Although my suffrage

---

* Leibnitz, Opera, Tom. V. pp. 56 – 62, (ed. Dutens.)

cannot be of any weight, I have nevertheless thought that gratitude obliged me not to withhold it, and to join to it some remarks for the satisfaction of a meritorious author, who ought to have much reputation and firmness, to have dared and been able to oppose with success the prejudiced crowd, and the unbridled tongue of mockers." Such language from Leibnitz must have been precious even to Saint Pierre. I cannot close this brief sketch of a philanthropist, ever constant in an age when philanthropy was little regarded, without offering him my unaffected homage. To him may be addressed the sublime salutation, which hymned from the soul of Milton:

> Servant of God, well-done! well hast thou fought
> The better fight, who single hast maintained
> Against revolted multitudes the cause
> Of truth, in word mightier than in arms;
> And for the testimony of truth hast borne
> . . . . reproach, far worse to bear
> Than violence; for this was all thy care
> To stand approved in sight of God, though worlds
> Judged thee perverse.

Our world hereafter, as it wakes from its martial trance, shall salute, with gratitude and admiration, the true greatness of his career. It may well measure its advance in civilization by its appreciation of his character.

Saint Pierre was followed in 1761 by that remarkable genius, Rousseau, in a small work to which he modestly gave the title, *Extract from the Project of Perpetual Peace by the Abbé Saint Pierre.* Without referring to those higher motives — as the love of true glory and of humanity, a regard for the dictates of conscience and the precepts of religion — for addressing which to sovereigns, Saint Pierre incurred the ridicule of what are called practical statesmen — Rousseau appeals to the common sense of rulers, and shows how much their actual worldly interests would be promoted by submitting their pretensions to the Arbitration of an impartial tribunal, rather than to the uncertain issue of arms, which cannot bring even to the victor adequate compensation for the blood and treasure expended in the contest. If this project, he says, fails to be executed, it is not because it is chimerical; but because men have lost their wits, and it is a sort of madness to be wise in the midst of fools. As no scheme more grand, more beautiful or more useful ever occupied the human mind, so, says Rousseau, no author ever deserved attention more than one proposing the means for its practical adoption; nor can any humane and virtuous man fail to regard it with something of enthusiasm.

The recommendations of Rousseau were encountered in Germany by a writer who will, probably, be remembered only by his hardihood on this occasion. I allude to Embser, who treats of Perpetual Peace in a work first published in 1779, under the title of *The Idolatries of our Philosophical Century*, (Die Abgötterei unsers philosophischen Jahrhunderts,) and, at a later day, appearing with a new title, under the *alias* of the *Refutation of the Project of Perpetual Peace* (Widerlegung des ewigen Friedens-projekts.) The objections, still common with superficial or prejudiced minds, are here vehemently urged; the imputation upon Grotius is reproduced; and the idea is pronounced visionary and impracticable, while war is held up as an instrument more beneficent than Peace, in advancing the civilization of mankind.

But the cause of Saint Pierre and Rousseau was not without champions. In 1763 appeared at Gottingen the work of Totze, entitled *Permanent and Universal Peace, according to the Plan of Henry IV.* (Ewiger und allgemeiner Friede nach der Entwurf Heinrichs IV.) And in 1767, at Leipzig, was published an ample and mature treatise on this subject, by Lilienfels, under the name of *New Constitution for States* (Neues Staatsgebäude.) Truth often appears contemporaneously to different minds, having no concert with each other; and this work, though in remarkable harmony with the labors of Saint Pierre and Rousseau, is said to have been composed without any knowledge of them. Lilienfels treats of the causes and calamities of war, the expenses of armaments in time of Peace, and the miserable chances of the battle-field, where controversies are determined, in defiance of all principles of justice, as by the throw of dice; and he urges the advantage of a submission of such matters to Arbitrators, unless a Supreme Tribunal should be established to administer the Law of Nations, and to judge between them. Such a Tribunal, according to him, should enforce its decrees by the combined power of the Confederacy.

It was left to another German mind, in intellectual preëminence the successor of Leibnitz, by especial and repeated labors, to illustrate this cause. At Königsberg, in a retired part of Prussia, away from the great lines of travel, Immanuel Kant consecrated his days to the pursuit of truth. During a long, virtuous, and disinterested life, stretching beyond the period appointed for man — from 1724 to 1804 — in retirement, undisturbed by the shocks of revolution and war, never drawn by the temptations of travel more than seven German miles from the place of his birth, he assiduously studied books, men, and things. Among the fruits of his ripened powers was that system of Philosophy, known as the *Critique of Pure Reason*, by which he was at once established as a master-mind of his country. His words became the text for writers almost without number, who vied with each other in expounding, in illustrating, or in opposing his principles. At this period — after an unprecedented triumph in philosophy — when his name had become familiar wherever his mother-tongue was spoken, and while his rare faculties were yet untouched by decay — in the Indian summer of his life — the great thinker published a work *On Perpetual Peace* (Zum ewigen Frieden, 1796.) The interest in the author, or in the cause, was attested by prompt translations of this philanthropic production into the French, Danish, and Dutch languages. The same cause was espoused in another effort, entitled *Idea for a General History in a Cosmopolitan View* (Idee zu einer allgemeinen Geschichte in weltbürgerlicher Absicht;) and finally in his *Metaphysical Elements of Jurisprudence* (Metaphysiche Anfangsgründe der Rechtslehre.) In the lapse of time, the speculations of the philosoper have lost much of their original attraction; and other systems, with other names, have taken their place. But these early and faithful labors for Perpetual Peace cannot be forgotten. Perhaps by these the fame of the applauded philosopher of Königsberg may yet be preserved.

By Perpetual Peace, Kant understood a condition of states, in which there could be no fear of war; and this condition, he said, was demanded by reason, which abhors all war, as little adapted to establish right, and which must regard this final development of the Law of Nations as a consummation worthy of every effort. To this all persons, and particularly the rulers of states, should bend their energies. A special leagu or treaty should be entered into, which may truly be called a *Treaty of Peace*, differing from other treaties in this regard, that, whereas these terminate a single existing war only, this should seek to terminate forever all war between the parties to it. Treaties of Peace, tacitly acknowledging the *right to wage war*, as all treaties now do, are nothing more than a *truce;* they are not Peace. By these treaties an individual War may be ended; but not the *state of war.* There may not be constant hostilities; but there will be constant fear of them, with constant threats of aggression and attack. The soldiers and armaments now nursed by civilized states, as a Peace establishment, become the fruitful parent of new wars. With real Peace, these would be abandoned. Nor should states hesitate to submit, like individuals, *to law.* They should form one comprehensive Federation of Nations, which, by the addition of other nations, should at last embrace the whole earth. And this, according to Kant, in the succession of years, by a sure progress, is the irresistible tendency of nations.

These views found immediate support from another German philosopher, Fichte, of remarkable acuteness and perfect devotion to truth, whose name, in his own day, awakened an echo inferior only to that of Kant. In his *Groundwork of the Law of Nature* (Grundlage des Naturrechts,) published in 1796, he urges a Federation of Nations, with a tribunal for the determination of international controversies, as the best way of securing the triumph of justice, and of subduing the power of the unjust. To the suggestion that by this Federation injustice might be done to an individual state, he replied, that it would not be easy for the confederate nations to find any common advantage to tempt them to do this wrong. This subject was again handled in 1804, by a learned German, Charles Schwab, whose work, entitled *Of unavoidable Injustice* (Uber das unvermeidliche Unrecht) is marked by great clearness and directness. He looks forward to the *Universal State*, in which nations shall be united together, as citizens are now united in a municipal state. He does not believe that in this condition justice will be always inviolate; for, as between citizens in the state, it is not so; but that it will become generally established. As in the municipal state war no longer prevails, but offences, wrongs, and sallies of vengeance often proceed from individual citizens, and insubordination and anarchy may sometimes show themselves;— so in the *Universal State* war will be extinguished; but here also, between the different nations, who will be as citizens in the Federation, there may be wrongs, and aggressions, and even the common power may be resisted. In short, the *Universal State* will be subject to the same accidents with the municipal state.

The cause of Permanent Peace now became a thesis for Universities. At Stuttgard, in 1796, there was an oration by J. H. La Motte, entitled *Utrum Pax Perpetua pangi possit, nec ne?* And again at Leyden, in Holland, in 1808, a Dissertation was written by Gabinus de Wal, on taking his degree as Doctor of Laws, entitled *Disputatio Philosophico-Juridica de Conjunctione Populorum ad Pacem Perpetuam.* This learned and elaborate performance reviews the previous efforts in the cause, giving a preëminence to those of Kant. Such a voice from a pupil of the University is a token of the sentiments of the time, and an example for the youth of our own day.

Meanwhile in England, that indefatigable jurist and reformer, Jeremy Bentham, entered upon similar speculations. In an Essay on International Law, bearing date from 1786 to 1789, and first published in 1839, by his Executor, Dr. Bowring,* he develops a plan for Universal and Perpetual Peace in the spirit of Saint Pierre. According to him, such is the extreme folly, the madness of War, that on no supposition can it be otherwise than mischievous. All trade, in its essence, is advantageous, even to that party to whom it is least so. All war, in its essence, is ruinous; and yet the great employments of government are to treasure up occasions of War, and to put fetters upon trade. To remedy this evil, Bentham proposes, first, "The reduction and fixation of the forces of the several Nations, that compose the European system," and in enforcing this proposition, he says, "Whatsoever nation should get the start of the other in making the proposal to reduce, and fix the amount of its armed force, would crown

* Bentham's Works, Part VIII. pp. 537 - 554.

itself with everlasting honor. The risk would be nothing — the gain certain. This gain would be, the giving an incontrovertible demonstration of its own disposition to peace, and of the opposite disposition in the other nation in case of its rejecting the proposal." He next proposes the establishment of a Court of Judicature for the settlement of international differences, with power to report its opinion, and cause it to be circulated in the territories of each state; and after a certain time, to put a refractory state under the ban of Europe. The whole arrangement he urges, can in no respect be styled visionary, for it is proved, *first*, that it is the interest of the parties concerned; *secondly*, that they are already sensible of that interest; and, *thirdly*, the situation in which it would place them is not new, but finds a parallel in the difficult and complicated conventions, which have already been effected between nations.

Coming to our own country, I find many names worthy of commemoration in our cause. No person, in all history, has borne his testimony against War in phrases of greater pungency and of more convincing truth than Benjamin Franklin. "There never has been," he says, "nor ever will be, any such thing as a good War, or a bad Peace;" and he asks, "When will mankind be convinced of this, and agree to settle their difficulties by Arbitration? Were they to do it even by the cast of a die, it would be better than by fighting and destroying each other." As a diplomatist, Franklin strove to limit the evils of War. From him, while Minister of the United States, at Paris, proceeded those instructions, more honorable to the American name than any battle, directing the naval cruisers of our country, among whom was the redoubtable Paul Jones, if they should encounter the returning expedition of the great English navigator, Capt. Cook, to allow it, in the sacred interests of universal science, a free and undisturbed passage. And still later to him belongs the honor of introducing, into a treaty with Prussia, a clause for the abolition of that special scandal, private War on the ocean. In similar strain with Franklin, Jefferson says, "Will nations never devise a more rational umpire of differences than Force? War is an instrument entirely inefficient towards redressing wrong, and multiplies instead of indemnifying losses." And he proceeds to exhibit the waste of War, and the beneficent consequences, if its expenditures could be diverted to purposes of practical utility.

To Franklin and Jefferson we freely render thanks for their authoritative words and example. But there are three names, fit successors of Saint Pierre, — I speak now, of course, only of those whose career is ended, and on whose good works is the heavenly signet of death, — which more than theirs deserve the affectionate regard of the friends of Peace. I refer to Noah Worcester, William Ellery Channing, and William Ladd. It would be a grateful task to dwell on the services of these our virtuous champions. The occasion will allow only a passing notice. In Worcester we behold the single-minded country clergyman, little gifted as a preacher, with narrow means, — and his example teaches what such a character may accomplish, — in his humble retirement pained by the reports of War, and at last, when the great European drama of battles closed at Waterloo, publishing that appeal, entitled "A Solemn

Review of the *Custom* of War," which has been so extensively circulated at home and abroad, and has done so much to correct the inveterate prejudices which surround our cause. He was the founder, and for some time the indefatigable agent, of the earliest Peace Society in the country. — The eloquence of Channing, both with tongue and pen, was often directed against War. He was heart-struck by the awful moral degradation which it caused, rudely blotting out in men the image of God their Father; and his words of flame have lighted in many souls those exterminating fires that shall never die, until this evil is scoured from the earth. — William Ladd, after completing his education at Harvard University, entered into commercial pursuits. Early blessed with competency, through his own exertions, he could not be idle. He was childless; and his affections embraced all the children of the human family. Like Worcester and Channing, his attention was arrested by the portentous crime of War, and he was moved to dedicate the remainder of his days to earnest, untiring efforts for its abolition; going about from place to place, to inculcate the blessed lesson of Peace; with simple, cheerful manner winning the hearts of good men, and dropping in many youthful souls the precious seeds, which shall ripen in more precious fruit. He was the founder of the American Peace Society, in which was finally merged the earlier association, established by Worcester. By a long series of practical labors in our cause, and especially by developing, maturing and publishing to the world, the plan of a Congress of Nations, has William Ladd enrolled himself among the benefactors of mankind.

Such are some of the names which, hereafter, when the warrior no longer receives from the world the "blessings" promised to the "peace-maker," shall be inscribed on immortal tablets.

And now at last, in the fullness of time, in our own day, by the labors of men of Peace, by the irresistible coöperating affinities of mankind, nations seem to be visibly approaching — even amidst tumult and discord — that Unity, so long hoped for, prayed for. By steamboats, railroads, and telegraphs, outstripping the traditional movements of governments, men of all countries are daily commingling; ancient prejudices are fast dissolving; while ancient sympathies are strengthening, and new sympathies are coming into being. The chief commercial cities of England send addresses of friendship to the chief commercial cities of France; and the latter delight to return the salutation. Similar cords of amity are woven between cities in England, and cities in our own country. The visit to London of a band of French National Guards is reciprocated by the visit to Paris of a large company of Englishmen. Thus are pacific conquests now achieved, where formerly all the force of arms could not prevail. Mr. Vattemare perambulates Europe and the United States to establish a happy system of literary international exchanges. By the daily agency of the press we are made sharers in the trials and triumphs of our brethren in all lands, and learn to live no longer in the solitude of insulated nationalities, but in the communion of associated states. By the multitudinous reciprocities of commerce are developed relations of mutual dependence, stronger than treaties or alliances written on parchment; while, from a truer appreciation of the ethics of government, we arrive at the conviction, that the divine injunction, "Do unto others as you would have them do unto you," was spoken to nations as well as to individuals.

From increasing knowledge of each other, and from a higher sense of our duties as brethren of the Human Family, arises an increasing interest in each other; and charity, which was once, like patriotism, exclusively national, is beginning to clasp the world in its loving embrace. Every discovery of science, every aspiration of philanthropy, in whatever country it may have its birth, is now poured into the common stock of mankind. Assemblies, whether of science or of philanthropy, are no longer merely municipal, but gladly welcome delegates from all the nations. Science has had her Congresses in Italy, in Germany, and in England. Great causes — grander even than science — like Temperance, Freedom, Peace — have drawn to London large bodies of men from different countries, under the title of *World Conventions*, in whose very name, and in whose spirit of fraternity, we discern the prevailing tendency. Such a convention, dedicated to Universal Peace, held at London in 1843, was graced by the presence of many persons well known for their labors of humanity. At Frankfort, in 1846, was assembled a large Congress from all parts of Europe, to consider what could be done for those who were in prison. The succeeding year witnessed, at Brussels, a similar Congress, convened in the same charity. And at last, in August, 1848, we hail, at Brussels, another

Congress, inspired by the presence of a generous American, Elihu Burritt,— who has left his anvil at home to teach the nations to change their swords into ploughshares, and their spears into pruning-hooks,— presided over by an eminent Belgian magistrate; and composed of numerous individuals, speaking various languages, living under diverse forms of government, differing in political opinions, differing in religious convictions, but all drawn together by a common sacred sentiment, to pledge themselves to united strenuous efforts for the abolition of War, and for the Disarming of the Nations.

The Peace Congress at Brussels constitutes an epoch in our cause. It is a palpable development of those international attractions and affinities which are now awaiting their final organization. The resolutions which it has put forth, are so important, that I cannot hesitate to introduce them here:

1st. That, in the judgment of this Congress, an appeal to arms for the purpose of deciding disputes among nations, is a custom condemned alike by religion, reason, justice, humanity, and the best interests of the people; and that, therefore, it considers it to be the duty of the civilized world to adopt measures calculated to effect its entire abolition.

2d. That it is of the highest importance to urge on the several Governments of Europe and America the necessity of introducing a clause into all International Treaties, providing for the settlement of all disputes by Arbitration, in an amicable manner, and according to the rules of justice and equity, by special Arbitrators, or a Supreme International Court, to be invested with power to decide in cases of necessity, as a last resort.

3d. That the speedy convocation of a Congress of Nations, composed of duly appointed representatives, for the purpose of framing a well digested and authoritative International Code, is of the greatest importance, inasmuch as the organization of such a body, and the unanimous adoption of such a Code, would be an effectual means of promoting universal Peace.

4th. That this Congress respectfully calls the attention of civilized Governments to the necessity of a general and simultaneous disarmament, as a means whereby they may greatly diminish the financial burthens which press upon them; remove a fertile cause of irritation and inquietude; inspire mutual confidence; and promote the interchange of good offices; which, while they advance the interests of each state in particular, contribute largely to the maintenance of general Peace, and the lasting prosperity of nations.

In France these resolutions have received the adhesion of Lamartine; in England, of Richard Cobden. They have been welcomed throughout Great Britain, by large and enthusiastic popular assemblies, hanging with delight upon the practical lessons of peace on earth and good will to men, poured by eloquent voices into their unaccustomed ears. At the suggestion of the Congress at Brussels, and in harmony with the demands of an increasing public sentiment, another Congress, in the approaching month of August, will be convened at Paris. The place of meeting is auspicious. There, as in the very cave of Æolus, whence have so often raged forth the conflicting winds and resounding tempests of War, will assemble delegates from various nations, including a large number from our own country, whose glad work will be to hush and imprison these winds and tempests, and to bind them in the chains of everlasting Peace. May God prosper the grand endeavor!

But not in voluntary assemblies only has our cause found welcome. It has effected an entrance into *legislative halls.* A document now before me in the hand-writing of Samuel Adams, an approved patriot of the Revolution, bears witness to his desires for action on this subject in the Congress of the United States. It is in the form of a Letter of Instructions from the Legislature of Massachusetts to the delegates in Congress from that State; and, though without date, seems to have been prepared some time between the Treaty of Peace in 1783, and the adoption of the Federal Constitution in 1789. It is as follows:

GENTLEMEN, —

Although the General Court have lately instructed you concerning various matters of very great importance to this Commonwealth, they cannot finish the business of the year until they have transmitted to you a further instruction which they have long had in contemplation; and which, if their most ardent wish could be obtained, might in its consequences extensively promote the happiness of man.

You are, therefore, hereby instructed and urged, to move the United States in Congress assembled to take into their deep and most serious consideration, whether any measures can by them be used, through their influence with such of the nations in Europe with whom they are united by Treaties of Amity or Commerce, that National Differences may be settled and determined, without the necessity of WAR in which the world has too long been deluged, to the destruction of human happiness, and the disgrace of human reason and government.

If after the most mature deliberation it shall appear that no measures can be taken *at present* on this very interesting subject, it is conceived, it would redound much to the honor of the United States, that it was attended to by their great Representative in Congress, and be accepted as a testimony of gratitude for most signal favors granted to the said states by Him who is the almighty and most gracious Father and Friend of mankind.

And you are further instructed to move that the foregoing

Letter of Instructions be entered on the Journals of Congress, if it may be thought proper, that so it may remain for the inspection of the delegates from this Commonwealth, if necessary, in any *future* time.

I am not able to ascertain whether this document ever became a legislative act; but it attests, in an authentic form, that a prominent leader of public opinion in Massachusetts, after the establishment of that Independence for which he had so assiduously labored, hoped to enlist not only the Legislature of this state, but the Congress of the United States, in efforts for the emancipation of nations from the tyranny of War. For this early effort at a period when the cause of Permanent Peace had never been introduced to any legislative body, Samuel Adams deserves grateful mention.

At last, many years later, the subject reached Congress. In 1838, the Committee on Foreign Affairs of the House of Representatives of the United States, in a report drawn up by the late Mr. Legaré, prompted by memorials from the friends of Peace, while injudiciously discountenancing the idea of an Association of Nations, as not yet sanctioned by public opinion, acknowledge, "that the union of all nations in a state of Peace, under the restraints and protection of law, is the ideal perfection of civil society; that they accord fully in the benevolent object of the memorialists, and believe there is a visible tendency in the spirit and institutions of the age towards the practical accomplishment of it, at some future period; that they heartily agree in recommending a reference to a Third Power of all such controversies as can be safely confided to any tribunal unknown to the Constitution of our country; and that such a practice will be followed by other powers, and will soon grow up into the customary law of civilized nations." The Legislature of Massachusetts, by a series of resolutions, in harmony with the early sentiments of Samuel Adams, adopted with exceeding unanimity in 1844, declare, that they "regard Arbitration as a practical and desirable substitute for War, in the adjustment of international differences;" and still further declare their "earnest desire that the government of the United States would, at the earliest opportunity, take measures for obtaining the consent of the powers of Christendom to the establishment of a General Convention or Congress of Nations, for the purpose of settling the principles of international law, and of organizing a high Court of Nations to adjudge all cases of difficulty which may be brought before them by the mutual consent of two or more nations." During the winter of 1849, the subject was again presented to the American Congress. On Tuesday, January 16th, Mr. Tuck asked the unanimous consent of the House of Representatives to offer the following preamble and resolution:

Whereas the evils of War are acknowledged by all civilized nations, and the calamities, individual and general, which are inseparably connected with it, have attracted the attention of many humane and enlightened citizens of this and other countries; and whereas, it is the disposition of the people of the United States to coöperate with others in all appropriate and judicious exertions to prevent a recurrence of national conflicts; therefore,

Resolved, That the Committee on Foreign Affairs be directed to inquire into the expediency of authorizing a correspondence to be opened by the Secretary of State with Foreign Governments, on the subject of procuring Treaty stipulations for the reference of all future disputes to a friendly Arbitration, or for the establishment instead thereof of a Congress of Nations, to determine International law and settle International disputes. Though, for the present unsuccessful, this excellent effort will prepare the way for another trial.

Nor does it stand alone. Almost contemporaneously, M. Bouvet, in the National Assembly of France, submitted a proposition of a similar character, the official record of which is as follows:

NATIONAL ASSEMBLY.

Proposition relative to the opening of a Universal Congress, having for its object a proportional disarmament among all recognized States. Presented the 8th of January, 1849, by the Citizen, Francisque Bouvet, representative of the People. Referred to the Committee of Foreign Affairs.

(*Urgency Demands.*)

Seeing that War between nations is contrary to religion, humanity, and the public well-being, the French National Assembly decrees:

First Article. — The French Republic proposes to the Governments and Representative Assemblies of the different States of Europe, America, and other civilized countries, to unite by their representation, in a Congress which shall have for its object a proportional disarmament among the powers, the abolition of War, and a substitution for that barbarous usage, of an Arbitral jurisdiction, of which the said Congress shall immediately fulfill the functions.

Second Article. — The Universal Congress shall commence on the 1st of May, 1849, at Constantinople.

Third Article. — The President of the Republic is charged to notify the present proposition to all the Governments and Representative Assemblies of civilized States, and to use all the means in his power to induce them to concur in it.

In an elaborate report, the French Committee on Foreign Affairs, while declining at present to recommend this proposition, distinctly sanction its object.

At a still earlier date, some time in the summer of 1848, Arnold Ruge brought the same measure before the German Parliament at Frankfort, by moving the following amendment to the Report of the Committee on Foreign Relations:

That, as armed peace, by its standing armies, imposes an intolerable burden upon the people of Europe, and endangers civil freedom, we therefore recognize the necessity of calling into existence a *Congress of Nations*, for the object of effecting a general disarmament of Europe.

Though this proposition failed to be adopted, yet the mover is reported to have sustained it by a speech, which was received with applause both in the assembly and in the gallery. Among other things, he used these important words:

There is no necessity of feeding an army of military idlers and eaters. There is nothing to fear from our neighboring barbarians, as they are called. You must give up the idea that the French *will* eat us up, and that the Prussians *can* eat us up. Soldiers must cease to exist; then shall no more cities be bombarded. These opinions must be kept up and propagated by a Congress of Nations. I vote that the nations of Europe disarm at once.

In the British Parliament, also, our cause has found an able representative in Mr. Cobden, whose name is an omen of success. He has not only addressed many large popular bodies in its behalf, but already by speech and motion, in the House of Commons, has striven for a reduction in the armaments of Great Britain, and has only lately given notice of the following motion, which he intends to call up in that assembly at the earliest moment:

That an humble address be presented to her Majesty,

praying she will be graciously pleased to direct her Principal Secretary of State for Foreign Affairs, to enter into communication with Foreign Powers, inviting them to concur in treaties, binding the respective parties, in the event of any future misunderstanding which cannot be arranged by amicable negotiation, to refer the matter in dispute to the decision of arbitrators.

Such is the Peace Movement. With the ever-flowing current of time it has gained ever-increasing strength; and it has now become like a mighty river. At first but a slender fountain, sparkling upon some lofty summit, it has swollen with every tributary rill, with the friendly rains and dews of heaven, and at last with the associate waters of various nations, until it washes the feet of populous cities rejoicing on its peaceful banks. By the voices of poets; by the aspirations and labors of statesmen, of philosophers, of good men; by the experience of history; by the peaceful union into nations of families, tribes, and provinces, divesting themselves of the "liberty" to wage War; by the example of leagues, alliances, confederacies and congresses; by the kindred movements of our age, all tending to Unity; by an awakened public sentiment, and a growing recognition of the Brotherhood of Mankind; by the sympathies of large popular assemblies; by the formal action of legislative bodes; by the promises of Christianity, are we encouraged to persevere in our work. So doing, we shall act not *against* nature, but *with* nature, making ourselves, according to the injunction of Lord Bacon, its ministers and interpreters. From no single man, from no body of men, does our cause proceed. Not from Saint Pierre or Leibnitz, from Rousseau or Kant, in other days; not from Jay or Burritt, from Cobden or

Lamartine in our own. It is the irrepressible utterance of longing with which the great heart of Humanity labors; it is the universal expression of the Spirit of the Age, thirsting after Harmony; it is the heaven-born whisper of Truth, immortal and omnipotent; it is the word of God, published in commands as from the burning bush; it is the soft voice of Christ, declaring to all mankind that they are brothers, and saying to the turbulent nationalities of the earth, as to the raging sea, "Peace, be still!"

GENTLEMEN OF THE PEACE SOCIETY,— Such is the War System of the Commonwealth of Nations; and such are the means and auguries of its overthrow. It is the chosen object of our Society, to aid and direct public sentiment so as most to hasten the coming of this day. All who have candidly attended me in this exposition, already too long protracted, will bear witness that we attempt nothing in any way inconsistent with the human character; that we do not seek to suspend or hold in check any general laws of nature; but simply to bring nations within that established system of social order, which has already secured such inestimable good to civil society, and which is as applicable to nations as to individuals.

The tendencies of nations, as revealed in history, teach that our aims are in harmony with those prevailing natural laws, which God, in his benevolence, has ordained for mankind.

Examples teach also that we attempt nothing that is not directly practicable. If the several states of the Helvetic Republic; if the thirty independent States of the North American Union; if the thirty-eight independent sovereignties of the German Confederation can, by formal stipulations, divest themselves of the *right of war with each other*, and consent to submit all mutual controversies to Arbitration, or to a High Court of Judicature, then can the Commonwealth of Nations do the same. Nor should they hesitate, while, in the language of William Penn, such surpassing instances show that *it may be done*, and Europe, by her incomparable miseries, that *it ought to be done*. Nay more; if it would be criminal in these several clusters of states to reëstablish the Institution of War, as the Arbiter of Justice, then is it criminal in the Commonwealth of Nations to continue it.

Changes already wrought in the *Laws of War* teach still further that the whole System may be abolished. The existence of laws implies an authority that sanctions or enacts, which in the present case is the Commonwealth of Nations. But this authority can, of course, modify or abrogate what it has originally sanctioned or enacted. In the exercise of this power, the Laws of War have, from time to time, been modified in many important particulars. Prisoners taken in battle cannot now be killed; nor can they be reduced to slavery. Poison and assassination can no longer be employed against an enemy. Private property on land cannot be seized. Persons, occupied on land exclusively with the arts of Peace, cannot be molested. It remains that the authority, by which the Laws of War have been thus modified, should entirely abrogate them. Their existence is a disgrace to civilization; for it implies the *common consent* of nations to the Arbitrament of War, as regulated by these laws. Like the Laws of the Duel, they should yield to some arbitrament of reason. If the former, once firmly imbedded in the systems of municipal law, could be abolished by individual states, so also can the Laws of War, which are a part of international law, be abolished by the Commonwealth of Nations. In the light of reason and of religion, there can be but one Law of War — the great law which pronounces it unwise, unchristian, and unjust, and forbids it forever as a crime.

In thus distinctly alleging the practicability of our aims, I may properly here introduce an incontrovertible authority. Listen to the words of an American statesman — whose long life was spent in the service of his country at home and abroad, and whose undoubted familiarity with the Law of Nations was never surpassed — John Quincy Adams. "War," he says, in one of the legacies of his venerable experience,* "by the common consent, and mere will of civilized man, has not only been divested of its most atrocious cruelties, but for multitudes, growing multitudes of individuals, has already been, and is abolished. *Why should it not be abolished for all?* Let it be impressed upon the heart of every one of you — impress it upon the minds of your children, *that this total abolition of War upon earth* is an improvement in the condition of man, entirely dependent on his own will. He cannot repeal or change the laws of physical nature. He cannot redeem himself from the ills that flesh is heir to; but the ills of war and slavery are all of his own creation.

* Oration at Newburyport, July 4, 1839.

He has but to will, and he effects the cessation of them altogether."

Well does John Quincy Adams say, that mankind have but to *will* it, and War shall be abolished. Let them will it; and War shall disappear like the Duel. Let them will it; and War shall skulk like the torture. Let them will it; and War shall fade away like the fires of religious persecution. Let them will it; and War shall pass among profane follies, like the ordeal of burning ploughshares. Let them will it; and War shall hurry to join the earlier Institution of Cannibalism. Let them will it; and War shall be chastised from the Commonwealth of Nations, as slavery has been chastised from their municipal jurisdictions, by England and France, by Tunis and Tripoli.

To arouse this powerful *public will*, which, like a giant, yet sleeps, but whose awakened voice nothing can withstand, should be our earnest endeavor. To do this, we must never tire in exposing the true character of the War System. To be hated, it needs only to be comprehended; and it will surely be abolished as soon as it is sincerely hated. See, then, that it is comprehended. Expose its manifold atrocities, in the light of reason, of humanity, of religion. Strip from it all its presumptuous pretences, its specious apologies, its hideous sorceries. Above all, let men no longer deceive themselves by the shallow thought that this System is a necessary incident of imperfect human nature, and thus continue to cast upon God the responsibility for their crimes. Let them see clearly, that it is a monster of their own creation, born with their consent, whose vital spark is fed by their breath, and without their breath must necessarily die. Let them see distinctly what I have so carefully presented to-night, that War, under the Law of Nations, is an Institution, and the whole War System is an Establishment for the administration of international justice, for which the Commonwealth of Nations is directly responsible, and which this Commonwealth can at any time remove.

As men come to recognize these things, they will instinctively cease to cherish War, and will refuse all appeal to its Arbitrament. They will forego their rights even, rather than wage an irreligious battle. But criminal and irrational as is War, unhappily we cannot — in the present state of human error — expect large numbers to appreciate its true character, and to hate it with that perfect hatred, which shall cause them to renounce its agency, unless we can offer an approved and practical mode of determining the controversies of nations, as a *substitute* for the imagined necessity of an appeal to the sword. This we are able to do; and so doing, we shall reflect new light upon the atrocity of a System, which discards reason, defies justice, and tramples upon all the precepts of Christian love.

1. The most complete and permanent substitute for War would be a Congress of Nations, and a High Court of Judicature organized in pursuance thereof. Such a system, while admitted on all sides to promise many excellent results, is opposed on two grounds. *First*, it is said, that, as regards the smaller states, it would be a tremendous engine of oppression, subversive of their political independence. Surely it could not be so oppressive as the War System. But the experience of the smaller states in the German Confederation, and in

the American Union — nay, the experience of Belgium and Holland, by the side of the overtopping power of France, and the experience of Denmark and Sweden in the very night-shade of Russia — all show the futility of this objection. And, *second*, it is said that the decrees of such a Court could not be carried into effect. Even if they were enforced by the combined power of the associate states, as the executive arm of the high tribunal, the sword would be the melancholy instrument of Justice only, but not the Arbiter of Justice. But there can be no occasion to entertain the question of the propriety or rightfulness of such a resort, so abhorrent to many of the friends of Peace, though clearly not obnoxious to the conclusive reasons against international appeals to the sword. We may learn, however, from the experience of history, and particularly from the experience of the thirty States of our Union, that there will be little occasion for any executive arm. The State of Rhode Island, in its recent controversy with Massachusetts, submitted, with much indifference, to the adverse decree of the Supreme Court of the United States; and I doubt not that Missouri and Iowa will submit with equal contentment to any determination of their present controversy by the same tribunal. The same submission would attend the decrees of any Court of Judicature, established by the Commonwealth of Nations. There is a growing sense of justice, combined with a growing might of public opinion, whereof the soldier knows little, which would maintain the judgments of the august tribunal, assembled in the face of the nations, better than the swords of all the marshals of France, better than the bloody terrors of Austerlitz or Waterloo.

The idea of a Congress of Nations and of a High Court of Judicature, established in pursuance thereof, is as practicable as its consummation is confessedly dear to all friends of Universal Peace. Whenever this Congress is convened, as surely it will be convened, I know not all the names that will deserve commendation in its earliest proceedings; but there are two, whose particular and long-continued advocacy of this Institution, will connect them forever indissolubly with its fame — the Abbé Saint Pierre, of France, and William Ladd, of the United States.

2. But there is still another substitute for War, which is not open even to the superficial objections made to a Congress of Nations. By formal treaties between two or more nations, Arbitration may be established as the mode of determining controversies between them. In every respect this is a contrast to War. It is rational, humane and cheap. Above all, it is consistent with the precepts of Christianity. As I mention this substitute, I should do injustice to the cause, and to my own feelings, if I did not express the obligations of all the friends of Universal Peace to its efficient introducer and advocate, our fellow-citizen, and the President of our Society, the honored son of an illustrious father, whose absence to-night enables me, without offending his known modesty of character, to introduce this tribute — I mean William Jay.

The complete overthrow of the War System, involving, of course, the disarming of the Christian States, would follow the establishment of a Congress of Nations, or of a general System of Arbitration. Thon at last would our aims be accomplished; then at last would Peace be organized among the nations, and once more angelic voices should fill the skies, and be echoed in every Christian breast. Then, indeed, might Christians repeat the fitful boast of the generous Mohawk, saying, " We have thrown the hatchet so high into the air, and beyond the skies, that no arm on earth can reach to bring it down." The incalculable sums, now devoted to armaments and the destructive industry of War, would be turned to the productive industry of Art, and to offices of Beneficence. As in the dead and rotten carcass of the lion, which roared against the strong man of Israel, after a time there was a swarm of bees and honey, so should crowds of useful laborers, and all good works take the place of the wild beast of War, and the riddle of Samson once more be interpreted; " Out of the eater came forth meat, and out of the strong came forth sweetness."

Put together the products of all the mines of the world — the glistening ore of California, the accumulated treasures of Mexico and Peru, with the diamonds of Golconda, and the whole shining heap shall be less than the means thus diverted from War to Peace. Under the blessed influence of such a change, civilization shall be quickened anew. Then shall happy labor find its reward, and the whole land be filled with its increase. There is no aspiration of knowledge, no vision of charity, no venture of enterprise, no fancy of art which may not then be fulfilled. The great unsolved problem of Pauperism will at last be solved. There will be no paupers, when there are no soldiers. The social struggles, that now so fearfully disturb the European states, would die away in the happiness of an era of unarmed

Peace, no longer cumbered by the oppressive System of War; nor can there be well-founded hope of any permanent cessation of these struggles so long as this System endures. The people ought not to rest; nay, they cannot rest, while this System endures. As King Arthur, prostrate on the earth, with bloody streams running from his sides, could not be at ease until his sword, the vengeful Excalibar, was thrown into the flood; so the nations, now prostrate on the earth, with bloody streams running from their sides, cannot be at ease until they fling far away the wicked sword of War.

Lop off the unchristian armaments of the Christian States; extirpate these martial cancers — that they may no longer feed upon the best life-blood of the people — and society itself, which is now so weary and sick, will become fresh and young: not by opening its veins, as under the incantation of Medea, in the wild hope of infusing new strength; but by the amputation and complete removal of a deadly excrescence, which is the occasion of unutterable debility and exhaustion. The energies, hitherto withdrawn from proper healthful action, shall then replenish it with unwonted life and vigor, giving new expansion to every human capacity, and new elevation to every human aim. And society at last shall rejoice, like a strong man, to run its race.

Imagination toils in vain to picture the boundless good that will be thus achieved. As war and its deeds are infinitely evil and accursed, so will this triumph of Permanent Peace be infinitely beneficent and blessed. Something of its consequences were seen, as in prophetic vision, even by that incarnate Spirit of War, Napoleon, when, from his prison-island of St. Helena, looking back upon his mistaken career, he was led to confess the True Grandeur of Peace. Out of his mouth let its praise be spoken. "I had the project," he said, mournfully regretting the opportunity he had lost, "at the general peace of Amiens, of bringing each Power to an immense reduction of its standing armies. I wished a European Institute, with European prizes, to direct, associate, and bring together all the learned societies of Europe. Then, perhaps, through the universal spread of light, it might be permitted to anticipate for the great European Family, the establishment of an American Congress, or an Amphyctionic Council; and what a perspective, at last, of grandeur, of happiness, of prosperity! What a sublime and magnificent spectacle!"

Such is our cause. In its mighty influence it embraces all the causes of human benevolence. It is the comprehensive charity, enfolding all the charities of all. There is none so vast as to be above its powerful protection; there is none so lowly as not to feel its generous care. Religion, Knowledge, Freedom, Virtue, Happiness, in all their manifold forms, depend upon Peace. Sustained by Peace, they lean as upon the Everlasting Arm. And this is not all. Law, Order, Government, derive new sanctions from our cause. Nor can they attain to that complete dominion which is our truest defence and safeguard, until, by the overthrow of the War System, they comprehend the Commonwealth of Nations;

And Sovereign LAW, *the world's collected will*,
O'er thrones and globes elate,
Sits empress, crowning good, repressing ill.

In the name of Religion profaned by War; of Knowledge misapplied and perverted; of Freedom crushed to earth; of Virtue dethroned; of human Happiness violated; in the name of Law, Order, and Government, I call upon you to unite in efforts to establish the supremacy of Peace. Let no person hesitate. With the lips you all confess the infinite evil of War. Are you in earnest? Let the confession of the lips be followed by corresponding action. Let all unite in endeavors to render the recurrence of this evil impossible. Science and humanity every where put forth their best energies against cholera and pestilence. Let equal energies be directed against an evil more fearful than cholera or pestilence. Let each man consider the cause his own concern. Let him animate his neighbors in its behalf. Let him seek, in all proper ways, to influence the rulers of the Christian states, and above all the rulers of this happy land.

Let the old, the middle-aged, and the young, combine in a common cause. Let the pulpit, the school, the college, and the public street, all be moved to speak in its behalf. Preach it, minister of the Prince of Peace! Let it never be forgotten in conversation, in sermon or in prayer; nor any longer seek, by subtle theory, to reconcile the monstrous War System with the precepts of Christ! Instil it, teacher of childhood and youth, in the early thoughts of your precious charge; exhibit the wickedness of War, and the beauty of Peace; let these sink deep among those purifying and strengthening influences which shall ripen into a character of true manhood. Scholar! write it in your books. Poet! let it inspire to higher melodies your

Christian song. Let the interests of commerce, whose threads of golden tissue interknit the nations, enlist all the traffickers of the earth in its behalf. And you, servant of the law! sharer of my own peculiar toils, mindful that the law is silent in the midst of arms, join in endeavors to preserve, uphold and extend its sway! Remember, politician! that our cause is too universal to become the exclusive possession of any political party, but that all are welcome beneath its white banner. And to you, statesman and ruler! let the principles of Peace be as a cloud by day and a pillar of fire by night. Let the Abolition of War, and the overthrow of the War System, with the Disarming of the Christian nations, be your constant aim! Be this your pious diplomacy! Be this your devoted Christian statesmanship!

As a measure, at once simple and practical, obnoxious to no objections, promising incalculable good, and presenting an immediate opportunity of labor in the cause, let me invite your instant active coöperation in the efforts now making by the friends of Peace, at home and abroad, to establish Arbitration Treaties among the nations. If there is a tendency only in this scheme to avert War; certainly, if we may hope through its agency to prevent a single war — and who can doubt that such may be its result? — we ought to adopt it. Make the initiative. Try it; and nations will be slow to return to their present System. They will begin to learn War no more. Let it be the high privilege of our country, through its representatives abroad, to volunteer the proposal to all civilized governments. Let it thus inaugurate the idea of Permanent Peace in the diplomacy of the world. Nor should it weakly wait for the movements of other governments. In a cause so holy, no government is justified in waiting for another to make the first advance. Let us, then, take the lead in this great work. Let our republic, the powerful child of Freedom, go forth, as the Evangelist of Peace. Let her offer to the world a Magna Charta of International Law, by which the crime of War shall be forever abolished. Let her do this; and hers will be a Christian glory, by the side of which all the glory of battle shall be as the flashing of a bayonet by the side of the heavenly light which beamed from the countenance of Christ.

And now, while I thus encourage you in the cause of Universal Peace, the odious din of War, mingled with pathetic appeals for Freedom, reaches us from struggling Italy, from convulsed Germany, from aroused and triumphant Hungary; the populous North, at the stern command of the Russian Autocrat, threatens to pour its barbarous multitudes upon the scene; and a portentous cloud, charged with "red lightnings and impetuous rage," seems to hang over the whole continent of Europe, as it echoes once again to the tread of mustering squadrons. Alas! must this dismal work be renewed? Can Freedom be born, can nations be regenerated, only through the abhorred baptism of blood? In our aspirations let us not be blind to the lessons of history, or to the actual condition of men, so long accustomed to brute force, that, to their imperfect natures, it seems the only means by which injustice can be crushed. With sadness let me say, I cannot expect the *domestic* repose of nations until tyranny is overthrown, and the principles of *self-government* established ; especially do I not expect imperturbable peace in Italy, so long as foreign Austria continues to tread, with insolent iron heel, upon any part of that beautiful land. But whatever may be the fate of the present crisis, whether it be doomed to the horrors of prolonged fraternal strife, or whether it shall soon brighten into the radiance of enduring concord, I cannot doubt that the nations are now gravitating, with resistless might, even through fire and blood, into peaceful forms of social order, where the War System shall no longer be known.

Nay, from the very experience of this hour, let me draw the happy auguries of Permanent Peace. Not in international strife ; not in duels between nation and nation ; not in the selfish conflicts of ruler with ruler ; not in the unwise " game " of War, as played by king with king, do we find the elements of the present commotions, " with fear of change perplexing monarchs." It is to overturn the enforced rule of military power, to crush the tyranny of armies, and to supplant unjust governments, — whose only stay is physical force, and not the consent of the governed, — that the people have at last risen in mighty madness. So doing, they wage a battle in which all our sympathies must be with Freedom, while, in our sorrow at the unwelcome combat, we confess that victory is only less mournful than defeat. But through all these bloody mists, with the eye of faith we may clearly discern the ascending sun of permanent Peace — struggling to shoot its life-giving beams upon the outspread earth, already teeming with the powerful products of a new civilization.

Everywhere the glad signs of Progress salute us; and the promised land seems to smile at our approach. His soul is cold, his eye is dull, who does not perceive these things. Vainly has he read the history of the Past, vainly does he feel the irrepressible movement of the Present. Man has waded through a red sea of blood, and for forty centuries wandered through a wilderness of wretchedness and error, but he stands at last on the top of Pisgah; like the adventurous Spaniard, he has wearily climbed the lofty mountain heights whence he may descry the vast, unbroken Pacific sea; like the hardy Portuguese, he is sure to double this fearful Cape of Storms, destined ever afterwards to be called the Cape of Good Hope. Let me not seem too confident. I know not, that the nations will, in any brief period, like kindred drops, commingle into one; that, like the banyan-trees of the East, they will interlace and interlock, until there is no longer a single tree, but one forest,

> . . . . . A pillared shade
> High overarcht, and echoing walks between;

but I am assured, that, without renouncing any essential qualities of individuality or independence, they shall yet, even in our own day, arrange themselves in harmony; as magnetized iron rings — from which Plato once borrowed an image — under the influence of the potent, unseen attraction, while preserving each its own peculiar form, all cohere in a united chain of independent circles. From the birth of this new order shall spring not only international repose, but domestic quiet also; and Peace shall become the permanent ruler of the Christian States. The stone shall be rolled away from the sepulchre in which men have laid their Lord; and we shall hear the new-risen voice, saying, in words of blessed import, "Lo, I am with you alway, even unto the end of the world."

And here I might fitly close. But, though admonished that I have already occupied more of your time than I could venture to claim, except for the cause in whose behalf I now speak, I cannot forbear to consider, for a brief moment, yet one other topic, which I have left thus far untouched, partly because it was not directly connected with the question of the War System, and therefore seemed inappropriate to any earlier stage of the discussion, and partly because I wished, with my last words, to impress it upon your minds and upon your hearts. I refer to that greatest, most preposterous and most irreligious of earthly vanities, the monstrous reflexion of War — more worthy of the beasts of the field than of intelligent Christian men — *Military Glory.*

Let me not disguise the truth. It is too true that this is still cherished by mankind; that it is still an object of regard and ambition; that men follow War, and count its pursuit "honorable;" that the feats of brute force in battle are pronounced "brilliant;" and that a yet prevailing public opinion animates unreflecting and mistaken mortals to "seek the bubble *reputation* e'en in the cannon's mouth." It is too true, that nations persevere in offering praise and thanksgiving — such as no labors of Beneficence can achieve — to the chief whose hands are red with the blood of his fellow-men.

But whatever may be the usage of the world, whether

during the long and dreary Past, or in the yet barbarous Present, it must be clear to all who are willing to confront this question with candor, and in the light of unquestioned principles and examples, that all "glory," won in bloody strife among God's children, must be fugitive, evanescent, unreal — unstable as water, worthless as ashes. It is the offspring of a deluded public sentiment, and must certainly disappear, as men learn to analyze its elements and to appreciate its true character. Too long, indeed, has mankind worshipped what St. Augustine called the *splendid vices*, neglecting the simple virtues. Too long has mankind cultivated the flaunting and noxious weeds, careless of the golden corn which produces the bread of life. Too long has mankind been insensible to those Christian precepts, and to that high example, which, whatever may be the apologies of self-defence, rebuke all the pretensions of military glory.

Look for one moment at this "glory." Analyze it in the growing light which is shed by the lamps of history. Regarding War as an established Arbitrament, for the adjudication of controversies among nations — like the Petty Wars of an earlier period between cities, principalities, and provinces, and the Trial by Battle between individuals — the conclusion is irresistible, that an enlightened civilization must condemn all the partakers in its duels, and all their vaunted achievements, precisely as we now condemn all the partakers in those miserable contests which disfigure the commencement of modern history. The prowess of the individual is all forgotten in unutterable disgust at the inglorious barbarism of the strife in which it was displayed.

Observe yet again this "glory," in the broad illumination of Christian truth. In all ages, even in Heathen lands, men have looked with peculiar reverence upon the relation of Brotherhood. Feuds among brothers, from that earliest "mutual-murdering" contest beneath the walls of Thebes, have been accounted dismal and abhorred; never to be mentioned without condemnation and aversion. This sentiment was revived in modern times; and men sought to extend the holy circle of its influence. According to curious and savage custom, valiant knights, desirous of associating as brothers, voluntarily caused themselves to be bled together, that the blood of each other, as it spirted from the veins, might intermingle, and thus constitute them of *one blood.* By this peculiar sanction, the powerful emperor of Constantinople confirmed an alliance of friendship with a crusading king. The two monarchs being first bled together, drank of each other's blood, in token of Brotherhood; and their attendants, following the princely example, bled each other, caught the flowing blood in a wine-cup, and then drank a mutual pledge, saying, "We are brothers of *one blood.*"

Alas! by such profane and superfluous devices have men, in their barbarism, sought to establish that relation of Brotherhood, whose beauty and holiness they perceived, though they failed to discern that, by the ordinance of God, without any human stratagem, it justly comprehended all their fellow-men. In the midst of Judaism, which hated all nations, Christianity proclaimed love to all mankind, and distinctly declared that God had made of *one blood* all the nations of men. And, as if to keep this sublime truth ever present to the mind, the disciples were taught, in the simple prayer of the Saviour, to address God as their Father in Heaven; not in phrase of exclusive worship, as "*my* Father;" but in those other words of high Christian import, "*Our* Father;" with the petition not merely "to forgive *me my* trespasses," but with a diviner prayer "to forgive *us our* trespasses;" thus in the solitude of the closet, recognizing all alike as children of God, and embracing all alike in the petition of prayer.

Confessing the Fatherhood of God, and the consequent Brotherhood of Mankind, we find at once a divine standard, of unquestionable accuracy and applicability, by which to estimate the achievements of battle. No brother can win "glory" from the death of a brother. Cain won no "glory" when he slew Abel; nor would Abel have won "glory," had he, in the exercise of strict self-defence, succeeded in slaying the wicked Cain. The soul recoils in horror from the thought of praise or honor, as the meed of any such melancholy, hateful success. And what is true of a contest between *two* brothers, is equally true of a contest between *many.* No army can win "glory" by dealing death or defeat to an army of its brothers.

The ancient Romans, ignorant of this sacred and most comprehensive relation, and recognizing only the exclusive fellowship which springs from a common country, accounted *civil war* as *fratricidal.* They branded the opposing forces — even under well-loved names in the Republic — as *impious;* and constantly refused "honor," "thanksgiving," or "triumph," to the conquering chief whose sword had been employed against his *fellow-citizens*, even though traitors and rebels. As the Brotherhood of Mankind — now professed by Christian lips — becomes practically recognized, it will be impossible to restrain our regard within the exclusive circle of country, and to establish an unchristian distinction of honor between *civil war* and *international war. As all men are brothers, so, by irresistible consequence,* ALL WAR MUST BE FRATRICIDAL. And can "glory" come from fratricide? No, no. Shame and sorrow must attend it; nor can any war, under whatever apology of necessity it may be vindicated, be justly made the occasion of "honor," of "thanksgiving," or of "triumph." Surely none can hesitate in this conclusion, who are not fatally imbued with the Heathen rage of nationality, that made the Venetians say, "they were Venetians first, and Christians afterwards."

Tell me not, then, of the homage which the world yet offers to the military chieftain. Tell me not of the "glory" of War. Tell me not of the "honor" or "fame" won on its murderous fields. All is vanity. It is a blood-red phantom, sure to fade and disappear. They, who strive after it, Ixion-like, embrace a cloud. Though seeming for a while to fill the heavens, cloaking the stars, it must, like the vapors of earth, pass away. Milton likens the early contests of the Heptarchy to the skirmishes of crows and kites; but God, and the exalted Christianity of the Future, must regard all the bloody feuds of men in the same likeness; looking upon Napoleon and Alexander, so far as they were engaged in war, only as monster crows and kites. Thus shall it be, as mankind ascend from the thrall of brutish passions. Nobler aims, by nobler means, shall fill the soul. A new standard of excellence shall prevail; and honor, divorced from all deeds of blood, shall become the inseparable attendant of good works alone. Far better, then, shall it be, even in the judgment of this world, to have been a door-keeper in the house of Peace, than the proudest dweller in the tents of War.

There is a legend of the early Church, that the Saviour left his image miraculously impressed upon a napkin which he had placed upon his countenance. The napkin was lost, and men attempted to portray that countenance from the Heathen models of Jupiter and Apollo. But the image of Christ is not lost to the world. Clearer than in the precious napkin, clearer than in the colors or the marble of modern art, it appears in every virtuous deed, in every act of self-sacrifice, in all magnanimous toil, in every recognition of the Brotherhood of Mankind. It shall yet be supremely manifest, in unimagined loveliness and serenity, when the Commonwealth of Nations, confessing the True Grandeur of Peace, shall renounce the wickedness of the War System, and dedicate to labors of Beneficence all the comprehensive energies now so fatally absorbed in its support. Then, at last, shall it be seen, that *there can be no Peace that is not honorable, and there can be no War that is not dishonorable.*

SPEECH AGAINST THE ADMISSION OF TEXAS AS A SLAVE STATE, MADE AT A PUBLIC MEETING IN FANEUIL HALL, BOSTON, NOV. 4, 1845.

Mr. Chairman,

I could not listen to the appropriate remarks of my friend, the Secretary of the Commonwealth, (Hon. John G. Palfrey,) who has preceded me, without being reminded of an important act in his life, and without feeling anew what all must feel, the beauty of the example he has afforded in the fraternal treatment of the slaves descended to him by inheritance; manumitting them as he has, and conducting them far away from slavery into these more cheerful precincts of freedom. In thus publicly offering him my humble tribute, I feel that I must awaken a response not only in every bosom in this assembly, but in every heart that has not ceased to throb at the recital of an act of self-sacrifice and humanity. By this act he has done, as a citizen, what Massachusetts is now called upon to do, as a State, — to divest herself of all responsibility for any accession of slave property.

There are occasions in the progress of affairs, when the attention of all, though ordinarily opposed to each other, is arrested; and even the lukewarm, the listless, the indifferent, unite heartily in a common object. Such is the case in great calamities, when the efforts of all are needed to avert a fatal blow. If the fire-bell startles us from our slumbers, we do not ask of what faith in politics or religion is the unfortunate brother whose house is exposed to destruction. It is enough that there is misfortune to be averted. In this spirit we have assembled, on this inclement evening, putting aside all distinctions of party, forgetting all disagreements of opinion, only to remember one point on which all are agreed; renouncing all discords only to cling to one ground on which we all meet in concord; I mean the opposition to the admission of Texas as a slave state.

The scheme for the annexation of Texas, begun in stealth and fraud, and with the view to extend and strengthen slavery, has not yet received the final sanction of Congress. Even according to the course pursued by the framers of this measure, it is necessary that Texas should be formally admitted into the family of States by a vote of Congress, and that her Constitution should be approved by Congress. The question on this measure will arise this winter, and we would, if we could, strengthen the hands and the hearts of the friends of freedom by whom the measure will be opposed.

Ours is no factious or irregular course. It has the sanction of the highest examples on a kindred occasion. In 1819, the question now before us arose on the admission of Missouri as a slave state. I need not remind you of the ardor and constancy with which this was opposed at the North, by men of all parties, with scarcely a dissenting voice. One universal chorus of protests thundered from the Free States against the formation of what was called another *black State*. Meetings were convened in all the considerable towns — in Philadelphia, Trenton, New York, New Haven, and everywhere throughout Massachusetts, in order to give expression to this opposition in a manner to be audible on the floor of Congress. At Boston, on December 3d, 1819, a meeting was held in the state-house, without distinction of party, and embracing the leaders of both sides. That meeting, in its objects, was precisely like this now assembled. A large committee was appointed to prepare resolutions. Of this committee, William Eustis, afterwards Governor of Massachusetts, was chairman. With him were associated John Phillips, at that time President of the Senate of Massachusetts — a name dear to every friend of the slave as the father of him to whose eloquent voice we hope to listen to-night — Timothy Bigelow, Speaker of the House of Representatives, William Gray, Henry Dearborn, Josiah Quincy, Daniel Webster, William Ward, of Medford, William Prescott, Thomas H. Perkins, Stephen White, Benjamin Pickman, William Sullivan, George Blake, David Cummings, James Savage, John Gallison, James T. Austin, and Henry Orne. A committee, more calculated to inspire the confidence of all sides, could not have been appointed. Numerous as were its members, they were all men of mark, high in the confidence and affections of the country. This committee reported the following resolutions, which were adopted by the meeting: —

Resolved, As the opinion of this meeting, that the Congress of the United States possess the constitutional power upon the admission of any new State created beyond the limits of the original territory of the United States, to make the prohibition of the further extension of slavery, or involuntary servitude, in such new State, a condition of its admission.

Resolved, That, in the opinion of this meeting, it is just and expedient that this power should be exercised by Congress upon the admission of all new States, created beyond the original limits of the United States.

The meeting in Boston was followed by one in Salem, called, according to the terms of the notice, "to consider whether the immense region of country extending from the Mississippi to the Pacific Ocean is destined to be the abode of Happiness, Independence, and Freedom, *or the wide prison of misery and slavery.*" Resolutions against the admission of any slave State were passed, being supported by Benjamin T. Pickman, Andrew Dunlap, and Joseph Story, a name of authority wherever found. In the meeting at Worcester, Solomon Strong and Levi Lincoln acted a prominent part. Resolutions were adopted here, "earnestly requesting their representatives in Congress to oppose the admission of any new slave State." By these assemblies, the Commonwealth was aroused. It opposed an unbroken front to slavery.

Twenty-five years have passed since these efforts in the cause of freedom. Some of the partakers in them are still spared to us, full of years and honors; but the larger part have been called from the duty of opposing slavery on earth, to His presence, whose service is perfect freedom. But the same question which aroused their energies, presents itself to us. Shall we be less faithful than they? Will Massachusetts oppose a less unbroken front now than then? In the lapse of these few years has the love of freedom diminished? Has the sensibility to human suffering lost any of the keenness of its edge?

Let us regard the question closely. Congress is called upon to sanction the Constitution of Texas, which not only supports slavery, but which contains a clause prohibiting the Legislature of the State from abolishing slavery. In doing this, it will give a fresh stamp of legislative approbation to an unrighteous system; it will assume a new and active responsibility for the system; it will again become a dealer, on a gigantic scale, in human flesh. Yes, at this moment, when the conscience of mankind is at last aroused to the enormity of holding a fellow-man in bondage; when, throughout the civilized world, a slave-dealer is a bye-word and a reproach, we, as a nation, are about to become proprietors of a large population of slaves. Such an act, at this time, is removed from the reach of the palliation often extended to slavery. Slavery, we are speciously told by those who seek to defend it, is not our original sin. It was entailed upon us, so we are instructed, by our ancestors; and the responsibility is often, with exultation, thrown upon the mother country. Now, without stopping to inquire into the truth of this suggestion, it is sufficient for the present purpose, to know that by welcoming Texas as a slave State we do make slavery our own original sin. Here is a new case of actual transgression which we cannot cast upon the shoulders of any progenitors, nor upon any mother country, distant in time or place. The Congress of the United States, the people of the United States, at this day, in this vaunted period of light, will be responsible for it;

so that it shall be said hereafter, so long as the dismal history of slavery is read, that in the year of Christ, 1846, a new and deliberate act was passed to confirm and extend it.

By the present movement we propose no measure of change. We do not offer to interfere with any institutions of the Southern States, nor to modify any law on the subject of slavery anywhere under the Constitution of the United States. Our movement is conservative in its character. It is to preserve the existing supports of freedom; it is to prevent a violation of the vital principles of free institutions.

Such a movement should unite in its support all but those few, in whose distorted or unnatural vision slavery seems to be a great good. Most clearly should it unite the freemen of the North; by all the considerations of self-interest, and by those higher considerations, founded on the rights of man. I cannot now dwell upon the controlling, political influence which the annexation of Texas will secure to the slave-holders in the councils of the country. This topic is of importance; but it yields to the supreme considerations of religion, morals, and humanity. I cannot banish from my view the great shame and wrong of slavery. The Judges of our Courts have declared it to be contrary to the law of nature, finding its support only in the positive enactments of men. Its horrors who can tell? Language fails in the vain effort to depict them.

By the proposed measure, we not only become parties to the acquisition of a large population of slaves, with all the crime of slavery; but we open a new market for the slaves of Virginia and the Carolinas, and *legalize a new slave trade.* A new slave trade! Consider this well. You cannot forget the horrors of what is called "the middle passage," when the crowds of unfortunate human beings, stolen, and borne by sea far from their warm African homes, are pressed on shipboard into spaces of smaller dimensions for each than a coffin. And yet the deadly consequences of this middle passage have been supposed to fall short of those, which are sometimes undergone by the wretched caravans, driven from the exhausted lands of the Northern slave States to the sugar plantations nearer to the sun of the South. It is supposed, that one quarter part often perish in these removals. I see them, in imagination, on this painful passage, chained in bands or troops, and driven like cattle, leaving behind what has become to them a home and a country (alas! what a home, and what a country!) — husband torn from wife, and parent from child, and sold anew into a more direful captivity. Can this take place with our consent, nay, without our most determined opposition? If the slave trade is to receive a new adoption from our country, let us have no part or lot in it. Let us wash our hands of this great guilt. As we read its horrors, may each of us be able to exclaim, with a conscience void of offence, "Thou canst not say I did it." God forbid, that the votes and voices of the freemen of the North should help to bind anew the fetter of the slave! God forbid, that the lash of the slave dealer should be nerved by any sanction from New England! God forbid, that the blood which spirts from the lacerated, quivering flesh of the slave, should soil the hem of the white garments of Massachusetts!

But voices of discouragement reach us from other parts of the country, and even from our own friends in this bracing air of freedom. We are told that all exertions will be vain, and that the admission of a new slave state is "a foregone conclusion." But this is no reason why we should shrink from our duty. "I will try," was the exclamation of an American general on the field of battle. "England expects every man to do his duty," was the signal of the British admiral. Ours is a contest holier than those which aroused these animating words. Let *us* try; let every man do his duty.

And suppose New England stands alone in these efforts; suppose Massachusetts stands alone; is it not a noble solitude? Is it not a position of honor? Is it not a position where she will find companionship with all that is great and generous in the past — with all the disciples of truth, of right, of liberty? It has not been her wont on former occasions, to inquire whether she should stand alone. Your honored ancestor, Mr. Chairman, who from these walls regards our proceedings to-night, did not ask whether Massachusetts would be alone, when she commenced the opposition which ended in the independence of the Thirteen Colonies.

But we cannot fail to accomplish great good. It is in obedience to a prevailing law of Providence, that no act of self-sacrifice, no act of devotion to duty, no act of humanity can fail. It stands forever as a landmark; as a point from which to make a new effort. The champions of equal rights and of human brotherhood shall hereafter derive new strength from these exertions.

Let Massachusetts, then, be aroused. Let all her

children be summoned to join in this holy cause. There are questions of ordinary politics in which men may remain neutral; but neutrality now is treason to liberty, to humanity, and to the fundamental principles of our free institutions. Let her united voice, with the accumulated echoes of freedom that fill this ancient Hall, go forth with comfort and cheer to all who labor in the same cause every where throughout the land. Let it help to confirm the wavering, and to reclaim those who have erred from the right path. Especially may it exert a proper influence in Congress upon the representatives of the free States. May it serve to make them as firm in the defence of freedom as their opponents are pertinacious in the cause of slavery.

Let Massachusetts continue to be known as foremost in the cause of freedom; and let none of her children yield to the fatal dalliance with slavery. You will remember the Arabian story of the magnetic mountain, under whose irresistible attraction the iron bolts which held together the strong timbers of a stately ship were drawn out, till the whole fell apart, and became a disjointed wreck. Do we not find in this story an image of what happens to many Northern men, under the potent magnetism of Southern companionship or Southern influence? Those principles, which constitute the individuality of the Northern character, which render it staunch, strong and seaworthy, which bind it together, as with iron, are drawn out one by one, like the bolts from the ill-fated vessel, and out of the miserable loosened fragments is formed that human anomaly — *A Northern man with Southern principles.* Such a man is no true son of Massachusetts.

There is a precious incident in the life of one whom our country has delighted to honor, furnishing an example that we shall do well to imitate. When Napoleon, having reached the pinnacle of military honor, lusting for a higher title than that of First Consul, caused a formal vote to be taken on the question, whether he should be declared Emperor of France, Lafayette, at that time in retirement, and only recently, by the intervention of the First Consul, liberated from the dungeons of Olmutz, deliberately registered his *No.* At a period, in the golden decline of his high career, resplendent with heroic virtues, revisiting our shores, the scene of his youthful devotion to freedom, and receiving on all sides that beautiful homage of thanksgiving, which is of itself an all-sufficient answer to the sarcasm against the alleged ingratitude of republics, here in Boston, this illustrious Frenchman listened with especial pride to the felicitation addressed to him, as "the man who knew so well how to say *no.*" Be this the example for Massachusetts, and may it be among her praises hereafter, that on this occasion she knew so well how to say NO!

SPEECH ON THE ANTI-SLAVERY DUTIES OF THE WHIG PARTY, BEFORE THE WHIG STATE CONVENTION, AT FANEUIL HALL, IN BOSTON, SEPT. 23, 1846.

MR. PRESIDENT AND FELLOW-CITIZENS,
WHIGS OF MASSACHUSETTS:

Grateful for the honor you have done me in calling upon me thus early to address you, I shall endeavor to speak with sincerity and frankness on the duties of the Whig party. It is of duties that I shall speak.

When it was first announced that the Convention was to be held in Boston, many were disposed to regret that it was not summoned to sit in the country; believing that the opinions of the country, free as its bracing air, more than those of Boston, would be in harmony with the tone which it becomes us to adopt at the present crisis. In the country, is the spirit of freedom; in the city, the spirit of commerce; and though these two spirits may, at times, act in admirable conjunction and with irresistible strength, yet it sometimes occurs that the generous and unselfish impulses of the one are checked and controlled by the careful calculations of economy suggested by the other. Even Right and Liberty are, in some minds, of less significance than dividends and dollars.

But I am happy that the Convention has been convoked in Faneuil Hall. This place is vocal with inspiring accents, and though, on other occasions, words have been uttered here, which the lover of morals, of freedom and humanity, must regret, these walls, faithful only to Freedom, refuse to echo them. The Whigs of Massachusetts, assembled in Faneuil Hall, must be true to this early scene of the struggles for Freedom; they must be true to their own name, which has descended to them from those who partook of those struggles.

We are a Convention of Whigs. And who are the Whigs? Some may say they are the supporters of the tariff; others, that they are the advocates of internal improvements; of measures to restrain the exercise of the veto power; or of a bank. All these are now, or have been, prominent articles in the faith of the party. But this enumeration does not do justice to the character of the Whigs.

The Whigs, as their name imports, are, or *ought to be*, the party of Freedom. They seek, or should seek, on all occasions, to carry out fully and practically the principles of our institutions. The principles which our fathers declared, and sealed with their blood, their Whig children should seek to manifest in their acts. The Whigs, therefore, reverence the Declaration of Independence, as embodying the vital truths of freedom, especially that great truth, "that all men are born equal." They reverence the Constitution of the United

States, and seek to guard it against infractions; believing that under the Constitution, Freedom can be best preserved. They reverence the Union of the States; believing that the peace, happiness and welfare of all depend upon this blessed bond. They reverence the public faith, and require that it should be punctiliously kept in all laws, charters and obligations. They reverence the principles of morality, of truth, of justice, of right. They seek to advance their country, rather than individuals; and to promote the welfare of the people, rather than of their leaders. A member of such an association, founded on the highest moral sentiments, recognizing conscience and benevolence as its animating ideas, cannot be said "to give to party what was meant for mankind;" for all the interests of the party must be coincident and commensurate with the manifold interests of humanity.

Such is, as I trust, or *certainly should be*, the Whig party of Massachusetts. It refuses to identify itself exclusively with those measures of transient policy, which may, like the Bank, become "obsolete ideas;" but connects itself with everlasting principles, which can never fade or decay. In doing this, it does not neglect other things; as the tariff, or internal improvements. But it treats these as subordinate. Far less does it show indifference to the Constitution or the Union; for it seeks to render these the guardians and representatives of the lofty principles to which we are attached.

The Whigs have been called by you, Mr. President, the *conservatives*. In a just sense, they should be conservatives; not of forms only, but of substance; not of the letter only, but of the living spirit. The Whigs should be the conservators of the spirit of our ancestors; conservators of the great animating ideas of our institutions. They should profess that truest and highest *conservatism*, which watches, guards and preserves the great principles of Truth, Right, Freedom and Humanity. Such a conservatism is not narrow and exclusive; but broad and expansive. It is not trivial and bigoted; but manly and generous. It is the conservatism of the Whigs of '76.

Let me say, then, that the Whigs of Massachusetts are — I hope it is not my wish only that is father to the thought — the party who seek the establishment of Truth, Freedom, Right and Humanity, under the Constitution of the United States, and by the Union of the States. They are Unionists, Constitutionalists, Friends of the Right.

And the question here arises, how shall this party, inspired by these principles, now act? The answer is easy. In accordance with their principles. It must utter them with distinctness, and act upon them with energy.

It will naturally express its opposition to the present administration for its treacherous course on the tariff; and for its interference, by the veto, with internal improvements; but it will be more alive to evils of greater magnitude, — the unjust and unchristian war with Mexico, which is not less absurd than wicked in its character; and beyond this, to the institution of Slavery.

The time, I believe, has gone by, when the question is asked, *What has the North to do with Slavery?* It might almost be answered, that, politically, it had little to do with anything else, so are all the acts of our government connected, directly or indirectly, with this institution. Slavery is every where. It constitutionally enters the halls of Congress, in the disproportionate representation of the slave States. It shows its disgusting front in the District of Columbia, in the shadow of the capitol, under the legislative jurisdiction of the nation; of the North as well as the South. It sends its miserable victims on the high seas, from the ports of Virginia to the ports of Louisiana, beneath the protecting flag of the republic. It follows into the free States, in pursuance of a provision of the Constitution, those fugitives, who, under the inspiration of freedom, seek our altars for safety; nay, more, with profane hands it seizes those who have never known the name of slave, colored freemen of the North, and dooms them to irremediable bondage. It insults and exiles from its jurisdiction the honored representatives of Massachusetts, who seek, as messengers of the Commonwealth, to secure for her colored citizens the peaceful safeguard of the laws of the Union. It not only uses the Constitution for its purposes, but abuses it also. It violates the Constitution at pleasure, to build up new slaveholding States. It seeks perpetually to widen its area, while professing to extend the area of freedom. It has brought upon the country war with Mexico, with its enormous expenditures, and more enormous guilt. By the spirit of union among its supporters, it controls the affairs of government; interferes with the cherished interests of the North, enforcing and then refusing protection to her manufactures; makes and unmakes presidents; usurps to itself the larger portion of all offices of honor and profit, both in the army and navy, and also in the civil department; and stamps upon our whole country, the character, before the world, of that monstrous anomaly and mockery, a *slaveholding republic*, with the living truths of freedom on its lips, and the dark mark of slavery printed on its brow.

In her opposition to slavery, Massachusetts has already, to a certain extent, taken the ground that becomes her character as a free Commonwealth. By successive resolutions of her Legislature, she has called for the abolition of slavery in the District of Columbia, and for the abolition of the slave trade between the States; and she has also proposed an amendment of the Constitution of the United States, putting the South upon an equality with the North in the representation in Congress. More than this, her judiciary, always pure, fearless, and upright, has inflicted upon slavery the brand of reprobation. I hope it will not appear too professional, if I refer to the opinion of the Supreme Court of Massachusetts, (18 Pick. Rep. 211,) where it is expressly declared that "Slavery is contrary to natural right, to the principles of justice, humanity, and sound policy." This is the law of Massachusetts.

And shall this Commonwealth continue in any way to sustain an institution which its laws declare to be contrary to natural right, to justice, to humanity and sound policy? Shall the Whigs support what is contrary to the fundamental principles of the party? Here the consciences of good men respond to the judgment of the court. If it be wrong to hold a single slave, it must be wrong to hold many. If it be wrong for an individual to hold a slave, it must be wrong for a State. If it be wrong for a State, in its individual capacity, it must be wrong also, in association with other States. Massachusetts does not allow any of her citizens within her borders to hold slaves. Let her be consistent, and call for the abolition of slavery wherever she is, to any extent, responsible for it, wherever she is a party to it, wherever it may be reached by her influence; that is, everywhere beneath the constitution and laws of the Federal Government. "If any practice exist," said Mr. Webster, in one of those earlier efforts which commended him to our admiration, his address at Plymouth in 1820 — "If any practices exist, contrary to the principles of justice and humanity, within the reach of our laws or our influence, we are *inexcusable, if we do not exert ourselves to restrain and abolish them.*" This is a correct sentiment, worthy of its author, and of Massachusetts. It points directly to Massachusetts, as inexcusable for not exerting herself to restrain and abolish slavery every where within the reach of her laws or her influence.

Certainly, to labor in this cause is far higher and nobler than to strive merely for a *repeal of the Tariff*, which was once mentioned as the tocsin to rally the Whigs. REPEAL OF SLAVERY UNDER THE CONSTITUTION AND LAWS OF THE FEDERAL GOVERNMENT, is a more Christian and more potent watchword, because it embodies a higher sentiment, and a more commanding duty.

The time has passed when this can be opposed on constitutional grounds. It will not be questioned by any competent authority, that Congress may, by express legislation, abolish slavery, 1st, in the District of Columbia; 2d, in the Territories, if there should be any; 3d, that it may abolish the slave trade on the high seas between the States; 4th, that it may refuse to admit any new State, with a constitution sanctioning slavery. Nor can it be questioned that the people of the United States may, in the manner pointed out by the Constitution, proceed to its amendment. It is, then, by constitutional legislation, and even by amendment of the Constitution, that slavery may be reached.

And here the question arises, Are there any *compromises* in the Constitution of such a character as to prevent action on this subject? The word *compromises* is invoked by many honest minds as the excuse for not joining in this cause. Let me meet this question frankly and fairly. It is said that the Constitution of the United States was the result of a compromise between the free and slave States, which it would be contrary to good faith to break. To this it might be replied, that the slave States, by their many violations of the Constitution, have already overturned all the original compromises, if there were any of a perpetual character. But I do not content myself with this answer. I wish to say, distinctly, that there is no compromise on the subject of slavery, of a character not to be reached *legally and constitutionally*, which is the only way in which I propose to reach it. Wherever power and jurisdiction are secured to Congress, they may unquestionably be exercised in conformity with the Constitution. And even in matters beyond existing powers and jurisdiction, there is a constitutional method of action. The Constitution contains an article pointing out how, at any time, amendments may be made thereto. This is an important element, giving to the Constitution a *pro-*

gressive character; and allowing it to be moulded to suit new exigencies and new conditions of feeling. The wise framers of this instrument did not treat the country as a Chinese foot, — never to grow after its infancy, — but anticipated the changes incident to its growth. "*Provided*, that no amendment which may be made prior to the year 1808 shall in any manner affect the 1st and 4th clauses, in the 9th section of the 1st article, and that no State, without its consent, shall be deprived of its equal suffrage in the Senate." These are the words of the Constitution. They expressly designate what shall be sacred from amendment, what compromises shall be perpetual; and in doing so, according to a familiar rule of law and of natural logic, virtually declare that the remainder of the Constitution may be amended. Already, since its adoption, twelve amendments have been made, and every year produces new projects. It has been pressed on the floor of Congress to abrogate the power of the veto, and also to limit the tenure of office of the President. Let it be distinctly understood, then, and this is my answer to the suggestion of binding compromises, that, in, conferring upon Congress certain specified powers and jurisdiction, and also in providing for the amendment of the Constitution, its framers expressly established the means for setting aside what are vaguely called the compromises of the Constitution. They openly declare, "Legislate, as you please, in conformity with the Constitution; and even make amendments in this instrument, rendered proper by change of opinion or character, following always the manner therein prescribed."

Nor can we dishonor the memories of the revered authors of the Constitution, by supposing that they set their hands to it, believing that slavery was to be *perpetual* — that the republic, which, reared by them to its giant stature, had snatched from Heaven the sacred fire of freedom, was to be bound, like another Prometheus, in the adamantine chains of fate, while slavery, like another vulture, preyed upon its vitals. Let Franklin speak for them. He was President of the earliest "Abolition Society" in the United States, and in 1790, only two years after the adoption of the Constitution, addressed a petition to Congress, calling upon them "to step to the very verge of the power vested in them for discouraging every species of traffic in our fellow-men." Let Jefferson speak for them. His desire for the abolition of slavery was often expressed with philanthropic warmth and emphasis. Let Washington speak for them. "It is among my first wishes," he said, in a letter to John Fenton Mercer, "to see some plan adopted by which slavery in this country *may be abolished by law*." And in his will, penned with his own hand, in the last year of his life, he bore his testimony again, by providing for the emancipation of all his slaves. It is thus that Washington speaks, not only by words, but by actions louder than words, "Give freedom to your slaves." The Father of his country requires, as a token of the filial piety which all profess, that his example should be followed. I am not insensible to the many glories of his character; but I cannot contemplate this act, without a fresh gush of admiration and gratitude. The martial scene depicted on that votive canvas may fade from the memories of men; but this act of justice and benevolence shall never perish;

Et magis, magisque viri nunc gloria claret.

I assume, then, that it is the duty of the Whigs, professing the principles of the fathers, to express themselves openly, distinctly and solemnly against slavery; *not only against its further extension, but against its longer continuance under the Constitution and laws of the Union.* But while it is their duty to enter upon this holy warfare, it should be their aim to temper it with moderation, with gentleness, with tenderness, towards slave owners. These should be won, if possible, rather than driven, to the duties of emancipation. But emancipation should always be presented as the cardinal object of our National policy.

It is for the Whigs of Massachusetts, now in convention assembled, to lay the corner-stone of a new edifice, in which all the Christian virtues shall be fellow-builders with them. The resolutions which they put forth, the platform of principles which they lay down, may be the foundation of a superstructure of true glory.

But it will not be sufficient to pass *resolutions* opposing slavery; we must choose *men*, who will devote themselves earnestly, heartily, to the work; who will enter upon it with awakened conscience, and with that valiant faith, before which all obstacles disappear; who will be ever loyal to Truth, Freedom, Right, Humanity; who will not look for rules of conduct, down to the earth, in the mire of expediency, but with Heaven-directed countenance seek those great "primal duties which shine aloft like stars," to illumine alike the path of individuals and of nations. They must be true to the principles of Massachusetts. They must not be Northern men with Southern principles; nor Northern men under Southern influences. They must be courageous and willing on all occasions to stand alone, provided Right is with them. "Though every tile were a devil," said Martin Luther, "yet will I enter Worms." Such a spirit is needed now by the advocates of Right. They must not be ashamed of the name which belongs to Franklin, Jefferson and Washington — and which expresses the idea to which they should be devoted — Abolitionist. They most be thorough, uncompromising advocates of the repeal of slavery, of its abolition under the laws and Constitution of the United States. They must be Repealers, Abolitionists.

There are a few such men now in Congress. — Massachusetts has a venerable representative,* whose aged bosom still glows with inextinguishable fires; like the central heats of the monarch mountain of the Andes, beneath its canopy of snow. To this cause he dedicates the closing energies of a long and illustrious life. Would that all would join him!

There is a Senator of Massachusetts, whom we had hoped to welcome here to-day, whose position is one of commanding influence. Let me address him with the respectful frankness of a constituent and a friend: — You have, Sir, by various labors, already acquired an honorable place in the history of our country. By the vigor, argumentation and eloquence with which you have upheld the Union, and that interpretation of the

* John Quincy Adams.

Constitution which makes us a Nation, you have justly earned the title of *Defender of the Constitution.* By the successful and masterly negotiation of the treaty of Washington, and by your efforts to compose the strife of the Oregon, you have earned another title — *Defender of Peace.* There are yet other duties, claiming your care, whose performance will be the crown to a life of high public service. Let me ask you, when again at your post in the Senate, not to forget them. Dedicate, Sir, the golden years of experience happily in store for you, to the grand endeavor, in the name of Freedom, to remove from your country its greatest evil. In this cause you shall find inspirations to eloquence, higher than any you have yet confessed;

> To heavenly themes sublimer strains belong.

Do not shrink from the task. With your marvellous powers, and the auspicious influences of an awakened public sentiment, under God, who always smiles upon conscientious labors for the welfare of man, we may hope for beneficent results. Assume, then, these unperformed duties. The aged shall bear witness to you; the young shall kindle with rapture, as they repeat the name of Webster; and the large company of the ransomed shall teach their children, and their children's children, to the latest generation, to call you blessed; while all shall award to you yet another title, which shall never be forgotten on earth or in heaven — *Defender of Humanity;* by the side of which that earlier title shall fade into insignificance; as the Constitution, which is the work of mortal hands, dwindles by the side of Man, who is created in the image of God.

And now let me say, in conclusion, that the time has arrived when the Whigs of Massachusetts, the party of Freedom, owe it to their declared principles, to their character before the world, and to conscience, to place themselves firmly on the ground which I have indicated. They need not fear to stand alone. They need not fear to be separated from brethren with whom they have hitherto acted in concert; better be separated even from them, than from the Right. Massachusetts can stand alone, if need be. The Whigs of Massachusetts can stand alone. Their motto should not be "our party *howsoever bounded;*" but our party bounded always by the Right. They must recognize the dominion of Right, or there will be none who will recognize the dominion of the party. Let us here then, in Faneuil Hall, beneath the images of our fathers, vow ourselves to perpetual allegiance to the Right — and to perpetual hostility to Slavery. Ours is a noble cause; nobler even than that of our fathers, inasmuch as it is more exalted to struggle for the freedom of *others*, than for our *own*. The love of Right, which is the animating impulse of our movement, is higher even than the love of Freedom. But Right, Freedom and Humanity all concur in demanding the abolition of slavery.

LETTER TO HON. ROBERT C. WINTHROP, REPRESENTATIVE IN CONGRESS FROM BOSTON, ON THE DECLARATION OF WAR AGAINST MEXICO, AND HIS VOTE FOR IT. Oct. 25, 1846.

Sir: —

From the columns of newspapers, and from the lips of some among your friends, have proceeded complaints of the manner in which many of your constituents are obliged to regard your vote on the Mexican War Bill. Your conduct has been defended with an ardor, such as even Truth, Freedom and Right do not always find in their behalf; while the honest strictures upon it have been attributed to personal motives; sometimes to a selfish desire to supplant you in the place which you now hold; sometimes even to a wanton purpose to injure you.

Perhaps this is a natural and inevitable incident of political controversy; though it cannot fail to be regretted, that personal feelings, and imputations of personal selfishness, should intrude into the discussion of an important question of public duty — I would say, of public morals. As a Whig, who never failed to vote for you whenever I had an opportunity, I have felt it proper on other occasions to review your course, and to express the sorrow it has caused. For this I have been arraigned; and the great question of public morals has been forgotten in the personal feelings excited on your side. Let this be my excuse for seeking, in this open manner, to recall attention to the true issue between you and your constituents. Conscious of no feeling towards yourself personally, except of good will, mingled with the recollection of pleasant social intercourse, I enter with pain upon the consideration of your vote, and of the apologies for it which you and others have set up. As one of your constituents, I feel that I do not transgress any rule of propriety in singling you, who are the representative of Boston, among the majority with whom you have acted. I am not a politician; and you will pardon me, therefore, if I decline to bring your conduct to any of the tests of party or of numbers, to any sliding scale of expediency, to any standard, except the golden rule of Right and Wrong.

To understand your course, it will be necessary carefully to consider the action of Congress in regard to the present war with Mexico. I shall endeavor to state the facts and conclusions thereupon, as briefly as possible.

By virtue of an unconstitutional act of our Congress, in conjunction with the *de facto* Government of Texas, this territory was annexed to the United States, some time in the month of December, 1845. If we regard it as a province of Mexico, its boundaries are to be sought in the geography of that Republic. If we regard it as an independent State, they are to be determined by the extent of jurisdiction which the State had been able to maintain. Now it seems to be clear that the river Nueces had always been regarded by Mexico, as the western boundary of the Province; and it is undisputed that the State of Texas, since its Declaration of Independence, had never exercised any jurisdiction beyond the Nueces. The Act of Annexation could not, therefore, transfer to the United States any title to the region beyond the Nueces, stretching to the Rio Grande. That region belonged to Mexico. *Certainly* it did not belong to the United States.

In the month of March, 1846, the President of the United States directed the troops under General Taylor, called the Army of Occupation, to take possession of this territory. Here was clearly an act of aggression, of wrong. As might have been expected, it produced collision. The Mexicans, in the exercise of the right of self-defence, sought to repel the invaders from their hearths and churches. Tidings unexpectedly reached Washington that the American forces were in danger. The President, by a message to Congress, called for succors.

And here the question arises, What was the duty of Congress in this emergency? Clearly to withhold all sanction from the unjust war; from the aggression upon a neighbor Republic; from the spoliation of our fellow-men. Our troops were in danger, because they were upon a foreign soil, forcibly and piratically displacing the jurisdiction and laws of the rightful government. In this state of things, the true and honorable way of safety was, by their instant withdrawal from the Rio Grande to the Nueces. Congress should have spoken like Washington, when addressed by the British General Braddock, "What shall I do, Col. Washington?"

"RETREAT, Sir — RETREAT, Sir!" — was the earnest reply. The American forces should have been directed to *retreat* — not from any enemy of human force, but from *wrong-doing*. Such a retreat would have been a true victory.

But alas! this was not the mood of our Representatives in Congress. With wicked speed a Bill was introduced, making large and unusual appropriations of men and money. In any just sense, such a provision was wasteful and unnecessary; but it would hardly be worthy of criticism, if it were confined in its object to securing the safety of the troops. But at the moment it was made, it must have been known, that the fate of the troops was already decided, while the magnitude of the appropriations, and the number of Volunteers called for, clearly showed that measures were contemplated *beyond mere self-defence*. Self-defence is easy and cheap. Aggression and injustice are difficult and costly.

The Bill, in its earliest guise, provided merely money and volunteers. Suddenly an amendment was introduced, in the nature of a preamble, which gave to it *another character*, in harmony with the covert design of the large appropriation. This was adopted by a vote of 123 to 67; and the Bill then leaped forth, fully armed, as a measure of open and active hostility against Mexico. As such, it was passed by a vote of 174 to 14. This was on the 11th May 1846, a day which will be ever accursed in our history.

The amendment, in the nature of a preamble, and the important parts of the Bill, were as follows: —

Whereas, *by the act of the Republic of Mexico, a state of war exists between that Government and the United States,*

Be it enacted, &c., *That for the purpose of enabling the Government of the United States to prosecute said War to a speedy and successful termination*, the President be authorized to employ the militia, naval, and military forces of the United States, and to call for and accept the services of any number of volunteers, not exceeding 50,000; and that the sum of ten millions of dollars be appropriated for this purpose.

It will be evident that this act cannot be regarded merely as a provision for the safety of General Taylor; nor, indeed, can this be considered the principal end proposed. It has other and ulterior objects, broader and more general, in view of which his safety, important as it might be, is of comparative insignificance; as it would be less mournful to lose a whole army, than to lend the solemn sanction of legislation to an unjust war.

This Act may be considered in six different aspects. It is six times wrong. Six different and unanswerable reasons should have urged its rejection. Six different appeals should have touched every Christian heart. Let me consider them separately.

First. It is practically a DECLARATION OF WAR against a sister Republic. In Congress is vested, by the Constitution of the United States, the power of declaring war. Before this Act was passed, the Mexican War had no legislative sanction. Without this Act, it would have no legislative sanction. It is *by virtue of this Act*, that the present war is waged. It is *by virtue of this Act*, that an American fleet, at immense cost of money, and without any gain of character, is now disturbing the commerce of Mexico, and of the civilized world, by the blockade of Vera Cruz. It is *by virtue of this Act*, that a distant expedition has seized, with pilfering rapacity, the defenceless province of California. It is *by virtue of this Act*, that General Kearney has marched upon and captured Santa Fe. It is *by virtue of this Act*, that General Taylor has perpetrated the massacre at Monterey. It is *by virtue of this Act*, that desolation has been carried into a thousand homes, — that mothers, sisters, daughters and wives have been plunged in the comfortless despair of bloody bereavement, while the uncoffined bodies of sons, brothers and husbands are consigned to premature graves. Lastly, it is *by virtue of this Act*, that the army of the United States has been converted into a *legalized band* of brigands, marauders, and banditti, in violation of the sanctions of civilization, justice and humanity. The American soldiers, who have died ignobly in the streets of a foreign city, in the attack upon a *Bishop's* palace, in contest with Christian fellow-men, who were defending fire-sides and altars, may claim the epitaph of Simonides: "Go, tell at Sparta, that we died here in obedience to her *laws*." It was in obedience to this Act of Congress that they laid down their lives in a barbarous war.

Second. This Act gives the sanction of Congress to an *unjust* war. War is barbarous and brutal; but this is unjust. It grows out of aggression on our part, and is continued by aggression. The statement of facts already made is sufficient to substantiate this point.

Third. It declares that war exists "*by the act of the Republic of Mexico*." This statement of brazen falsehood is inserted in the front of the Act. But it is now admitted by most, if not all of the Whigs, who unhappily voted for it, that it is not founded in fact. It is a National lie.

> ——— Whose tongue soe'er speaks false,
> Not truly speaks ; *who speaks not truly*, LIES.

Fourth. It provides for the prosecution of the war "*to a speedy and successful termination*," that is, for the successful prosecution of an *unjust* war. Surely no rule can be more firmly founded in morals, than that that we should seek the establishment of *right*. Never strive for the triumph of *wrong*.

Fifth. The war has its origin in a series of measures to extend and perpetuate Slavery. A wise and humane legislator should have discerned its source, and derived therefrom fresh impulses to oppose it.

Sixth. The war is dishonorable and *cowardly*, as being the attack of a rich, powerful, numerous and united Republic, upon a weak and defenceless neighbor, distracted by civil feuds. Every consideration of true honor, manliness and Christian duty, prompted gentleness and forbearance towards our unfortunate Sister.

Such, Sir, is the Act of Congress, which received your sanction. It will hardly yield in importance to any measure of our Government since the adoption of the Federal Constitution. It is certainly the most wicked in our history, as it is one of the most wicked in all history. The recording Muse will drop a tear over its turpitude and injustice, while she gibbets it for the disgust and reprobation of mankind.

Such, Sir, is the Act of Congress to which, by your affirmative vote, the people of Boston have been made parties. Through *you*, they have been made *to declare an unjust and cowardly war, with falsehood, in the cause of slavery.* Through *you*, they have been made partakers in the blockade of Vera Cruz, in the seizure of California, in the capture of Santa Fe, in the bloodshed of Monterey. It were idle to suppose that the poor soldier, or officer only, is stained by this guilt. It reaches far back, and incarnadines the Halls of Congress; nay more, through you, it reddens the hands of your constituents in Boston. Pardon this language. Strong as it may seem, it is weak to express the aggravation of your act, *in joining in the declaration of an unjust war.* Oh! Mr. Winthrop, rather than lend your vote to this wickedness, you should have suffered the army of the United States to pass submissively through the Caudine Forks of Mexican power — to perish, it might be, irretrievably, like the legions of Varus. Their bleached bones, in the distant valleys where they were waging an unjust war, would not tell to posterity such a tale of ignominy as this lying Act of Congress.

From this survey of the character and consequences of your vote, I proceed to examine the grounds on which it is vindicated; for it is vindicated, both by yourself and by some of your friends!

1. The first apology, extenuation, or vindication, appears in your speech on the Tariff, delivered in the House of Representatives, June 25th. This was a deliberate effort, more than six weeks subsequent to the vote, and after all the disturbing influences of haste and surprise had subsided. It may be considered, therefore, to express your own view of the ground on which it is to be sustained. And here, while you declare, with commendable frankness, that you "cannot

vindicate the justice (why not say the *truth?*) of the declaration that war exists by the act of Mexico," yet you adhere to your vote, and proceed to animadvert upon the conduct of Mexico, in refusing to receive a minister, instead of a commissioner, as if that were an apology, an extenuation, or a vindication of the Declaration of War! Do we live in a Christian land? Is this the nineteenth century? Does an American statesman venture even an allusion to such a matter in excuse, or extenuation of War? On this point, let me join issue with you. By the law of nations, as now enlightened by civilization — by the law of common sense — by the higher law of Christian duty, the fact you have introduced into your vindication, can form no ground of war. Sir, this vindication has given pain to many of your constituents, hardly less than the original vote. It shows an insensibility to the true character of war, and a perverse adherence to the fatal act of wrong. It were possible to suppose a person, not over-tenacious of moral purpose, shaken from his firm resolve, by the ardors of a tyrannical majority ordaining wicked things; but it is less easy to imagine a deliberate vindication of the hasty wrong, when the pressure of the majority has been removed, and time has afforded opportunity for the recovery of that sense of Right, which had been for a while overturned.

2. Another apology, suggested by yourself, and vouchsafed by your defenders, is founded on the alleged duty of voting succors to General Taylor's troops, and the impossibility of doing this, without voting also for the Bill, after it had been converted into a Declaration of Falsehood and of War. It is said that patriot-

ism required this vote. Patriotism! is not thy name profaned by this apology! Let one of your honored predecessors, Sir, a representative of Boston on the floor of Congress, Mr. Quincy, give the reply to this apology. On an occasion of trial not unlike that through which you have passed, and in the same place, he gave utterance to these noble words: —

> But it is said this resolution must be taken "as a test of patriotism." To this I have but one answer. If patriotism ask me to assert a falsehood, I have no hesitation in telling patriotism, "I am not prepared to make that sacrifice." The duty we owe to our country is indeed among the most solemn and impressive of all obligations. But, high as it may be, it is nevertheless subordinate to that, which we owe to that Being, with whose name and character *truth* is identified. In this respect, I deem myself acting, upon this resolution, under a higher responsibility than either to this House, or this people.

These words were worthy of Boston. May her representatives never fail to be inspired by their spirit! But, say your too swift defenders, "Mr. Winthrop voted against the falsehood *once*." That, certainly, is no reason for not voting against it *always*. But the excuse is still pressed, "Succors should have been voted to General Taylor." The result has shown, that even these were unnecessary. Before the passage of this disastrous Act of Congress, his troops had already achieved a success, to which may fitly be applied the words of Milton: —

> ——— That *dishonest* victory
> At Cheronæa, *fatal to liberty*.

But it would have been certainly less wrong to leave him without fresh succors, even if needful to his safety, than to vote a falsehood and an unjust war. In seeing that the republic received no detriment, you should not have regarded its army only ; *your highest care should have been, that its good name, that its moral and Christian character received no detriment.* You should have said, Sir, with the virtuous Andrew Fletcher, of Saltoun, that you would lose your life to *serve* your country, but would not do a base thing to *save* it. You should have adopted the words of Sheridan, in the British Parliament, during our Revolution, that you "would not assent to a vote that would imply a recognition or approbation of the war."

3. Another apology, which is often supplied by your defenders, is, that the *majority* of the Whig party joined with you, or, as it has been expressed, that "Mr. Winthrop voted with all the rest of the weight of moral character in Congress, from the Free States, belonging to the Whig party, *not included in the Massachusetts delegation;*" and suggestions have been made in disparagement of the *fourteen*, who remained unshaken in their loyalty to Truth and Peace. In the question of Right or Wrong, it can be of little importance, that a few fallible men, constituting what is called a majority, were all of one mind. In every age supple or insane majorities have been found to sanction injustice. It was a majority which passed the Stamp Act, and Tea Tax; which smiled upon the persecution of Galileo; which stood about the stake of Servetus; which administered the hemlock to Socrates; which called for the crucifixion of our Lord. But these majorities cannot make us withhold condemnation from the partakers in these acts. Aloft on the throne of God, and not below

in the footprints of a trampling multitude of men, are to be found the sacred rules of Right, which no majorities can displace or overturn. And the question returns, Was it *right* to vote for an unjust and cowardly war, with falsehood, in the cause of slavery?

Thus have I briefly set forth the character of your act, and the apologies by which it has been shielded. I had hoped that you would see the wrong you had done, and with Christian magnanimity seek to repair it. I had hoped that your friends would all join in assisting you to recover the position of moral uprightness, which becomes a Representative from Boston. But I am disappointed.

Let me add that, in other respects, your course has been in disagreeable harmony with your vote on the Mexican War Bill. I cannot forget — for I sat by your side at the time — that on the 4th of July, 1845, in Faneuil Hall, you extended the hand of fellowship to Texas; although she had not yet been received among the States of the Union. I cannot forget the toast, which you uttered on the same occasion, by which you have connected your name with an epigram of dishonest patriotism. I cannot forget your apathy at a later day, when many of your constituents entered upon holy and constitutional efforts to oppose the admission of Texas, *with a slaveholding constitution* — conduct strangely inconsistent with your recent avowal of "uncompromising hostility to all measures for introducing new slave States and new slave Territories into the Union." Nor can I forget the ardor with which you devoted yourself to the less important question of the Tariff — indicating the relative position of the two questions in your mind. As I review your course, the vote on the Mexican War Bill seems to be the dark consummation.

And now let me ask you, when you resume your seat in Congress, to bear your testimony *at once*, without hesitation or delay, against the further prosecution of this war. Forget for a while the Sub-Treasury, the Veto, even the Tariff; and remember this wicked war. With the eloquence which you command so easily, and which is your pride, call for the instant cessation of hostilities. Let your cry be that of Falkland in the civil wars, "Peace! Peace!" Think not of what you have called, in your speeches, "An *honorable* peace." There can be no peace with Mexico which will not be more honorable than this war. Every fresh victory is a fresh dishonor. "Unquestionably," you have strangely said, "We must not forget that Mexico must be willing to negotiate!" No! No! Mr. Winthrop. We are not to wait for Mexico. Her consent is not needed; nor is it to be asked, by a Christian statesman, while our armies are defiling her soil by their aggressive footsteps. She is *passive*. We alone are *active*. Stop the war. Withdraw our forces. In the words of Colonel Washington, RETREAT! RETREAT! By so doing, we shall cease from further wrong; and peace will ensue.

Let me ask you, Sir, to remember in your public course the rules of Right, which you obey in your private capacity. The principles of morals are the same for nations and for individuals. Pardon me, if I suggest that you do not appear to have acted invariably in accordance with this truth. You would not, in your private capacity, set your name to a falsehood; but you have done so, as a Representative in Congress. You would not, in your private capacity, countenance wrong, even in your friend or your child; but, as a Representative, you have pledged yourself "not to withhold your vote from any reasonable supplies which may be called for" in the prosecution of this wicked war. Do by your country as by your child. You would not furnish to him means of offence against his neighbors; do not furnish them to your country. Do not vote for any supplies to sustain this unrighteous purpose. Again, you would not hold slaves. I doubt not you would join with Mr. Palfrey, in emancipating any who should become yours by inheritance or otherwise. But I have never heard of your joining in efforts, or sympathy, with those who seek to carry into our institutions that practical conscience, which declares it to be equally wrong in individuals and in States to sanction Slavery.

Let me ask you still further — and you will know if there is any reason to justify this request — to bear your testimony against the Mexican War, and all supplies for its prosecution, regardless of the minority in which you may be placed. Think, Sir, of the cause, and not of your associates. Forget for a while the tactics of party, and all its subtle combinations. Emancipate yourself from its close-woven web, spun as from a spider's belly, and walk in the luminous pathway of Right. Remember that you represent the conscience of Boston, the churches of the Puritans, the city of Channing.

Meanwhile a fresh election is at hand, and you are again a candidate for the suffrages of your fellow-citizens. I shall not anticipate their verdict. Your blameless private life, and your respectable attainments, cannot fail to receive the approbation of all; but more than one of your neighbors will be obliged to say,

> — "Cassio, I love thee,
> But never more be officer of mine."

I am, sir, your obedient servant,

CHARLES SUMNER.

Oct. 26, 1846.

SPEECH AGAINST THE MEXICAN WAR, AND ALL SUPPLIES FOR ITS PROSECUTION, AT A PUBLIC MEETING IN THE TREMONT TEMPLE, BOSTON, NOV. 4, 1846.

[This was made on the eve of a Congressional election, in which Dr. Howe was brought forward as the Anti-War candidate in Boston. Mr. Winthrop was the regular Whig candidate.]

Mr. Chairman,

When in the month of July, 1830, the people of Paris rose against the arbitrary ordinances of Charles X., and, after three days of bloody combat, succeeded in that Revolution, by virtue of which the Dynasty of Orleans now occupies the throne of France, Lafayette, votary of Liberty in two hemispheres, placing himself at the head of the movement, on the second day, walked from his residence to the City Hall, through streets impassable to carriages, filled with barricades, and strewn with the wrecks of war. Moving along with a thin attendance, he was unexpectedly joined by a gallant Bostonian, who, though young in life, was already eminent by seven years of disinterested service in the struggle for Grecian independence against the Turks, who had himself listened to the whizzing of bullets, and had narrowly escaped the descending scimitar. Lafayette, considerate as he was brave, turned to his faithful friend, and said, "Do not join me; this is a danger for Frenchmen only; reserve yourself for your own country, where you will be needed." Our fellow-citizen heeded him not, but continued by his side, sharing his perils. That Bostonian was Dr. Howe. And now the words of Lafayette are verified. He is needed by his country. At the present crisis, in our Revolution of "Three Days," he comes forward to the post of danger.

I cannot disguise the satisfaction I shall feel in voting for him — beyond even the gratification of personal friendship — because he is not a politician. His whole life is thickly studded with various labors in the highest of all causes, the good of man. He is the friend of the poor — the friend of the blind — the friend of the prisoner — the friend of the slave. Wherever there is suffering, there his friendship is manifest. Generosity, disinterestedness, self-sacrifice and courage, have been his inspiring sentiments, directed by rare sagacity and intelligence; and now, wherever Humanity is regarded, wherever there are bosoms that beat responsive to philanthropic exertions, his name is cherished and beloved. Such a man reflects lustre upon the place of his birth; far more than any one who has excelled only in the strife of politics, or the servitude of party.

He has qualities which commend him, especially at this time. He is firm, ever true, honest, inflexible, a lover of the Right. With a courage that charms opposition, he would not fear to stand alone against a fervid majority. Knowing War by a fearful familiarity, he is an earnest defender of Peace. With a singular experience of life in other countries, he now brings the stores which he has garnered up, and his noble spirit, to the service of his fellow-citizens. May they know how to value them!

But we are assembled to-night, less to consider his praises — grateful as these would be to me, who claim him as a friend — than to examine the principles in issue at the present election. This does not depend upon names, but upon principles. And proud as we may be of our candidate, we feel, and he feels, that his principles on the important questions now before the public are his truest recommendation.

In examining these questions, I purpose to regard those only which have been directly put in issue by the Whigs. It is with the Whigs that I have heretofore acted, and may hereafter act; always confessing a loyalty to principles higher than any party ties.

The recent Whig State Convention, by its resolutions which I hold in my hand, have brought forward five different questions, on which they have expressed the opinions of the party. These are the Veto of the President, the Sub-Treasury, the Tariff, *Slavery*, and *the Mexican War*. Now, of these five questions, it will not be disguised, that the last two are the most important. Slavery is a wrong which justice and humanity alike condemn. The Mexican War is an enormity born of Slavery. Viewed as a question of dollars and cents, it overshadows the other questions; while, if viewed in the darkness of its guilt, it compels them to the obscurity of a total eclipse. It is a war base in its object, atrocious in its beginning, immoral in all its influences, and vainly prodigal of treasure and life. It is a war of infamy, destined to blot the pages of our history with indelible blackness. No success, no bravery, no victory can change its character. If our flag should wave in triumph over twenty fields, there could be no True Honor therefrom. Shame, and not glory, will attend our footsteps, while, in the spirit of a bully, we employ our superior resources of wealth and numbers in carrying death and destruction to a poor, distracted, long-suffering sister republic. Without, then, disparaging the other questions, every just and humane person will recognize Slavery and the Mexican War as paramount to all else; so much so, that whoever is wrong on these, must be so entirely wrong as not to deserve the votes of the Whigs of Massachusetts.

But the Whig Convention has furnished a rule or measure of opinion on these subjects. It has expressly pledged the Whigs "to promote all constitutional measures for the overthrow of *Slavery*, and to oppose at all times, with uncompromising zeal and firmness, any further addition of slave-holding States to this Union, out of whatever territory formed." The Mexican War, it has denounced as having its origin in an *invasion* of Mexico by our troops.

Now, on these subjects, Dr. Howe's opinions are clear and explicit. He is an earnest, hearty, conscientious opponent of Slavery; and, in his speech, made at your former meeting, he has denounced the injustice of the Mexican war, and, as a natural consequence, demanded the instant *retreat* of General Taylor's troops to the Neuces.

And this brings me to Mr. Winthrop. But, as I begin to consider his position, let me carefully disclaim any sentiment except of kindness towards him as a private citizen. It is of Mr. Winthrop, the politician, that I speak; and not of Mr. Winthrop, the acceptable gentleman.

And, *first*, what may we expect from him against *Slavery*? Will he promote all constitutional measures for its overthrow? One of these clearly is the Abolition of Slavery in the District of Columbia. This is within the constitutional powers of Congress. It has sometimes occurred to me, indeed, that Slavery in our country was, like the image in Nebuchadnezzar's dream, whose feet of clay are in the District of Columbia, where they may be shivered by the iron hammer of Congressional legislation, directed by an enlightened Northern sentiment, so that the whole image shall tumble to the earth. This and still other measures against Slavery have been sanctioned by the Massachusetts Whigs, and by the legislature of our State in formal resolutions, which have been duly transmitted to Washington. I have never heard of Mr. Winthrop's voice in their favor. Nor, judging by the past, have I any reason to believe that he will support them earnestly and heartily on the floor of Congress. On these points he fails, if tried by Whig standards.

Will he oppose at all times, with uncompromising zeal and firmness, any further addition of slave-holding States to the Union? And here, if we judge him by the past, he will be found wanting. None of us can forget that on the 4th of July, 1845, a day sacred to memories of freedom, in a speech at Faneuil Hall, he swiftly volunteered, in advance of any other Northern Whig, to receive Texas with a welcome into the family of States, although on that very day she was preparing a Constitution, placing slavery beyond the reach of legislative change. I dismiss his toast on that occasion, the fit conclusion of such a speech, to the limbo of political immoralities, there to keep company with its kindred sentiments, "Our Party always," and "Our Country, Right or Wrong."

The conclusion is irresistible, that Mr. Winthrop cannot fitly represent the true feeling palpitating in Massachusetts bosoms, and so often expressed by the Resolutions of our Legislature on the subject of slavery.

And, secondly, what may we expect from him on the subject of the *Mexican War?* This brings me to a melancholy part of this inquiry, on which I am the less disposed to dwell, because it has already been so fully considered. Will he ascend to the true heights of Christian duty, and, while branding the war as unjust, call at once for its cessation, and for the withdrawal of General Taylor's forces? Unhappily, there is no reason to believe that he will. He voted for the act of Congress, under which it is now waged; and, by that disastrous vote, made his constituents partakers in an unjust and bloody war. At a later day, in an elaborate speech, he vindicated his act, and promised "not to withhold his vote from any reasonable supplies which may be called for" in the prosecution of the war; adding, that he should vote for them "to enable the President to achieve that *honorable peace*, which he has solemnly promised to bring about at the earliest possible moment" *by the sword*. And, pray, what is Mr.

Winthrop's idea of an "honorable peace?" Is it peace imposed by brute force upon a weak neighbor, the successful consummation of unrighteous war?" Is it the triumph of wrong? Is it the Saturnalia of slave-holders? Is it the fruit of sin? Is it a baptism of blood unjustly shed? In the same speech, with a grievous insensibility to the sordid character of the suggestion, he pleads for the existence of the old Tariff, as necessary to meet "the exigencies" of the Mexican War. "In a time of war, like the present," he says, "more especially, *an ample revenue should be the primary aim and end of all our custom-house duties.*" Perish manufactures, let me rather say, if the duties by which they seem to be protected, are swollen to feed "the exigencies" of an unjust war! At a still later day, in his speech at Faneuil Hall, before the Whig Convention, he failed to appreciate the becoming Christian course for his country. He nowhere sounds the word *duty.* He nowhere tells his country, to begin by doing Right. He nowhere gives assurance of his aid in calling for the instant stay of the Mexican War.

But it is said, sometimes, that his vote was a mistake; and that we are not to judge him for this mistake. Can we afford to send a man to Congress, who can make such a mistake? But it is a mistake, which has never been acknowledged as such by him. It is still persisted in, and hugged to his bosom. Among the last words of warning which came from the lips of Chatham, as he fell at his post in the British Senate, almost his dying words, were, "not to put trust in a man who perseveres in unretracted error."

In his vote for the Mexican War Bill, Mr. Winthrop

is not a true Whig. He left the party; for the party is not to be found where numbers prevail, but where its principles are recognized. The true Whigs are the valiant minority of *fourteen*. Once in Roman history, the vestal fire, the archives, the sacred volumes of the Republic, were in the custody of a single individual, in a humble vehicle, fleeing from the burning city. With him was the life of the Republic. So in that small minority was preserved the life, the principles, the sacred fire of the Whig party.

The true Whig ground, the only ground, consistent with our professed loyalty to the higher sentiments of duty, is constant uncompromising opposition to the war, in all the forms in which opposition may be made. Expecting right from Mexico, we must begin by doing right. We are the aggressors. We must cease to be the aggressors.

This is the proper course of duty, having its foundations in the immutable laws of God. Our country must do as an individual in similar circumstances; for though politicians may disown it — and this principle cannot be too often repeated — there is but one rule of duty for nations and for individuals. If any one of you, fellow-citizens, finding yourself in dispute with a neighbor, had unfortunately resorted to blows and felled him to the earth, but, with returning reason, discovered that you were in the wrong, what would you do? Of course, cease instantly from *wrong-doing*. You would help your neighbor to his feet. With Christian benevolence you would seek to soothe his wrongs. You would not, in the language of President Polk, seek "to conquer a peace," nor, in the language of Mr. Winthrop, "to achieve an honorable peace" by force. Precisely so must our country act now. We must help our down-trodden Mexican neighbor to her feet. We must withdraw our forces to the Neuces, and then, when ample justice has been done on our side, seek justice and peace from her. Be assured these would easily follow. Perhaps the same response might come from the Mexicans, that the Falerii sent to the Roman Senate, through Camillus: "The Romans having preferred *justice* to *conquest*, have taught us to be satisfied with submission instead of liberty."

That I may not seem to found these conclusions upon general principles of morals only, let me invoke the example of the Whigs of England, of Chatham, Camden, Burke, Fox and Sheridan, in their opposition to the war of our Revolution; denouncing it, at the outset, as unjust, and never, during its whole progress, failing to declare their condemnation of it; voting against supplies for its prosecution, and against thanks for the military services by which it was waged. Holding their example, as of the highest practical authority on the present question of political duty, and as particularly fit to be regarded by persons professing to be Whigs in America, I shall make no apology for introducing at some length the authentic evidence which places it beyond doubt. This is to be found in the volumes of the Parliamentary Debates. I am not aware that it has ever before been applied to the present discussion.

In the Debate in the Lords on the address of Thanks in Oct. 1775, after the battle of Lexington and Bunker Hill — the Duke of Grafton said:

I pledge myself to your lordships and my country, that, if necessity should require it, and my health not otherwise permit it, I mean to come down to this House in a litter, in order to express my full and hearty disapprobation of the measures now pursuing ; and, as I understand from the noble lords in office, meant to be pursued. I do protest, that if my brother or dearest friend were to be affected by the vote I mean to give this evening, I cannot, possibly, resist the faithful discharge of my conscience and my duty. Were I to lose my fortune, and every other thing I esteem, were I to be reduced to beggary itself, the strong conviction and compulsion at once operating on my mind and conscience, would not permit me to take any other part on the present occasion, than that I now mean to adopt.

At the close of this Debate, a protest was signed by several peers, containing the following clause :

Because we cannot, as Englishmen, as Christians, or as men of common humanity, consent to the prosecution of a cruel civil war, so little supported by justice, and so very fatal in its necessary consequences, as that which is now waging against our brethren and fellow-subjects in America.

In the House of Commons, on the same Address, Mr. Wilkes said :

I call the war with our brethren in America, an unjust felonious war. * * * I assert that it is a murderous war, because it is an effort to deprive men of their lives for standing up in the just cause of the defence of their property, and their clear rights. It becomes no less a murderous war, with respect to many of our fellow-subjects of this Island ; for every man, either of the army or navy, who has been sent by Government to America, and fallen a victim in this unnatural and unjust contest, has, in my opinion, been murdered by the administration, and his blood lies at their door. Such a war,

I fear, Sir, will draw down the vengeance of Heaven upon this devoted kingdom.

Mr. Fox said:

He could not consent to the bloody consequences of so silly a contest about so silly an object, conducted in the silliest manner that history, or observation, had ever furnished an instance of; and from which we were likely to derive nothing but poverty, misery, disgrace, defeat and ruin.

Mr. Serjeant Adair said:

I am against the present war, because I think it unjust in its commencement, injurious to both countries in its prosecution, and ruinous in its event. * * * I think from the bottom of my soul, that the Colonies are engaged in a noble and glorious struggle. * * * Sir, I could not be easy in my own mind, without entering the strongest and most public protestations against measures which appear to me to be fraught with the destruction of this mighty Empire. *I wash my hands of the blood of my fellow-subjects;* and shall at least have this satisfaction, amidst the impending calamities of the public, not only to think that I have contributed to, but that I have done all in my power to oppose and avert the ruin of my country.

In another debate in the Lords, Nov. 15th, 1775, that strenuous friend of freedom, and upholder of Whig principles, Lord Camden, said:

Peace is still within our power; nay, we can command it. A suspension of arms on our part, if adopted in time, will secure it for us; and I may add on our own terms. *From which it is plain, as we have been the original aggressors in this business, if we obstinately persist, we are fairly answerable for all the consequences.* I again repeat, what I often urged before, that I was against this unnatural war from the beginning. I was equally against every measure from the instant the first tax was proposed, to this minute. When, therefore, it is insisted, that we are only to defend and enforce our own right, I positively deny it. I contend that America has been driven by cruel necessity to defend her rights from the united attacks of violence, oppression and injustice. I contend that America has been indisputably aggrieved. * * * I must still think, and shall uniformly continue to assert, that Great Britain has been the aggressor; that most, if not all, the acts were founded on oppression, and that if I was in America, I should resist to the last such manifest exertion of tyranny, violence and injustice.

In another debate in the Commons, Dec. 8th, 1785, Mr. Fox said:

I have always said that the war carrying on against America is unjust.

In the Lords, March 5th, 1776, the Earl of Effingham said:

I can never stand up in your lordship's presence without throwing in a few words on the justice of this unnatural war.

In the Commons, March 11th, 1776, Col. Barré, Mr. Burke, Mr. Fox, all vied in eulogies upon General Montgomery, the account of whose death before Quebec had arrived some days before.

In the Commons, April 24th, 1776, a debate arose on the Budget, containing resolutions to raise taxes to carry on the war against America. Mr. Fox then said:

To the resolutions he should give a flat negative, and that not because of any particular objection to the taxes proposed (although it might be a sufficient ground for urging many) *but because he could not conscientiously agree to grant any money for so destructive, so ignoble a purpose as the carrying on a war commenced unjustly, and supported with no other view than to the extirpation of freedom,* and the violation of every social comfort. THIS HE CONCEIVED TO BE THE STRICT LINE OF CONDUCT TO BE OBSERVED BY A MEMBER OF PARLIAMENT. He then painted the war with America as unjust, and the pursuance of the war as blood-thirsty and oppressive.

Col. Barré followed, and adopted the phrase of Mr. Fox, giving his flat negative to the Resolutions, *as they were calculated to tax the subject for an unjust purpose.*

In the Lords, Oct. 31st, 1776, the Duke of Grafton said:

He pledged himself to the House, and to the Public, that while he had a leg to stand on, he would come down day after day to express the most marked abhorrence of the measures hitherto pursued, and meant to be adhered to in respect to America.

In the Commons, on the same night, Mr. Fox said:

The noble Lord who moved the amendment, said that we were in the dilemma *of conquering or abandoning America; if we are reduced to that, I am for abandoning America.*

In the Commons, Nov. 6th, 1776, Mr. Burke said:

You simply tell the Colonists to lay down their arms, and then you will do just as you please. Could the most cruel conqueror say less? Had you conquered the devil himself in hell, could you be less liberal? No!

In the Commons, Feb. 18th, 1777, Col. Barré said:

America must be reclaimed, *not conquered or subdued.*

Conciliation or concession are the only sure means of either gaining or retaining America.

In the Commons, May 14th, 1777, another debate occurred on the Budget, in the course of which Mr. Burke said:

He was and ever would be ready to support a just war, whether against subjects or alien enemies; but where justice, or a color of justice, was wanting, he should ever be the first to oppose it.

In the Lords, May 28th, 1777, Lord Chatham brought forward a motion to put a stop to American hostilities, and said:

We have tried for unconditional submission; *try what can be gained by unconditional redress.* We are the aggressors. We have invaded them. We have invaded them as much as the Spanish Armada invaded England. * * * * In the sportsman's phrase, when you have found yourselves at fault, *you must try back.* I shall no doubt hear it objected, Why should we submit or concede? Has America done any thing, on her part, to induce us to agree to so large a ground of concession? I will tell you, my lords, why I think you should. *You have been the aggressors from the beginning. If then we are the aggressors, it is your lordships' business to make the first overture.* I say again, this country has been the aggressor. You have made descents upon their coasts; you have burnt their towns, plundered their country, made war upon the inhabitants, confiscated their property, proscribed and imprisoned their persons. *I do therefore affirm, that, instead of exacting unconditional submission from the Colonies, we should grant them unconditional redress.* We have injured them; we have endeavored to enslave and oppress them. Upon this clear ground, instead of chastisement they are entitled to redress. If I were an American, as I am an Englishman, while a foreign troop was landed in my country, I never would lay down my arms — never — never — never.

And again Lord Chatham said:

I would sell my shirt from off my back to assist in proper measures, properly and wisely conducted; *but I would not part with a single shilling to the present ministers.* Their plans are founded in destruction and disgrace. It is, my lord, a ruinous and destructive war; it is full of danger; it teems with disgrace, and must end in ruin.

In the Lords, Nov. 18th, 1777, the Duke of Richmond said:

Can we too soon put a stop to such a scene of carnage? I know, that what I am going to say is not fashionable language, but a time will come when every one of us must account to God for his actions; and how can we justify causing so many innocent lives to be lost?

In the Commons, Dec. 5th, 1778, Mr. Hartley, the constant friend of America, brought forward a motion:

That it is unbecoming the wisdom and prudence of Parliament, to proceed any further in the support of this fruitless, expensive, and destructive war; more especially without any specific terms of accommodation declared.

In the Lords, Feb. 16th, 1778, the Marquis of Rockingham said:

He was determined to serve his country, *by making peace at any rate.*

In the Lords, March 23d, 1778, the Duke of Richmond brought forward a motion for the withdrawal of the forces from America.

In the Commons, Nov. 27th, 1780, on a motion to

thank General Clinton and others, for their military services in America, Mr. Wilkes said :

I think it my duty to oppose this motion, because in my idea every part of it conveys an approbation of the American war ; a war unfounded in principle, and fatal in its consequences to this country. * * *Sir, I will not thank for victories which only tend to protract a destructive war.* * * As I reprobate the want of principle in the origin of the American war, I the more lament all the spirited exertions of valor and the wisdom of conduct, which, in a good cause, I warmly applaud. Thinking as I do, I see more matter of grief than of triumph, of bewailing than thanksgiving, in this civil contest, and the deluge of blood, which has overflowed America. * * I deeply lament that the lustre of such splendid victories is obscured and darkened by the want of a good cause, without which no war, in the eye of truth and reason, before God or man, can be justified.

Mr. Fox said :

He allowed the merits of the officers now in question, but he made a distinction between thanks and praise. He might admire their valor, but he could not separate the intention from the action ; they were united in his mind ; there they formed one whole, and he would not attempt to divide them.

Mr. Sheridan said :

There were in that House different descriptions of men *who could not assent to a vote of thanks that seemed to imply a recognition or approbation of the American war.*

Such is the doctrine of morals, sanctioned by high English examples. Such should be the doctrine of an American statesman. If we apply this to the existing exigency ; nay, more, if we undertake to try the candidates on the present occasion by this standard, we shall find, that, as Dr. Howe is unquestionably right, so Mr. Winthrop is too certainly wrong. In thus exalting our own candidate, I would not unduly disparage another. It is for the sake of the cause in which we are engaged, — by the side of which all individuals dwindle into insignificance, — that we now oppose Mr. Winthrop. We desire to bear our testimony earnestly, heartily, sincerely, against Slavery, and the longer continuance of the Mexican war. We demand the retreat of General Taylor, and the instant withdrawal of the American forces. And even if we seem to fail, in this election, we shall not fail in reality. The influence of this effort will be felt. It will help to awaken and organize that powerful public opinion by which this war will at last be arrested.

Hang out, then, fellow-citizens, the white banner of Peace. Unfurl all its ample folds, streaming with Christian trophies. Let the citizens of Boston rally about it; and let it be borne by an enlightened, conscientious people, aroused to the condemnation of this murderous war, until Mexico, wet with blood unjustly shed, shall repose undisturbed at last beneath its celestial folds.

ARGUMENT BEFORE THE SUPREME COURT OF MASSACHUSETTS, AGAINST THE VALIDITY OF ENLISTMENTS IN THE MASSACHUSETTS REGIMENT OF VOLUNTEERS FOR THE MEXICAN WAR, JAN. 1847.

[By the Mexican War Bill (approved May 13th, 1846,) the President was authorized " to call for and accept the services of volunteers to a number not exceeding 50,000," and provisions were made for their organization. The Governor of Massachusetts, by proclamation, called for a Regiment in this Commonwealth, which was organized under the Act of Congress. Before it had left the Commonwealth, applications for discharge from it were made to the Supreme Court of Massachusetts, in behalf of several persons, who had repented their too hasty enlistment. At the hearing of these cases, the proceedings, by which the Regiment had been organized, were called in question. Their validity was denied on the ground that the Act of Congress, in some of its essential provisions on the subject of volunteers, was unconstitutional; that the enlistments were not in conformity with the Act; and also that the militia laws of Massachusetts had been fraudulently used in order to form the Regiment. These points, and the further question, whether a minor was bound by his contract of enlistment under the Act, were argued by Mr. Sumner, who appeared as counsel for one of the petitioners.

The Court sustained the validity of the proceedings, but discharged the minors. See *In re* Kimball, Murray & Stone, 9 Law Reporter, 500, where the case is reported.]

MAY IT PLEASE YOUR HONORS,

THIS cause has a strong claim upon the careful consideration of the Court. It comes with a *trinoda necessitas*, a triple cord, to bind its judgment. It is important as respects the parties, the public, and the principles involved.

To the *parties*, it is one of the highest questions known to the law, — a question of *human freedom*. It is proposed to hold the petitioner in the servitude of the army for an indefinite space of time, viz., "for the duration of the war with Mexico." During all this period, he is to be subject to martial law, to the articles of war, with the terrible penalties of desertion. He is to be under the command of officers, at whose word he will be obliged to move from place to place beyond the confines of the country, and to perform unwelcome duties, involving his own life and the lives of others.

To the *public*, it is important, as it is surely of high consequence, in whose hands it places the power of life and death. The soldier is vested with extraordinary attributes. He is at times more than marshal or sheriff. He is also surrounded expressly by the law with certain immunities, one of which is exemption from imprisonment for debt.

It is important from the *principles* involved in the inquiry. These are the distinctions between the different kinds of military force to be employed under the Constitution of the United States; the *constitutionality* of the Act of Congress of May, 1846, and the legality of the enlistments under it. The determination of these questions will establish or annul the immense and complex Volunteer System now in action in the United States.

In a case of such magnitude, I shall be pardoned for dwelling with some care upon the different questions. In the course of my argument, I shall seek to establish the following propositions:

I. That the forces contemplated by the Act of May, 1846, are a part of the "army" of the United States or its general military force, and not of the "militia" thereof.

II. That the part of the Act of Congress of 1846, providing for the officering of the companies is unconstitutional, and the whole proceedings thereunder void.

III. That the present contract is illegal, inasmuch as it is not according to the terms of the Statute, which prescribes that it shall be for "12 months or the war," whereas it is "for the war" only.

IV. That it is illegal, being entered into by an improper use of the militia laws of Massachusetts, so as to be a *fraud* on those laws.

V. That minors cannot be held by the contract of enlistment under the present Act.

I shall now consider these different propositions.

First. The force contemplated by the Act of May, 1846, is a part of the *army* of the United States, or of its general military force, and not of the *militia* thereof.

It is called "volunteers;" but, on inquiry, it will appear, that it has elements which are *inconsistent* with its character as militia, while it wants some elements which are *essential* to the character of militia.

Without stopping now to consider what these elements are, it will be proper, first, to consider the powers of Congress over the land forces. Congress is not omnipotent, like the British Parliament. It can do only what is permitted by the Constitution of the United States, and *in the manner in which it is permitted.* We are, then, to search the Constitution.

Here we find *two* different species of *land forces*, and only *two.* These are "armies" and "militia." There is no mongrel, or hybrid, a cross between the two — no *tertium quid.*

These are referred to and sanctioned by the following clauses, and by no others: "Congress shall have power to *raise and support armies;* to provide for calling forth *the militia* to execute the laws of the Union, suppress insurrections, and repel invasions; — to provide for organizing, arming, and disciplining *the militia*, and for governing such part of them as may be employed in the service of the United States, *reserving to the States, respectively, the appointment of the officers*, and the authority of training the militia, according to the discipline prescribed by Congress." (Art. I. § 8.) And again; "The President shall be commander-in-chief of the *army* and navy of the United States, and of *the militia of the several States, when called into the actual service of the United States.*" (Art. II. § 2.)

It has been ably argued by Mr. Lanier, in a recent debate in the Virginia Assembly, that the distinction between the *army* and the *militia* is, that the first stands on *contract* or *voluntary enlistment*, and the second, on the *law compelling parties to serve;* that this simple test determines the character of the service, Did the party enter it *voluntarily*, or by *operation of law?* If voluntarily, then he is in the "army;" if compulsorily, or by operation of law, then he is in the "militia." This distinction is plausible, and is true, I think beyond question, with regard to the "army" and "militia" under existing laws. I am not prepared to say, that Congress, under the clause authorizing it "to raise and support armies," may not, following the example of other countries, enforce a conscription, or levy, which shall act compulsorily, throughout the country, being in this respect like the *militia*, although unlike it in other respects. Such a plan was recommended by Mr. Monroe, when Secretary of War, October 17th, 1814, (Niles' Register, Vol. 7, p. 139; November 5th, 1814.) He speaks of it as follows: —

The limited power which the United States have in organizing the militia, may be urged as an argument against their right to raise *regular troops in the mode proposed*. If any argument could be drawn from that circumstance, I should suppose that it would be in favor of an opposite conclusion. The power of the United States over the militia has been limited, and that for raising regular armies granted, without limitation. There was, doubtless, some object in this arrangement. The fair inference seems to be, that it was made on great consideration; that the limitation in the first instance was intentional, the consequence of the unqualified grant of the second.

But it is said, that by drawing the men from the militia service into the regular army, and putting them under regular officers, you violate a principle of the Constitution, *which provides that the militia shall be commanded by their own officers*. If this was the fact, the conclusion would follow. But it is not the fact. The men are not drawn from the militia, but from the population of the country; *when they enlist voluntarily, it is not as militia-men that they act, but as citizens*. If they are drafted, it must be in the same sense. In both instances they are enrolled in the militia corps; but that, as is presumed, cannot prevent the voluntary act in one instance, or the compulsive in the other. The whole population of the United States, within certain ages, belong to these corps. If the United States could not form regular armies from them, they could raise none.

If Mr. Monroe's views are sound, the "army" of the United States may be raised by draft, as well as the "militia." It may consist of *regulars* and *irregulars*.

But whatever may be the powers of Congress on this subject, it is certain that there is no legislation now in force, providing for the "army," except by means of *voluntary enlistment*. The whole army of the United States is, at present, an army of *volunteers;* and all persons who are *volunteers* are of the *army*, and not of the *militia*. To call them *volunteers* does not take them out of the category of the *army*, or general military force of the United States.

On the other hand, the *militia*, when in the service of the United States *as militia*, are not *volunteers*. They come by draft or conscription. This distinction is derived from England, to which we are indebted for so much of our jurisprudence, and so many of our principles of constitutional law. We may find from Blackstone (Vol. 1, p. 412,) that the English militia consist of "the inhabitants of the county, chosen by lot for three years." They are called "the constitutional security which the laws have provided for the public peace, and for protecting the realm against foreign or domestic violence; and they are *not compellable to march out of their countries, unless in case of invasion or actual rebellion within the realm, nor in any case compellable to march out of the kingdom.*" They are "officered by the lord-lieutenant, the deputy-lieutenants and the principal landholders, under a commission from the crown." It will be observed, from this description, that there are four distinct elements in the English militia. 1. It is in its nature a draft or conscription. 2. It is local in its character. 3. It is officered by persons in the county. 4. It can be called out only on peculiar exigencies, which are expressly designated. In all these respects, it is distinguishable from what is called the *army* of England.

Mr. Burke somewhere says that more than half of the first edition of Blackstone's Commentaries found its way to America. The framers of our Constitution were familiar with this work, and they have reproduced all these four features of the English militia, substituting "State" for "county," and adopting even the peculiar exigencies when they are compellable to march "out of the State." Thus following Blackstone, they have recognized an "*army*" and a "*militia*," without any third or intermediate military body.

This same distinction between the militia and army is recognized by Mr. Charles Turner, in the British Parliament, in a speech on the Bill for embodying the militia, Nov. 2d, 1775. "The proper men," he says, "*to recruit and supply your troops* are the scum and outcast of cities and manufactures — fellows who *voluntarily submit to be slaves* for an apprenticeship of seven years are the proper persons to be military ones. But to take the honest, sober, industrious fellow from the plough is doing an essential mischief to the community, and laying a double tax." Parl. History, Vol. 18, p. 846.

Let us now apply these general considerations to the present case.

The Act of May, 1846, recognizes a clear distinction between the *militia* and *volunteers*. It authorizes the President "to employ the *militia*, naval and military forces of the United States, and to call for and accept the services of any number of *volunteers*, not exceeding 50,000 — to serve twelve months after they shall have arrived at the place of rendezvous, or to the end of the war, unless sooner discharged." The next section (§ 2) provides that "the *militia*, when called into the service of the United States by virtue of this act or of any other act, may, if in the opinion of the President the public interest requires it, be compelled to serve *for a term not exceeding six months*, after their arrival at the place of rendezvous." The 9th section speaks of "militia or volunteers," referring to the two distinct classes.

Now on the face of this Act there are at least two distinct recognitions that the "volunteers" are not of the *militia*. 1st. In providing for the employment of *volunteers* and also of the *militia*, treating the two as distinct; and 2d. In providing the term of service of volunteers to be "twelve months or the war," while that of the militia is "six months" only.

There are still other reasons derived from the circumstances of the case. 1st. The volunteers do not come by draft, but by contract. 2d. According to § 2, it is provided that the President shall, "by and with the advice and consent of the Senate, appoint the generals of brigade and division and of general staff, as now authorized by law; *provided*, however, that major generals and brigade generals shall have the appointment of their own aids-de-camp, and the President shall, if necessary, apportion the staff, field and general officers among the respective States and Territories from which the volunteers shall tender their service as he may deem proper." This proviso in one of its characteristics is a sop to the States, to whom the appointment of the officers of the *militia* is due. But the appointment of the officers by the President is inconsistent with the character of *militia*. 3d. A third reason why these cannot be the *militia* is, that no such exigency has occurred as will authorize the President to call for the militia; as, for instance, "to execute the laws of the Union, suppress insurrections, and repel invasions."

Thus far I have sought to bring the proposed body of volunteers to the touchstone of the Constitution and laws of the United States. Let us now see how they conform with the Constitution and laws of Massachusetts.

1. By the Constitution of Massachusetts, the Governor is Commander-in-Chief of the Militia; but he could not command these volunteers.

2. By our laws, (cap. 92, March 24, 1840,) volunteers in the militia are "to do duty for five years;" while our volunteers are for "one year or the war."

3. A "uniform such as the Commander-in-Chief

shall prescribe," is appointed for the volunteer militia, while our volunteers are subject to no such regulations.

4. The statute of 1846, cap. 218, § 10, provides that each company shall have "one first, one second, one third, and one fourth lieutenant." Mr. Secretary Marcy's requisition (p. 30 of Mr. Cushing's report,) allows to each company, "one first lieutenant, and two second lieutenants."

It is by provisions like these, that Massachusetts has marked her militia that she may know them. She tells them how they shall be appareled and officered. But the body now called out is so appareled and officered that the Commonwealth cannot recognize it as her militia.

From this survey, it seems clear that, in the light of the Constitution and laws of the United States, and also of the Constitution and laws of Massachusetts, this body cannot be a part of the *militia.*

But it has been suggested, on the other side, that the companies now raised may be regarded as companies of militia, who *volunteer as companies* into the army of the United States; and it is urged that the requisitions of the Constitution are complied with, inasmuch as the officers of the regiment are commissioned by the Governor. To this it may be replied that the militia of the Commonwealth have certain specific duties detailed in the statute on the subject, (cap. 92, 1840.) For instance, (§ 23,) three parades in each year, and inspection on the last Wednesday of May; (§ 24) an inspection in each year; (§ 27) and particularly to aid the *posse comitatus* in case of riot. These all contemplate that they shall remain *at home.* Now, it is not to be questioned, that, in any of the *exigencies* mentioned in the Constitution, they may be ordered from home, *in the manner prescribed by the Constitution and law.* But it certainly cannot be allowable for a company of militia, to VOLUNTEER as a *company* into a service *inconsistent with the duties prescribed by the laws under which it is established.* Adopting Mr. Monroe's distinction, the individuals can volunteer as *citizens*, but not as a *company.*

Let us try this point by an analogy. The Commonwealth by its legislation, (Rev. Stat. cap. 18,) establishes companies of engine-men, who are to be appointed by the selectmen of towns, in order to guard against fires. Can it be supposed that these companies can volunteer *as companies,* — to enter the army of the United States, and go far away from the scene of duties for which they were established? But the companies of militia are hardly less local and home-keeping in their character than the companies of engine-men. It is impossible to suppose that they may volunteer, as companies, into the "army" of the United States.

But suppose, for the sake of argument, that companies of militia, as such, may volunteer into the service of the United States, under the Act of May, 1846, — do they continue to be *militia?* Clearly not. They are in no wise subject to the laws of Massachusetts. Her Governor, who was so unfortunately prompt to put them in motion, cannot recall them, although he is commander-in-chief of her militia. They have not her uniform. Their officers are not her officers; but officers of the United States. The corps has become part of the *army* of the United States, or of its general military force.

And this is the legal character of the present Massachusetts regiment, if it have any *legal character ;*

> If shape it may be called, that shape has none
> Distinguishable in member, joint or limb,
> Or substance may be called that shadow seems.

It is a part of the "army" of the United States, and not of the "militia."

Second. It being established that it is not of the *militia*, but of the *army*, the way is prepared for the consideration of the other questions. The first of these relates to the *constitutionality* of a part of the act under which the Regiment is raised. Looking at Capt. Webster's return in the present case, it will be perceived that he claims to hold the petitioner "because the said Samuel A. Stone has been duly enrolled and enlisted as a member of Company A, of the first Regiment of Massachusetts Infantry, whereof the said Edward Webster has been duly commissioned Captain by his Excellency the Governor of this Commonwealth." Now on this return a question is presented of a double aspect. 1. Has Edward Webster a right to detain the petitioner? 2. Is the petitioner liable to be detained by any body? For it is possible that the petitioner may be liable, although Edward Webster may have no right to detain him. In other words, he may be legally enlisted as a soldier in the "army" of the United States, although Webster is not a legal officer.

And, first, Is Edward Webster legally commissioned as "an officer of the United States?" This is an important question, which concerns the validity of his acts. He should be anxious to know if he is a legal officer, that he may not bear the sword in vain. The attributes of a military officer are of a high order. He has power over human life and property to an extraordinary degree. He has at once executive and judicial power; he is sheriff and judge. In these peculiar powers he is distinguishable from his fellow-citizens. These powers the Government can impart; but only in certain ways *precisely prescribed* by the Constitution and laws — only constitutionally, legally and rightfully. And the question recurs, Have these powers been imparted in such wise to Edward Webster?

This is to be determined by the Constitution of the United States. That instrument provides explicitly the manner of appointing "officers of the United States." It says, (Art. 2, § 2,) "The President shall nominate, and by and with the advice and consent of the Senate, shall appoint ambassadors, other public ministers and consuls, judges of the supreme court, *and all other officers of the United States*, whose appointments are not herein otherwise provided for, and which shall be established by law; but the Congress may by law vest the appointment of such *inferior officers* as they think proper, in the courts of law, or in the heads of departments." In the next clause it is declared, that "The President shall have power to fill all vacancies that may happen during the recess of the Senate, *by granting commissions*, which shall expire at the end of their next session."

From these clauses it appears that all "officers of the United States" are to be nominated, and by and with the advice of the Senate are to be appointed by the President; and it is to be inferred that they are to be "commissioned" by the President.

Now two questions arise, whether an officer in the "army" of the United States is an "officer of the United States" in the sense of the Constitution, and whether he is an "inferior officer."

He is not an "inferior officer" in the sense of the Constitution; for his appointment has never been vested "in the President alone, in the courts of law, or in the heads of departments."

He is an "officer of the United States." In favor of this is universal custom, which has always regarded him as such; the express action of President Monroe and Congress in 1821, in regard to the office of Adjutant General, (3 Story, Com. on Const. § 1531,) and sundry precedents.

I conclude, therefore, that Edward Webster, assuming to be an "officer of the United States," but not having been "nominated by the President, and by and with the advice and consent of the Senate appointed;" nor being "commissioned" by the President; is not constitutionally an officer of the "army" of the United States, nor entitled to detain the petitioner. He is commissioned by the Governor of Massachusetts, who cannot give any power in the "army" of the United States.

The question next arises, whether any person is authorized to detain the petitioner. Webster is not. Who is?

He has been mustered into the service of the United States; but it is not as an individual citizen; but *as a member of the company of which Webster assumed to be Captain.* If the company has no legal existence as a company, all the proceedings are void. But the company becomes such, only through its officers. Until its officers are chosen, it is an embryo — not a legal body. But its officers never have been chosen in any constitutional way. The company is, therefore, still unborn. Or rather, to adopt the illustration of the Roman Tribune, the " belly " is produced, but the " head and hands " are wanting; so that it is impossible to present a complete body.

The conclusion is, that the petitioner is not liable to be held in the service of the United States. This stands upon the *unconstitutionality* of that part of the law of Congress, relating to the peculiar organization of this corps.

This same error Congress has committed before. By Act of Feb. 24, 1807, (Little & Brown's edit. Vol. 2, p. 419,) it provides for volunteers in companies, whose " commissioned officers shall be appointed in the manner prescribed by law in the several States and Territories to which such companies shall respectively belong." Also by Act of Feb. 6th, 1812, (Little & Brown's edit. Vol. 2, p. 676,) the same words are repeated. But at a later day it seems the mistake was discovered. In the Act of Jan. 27th, 1815, it is provided " that the officers of the said volunteers shall be commissioned by the President of the United States," (§ 4); and also " that the appointment of the officers of the said volunteers, if received into the service of the United States for the term of twelve months, or for a longer term, shall be submitted to the Senate for their advice and consent, at the next session, after commissions for the same shall have been issued," (§ 8). This bill was much considered in Congress. See Niles's Register, Vol. 7th, pp. 313, 333, 352. But the same error is repeated in the act of May, 1846.

It is submitted, however, that it will be the duty of the Court to declare the Act of May, so far as it relates to the organization of the *volunteers*, unconstitutional, and all the proceedings under it a nullity.

Third. But, if the law should be regarded as constitutional, it is further submitted, that the proceedings under it in Massachusetts have been *illegal* in two respects; *first*, by the action of the Federal Government, and *second*, by the action of the Commonwealth.

At present, let us consider the illegality on the part of the Federal Government.

The Act of May provides for Volunteers "to serve twelve months, after they shall have arrived at the place of rendezvous, or to the end of the war, unless sooner discharged." But by the requisition of Mr. Secretary Marcy, they are "to serve during the war with Mexico, unless sooner discharged," which is a different term from that in the law.

The right to enlist soldiers is determined by the laws. Its exact extent is to be measured there. It is not dependent upon the judgment or conscience of any Secretary — as if his foot were to be the standard of physical measure. The law has expressly said, that the enlistment is to be for "twelve months or the war." Now, it could not have been the intention of Congress, to obtain enlistments for the indefinite period of the war — for ten years, like the Trojan war, or thirty years, like that of Wallenstein, in Germany. They wished to hold volunteers for twelve months, or even for a shorter time, if the war should be ended sooner; and, at the time of this untoward act, it was supposed that it would be ended sooner. The militia, in this Act, are to be called out for "six months" only.

By the Act of Feb. 24th, 1807, (Little & Brown's edit. Vol. 2, p. 419,) the volunteers are "for the term of twelve months, after they shall have arrived at the place of rendezvous, unless sooner discharged." So also for the same term, by the Act of Feb. 6th, 1812, (Vol. 2, p 676.) But by Act of Feb. 24th, 1814, (Vol. 3, p. 98,) the term was "five years or during the war." By Act of Jan. 27th, 1815, (Vol. 3, p. 193,) the term was "not less than twelve months." By the Act of Jan. 27th, 1814, (Vol. 3, p. 94,) the term of soldiers in the regular army is "five years, or during the war." I mention these precedents, to show that this question may have arisen before, although we have no reports of it from any judicial tribunal. But we have the express opinion of the late Mr. Justice Johnson, of the Supreme Court of the United States, in a note to his elaborate Life of General Greene, which was, probably, written not long after the Acts of Congress, to which I have referred. It was printed in 1822. He says: "The point on which the Pennsylvania line really grounded their revolt, was the same which has been more recently agitated between the American Government and its army. The soldiers were enlisted for a certain number of years, *or the war.* At the expiration of the term of years they demanded their discharge, and after resisting this just claim, and sustaining all the terrors and real dangers of a revolt, the Government was obliged to acquiesce. *For so many years or the war*, certainly meant for that time, if the war should so long last. Else why specify a term of years, as enlistment for the war would have expressed the sense of the contracting parties." (Vol. 2, p. 53.)

On the authority of Mr. Justice Johnson, the question would seem to be clear. But if there should be any doubt, the inclination should be against the Government. They are the powerful and intelligent party; the soldier is powerless and ignorant. The Government are the inviting, offering, promising party. To them applies the rule, *Verba fortius accipiuntur contra proferentem.* (Lord Bacon's Maxims, Reg. iii.)

But it has been s.id on the other side, that the "twelve months" have not yet expired; and it does not follow that the volunteers will be detained beyond that period. But the case now is to be judged on the *contract.* Is it legal, under the Act of Congress, or illegal? It is submitted that it is illegal.

I now approach the fourth point of inquiry.

Fourth. The proceedings in Massachusetts under the Act of March are *illegal,* inasmuch as they are a *fraud* upon the militia laws of the Commonwealth. This brings me to a part of the case humiliating to our Commonwealth.

We have already seen the purpose of these laws, contemplating the performance of duties *at home,* as in preserving the peace, and aiding the *posse comitatus.* These purposes are distinctly declared by the Legislature. (Cap. 92, 1840.) These *laws* have been, by the agency of State officers, employed, — I would say, prostituted — to a purpose widely different; not to help preserve the peace at home, but to contribute means to destroy peace abroad. It appears from the communication of the Adjutant-General, that he resorted to the device or invention of using the militia laws of the State, in order to enlist soldiers to make war on Mexico. The following is the form of an application to be organized as a company of the Massachusetts militia; the applicant expressly setting forth objects inconsistent with the duties of the militia.

Charlestown, January 4, 1847.

To His Excellency George N. Briggs, Governor and Commander in Chief of the Commonwealth of Massachusetts:

SIR, — The undersigned, in behalf of himself and his associates, whose names are duly enrolled therefor, respectfully requests that they may be duly organized as a company, to be annexed to the First Regiment of Massachusetts Infantry; *it being understood, that when so organized, they desire and assent to be placed at the disposal of the President of the United States, to serve during the existing war with Mexico.* And as in duty bound will ever pray.

(Signed,) JOHN S. BARKER.

Thus it is, that the Executive of the Commonwealth placed all the apparatus and energy of the office of the Adjutant-General, and of the militia laws, at the service of certain petitioners, well knowing that they were not to enlist *bonâ fide* in the honest militia of Massachusetts, but with the distinct understanding that they should be placed at the disposal of the President of the United States, to serve during the existing war with Mexico. I do not complain that the Governor or the Adjutant-General has lent himself officially or personally to this purpose, though I have my regrets on this score; but

I do complain that *the laws of Massachusetts* have been prostituted to this purpose.

It has been decided by the Supreme Court of the United States, in *Pennsylvania* v. *Prigg*, (16 Peters, 539,) that State officers are not obliged to enforce United States' laws. Congress must execute its laws by its own officers. Under the lead of this decision, the Legislature of Massachusetts passed a law making it penal for any State officers to arrest or detain in public buildings any person, for the reason that he is claimed as a fugitive slave, (Act of 1843, cap. 69,) although they were expressly empowered thereto by the Act of Congress of 1793. By this legislation, Massachusetts has clearly shown her determination to take advantage of the principle in Prigg's case. The Governor and the Adjutant-General — not heeding the spirit of our Commonwealth — made themselves *recruiting officers* of the United States, as much as if they had enlisted sailors for the Ohio. They made themselves *Volunteers*.

But how much soever this may be deplored, it forms no ground for any legal questioning of their acts. What they did, under the directions of an act of Congress, as *agents* of the United States, would be legal, provided it was not forbidden by the laws of the State. But although they might volunteer to act as *agents* of the United States in raising troops for the Mexican war, acting under the law of Congress, *they could not employ the State laws for this purpose*. They cannot be justified in *diverting* the laws of the State to purposes not originally contemplated by these laws, and also *inconsistent with their whole design and character*. Such was the employment of the militia laws of Massachusetts.

These laws have been made, by the Executive, the instruments, the "decoy-ducks," to get together the Falstaff regiment, whose existence is now drawn in question. The whole proceeding is a *fraud* on those laws.

It is the duty of this Court, as the high conservators of the laws of this Commonwealth, bound to see that they receive no detriment, to guard them from such a perversion from their true and original purpose. This can be done only by annulling the proceedings that have taken place under them.

Such are the objections to the legal character of the Massachusetts Regiment. If either of these should prevail, then the whole Regiment is virtually dissolved. It becomes a mere name. *Stat nominis umbra.* Or it is left a mere voluntary association, without that quickening principle, which is necessary to a military organization under the Constitution and laws of the United States. It is like the monster Frankenstein, the creation of audacious human hands, endowed with a human form, but wanting a soul.

Fifth. But suppose the Court should hesitate to pronounce the nullity of these proceedings, and should recognize the legal existence of the regiment, it then becomes important to determine, whether there are any special circumstances in the case of the petitioner now before the Court, which will justify his discharge. The party that I represent is a *minor*, and as such entitled to his discharge. The question on this point I have reserved to the last, because I wished to consider it after the inquiry, whether the regiment was a part of the "army" or the "militia," in order to disembarrass it of some considerations that might arise from the circumstance that the militia laws embrace minors. I assume now that the regiment, if it have any legal existence, is a part of the "army."

The jurisprudence of all countries wisely provides a certain period of majority at which persons are supposed to be able to make contracts. This by the common law is twenty-one.

Now the enlistment in the army of the United States is a *contract.* The parties are volunteers; and the term implies contract. And the question arises whether this contract is governed by the common law, so as to be voidable when made by a minor. Is the circumstance that the contract is made with the *Government*, any ground of exception? If an infant were to contract with the Government to sell a piece of land, he would not be bound by it any more than if the contract were with a private person. Is the circumstance, that the contract is *military*, any ground of exception? If an infant were to contract to furnish military supplies to Government, he could not be held more than by any private individual.

The rule of the common law as to the incapacity of infants is specific. An exception to it must be established, by express legislation, as in the case of capacity to make a will, to marry, or to serve in the militia. Congress has recognized this principle by expressly declaring, on several occasions, that persons between eighteen and twenty-one might be enlisted. The argument from this is clear, that without this *express provision*, such enlistments would not be binding. The Act of Jan. 11, 1812, (Little & Brown, Vol. 2, p. 671) and of Dec. 10, 1814, (Ibid. Vol. 3, p. 146,) contain such provisions. And we are able from contemporary history to ascertain what was the true understanding. See Niles's Register, Vol. 3, p. 207, where is a discussion on the first of these acts; and also Vol. 7, p. 308, where it appears that this legislation of Congress formed a special subject of complaint.

It has been argued, however, that the United States have no common law, and cannot, therefore, be governed by the rules of majority therein established. Although it may be decided that the United States have no common law as a source of jurisdiction, yet it cannot be questioned that they have a common law, so far as it may be necessary in determining the signification of words and the capacity of persons. Idiots and feme coverts would not be held as *volunteers* in the army of the United States; but their capacity is determined by the common law, and not by any special legislation.

I conclude, therefore, that the contract of enlistment in this regiment may be avoided by a minor.

It may possibly be in the power of the Court to discharge the petitioner, without passing upon all the grave questions which have been presented. But it is submitted that, if these proceedings are unconstitutional and illegal as has now been urged — if the regiment is a nullity, as is believed — the truth should be declared. The regiment is soon to embark for foreign war, when its members will be beyond the kindly protection of this Court. It will be for the Court to determine whether it may not, by a just judgment, vindicate the injured laws of Massachusetts, and discharge many fellow-citizens from obligations imposed in violation of the Constitution and laws of the land.

SPEECH CALLING FOR THE WITHDRAWAL OF THE AMERICAN TROOPS FROM MEXICO, AT A PUBLIC MEETING IN FANEUIL HALL, BOSTON, FEB. 4, 1847.

MR. CHAIRMAN AND FELLOW CITIZENS,

In the winter of 1775, five years after the "massacre" in King Street, now called State Street, a few months only before the battles of Lexington and Bunker Hill, Boston was occupied by a British army under the command of General Gage — as Mexican Monterey, a town of the same size with Boston in those days, is now occupied by American troops under the command of General Taylor. The people of Boston deeply felt the grievance of this garrison, holding by an iron hand the control of the province of Massachusetts Bay. With earnest voices they called for its withdrawal, as the true beginning of reconciliation and peace. Their remonstrances found an unexpected echo in the House of Lords, when Lord Chatham, on the 20th January, brought forward his memorable motion for the withdrawal of the troops from Boston. Josiah Quincy, Jr., dear to Bostonians alike for his own services, and for the services of his descendants in two generations, was present on this occasion, and has preserved an interesting and authentic sketch of Lord Chatham's speech. From his report I take the following important words: —

There ought to be no delay in entering upon this matter. We ought to proceed to it immediately. We ought to seize the first moment to open the door of reconciliation. The Americans will never be in a temper or state to be reconciled — they ought not to be, till the troops are withdrawn. The troops are a perpetual irritation to them; they are a bar to all confidence and all cordial reconcilement. I, therefore, my Lords, move — "That a humble address be presented to His Majesty, most humbly to advise and beseech his Majesty that, in order to open the way to a happy settlement of the dangerous troubles in America, by beginning to allay ferments and soften animosities there — and above all, in preventing, in the mean time, any sudden and fatal catastrophe at Boston, now suffering under the daily irritation of an army before their eyes, posted in their town — it may graciously please his Majesty, *that immediate orders may be despatched to General Gage for removing his Majesty's forces from the town of Boston* — as soon as the rigor of the season, and other circumstances indispensable to the safety and accommodation of the said troops, may render the same practicable."

It is to promote a similar measure of justice and reconciliation that we are now assembled. We ask the cessation of this unjust war, and the withdrawal of the American forces from Mexico, "so soon as the rigor of the season, and other circumstances indispensable to the safety and accommodation of the said troops, may render the same practicable."

It is hoped that this movement will extend throughout the country. It is proper that it should begin here.

Boston herself, in former times, has suffered. The war horse has been stalled in one of her most venerable churches. Her streets have echoed to the tread of hostile troops. Her inhabitants have been waked by the morning drum-beat of their oppressors. They have seen, on their own narrow peninsula, the smoke of an enemy's camp. Though these things are beyond the memory of any in this multitude, yet faithful History has entered them on her record, so that they can never be forgotten. It is proper, then, that Boston, mindful of the past, and of her own trials, mindful of her own pleadings for the withdrawal of the troops of General Gage, as the beginning of reconciliation with England, should now come forward and ask for *others*, what she once so earnestly asked for *herself*. It is proper that Boston should confess her obligations to the generous eloquence of Chatham in her behalf, by vindicating his high arguments of policy, humanity and justice, in their application to the citizens of a sister Republic. Franklin, in dispensing a charity, said to the recipient, return this when you are able, not to me, but to some one in need, like yourself now. In the same spirit, Boston should seek to repay the debt of a former generation, by striving for the withdrawal of the American troops from Mexico.

Other considerations call upon her to take the lead. Boston has always led the generous and magnanimous actions of our history. Boston led the cause of the Revolution. Here was commenced that discussion, pregnant with the independence of the colonies, which, at first occupying a few warm but true spirits only, finally absorbed all the best energies of the continent, the eloquence of Adams, the patriotism of Jefferson, the wisdom of Washington. Boston is the home of noble charities, the nurse of true learning, the city of churches. By all these tokens, she stands conspicuous; and other parts of the country are not unwilling sometimes to follow her example. Athens was called "the eye of Greece." Boston may be called "the eye" of America; and the influence which she exerts is to be referred not to her size — for there are other cities larger far — but to her moral and intellectual character. It is only just, then, that a place foremost in the struggles of the Revolution, foremost in all the humane and enlightened labors of our country, should take the lead on the present occasion.

The war, in which the United States are now engaged, has been pronounced, from this platform, unconstitutional. Such was the judgment of him, who has earned the title of Defender of the Constitution. Would that he had not confined himself to an innocuous threat of impeachment against its alleged author; but had spoken in the spirit of another time, when, on branding a certain appropriation as unconstitutional, he boldly said he would not vote for it, if the enemy were thundering at the gates of the Capitol!

Assuming that the war was commenced in violation of the Constitution, we have ample reason, on this account alone, to call for its arrest. Let the troops be withdrawn to the place where they were, when, in defiance of the Constitution, they were moved upon the disputed territory.

But the war is not only unconstitutional; it is unjust; it is vile in its object and character. It has its origin in a well known series of measures to extend and perpetuate slavery. It is a war which must ever be odious in history, beyond the common measure allotted to the outrages of brutality which disfigure other nations and times. It is a slave-driving war. In its principle, it is only a little above those miserable conflicts between the barbarian chiefs of Central Africa, to obtain slaves for the inhuman markets of Brazil. Such a war must be accursed in the sight of God. Why is it not accursed in the sight of man?

We are told that the country is engaged in the war, and that, therefore, it must be maintained, or, as it is sometimes expressed, vigorously prosecuted. In other words, the violation of the Constitution, and the outrage upon justice, are to be disregarded, while all are to join in a continuance and repetition of the violation and the outrage. By what necromancy do these pass from wrong to right? In what book of morals is it written, that what is bad before it is commenced, may become righteous merely by the fact that it has been commenced? Who on earth is authorized to transmute wrong into right? They, who admit the unconstitutionality and injustice of the war, and yet sanction its prosecution, must recognize the heaven-defying sentiment, "Our country, right or wrong." Can this be the sentiment of the people of Boston? If it be so, in vain have they been nurtured in the churches of the Pilgrims; in vain have they been fed from the common table of knowledge, bountifully supplied by our public schools. Who would confess allegiance to wrong? Who would deny allegiance to right? Right is one of the attributes of God, or rather, it is a part of the

Divinity, immortal as himself. Surely nothing mortal can be higher than what is immortal. Suppose this sentiment had been received by our English defenders in the war of the Revolution, the fiery tongues of Chatham, Burke, Fox and Camden, would not have been heard in our behalf. They would all have been silenced by the dogma, that, whether the country was right or wrong, it must be carried through the war.

The saying, that the country must be maintained in the war, because it is already commenced, confounds the opposite duties in cases of *defence* and of *offence*. When the country is invaded, when its soil is pressed by hostile footsteps, when its churches are desecrated, when its inhabitants are despoiled of their homes, when its national life is assailed, then the indignant spirit of a free people will rise to repel the aggressors. Such an occasion challenges all the energies of *self-defence*. It has about it all of that dismal glory which can be earned in any scenes of human strife. But if it be right to persevere in *defence*, it must be wrong to persevere in *offence*. If the Mexicans are right in defending their homes, we certainly are wrong in invading them.

The present war is *offensive* in its character. As such, it loses all shadow of title to our support. The acts of courage and hardihood, which, in a just cause, might excite our regard, when performed in an unrighteous cause, have no quality that can commend them to any virtuous sympathy. The victories of aggression and injustice are sources of grief and shame. The blood, which is wrongfully shed, cries from the ground, as the blood of Abel cried against Cain.

The enormous expenditures already lavished upon

this war, now extending to fifty millions of dollars, — we have recently been told on the floor of the Senate that they were near one hundred millions, — form another reason for calling for its cessation. The soul sickens at the contemplation of this incalculable sum, diverted from purposes of usefulness and beneficence, from railroads, colleges, hospitals, schools, and churches, — under whose genial influences, the country would blossom as a rose, — and prostituted to the wicked purposes of an unjust war. In any righteous cause of self-defence, even these expenditures would be readily incurred. The saying of an early father of the Republic, which roused its enthusiasm to an unwonted pitch, was "Millions for Defence, but not a cent for Tribute." Another sentiment more pertinent to our times, would be, "Not a cent for OFFENCE."

And why is this war to be maintained? According to the jargon of the day, "to conquer a Peace." But, if we ask for Peace, in the spirit of Peace, we must begin by doing justice to Mexico. We are the aggressors. We are now in the wrong. We must do all in our power to set ourselves right. This surely is not by brutal efforts to conquer Mexico. Our military force confessedly is greater than hers. There can be nothing even of the wretched glory of conquest, where there is such disparity of power. Nor can there be any true honor in a successful adherence to our original acts of wrong. "To conquer a Peace" may have a sensible signification when a nation is acting in *self-defence;* but it is base, unjust, and atrocious, when the war is of *offence.* Peace, in such a war, if founded on conquest, must be the triumph of injustice, the consummation of wrong. It is unlike that true peace, which is won by Christian forbearance and justice. It cannot be sanctioned by the God of Christians. It would be offensive to the better divinities of heathenism. It is of such a Peace, that the Roman historian, whose pen has the sharpness of the point of a sword, says, — "*Auferre, trucidare, rapere, falsis nominibus,* IMPERIUM; *atque, ubi solitudinem faciunt,* PACEM *appellant.*" "With lying names, they call spoliation, murder, and rapine, *Empire;* and, when they have produced the desolation of solitude, they call it *Peace.*"

The present course of our country is inconsistent with the principles of conduct which govern individuals in private life. There are few, if any, of the conspicuous advocates for the maintenance of this war, who would hesitate, if found wrong in any private transaction, to *retreat* at once. With Christian apologies they would seek to repair their error, while they recoiled from even any appearance of perseverance in it. Such should be the conduct of our country; for the general rules of morals are the same for individuals and states. "A commonwealth," says Milton, "ought to be but as one huge Christian personage, one mighty growth or stature of an honest man, as big and compact in virtue as in body; for look what the grounds and causes are of single happiness to one man, the same you shall find them to a whole state; by consequence, therefore, that which is good and agreeable to the state, will appear soonest to be so, by being good and agreeable to the true welfare of every Christian, and that which can be justly proved hurtful and offensive to every true Christian, will be evinced to be alike hurtful to the state."

Is it not hurtful and offensive to every true Christian to persevere in wrong-doing? Is it not hurtful and offensive to every Christian Commonwealth to persevere in wrong-doing? This becomes doubly so, when the opposite party is weak, and we are strong.

There are other considerations, arising from our peculiar fellowship with Mexico, which plead in her behalf. She is our neighbor and sister republic, who caught her first impulse to independence from our example, and rejected the ensigns of royalty to follow our simpler, purer forms. She has erred often, and has suffered much under the rule of selfish and bad men. But she is our neighbor and sister still, and is entitled to the rights of neighborhood and sisterhood. Many of her citizens are well known in our country, where they have established relations of respect and amity. One of them, General Almonte, her recent minister at Washington, has been a favored guest in the social circles of the capital. He is familiar doubtless with many members who voted the supplies for the prosecution of this cruel war upon his country. The representative from Boston has referred to him in terms of personal regard. In addressing any of these friends, how justly might this Mexican adopt the words of Dr. Franklin, in his remarkable letter to Mr. Strahan, of the British Parliament!

PHILADELPHIA, July 5th, 1775.

MR. STRAHAN, — You are a member of Parliament, and one of that majority which doomed my country to destruction. You have begun to burn our towns and murder our people. *Look upon your hands! They are stained with the blood of your relations!* — You and I were long friends. You are now my enemy, and I am, yours,

B. FRANKLIN.

The struggle in Mexico against the United States, and that of our fathers against England, have some peculiar points of resemblance. Prominent among these is the aggressive character of the proceedings instituted by the more powerful nations, in the hope of crushing their weaker brethren. But the parallel fails as yet in an important particular. The injustice of England roused, in her own Parliament, some of her most distinguished sons to call for the cessation of the war. It inspired the eloquence of Chatham to those strains of undying fame. In the Senate of the United States, there is a favorite son of Massachusetts, to whom has been accorded, by a bountiful Providence, powers unsurpassed by those of any English orator. He has now before him the cause of Chatham. His country is engaged in an unrighteous war. Let us join in asking him to raise his powerful voice in behalf of justice, and of peace founded on justice ; and may the spirit of Chatham descend upon him !

Let us call upon the whole country to rally in this cause. Let a voice go forth from Faneuil Hall to-night, awakening fresh echoes throughout the kindly valleys of New England ; swelling as it proceeds, and gathering new reverberations in its ample volume ; traversing the whole land, and still receiving other voices, till it reaches our rulers at Washington, and, in tones of thunder, demands the cessation of this unjust war.

SPEECH BEFORE THE BOSTON PRISON DISCIPLINE SOCIETY, AT THE TREMONT TEMPLE, JUNE 18, 1847.

[At the Anniversary of the Prison Discipline Society, May 26, 1846, on motion of Mr. Sumner, a committee was appointed to examine and review the printed Reports of the Society; also the course of the Society; and to consider whether its course could in any way be varied or amended, that its usefulness might be extended. At the succeeding Anniversary, May 29, 1847, Mr. Sumner, for himself and his associates on the Committee, George S. Hillard, Esq. and Rev. Francis Wayland, presented a Report, concluding with the following resolutions: —

Resolved, That the object of our Society is to promote the improvement of public prisons.

Resolved, That our Society is not, and ought not to be considered, the pledged advocate of the Auburn system of prison discipline, or of any other system now in existence; and that its reports should set forth, with strict impartiality, the merits and demerits of any and all systems.

Resolved, That we recognize the Directors of the Eastern Penitentiary of Pennsylvania as sincere, conscientious and philanthropic fellow-laborers in the great cause of prison discipline.

Resolved, That if any expressions of disrespect have appeared in our reports, or been uttered at any of our public meetings, which have justly given pain to our brethren, our Society sincerely regrets them.

Resolved, That our Society should strive, by increased action on the part of its officers, and of its individual members, to extend its usefulness.

Resolved, That the Board of Managers be requested to organize a new system of action for the Society, which shall enlist the coöperation of its individual members.

The acceptance of these by the Society being opposed, its meeting was adjourned for further consideration till the evening of June 2d, when Mr. Sumner sustained the report and resolutions in a speech of some length. Other meetings, by adjournment, took place on the evenings of June 4th, June 9th, June 11th, June 16th, June 18th, and June 23d. These were at the Tremont Temple, and were attended by a large and most intelligent audience. They were presided over by Hon. Theodore Lyman. In the course of the debate, the resolutions were supported by Dr. Howe, George S. Hillard, Esq., Rev. Francis Parkman, and Henry H. Fuller, Esq. They were opposed by Hon. S. A. Eliot, (the Treasurer of the Society,) Hon. Francis C. Gray, Bradford Sumner, Esq., Rev. George Allen, Dr. Walter Channing, and J. Thomas Stevenson, Esq. On the evening of June 18th, Mr. Sumner took the floor, and spoke as follows :]

MR. PRESIDENT,

As Chairman of the Committee, whose report and resolutions are now under consideration, it becomes my duty to review and to close this debate. The reapers have been many, and the sickles keen; but the field is ample and the harvest abundant; so that I may hope, even at this late period, to be no superfluous gleaner.

And now, before entering upon our labor, let us refresh ourselves by the contemplation of the unquestioned good which has arisen from these protracted meetings. All will feel that it is well for our society that its attention has at last been turned within itself, and that it has been led to do what is enjoined upon every good man, by self-examination to endeavor to improve the character, with a view to future usefulness. All, too, will feel that, whatever may be the immediate vote on the question before us, this discussion has excited, among large circles of men, an unwonted interest in behalf of those who are in prison, and that, under its generous influences, a sacred sympathy has vibrated from heart to heart. Thus much for the unquestioned good of our meetings.

Mr. President, I approach this discussion with regret; feeling that I must say some things which I would gladly leave unsaid. I shall not, however, decline the duty which seems to be cast upon me. In its performance I hope to be pardoned, if I speak frankly and freely; I hope it will be gently and kindly. I will borrow, with his permission, from the honorable Treasurer [Mr. Eliot] something of his frankness, without his temper. And as I propose to refer to facts, I shall be grateful to any gentleman who will correct me, where I may seem to be wrong. For such a purpose, I will cheerfully yield the floor; even to the Treasurer, though his sense of justice did not suffer him, while on the floor, to give me an opportunity of correcting a misstatement he made of what I had said on a former occasion.

Let me begin by a reference — which I should be pleased to avoid — to myself and my own personal relations to this inquiry. I was brought up at the feet of our society. My earliest recollection of matters, like those to which it is devoted, does not extend beyond the period of its origin. All my early partialities were in favor of its course, and of the system of Prison Discipline which it has advocated. I had read and circulated its reports at home and abroad, and felt grateful to their author. Other studies, and some acquaintance with the elaborate labors, by which the science of Prison Discipline has been so much advanced in Europe, led me at first to doubt the course of our society, and finally to the conviction that it had not been candid and just, particularly in the treatment of the Pennsylvania System. With this impression, I attended the anniversary of 1845, where I listened to what seemed to be a discreditable report from the Board of Managers, in which this system was treated ignorantly, ungenerously, and unjustly, while the officer of our society, whose duty it was to read the report — in words which fell from him while reading it — seemed to impeach the veracity of the Inspectors of the Penitentiary at Philadelphia. I was emboldened, in conjunction with my friend on my right, [Dr. Howe,] to move a reference of the report to a select committee, with power to review and modify it, and to visit Philadelphia, in order to ascertain on the spot the true character of the System of Prison Discipline there practised, *and to incorporate a report of their proceedings in the next annual report of the society.* What I said at the time was unpremeditated. I was moved to speak in behalf of the absent, and, in a certain sense, as the representative of the unrepresented, believing that gross injustice had been done to them and to their system. My aim was to recall the society to that position of candor and justice, which self-respect, to say nothing of its Christian professions, seemed to require.

Here let me indulge in a reminiscence. It is the custom to open our meetings with prayer. By the records of our society, it appears that, at its earliest anniversary, as long ago as 1826, this service was performed by an eminent clergyman, the deserved favorite of his own denomination, and much respected by all others. This public profession of interest in our cause was followed by other manifestations of it. He became a manager of our society. Subsequently, yielding to the call of the University at Providence, he left Boston and became the President of that important seat of learning. His labors were not restrained to academic duties. By his pen, and the wide influence of his remarkable character, he was felt in various fields of labor in all parts of the country. His interest in the cause of Prison Discipline was constant, and in 1843 he was chosen President of our society. In placing him at its head, we justly honored one of our earliest and most distinguished friends. He was in the chair on the anniversary to which I have referred. His sense of the injustice done to the gentlemen of Philadelphia was great. As the most authentic expression of his opinions on that occasion, influencing as they have the subsequent proceedings of those who seek a change in the course of our society, I shall read a letter from him written on the evening of that anniversary:

PROVIDENCE, May 27, 1845.

MY DEAR SIR, — I cannot resist the impulse, to thank you again for your remarks this morning. I had resolved, before you rose, to return home and immediately resign office in the society; for I could not allow my influence, though ever so small, to be used for the purpose of (as it seemed to me) vilifying the intentions of good and honorable men. I cannot perceive how we can, with any share of propriety, use language in respect to absent gentlemen, which, in the ordinary intercourse of society, would be just cause of irreconcilable variance. I agree with you entirely as to the object of the society. It is to improve the discipline of prisons, and it should hail, as fellow-laborers, all who are honestly engaged in the same cause. The cause requires the trial of various experiments, and our business is to collect in good faith and with catholic liberality, the results of all, that so, by the comparison of results, the best end may be attained. I thank you over and over again, for coming forward so nobly in defence of the absent, and for placing the object of the society on its true basis, instead of allowing it to be a mere antagonist to the gentlemen at Philadelphia. In all this, of course, I mean no unkindness to any one. I only feel that, by looking at an object steadily and earnestly in only one light, we are all liable to lose sight of its wider relations.

I am, so far as I see, in favor of the Auburn System; but I want to know something of all of the systems, and am, I trust, anxious to learn the facts. I wrote an article in the North American Review some time since, on the subject. I am inclined to the same view still. But this is no reason why I should disparage the labor of others.

You seem interested in this matter, and I feel rejoiced at it. I cannot but hope that good will come of it. Let me suggest a few things, by way of indication, that may possibly be improved: —

1. Is it wise to have our annual reports so far *extempore?* What we sanction should be *ipsissima verba.* Our character as men is involved in what we hear and order to be published.

2. It seems to me that our expenditure should be used with great attention to results. The statistics which we have are

important, but I doubt whether they always bear so closely on our object as they might. Why would it not be desirable to investigate the great subject of *Pauperism*, and that of *Criminal Law*, which, together, do almost the whole work of filling our prisons?

3. Do the Executive Committee really take these subjects in hand, and give direction to the labors of the Society? They have a very responsible situation, and cannot discharge it by simply auditing bills. Can they not be induced to labor earnestly in this matter?

4. It seems that John Augustus, a poor man, has done much. We praise him. This is well. Can we not take means for following his example?

These things have occurred to me, and I know that you will pardon me for suggesting them. I believe that there is here a field for doing great good. When I think of the good which Miss Dix, alone and unaided, has done, I cannot but believe that we might do more. To the gentlemen of your profession, we specially look for aid in this matter. Can you labor in any philanthropic object with better prospect of success? Excuse my freedom. I have no right to set you or any one else at work. I am ashamed to be President of a society for which I do so little, and will gladly remove myself out of the way, and have earnestly desired to do so. I, however, hold myself ready to do any thing that may be in my power to advance the cause in which we are engaged.

I am, my dear Sir, yours very truly,

F. WAYLAND.

C. SUMNER, Esq.

The Committee, appointed under the resolution, examined the report of the Board of Managers, and visited Philadelphia. A report, prepared by their chairman, Dr. Howe, was made a minority report by the votes of *the Treasurer and the Secretary*, officers of the society and both of them, as it appears from the records of the society, connected with the authorship of the original report, which gave occasion to the inquiry, and therefore, it would seem, in the light of delicacy, if not of parliamentary rules, hardly competent members of the committee. It was next proposed that the report, although by a minority of the committee, should, in pursuance of the instruction contained in the original resolution, "be incorporated in the next annual report." This, it appears from the records of the society, was submitted to the Board of Managers, May 7th, 1846, where it was opposed *by the Treasurer*. On May 21st, it was referred to a meeting of the whole society, convened at the dwelling-house of the *Secretary;* for our association, not unlike the enchanted carpet in the Arabian Nights, dilates at times to dimensions ample to embrace this large audience, and then again shrinks, if need be, to the narrow space occupied by its Secretary. At this meeting, on motion of *the Treasurer*, still another impediment was thrown in the way of printing the report, in pursuance of the original resolution. At the business meeting of the society, May 25th, on the day preceding the anniversary, I made still another ineffectual attempt to have this report appear among the transactions of the society. This was followed by a resolution, on motion of Mr. Nathaniel Willis, *a near connection of the Secretary*, as follows: —

Voted, That it is not expedient to discuss the subject at the anniversary meeting.

It was at the anniversary meeting, however, that I was determined to discuss the subject, being well assured that, in the presence of a wakeful public, the will of one or two individuals could not control the course of the society. Accordingly I took the floor and proceeded to speak, when I was strangely encountered by the *Secretary*, who ejaculated, " Mr. President, the annual meeting was interrupted in this manner last year; there are gentlemen present who are invited by the Committee of Arrangements to address us." On this remarkable fragment of a speech I made no comment at the time. I shall make none now; but I cannot forbear quoting the words of the able editor of the Law Reporter, with regard to it. " It would seem," he says, " that the addresses at the public meetings of the society are all cut and dried beforehand, a fact that might as well have been kept back, under the circumstances, for the credit of all concerned." Notwithstanding this interference, I proceeded to expose the prejudiced and partisan course of the society, and its consequent loss of credit, concluding by a motion for a committee to consider its past conduct, and the best means of extending its usefulness. The motion, though opposed at the time, was passed. It is the report of that committee which is now before you.

This report, when offered to the society, was first opposed on grounds of *form*. It is now opposed on other grounds, hardly less pertinent, though seeming to be not of form only. Thus at every step have our honest efforts to elevate the character of our society, and to extend its usefulness, been encountered by opposition. Under the auspices of the *Treasurer and the Secretary*, the society has seemed to shrink from examination and inquiry. Like the sensitive leaf, it has closed at the touch. Nay, more: it has repelled all endeavors to wake it to new life. It seems to have adopted, as its guardian motto, that remarkable epitaph which, for more than two centuries, has preserved from examination and intrusion the sacred remains of the greatest master of our tongue: —

> Good friend, for Jesus' sake, forbear
> To digg the dust enclosed here!
> Blest be the man that spares these stones,
> And cursed be he that moves my bones!

The Boston Prison Discipline Society is not William Shakspeare; nor is it yet dead. But the maledictions of the epitaph seem to have fallen upon those of us, who have undertaken "to move its bones."

The amiable Treasurer has impeached our motives. Sir, I impeach no man's motives; but I do submit that if the motives of any person are to be drawn in question, it cannot be those of gentlemen who have originated this inquiry; but rather of those few whose pride of opinion is intertwined with the whole course of the society. Again, it has been said that we are "intruders." That was the word. Is your predecessor, Sir, the Rev. Dr. Wayland, who is one of the authors of the report, an intruder? Are the gentlemen who have sustained the report, in this debate, intruders? Are we not all members of this society, and as such bound to exert ourselves to the best of our abilities to carry out its objects? Who shall call us intruders? Sir, I apply this term to no man, and to no set of men; but I cannot forbear saying that if the injurious suggestion which it is calculated to convey, is applicable any where, it cannot be to those who have honestly striven to elevate the character of the society, and to extend its usefulness; but rather to those who have met these efforts with constant opposition, and have declared in this debate, that "It was the policy of the society to act by one man only." It has also been insinuated that one of the gentlemen who has supported the report, a valued friend of mine, has shown an undue degree of confidence in his own opinions: I do not remember the word that was employed. Sir, his modest character and services, which have been gratefully recognized in two hemispheres, and his intimate acquaintance with the subject, entitle him to speak with firmness. I do not charge the gentleman, who dealt this insinuation, with vanity or self-esteem; though it did seem to me, that it came with an ill-grace from one, who, in the course of a short speech, contrived to announce himself as the Treasurer of the Boston Prison Discipline Society, next as the Treasurer of Harvard College, and not content with this, told us that he had once been a member of the City Government, and a Senator of the Commonwealth! But I will not follow these personalities further. I have alluded to them with regret. They are a part of the poisoned ingredients — "eye of newt and toe of frog," — which the Treasurer has dropped into the cauldron of this debate.

I advance now to other fields. The report and the accompanying resolutions present three principal points. First, the duty and pledge on our part of candor and impartiality between the different systems of Prison Discipline. Second, the duty of offering some expressions of Christian regret to our brethren in Philadelphia on account of the past. Third, the duty of our officers to make increased exertions to extend the usefulness of the society, particularly by enlisting the coöperation of individual members.

To these several propositions we have had various replies, occupying no inconsiderable portion of time. We have listened to the humane sentiments of my friend on the left (Dr. W. CHANNING;) to the inappropriate twice-told statistics of my other friend (Mr. F. C. GRAY;) to the labored argument of my professional brother (Mr. BRADFORD SUMNER;) to the two addresses of the reverend gentleman from Worcester (Mr. ALLEN.) Let me say, that I have many sympathies with this gentleman. I have recently read a production of his, entitled, "Resistance to Slavery is Duty to God," with admiration and delight. Here his own powers answered to the grandeur of his cause. If he has failed in the present debate to impress his hearers, it cannot be from lack of ability, or from shortness of time, but from the weakness of his cause. And lastly, we have been made partakers of that singular utterance from our Treasurer, (Mr. ELIOT,) which abounded so largely in the excellence, that Byron found in Mitford, the historian of Greece, and which he said should characterize all good historians, — "wrath and partiality."

It is my purpose to consider and sustain the positions of the report and resolutions, and in the course of my remarks to reply to the various objections that have been raised against them. In doing this, I shall confine myself to those topics which occupied the attention of the committee. This will lead me to place aside one suggestion of an interesting character, which has been introduced into this debate by a friend not of the committee. I refer to the charge of sectarianism. This did not enter into the deliberations of the committee, and formed no part of the basis of the report. If there be in the past course of the society any ground for this charge — and on this I express no opinion — it will doubtless find a corrective in what has been said here. As I do not ask your acceptance of the report and resolutions on this ground, so I appeal to your candor to entertain them irrespective of any considerations arising from the introduction of this topic.

I. The first point for consideration is, the duty and pledge on our part of candor and impartiality between the different systems of Prison Discipline. And here I might, perhaps, content myself by the bare enumeration of these systems, and ask my hearers, if they were so fully convinced with regard to the respective merits of each, as to be willing to embrace one, and to reject, absolutely, all the others. For instance, I may mention four different systems: *First*, that of Pennsylvania, which has been so much discussed, the principal feature of which is separation of the prisoners from each other both by day and night, with labor in cells. *Second*, that of Auburn, where the prisoners are in separate cells by night, but work in common workshops, in *enforced silence*, by day. *Third*, there is a system, compounded of these two, according to which, certain prisoners are treated as at Auburn, and certain others as in Pennsylvania. This is sometimes called the *Mixed* System, and sometimes that of Lausanne, from the circumstance that at this place in Switzerland — interesting to us as the scene of the labors of the historian of the Decline and Fall of the Roman Empire — there is a prison of this character. *Fourth*, there is still another system, — or, perhaps, absence of system, — which is followed at Munich, and has been called that of *Obermayer*, the benevolent head of the prison in that place, who has rejected the separate cell of Pennsylvania by day, and also the corporal punishment and enforced silence of Auburn. Our own prison at Charlestown, which is also marked by the absence of system, seems to me not unlike that of Obermayer. A similar benevolence emanates from the head of each of these institutions.

In each and all of these systems there is, doubtless, much which we should hesitate to condemn, and which it becomes us, as honest inquirers, to examine carefully and to seek to comprehend. In calling upon our society to pledge itself to candor and impartiality in its treatment of these, it will not be disguised, that there are special reasons to be found in its past course. In order properly to appreciate this course, and to understand the unfortunate position of ungenerous antagonism to the Pennsylvania System which we now occupy, it will be necessary to revert to the origin and true character of that system. This will lead us to some minuteness of historical detail.

Turning our eyes to the condition of prisons during the last century, we shall perceive that scarcely a single ray of humanity had then penetrated their dreary confines. In them idleness, debauchery, disease, blasphemy, squalor, wretchedness, brutality, mingled as in a hateful sty. All the unfortunate children of crime, the hardened felon, whose soul was blotted by repeated guilt, and the youthful victim, who had just yielded to temptation, but whose countenance still mantled with the blush of virtue, and whose soul had not lost all its original brightness, without any separation or classification, were crowded together, in one promiscuous, fermenting mass of wickedness, with scanty food and raiment, with few or no means of cleanliness, the miserable prey of the contagion of disease, and the worse contagion of vice and sin. The abject, social degradation of the ancient Britons, in the picture drawn by Julius Cæsar, excites our wonder to a less degree than the well-authenticated misery of the poor prisoners in the polite annals of George III.

Of all the circumstances which conspired to produce this misery, it cannot be doubted that the promiscuous commingling of the prisoners in one animal herd, was the most to be deplored. This evil especially arrested the attention. It enkindled in France the fiery eloquence of Mirabeau, as in England, it inspired the heavenly charity of Howard. It was felt not only in Europe, but here in our own country. Nay, it still continues, the scandal of this age and place, in the jail of Boston!

In the effort to escape from this evil, persons, with the best intentions, but by a not unnatural error, rushed to the opposite extreme. It was proposed to *separate* prisoners from each other, by a system of *absolute solitude*, without labor, books, or solace of any kind. This was actually done in Maine, New York, New Jersey, Virginia and Pennsylvania. Without referring particularly to the other States, let us follow the course of things in Pennsylvania. In 1818, a law was passed authorizing the building of a penitentiary at Pittsburg "on the principle of solitary confinement of the convicts;" and "provided always that the principle of the solitary confinement of the prisoners be preserved and maintained." In 1821, another law was passed authorizing the same at Philadelphia. Both of these prisons were conceived in a system of *solitude without labor.*

As such, they were justly obnoxious to criticism and censure. God bless all who interfered to arrest this design! God bless our Secretary, whose early energies were rightly directed to this purpose! The soul shrinks with horror from the cell of constant and unoccupied solitude, as repugnant to the unceasing yearnings of the nature of man. The *leads* of Venice, — the cruel cages of prisoners of state, — inspire us with indignation against that heartless republic. The terrors of the Bastile, whether revealed in the pictured page of Victor Hugo, or in the grave descriptions of dungeons, where toads and rats had made their home, contain nothing to fill us with such dread as the unbroken solitude which was the lot of many of its victims. Lafayette, — whose own experience at Olmutz should not be forgotten, — has left his testimony of its melancholy influences, as apparent in the condition of those who tasted of the cheerful day and pleasant companionship on the morning which dawned upon the destruction of that gloomy prison. Their sufferings have been revived almost in our own time, in the Austrian dungeons of Spielberg; and Silvio Pellico has left, to the literature of mankind, the record of the horrors filling the perpetual solitude of his cell, which he vainly strove to relieve by crying out to the iron bars of his window, to the hills in the distance, and to the birds which sported with freedom in the air.

A system of absolute solitude excludes every rational idea of health, improvement or reformation. It hardens, abases, or overthrows the intellect and character. Such a punishment is justly rejected in a Christian age, which has learned to temper justice with mercy, and to regard the reformation of the offender among its essential aims.

Under the pressure of these considerations, the subject was reconsidered in those States where this system had been adopted. The discussion in some of the States was affected materially by the opinions of two remarkable men, William Roscoe and Lafayette. The former is cherished as the elegant historian of Lorenzo di Medicis, and Leo X.; though, perhaps, he should be more justly dear to us by those labors which crowned the close of his life, in the sacred fields of humanity. Lafayette, — on his visit, in 1825, to the country which had been the scene of his youthful devotion, — was induced, by a letter from Roscoe, to interest himself in the cause of Prison Discipline. He did not surrender himself merely to the blandishments of that unparalleled triumph, — a more than royal progress, forming one of the most touching incidents in history, — when in advanced years he received the gratitude of the giant republic, whose mewling infancy he had helped to cradle and protect. It appears, from his correspondence, that he strove, by conversation in Maine, New Hampshire, New York, and particularly in Pennsylvania, to influence public opinion on the subject of Prisons, and most especially against the system of *solitary confinement*, which he justly likened to the Bastile. His own opinions, and those of Roscoe, were widely circulated, and were quoted in official documents. Their precise influence it is impossible to calculate. The system, so abhorrent to our feelings, after brief experiments, was discarded in those States where it had been in operation; and in New York, that of Auburn, consisting of solitude by night with labor in common by day, was confirmed, to the great joy of Roscoe, who feared that it would yield to that of absolute solitude, which had been tried there in 1822.

In Pennsylvania, this important change took place previous to the occupation of the new penitentiary at Philadelphia. By a law bearing date April 23, 1829, it was expressly provided, that, after July 1st, 1829, convicts "shall, instead of the penitentiary punishment heretofore prescribed, be sentenced to *suffer punishment by* SEPARATE *or solitary confinement at* LABOR." It is further provided, that the warden "shall visit every cell and apartment, and see every prisoner under his care, at least once a day;" that "the overseers shall inspect the condition of each prisoner at least three times in every day;" "that the physician shall visit every prisoner in the prison twice in every week;" and further provision was made for "visitors," among whom are "the acting committee of the Philadelphia Society for the alleviation of the miseries of public prisons." Here is the first legislative declaration of what has since been called, both at home and abroad, the *Pennsylvania System*. As it has been administered there and elsewhere, it will be found to have, in greater or less degree, the following elements: 1. Separation of the prisoners from each other; 2. labor in the cell; 3. exercise in the open air; 4. visits; 5. books;

6. moral and religious instruction. Its fundamental doctrine and only essential element is *the separation of the prisoners from each other*, on which may be ingrafted solace of any kind needful to the health of body or mind. In 1840, M. de Tocqueville, in his masterly report to the French Chamber of Deputies, recommending the adoption of this system throughout France, accorded to it these characteristics.

In considering the history of this system, its origin is often referred to various places. It is sometimes said to have been first recognized in Rome as long ago as 1703, by Clement XI., in the foundation of a House of Refuge; and again, it is said to have appeared some time during the last century in a prison in Holland; also in one at Gloucester, in England, while it seems to be described with tolerable clearness in the preamble to an act of Parliament, which was drawn by Howard, in conjunction with Sir William Blackstone, as early as 1779. But, whatever may be the claims of these different places, it is now admitted that this system was first reduced to permanent practice, on an extended scale, in Pennsylvania. Indeed, this State is hardly more known in Europe for her shameful neglect to pay the interest of her public debt, than for her admired system of Prison Discipline.

Now, waiving for the present, as entirely irrelevant, the question whether this system can be practically administered, so as to be consistent with health, all will admit that it is not the constant, unoccupied, cheerless solitude of the Bastile. Its main object is not solitude, but the separation of criminals from each other, and the bringing them under good influences only.

In considering the Pennsylvania or Separate System, as it has already been explained, several questions properly arise:

1. Shall it be applied to persons before trial? Here the answer is prompt. It is the right of every person whom the law presumes to be innocent, as is the case with all before trial, to be kept free from the touch or contamination of those who may be felons. I well remember the indignation expressed by the late William Ellery Channing, at an incident which occurred in our streets, where a stranger who had fallen under suspicion, but who proved to be innocent, was marched from the jail handcuffed, in company with a hardened offender. He held it to be the duty of the State to prevent such an outrage. The principle of justice and humanity, which led him to condemn this, requires the *absolute separation* of all prisoners before trial.

2. A question, which is more perplexed, arises with regard to the application of the system to convicts for short terms. But here, it would seem, that the principle of *absolute separation* ought to prevail.

3. A question of greater doubt arises with regard to the application of the System to juvenile offenders. When we observe the admirable success of the House of Reformation at South Boston, and of the Penal Colony at Mettray, in France, both of which are conducted on the social principle, we may well hesitate; though, on the other hand, the marked success of the institution of La Roquette, at Paris, under peculiar difficulties, shows that the principle of *absolute separation* may be applied even to this class of offenders. Here certainly is a question worthy of consideration.

4. Shall the Separate System be applied to women in any cases? The authority of Mrs. Fry, in England — who, at first, disapproved of the system, but, at the close of her valuable life, approved it, even for her own sex — also, that of Mademoiselle Josephine Mallet, in France, who has declared herself warmly for this system, seem to entitle this question to the most careful attention.

5. And, lastly, shall the Separate System be applied to convicts for long terms? This is, indeed, the crucial questial, involving the statistics of health and insanity, and many other considerations, on which much light has been shed by the experience of Europe, as well as our own country, and also by the writings of eminent characters, devoted to this subject. Here we may well hesitate, and open our minds to influences from all quarters.

The way is now prepared to consider the point, whether our society, in unfolding what may be called the science of Prison Discipline, has treated the Pennsylvania System, involving the several questions already stated, with candor and justice. The question is not, whether this system is preferable, in all cases, to every other, or whether there is any other which is preferable to this; but simply, has our society been candid and just towards it? An examination of our course will furnish an easy answer to this inquiry.

It will appear that our society has failed to make any discrimination with regard to the different classes of cases which have been set forth. It has indulged in one constant, sullen, undistinguishing, uncompromising opposition to the system in all cases — so much so as to give occasion to an eminent foreign writer to say, that it had sworn against it "war to the knife." Early in its existence, it gave in its adhesion to the Auburn Prison, saying — "Here, then, is exhibited what Europe and America have been long waiting to see, a prison which may be made a model of imitation." This adhesion was confirmed by the declaration of an officer of our society, at a public anniversary in 1837, that the System of Auburn was "our system" — and still more by a resolution of similar effect offered in 1838, by the *Treasurer* — who now opposes, not unnaturally, the efforts to release the society from the bands which he helped to tie.

But I do not found my complaints merely on the character of advocacy, which our reports have assumed, though it were well worthy of inquiry, whether this is not improper in an association like ours. I go further. I wish to state distinctly, that, in the zeal of our devotion to Auburn, and in the frenzy of our hostility to Pennsylvania, we have been betrayed into a course which no candid mind can fail to regard with regret. I will not dwell now on the language that fell from our Secretary, at the anniversary of 1845, which was in part the occasion of the letter from President Wayland, already read; nor shall I be able to review all our reports. One will be enough. I shall confine myself to the 18th report, which appeared in 1843.

This report has already been the subject of much remark here and elsewhere. A French writer of authority, M. Morau Christophe, Inspector General of Prisons in France, has characterized it as "*a perversion of truth*" — (*Revue Penitentiare*, 1844, p. 421;)

while an English author has spoken of it in stronger terms: "With the nature of framing recurring documents," says Mr. Adshead in his work on Prisons, "connected with public institutions, we are not unacquainted, *and we believe a more flagrant instance of trickery has never come within the range of our experience.*" (P. 128.) I am unwilling to adopt this language; but I cannot forbear terming the report uncandid and unjust. This, I shall endeavor to show, and I am especially moved to do it, since the *Treasurer* has undertaken to vindicate it, and to vouch for the accuracy of its quotations. I shall consider it under *six* different heads.

First. It adduces against the Pennsylvania System the failure of the experiments in Maine, New York, New Jersey, and Virginia, on the principle of *absolute solitude without labor*, which, of course, were entirely inapplicable in the discussion of a system, recognizing labor and many other solaces, as essential parts of the system. Was this candid? Was it just?

Second. But here is a more pungent instance, though not more objectionable than the preceding. The report adduces the authority of Mr. George Combe against "the Pennsylvania System." The article or chapter on this point is entitled, in capitals, "DR. [Mr.] COMBE'S OPINION OF THE PENNSYLVANIA SYSTEM." Under this head, several extracts are presented from his book of travels in America, where this eminent phrenological observer has considered the character of this system. But will the society believe that at least one of these extracts is garbled, so as not to express his true and full opinion of the system? The 18th report quotes from Combe as follows: —

The Auburn system of social labor is better, in my opinion, than that of Pennsylvania, in so far as it allows of a little more stimulus to the social faculties, and does not weaken the nervous system to so great an extent.

The sentence in Combe is as follows: —

The Auburn system of social labor is better, in my opinion, than that of Pennsylvania, in so far as it allows of a little more stimulus to the social faculties, and does not weaken the nervous system to so great an extent; *but it has no superiority in regard to providing efficient means for invigorating and training the moral and intellectual faculties.*

Thus does our report, while pretending to give Combe's "Opinion of the Pennsylvania System," stop at a semicolon, and omit the latter branch of the sentence, where the opinion is *in favor* of the system. And yet the Treasurer has vouched for the accuracy of this quotation. "I think I can read English," he says, "and I think the extract from Combe properly made."

Mr. Eliot here rose and said; I did not mean to vouch for the verbal accuracy of the quotation, but that it gave the substance of Mr. Combe's opinion, which was against the Pennsylvania system.

Mr. Sumner. The Treasurer, then, relies upon Mr. Combe's authority as adverse to the Pennsylvania system. I hold in my hand a letter from that gentleman, dated Edinburgh, March 24th, 1847, addressed to the author of the minority report to this society, (Dr. Howe,) since published as an essay, and which has been characterized in this debate as an uncompromising plea for that system. In this letter Mr. Combe says —

I have read every word of your Prison Essay with attention, and do not perceive any difference of principle between your views and mine. Your Essay is a special pleading in favor of the Pennsylvania system; but I do not object to it on this account. Such a pleading was called for in the circumstances mentioned in your preface; it was the thing needed to make an impression, and while it states strongly and eloquently the advantages of the Separate System, it does not conceal, although it does not dwell upon, its defects.

And yet Mr. Combe is pressed by our report, and now by our Treasurer, into opposition to this system; and the work is aided by publishing a maimed sentence, and entitling it *his opinion.*

Third. We have already observed the timely opposition of William Roscoe to the system of *solitude without labor*, which promised to prevail extensively in the United States. Our 18th report in 1843 draws forth a passage from his publication on this subject in 1827, and entitles it in capitals, "MR. ROSCOE'S OPINION OF THE PENNSYLVANIA SYSTEM." But I will give the whole article or chapter which relates to this. It is as follows: —

MR. ROSCOE'S OPINION OF THE PENNSYLVANIA SYSTEM.

Mr. Roscoe, of Liverpool, said, before the new Penitentiary was built —

At Philadelphia, as has before been observed, it is intended to adopt the plan of "solitary confinement in all cases," "*the duration of the punishment to be fixed,*" and "*the whole term of the sentence to be exacted,*" except in cases where it shall be made to appear, to the satisfaction of the governor, that the party convicted was innocent of the charge.

By the establishment of a general system of solitary confinement, a greater number of individuals imprisoned for *minor offences, will probably be put to death*, by the superinduction of diseases inseparable from such a mode of treatment, than will be executed through the whole State, for the *perpetuation of the most atrocious crimes;* with this remarkable difference, that the law has provided for the heinous offender a brief, and perhaps an unconscious fate, whilst the solitary victim passes through every variety of misery, and terminates his days by an *accumulation of sufferings which human nature can no longer bear.*

With regard to this, several things are to be observed. 1st. It sets forth as Mr. Roscoe's opinion of the Pennsylvania System, what, in fact, was not his opinion of that system, but of the system of *solitude without labor*, and what was written two years before the Pennsylvania System came into existence. It misapplies his opinion, and therefore misrepresents it. 2d. It withholds or suppresses the date of the extract, and the source from which it is drawn. It, indeed, appears that it was written before the new penitentiary was built; but it is nevertheless entitled as "Mr. Roscoe's opinion of the Pennsylvania System," so that the reader, who was not familiar with the subject, would suppose it to be in reality his opinion of that system. 3d. It omits an important passage after the word "charge," without any asterisk, or other mark denoting omission — which, if printed, would have shown conclusively that Roscoe's remarks did not apply to the Pennsylvania system of absolute solitude, without solace of any kind. Is it not proper, then, to say that this passage is garbled? And yet the Treasurer's voucher for the accuracy of the quotations extends to this also.

Fourth. The opinions of Lafayette have received similar treatment with those of Roscoe; though this case is still stronger against that most discreditable 18th report. The article or chapter in which this is done is as follows: —

GEN. LAFAYETTE'S OPINION OF THE PENNSYLVANIA SYSTEM.

"As to Philadelphia," says the General, in a letter to Mr. Roscoe, "I had already, on my visit of the last year, expressed my regret, that the great expenses of the new Penitentiary building had been chiefly calculated on the plan of solitary confinement. This matter has lately become an object of discussion; a copy of your letter, and my own observations, have been requested; and as both opinions are actuated by equally honest and good feelings, as solitary confinement has never been considered but with a view to reformation, I believe our ideas will have their weight with men who have been discouraged by late failures of success in the reformation plan. It seems to me, two of the inconveniences most complained of might be obviated, in making use of the solitary cells to separate the prisoners at night, and multiplying the rooms of common labor, so as to reduce the number of each room to what it was when the population was less dense — an arrangement which would enable the managers to keep distinctions among the men to be reclaimed, according to the state of their morals and their behavior." "In these sentiments," says Mr. Roscoe, "I have the pleasure most fully to concur, and I hold it to be impossible to give a more clear, correct, and impartial decision on the subject."

"The people of Pennsylvania think," said Lafayette, "that the system of solitary confinement is a new idea, a new discovery. Not so; — it is only the revival of the system of the Bastile. The State of Pennsylvania, which has given to the world an example of humanity, and whose code of philanthropy has been quoted and canvassed by all Europe, is now about to proclaim to the world the inefficacy of the system, and to revive and restore the cruel code of the most barbarous and unenlightened age. I hope my friends of Pennsylvania will consider the effect this system had on the poor prisoners of the Bastile. I repaired to the scene, (said he,) on the second day of the demolition, and found that all the prisoners had been deranged by their solitary confinement, except one. He had been a prisoner twenty-five years, and was led forth during the height of the tumultuous riot of the people, whilst engaged in tearing down the building. He looked around with amazement, for he had seen nobody for that space of time, and before night he was so much affected, that he became a confirmed maniac, from which situation he has never recovered."

With regard to this also, several things are to be observed. 1st. It invokes the authority of Lafayette against the Pennsylvania System, and quotes as his *opinion* of that system words which he had used with regard to *solitude without labor*, as in the Bastile. In fact, Lafayette never condemned what in 1843 was known as the Pennsylvania System, nor ever expressed any opinion impugning it in any degree. His family are at this moment among its warmest advocates in France. 2d. It withholds or suppresses the date of the extract, and the book from which it is drawn, and does not in any way disclose to the uninformed reader that it was actually written before the origin of the Pennsylvania System. 3d. The extract purports to be from a letter of Lafayette to Roscoe, whereas this is true only of the first paragraph. The second is from an anonymous letter from Paris, in the *National Intelligencer* of November 17th, 1826, where the writer relates a conversation with Lafayette concerning the prison then building in Philadelphia, in which it was proposed to introduce *solitude without labor.* 4th. After the words " unenlightened age," in the very heart of this extract, there is an important passage omitted — without any asterisk, or other mark denoting omission — which, if inserted, would have shown conclusively that Lafayette's opinion was directed to a system of solitude " without the least employment, and without the use of books." May it not be justly said, that the opinions of Lafayette are here misrepresented and garbled?

Fifth. And here I must glance only at a matter to which I have alluded on a former occasion. Our 18th report sets forth at length the disparaging pictures, by Mr. Dickens, of the Pennsylvania System, while it makes no mention of the opinions of Captain Hamilton, — the accomplished author of Cyril Thornton, — of Miss Martineau, Dr. Reed, Dr. Matherson, Dr. F. A. Cox, Dr. Hoby, Captain Marryatt, Mr. Buckingham, and Mr. Abdy, all of whom are said to have expressed themselves with more or less distinctness in favor of that system. Nor does it make any allusion to the authoritative opinions of different commissioners from foreign governments, as of Crawford, from England, in 1834; Demetz and Blouet, from France, in 1836; Pringle, from England, in 1836; Julius, from Prussia, in 1836; and Neilson and Mondolet, from the Canadian government, in 1836 — all of whom reported emphatically in favor of the Pennsylvania System. Surely it was not candid and just in our society to neglect all allusion to these travellers and commissioners, while it brought forward the imaginings of Mr. Dickens, and, as I have already said, unearthed the dateless letters of Roscoe and Lafayette, to employ them in a cause for which they were never written.

Sixth. But our 18th report is open to still another objection; either of gross ignorance, or of a most uncandid withholding of information on the subject. It employs these words, which will appear most remarkable when we consider the actual facts: "*What will be done in other countries, is evidently suspended, in a great degree*, on the results of more experience in regard to the effects of the system." Nothing more is said on what had been done in other countries, and the reader is left to infer that *nothing* had been done. This was in May, 1843. Now what had been done in other countries *at that time?* In *England*, the inspectors of public prisons had made two or more able and extensive reports in favor of the Separate System, in which the principles on which it is founded had been developed with great fullness and clearness. Parliament had passed a law, authorizing the creation of a model prison on this system at Pentonville. This had already been built, and also various other prisons on the same system in different parts of the kingdom.

Mr. Dwight. Will the gentleman please to state the difference between the prisons at Philadelphia and Pentonville?

Mr. Sumner. With great pleasure, so far as any exists. The two are founded on the same principle of *separation*, though that of Pentonville is probably administered with less austerity than that of Philadelphia. They may differ in degree, but not in kind. But to proceed with a review of what had been done in 1843 in other countries. In *France*, the subject had undergone the most thorough discussion in various ways, in journals, in pamphlets, among professional men, and in official documents. The government and the highest authorities in the State and in medicine had declared in favor of the separate system. Their conclusions had been founded on the most ample inquiries by commissions, that had visited America, England, Scotland, Holland, Belgium, Switzerland, Italy, Germany, Prussia, Spain, and even Turkey. In 1836, Count Gasparin, the Minister of the Interior, had written a circular, informing the prefects of the departments that the government had decided to adopt exclusively the Separate System in the *maisons d'arret*, or what may be called the county jails. In 1839, the grave question of the influence of this system on the health, bodily and mental, was submitted to the highest living authority, the Academy of Medicine, who referred it to a committee, consisting of MM. Pariset, More, Villerme, Louis, and Esquirol. Their report, which was by the latter distinguished name, expressly declared that "Separate imprisonment by day and night, with labor, and conversation with the overseers and inspectors, does not abridge the life of the prisoners, nor compromise their reason." This report afterwards received the sanction of the learned body to which it was addressed. In 1840, M. Remusat, Ministor of the Interior, submitted the project of a law for the building of prisons on the principle of *separation*. This was sustained by a masterly report from M. de Tocqueville, dated June 25th, 1840. It was followed in 1841 by another circular from the Home Department, sending an atlas of plans to the departments as their guide in building prisons. I hold one of them in my hand now.

Mr. Dwight, looking at the atlas, said — The cells here are on a circumference, whereas in Philadelphia they are on radii.

Mr. Sumner. In some of the plans the cells are on a circumference, and in some on radii. But does this make any difference in the system?

I will proceed. In 1843, 17th April, Count Duchatel, in behalf of the government, offered another project of a law providing for the extension of the principle of *separation* to all the *maisons de force* throughout France. It was calculated that this could not be carried into execution under an expense of one hundred and seven millions of francs, or twenty-one millions of dollars. At the same time it appeared that the extensive prison La Roquette, in Paris, had been for several years in most successful operation in France. Still further it was stated in 1843, by M. de Tocqueville, that since 1838, *thirty* prisons, containing two thousand seven hundred and forty cells on the Separate System, had been built, or were in an advanced state of building, in the departments of France. But nothing of all this is in our report.

In *Poland*, it appears that a prison on the Separate System was commenced as long ago as 1831, and had been in successful operation since 1835, while in 1843 appropriations had been made to build three more. But nothing of this appears in our report.

In *Denmark*, after an elaborate report from a committee, a royal ordinance had declared, in 1841, that "All houses of detention, to be built for the accused, shall be on the Separate System, and that all new constructions or reconstructions, which the old prisons should require, should be on this system, to prepare for its general adoption." And again, another ordinance followed, June 25th, 1842, on the report of a commission that had visited England, directing the building of certain prisons on this system. But nothing of this appears in our report.

Look at *Norway.* In 1838, a commission from this region was sent to visit the principal prisons in England, Ireland, Belgium, France, Switzerland, Germany and Denmark. Their report was made in 1841. "Its unanimous and *absolute* advice was, to demand the introduction into the prisons of Norway of the Pennsylvania System." But nothing of this appears in our report.

In *Sweden*, in 1841, the States General declared that the Separate System was the most rational, and voted 1,300,000 florins for the construction of new prisons on this system. And already before this time, the present King of Sweden, then the Crown Prince, had secured a new honor for his throne, by writing a book on prisons, in which he had compared the Auburn and Pennsylvania Systems, and given his preference to the latter. But nothing of this is alluded to in our report.

And here, as I refer to this royal author, let me pause to offer him my tribute of gratitude. His work, originally written in Swedish, has already been twice translated into German, twice into French, once into Norwegian, and once into English. It deserves to be translated into every language of the globe. Such words from a throne find no parallel in history. All the productions of the sixteen royal authors of England, and the six of Scotland, mentioned in Walpole's Catalogue, could not confer the same true honor as these few pages. A work on *Punishments* and *Prisons* by a king, written in a spirit of simplicity and gentleness, with sympathy for the poor, the humble, the wicked, teaches us to appreciate new and higher forms of grandeur than any found in the ordinary pursuits of royal ambition. Oscar is the son of one of the marshals of the empire, Bernadotte, the elected king of Sweden; but — pardon me while I speak what my heart feels — the author of this little book of humanity and wisdom inspires a warmer glow of admiration, than the commander of the centre in the victory of Austerlitz, or of the timely succors that hurried the close of the giant struggle at Leipzig. He sits on a throne which has been illustrated by two of the greatest sovereigns of modern Europe; but his is a truer glory than that of Gustavus Vasa in the mines of Dalecarlia, or of Gustavus Adolphus on the field of Lutzen.

In *Holland*, the penal code, in 1840, established, as the basis of prison discipline, separation by night, and labor in common by day. "But they were not slow to recognize the insufficiency of this," says one of the eminent authorities on this subject. Wherefore the States General ordered the system of separate imprisonment as it is practised at Philadelphia, with the modifications which excluded *solitude*, separating the prisoners from each other, and securing communication with good people without. In the States General there was only *one voice* against this system. But nothing of this appears in our report.

And lastly, at *Geneva*, in Switzerland, a plan of a prison on the Separate System was adopted in 1842. I have here the atlas, containing a full representation of all parts of this prison. But nothing of this is in our report.

In view of all these facts, is it not justly humiliating that our society should have made the statement it did with regard to "other countries?" Most certainly, if the authors of the 18th report were ignorant of the extensive adoption of the Pennsylvania System in Europe, their ignorance was reprehensible, and not to be vindicated by the apology of the Secretary, *that he could not read French.* If they uncandidly withheld or suppressed this information, as I cannot suppose, they are equally reprehensible.

Such is the 18th report of our society! And yet this document, seamed and botched with errors and uncandid statements, injuriously affecting the Pennsylvania System, was sent by our society, as I have been credibly informed, to every member of the legislature of that State. Surely, we need not wonder that the humane and upright gentlemen, connected with the administration of prisons there, felt that we had done them wrong.

II. I am now conducted to the second proposition contained in the report and resolutions under consideration; and here I shall be brief. It is proposed that we shall recognize the directors of the Eastern Penitentiary of Pennsylvania as sincere fellow-laborers in the cause of prison discipline; and shall declare that *if* any expressions have appeared in our reports, or been uttered at any of our public meetings, which have justly given pain to our brethren, our society sincerely regrets them. Is not this a proper and most Christian resolution? What candid or generous mind can hesitate with regard to it, particularly after becoming acquainted with the course of our society towards those gentlemen and the system which they have administered? But here we again encounter the Treasurer, the Achilles of this debate, according to the description of that martial character, by Horace,

> Impiger, iracundus, inexorabilis, acer.

The Treasurer objects, with passionate emphasis, to any expressions of confidence in the gentlemen of Philadelphia. He is not personally acquainted with all of them. He is conscientious on the point. He will not commit our tender society by any such extravagant declaration. To be sure he made no opposition when our own association passed a formal vote, that it was "entitled to the thanks of every friend of humanity for its successful efforts in the cause of Prison Discipline." It was all right for us to praise ourselves; but the Treasurer cannot praise the gentlemen of Philadelphia. He never objected to any of the hard words which we have employed with regard to them and their system. It is those soft words, turning away wrath, which disturb his propriety.

Then, again, he dislikes what he calls an hypothetieal apology. He is startled by the *if.* He cannot say, — *if* I have uttered words which have justly given pain to my brother, I sincerely regret it. It is Shakspeare who says —

> *If* is a gaoler to lead out
> Some horrid malefactor.

And this little word, true to its vocation, leads before the Treasurer a frightful proposition, which he cannot receive. No — he will have nothing to do with it. But his sudden sensitiveness, with regard to the course of the society, should not surely prevent us from performing a simple Christian duty.

III. The third and last proposition involved in the report and resolutions of our committee is, that our society, by its officers and individual members, ought to strive for increased usefulness; and it is particularly urged upon the Board of Managers, to devise some means to enlist the coöperation of individual members. This, too, has been opposed most violently, as if it were not the duty of all persons to seek new opportunities of doing good. The Treasurer, of course, is ardent. He does not ask the coöperation of others. It is the policy of the society, he says, to act by one mind only.

Look at our grandiose organization. We have a President and *forty* Vice-Presidents — or, perhaps, it might be said, borrowing an illustration from Turkey, "a pacha with forty tails." Then we have a large body of foreign correspondents — whose names we print in capitals — "fancy men," as they have been called, because they are for show, I suppose, like our Vice-Presidents. Then there are scores of Directors, and a Board of Managers. Now I know, full well, that very few of these interest themselves so much in our society as to attend its sessions. At the meeting last year for the choice of officers, there were but *ten* persons. We *ten* chose the whole array of Vice-Presidents, and all. And then, too, the Secretary politely furnished us printed tickets bearing their names and his own. Certainly, Sir, something should be done to mend this matter. We must cease to have so many officers, or they must participate actively in the duties of the society.

Look now at our annual income. Notwithstanding the special pleading of the Treasurer, I must insist that this is upwards of $3000, derived partly from interest on our capital stock of $7000, and the remainder from subscriptions obtained mainly through the solicitations of the Secretary.

Mr. DWIGHT, the Secretary. But this is not a permanent income. It is derived from the charity of Boston.

Mr. SUMNER. And is not the charity of Boston permanent, perennial? I have stated the facts, precisely as they are. Now, it becomes a society so richly endowed, to do much for the cause to which it professes to be devoted. It should make itself felt widely, not only in our own State, but wherever the subject of Prison Discipline claims attention.

But what does it accomplish? By looking at its journal for the last three years, it will appear that the chief business of the Board of Managers, who have met some three or four times in the year only, has been to vote a salary of $1700 to the Secretary, with fuel and rent for his office sometimes, and also to vote to him a vacation of four months in the country during our pleasant summers. This, certainly, so far as the managers are concerned, is not doing much in the cause of Prison Discipline. But the Managers are responsible for the annual reports of the society. I think it may be safely said, that, for several years, our society has done little besides publish these reports. Its annual income, and the labors of its galaxy of officers are all substantially absorbed in these. I do not wish to disparage these documents; but, professing as I do, some familiarity with the kind of labor required in their preparation, I cannot forbear repeating what I have said before, that if we take our last report for an example, one month would be a large allowance of time for its production, by any one man competent to the task. But the Treasurer says our society has devised a plan for a new jail in Boston, which of itself is no inconsiderable labor — and the Treasurer praises this plan. My own judgment with regard to it, is of very little consequence — but I have here a letter from Dr. Julius, of Prussia, one of the highest living authorities on the subject, — to whom the plan has been shown, — who expresses an opinion different from that of the Treasurer.

Certainly, Sir, our society must do more. It becomes us to imitate our sister associations in Philadelphia and New York, whose incomes are less than ours, and whose array of organization is less imposing, but who, by means of committees and sub-committees, and committees of ladies too, make their beneficence practically felt by those who are in prison, while by their influence they widely affect public opinion. It becomes us also to imitate the Board of Education in our own Commonwealth, which not only publishes an annual report, but by its Secretary makes annual visits to every part of the State, and by lectures and speeches, by the glowing pen, and the living voice, arouses the indifferent and confirms the wavering. I trust soon to hear of lectures on Prison Discipline, and of local societies under our auspices in every county of our State.

Ours is a large and powerful organization; abundant in its resources of all kinds; plenteously supplied by never-failing streams of charity. It becomes us to administer it in the spirit of charity, that we may promote the greatest good of those who are its objects. The contributions, of which we are the almoners, should not be allowed to run to waste. All should join in efforts to give them the widest influence. All should join in influence to place our society in cordial fellowship with other laborers in the same pursuits. Let me ask you, Mr. President, to unite with your honored predecessor [Rev. Dr. Wayland] in promoting these worthy objects. Auspicate your new duties, by guiding us in a path where we may find that universal confidence, which we have somewhat forfeited, and where the blessings of those who, being in prison, have experienced kindness, may be ours.

I believe I might leave the report and resolutions here, feeling that they stand on impregnable ground. But there are two objections, each brought by different speakers, which I have reserved to the close; one founded on the private character of the Secretary of our society; the other, on the alleged superiority of the Congregate System over the Separate System.

In interposing the private character of the Secretary, a new issue has been presented, which is entirely immaterial to the question of the adoption of the resolutions. This will be discerned merely by repeating the grounds of these. *First*, our society ought to be candid and just. *Second*, it should offer a hand of fellowship to our brethren in Philadelphia. *Third*, it should be more useful. It is certainly no answer to these propositions, to declare, in eloquent phrase, that the private character of the Secretary is good. Let me give my homage to his private character. I have never failed to render my tribute to his early merit in founding and organizing this society; nor in this discussion, painful as it has been, and calling for a severe criticism of matters with which he is intimately connected, have I made any impeachment of the motives by which his course has been controlled. It is my earnest desire, that the society, under his auspices, may be more widely felt, and develop new capacities for usefulness.

The other remaining objection is, that the Congregate System is superior to the Separate System, and that the acceptance of the report and resolutions will be giving an adhesion to the latter. This conclusion is not correct. Your committee ask for candor and justice; they do not ask for adhesion to any system. On the contrary, they expressly disclaim any such desire. But it may well be asked — and I allude to this point, not because I regard it as material to the issue — whether *experience* does conclusively establish the superiority of the Congregate System. My learned friend, [Mr. Gray] who first introduced this topic, founds his conclusion mainly on a comparison of the statistics of the prisons at Philadelphia and Charlestown, which are said to show a much larger proportion of deaths, and of cases of insanity in the former, than in the latter. Admitting that the statistics he has adduced are accurate, (and I do not propose to question them,) it certainly is very hasty in my friend to rush to his conclusion, with regard to the comparative merits of the two systems. In the first place, the limited experience of these prisons, or any small number of prisons, may be affected by circumstances irrespective of the two systems, as for instance, their administration, which may be more or less defective. And permit me to say, that the argument of my friend seems rather to show a defect in the administration of the system at Philadelphia, than in the system itself. The system has but *one essential idea*, the absolute separation of prisoners from each other. But it is said, that this cannot be practically carried out, consistent with the health of the body and mind. It may be so. But to this the highest authorities have given a negative. The College of Medicine in France, and the Scientific Congress at Padua in 1843, and of Lucca in 1844, have pronounced it practicable. But my friend urges, that each prisoner should be indulged with at least two hours of society daily, and that this is impracticable. I doubt if so much is requisite. But if this, and much more be needed, in order to introduce into our prisons those influences which will most conduce to the reformation of offenders, will it not be found? There are Christian clergymen still, who find time to bless with their presence, with prayers and texts, the gaudy celebrations of military companies; there are young men, who partake of these pomps. Cannot as many be found who will visit those who are in prison?

In the next place, the conclusion is fallacious, as it is founded on a comparison of prisons in different places, under the influence of different circumstances of climate and situation ; whereas, to render the comparison exact, it should be between prisons in the same place, and under the same circumstances. This I am enabled to do. There are now at Geneva two prisons, one on the Auburn System, built in 1825, and the other on the Pennsylvania System, built in 1843. M. Ferriere, the chaplain of both these prisons, — and, therefore, it is to be supposed, equally conversant with both, — presented to the Penitentiary Congress at Frankfort a comparison between these two, which he states to be in the same locality, with a unity of conditions in all respects, except what touches the system itself. He gives the preference in every particular to the Pennsylvania prison, and expressly declares that there have always been persons in the Auburn prison who were insane, while, down to the present time, there have been none in the other prison.

And, lastly, the conclusion of my friend is fallacious, inasmuch as it is founded on a narrow induction, closing his eyes to the experience of Europe. There is the prison of Warsaw, on the Separate System, which has been in operation since 1835. During the ten years since its occupation, there have been only two cases of mental alienation, one of which declared itself on the morning after the arrest, and the other was caused by too hasty treatment of the *plique*. In France, as we learn from an address before the Penitentiary Congress, there are nineteen prisons on the Separate System, which have been *occupied* since 1843. "The experience," it is said, "is not of long duration ; but it is sufficient to assure the spirits of the most fearful. The most harmonious unanimity prevails in the observations of the physicians. All recognize that maladies are less frequent, and shorter in duration. It is the same with mental alienation in the period of one to four years, to which the observations relate. No case of insanity is attributed by the physicians to the Separate System, as it is practised in France, with frequent visits, labor, and an hour at least of exercise in the open day." In England there are at this moment *thirty* prisons on the Separate System, with 3500 cells, which are so successful in their influences, that upwards of 3000 additional cells are to be constructed. There are also on the Continent many directors of Auburn prisons who have become dissatisfied with their operation, and openly pronounced in favor of the Pennsylvania System. I might dwell on the experience of Europe till the chimes of midnight sounded in our ears; but I forbear. I cannot dismiss this topic, however, without alluding to one suggestion, which came in such a questionable shape that I am at a loss how to treat it.

The sentiment of patriotism has been invoked, and it has been intimated that the reference to European authorities and experience, which has occurred in this debate, was not consistent with a proper regard to our own country. We incline, Sir, by a natural emotion, to the spot where we were born, to the fields which witnessed the sports of childhood, to the seat of youthful studies, and to the institutions under which we have been trained. The finger of God writes all these things in indelible colors on the heart of man, so that in the dread extremities of death he reverts in fondness to early associations, and longs for a draught of cold water from the bucket in his father's well. This sentiment is independent of reflection, for it begins before reflection, grows with our growth, and strengthens with our strength. But it should not be allowed to interrupt with malign influence the course of truth, nor interfere with the consideration of questions to which it is alien. The subject now before us belongs to science and philanthropy, and I have yet to learn that the prejudices of patriotism have any just foothold in these sacred demesnes. Let us welcome knowledge wherever it may be found. Hail, holy light! from whatever sun or star it may pour upon the eyes, from whatever country or clime it may penetrate the understanding or the heart!

Again, let me say that our report and resolutions stand on impregnable grounds. And now, Mr. President, as I conclude, let me render to you my thanks for the impartiality and amenity with which you have presided over these debates, and may these high qualities be reflected in the future course of our society. Let us all unite in efforts for increased usefulness, in harmony with each other, and with kindred associations in our own country and in other lands. And if, from the collisions of this discussion, there have been any sparkles of unkindly feeling, may they all be quenched in the vote which is now to be taken.

NOTE. The result of these debates called forth the following letter from M. de Tocqueville, of France, addressed to Mr. Sumner: —

[TRANSLATION.]

My dear Sir, — I have read in the Daily Advertiser of June 1st, the account of a meeting of the Boston Prison Discipline Society, in which you proposed a resolution, the effect of which was to declare that this society ought not to be considered "the pledged advocate" of the Auburn System, or of any other system, and that it should judge all systems without taking sides in advance and without prejudice. I have since learned, by the same paper, that the society refused to adopt the resolution. This vote has surprised and pained me. I take a very lively interest in the reform of prisons, and I have always cherished a respectful attachment for the society, which has, of its own accord, done me the honor to make me one of its members, and which enjoys so just a reputation in the philanthropic world. It is under the influence of these two sentiments, that I feel an impulse to write to you.

The vote, of which I have spoken, will cause, I do not fear to say, a painful surprise to almost all those in Europe who are devoted to the Prison question. They will interpret it as a solemn determination taken by the society to make itself the champion of the Auburn System, and the systematic adversary of the Separate System. Instead of a judge, it will seem to become a party.

I need not inform you that at the present day in Europe, discussion and experience have, on the contrary, led almost all persons of intelligence to adopt the Separate System, and to reject the Auburn System. Most of the governments of the old world have declared themselves more or less in this way, not hastily, but after serious inquiry and long debates. I will speak only of the two great free nations of Europe — those which I know the best, and which are the most worthy of being regarded as an authority wherever questions are decided only after discussion before the country, and obedience is rendered to public opinion alone — France and England. Among these two nations, I can assure you that the Auburn System is almost universally rejected. The greater part of those, who have already inclined towards this system, have completely abandoned it, when they came to discuss it, or to see it in operation, and have adopted, wholly or in part, the system of separate imprisonment. The two governments have followed the same tendencies. You know that the French government brought forward, a few years since, a law of which separate imprisonment formed the basis. This law, after a discussion of five weeks, the longest and most thorough which has ever taken place in our parliament on any question, was voted by an *immense majority*. If this same law has not yet been discussed in the Chamber of Peers, the reason is to be found in circumstances entirely foreign to the Penitentiary Question. The Chamber of Peers will take it into consideration at the opening of the approaching session; and among the men the most considerable in this Chamber, the greater part have already pronounced openly in favor of its principle. As to the press, almost all the journals sustain the system of Separate Imprisonment. The journal, which had most skilfully and earnestly combatted the system, has recently declared itself convinced of its excellence. This change has been produced, in part by the experience had for many years in a large number of our prisons. Indeed, it may be doubted whether, when the law shall be reported to the Chamber of Deputies, there will be found a single person to combat its *principle*.

In this state of facts and opinions, the vote, which a society so enlightened and celebrated as that of Boston has just passed, will not be comprehended among us; and I cannot, I confess to you, prevent myself from fearing that it will be injurious to the high consideration which the society enjoys on this side of the ocean, or that, at least, it will weaken its authority. I should strongly regret this, not only from my interest in an association to which I have the honor to belong, but also from my interest in humanity, whose cause it can so powerfully serve.

Be pleased to receive, Sir, the assurance of my very distinguished consideration,

ALEXIS DE TOCQUEVILLE,
Member of the Institute and of the
Chamber of Deputies.

Tocqueville, Aug. 6th, 1847.

CHARLES SUMNER, Esq., Boston.

SPEECH FOR POLITICAL ACTION AGAINST THE SLAVE POWER AND THE EXTENSION OF SLAVERY, IN THE WHIG STATE CONVENTION OF MASSACHUSETTS, AT SPRINGFIELD, SEPT. 29, 1847.

[This was made in support of the following resolution, moved by the Hon. John G. Palfrey :

Resolved, That the Whigs of Massachusetts will support no man for the offices of President and Vice-President of the United States, but such as are known by their acts or declared opinions to be opposed to the extension of Slavery.]

Mr. President,

It is late, and I am sorry to trespass upon your unwilling attention; but the importance of the cause is my apology. The question is, What form of expression shall we give to our opposition to the extension of Slavery? And here it is satisfactory to know that there can be no embarrassment from constitutional scruples. It is not proposed to interfere with Slavery in any of its constitutional strongholds, or to touch any of the so-called compromises of the Constitution. Adopting the principle, so often declared by our Southern friends, that Slavery is a local institution, drawing its vitality from the municipal laws of the States in which it exists, we solemnly assert that the power of the nation — of Congress — of the North as well as the South — shall not be employed to extend it, and that this curse shall not be planted in any territory which may be hereafter acquired by the United States.

And is it not strange, Mr. President, that we, in this nineteenth century of the Christian era — in a country whose earliest charter declares that " All men are born equal " — under a Constitution, one of whose express objects is, " to secure the blessings of liberty " — is it not passing strange, that we should be now occupied in considering how best to prevent the opening of new markets in human flesh? Slavery, which has been expelled from distant despotic states, seeks shelter here by the altars of freedom. Alone in the company of nations does our country assume the championship of this hateful institution. Far away in the East, at " the gateways of the day," by the sacred waters of the Ganges, in effeminate India, Slavery has been condemned; in Constantinople, the queenly seat of the most powerful Mahomedan empire, where barbarism still mingles with civilization, the Ottoman Sultan has fastened upon it the stigma of disapprobation; the Barbary states of Africa have been changed into Abolitionists; from the untutored ruler of Morocco comes the expression of his desire, stamped in the formal terms of a treaty, that the very name of Slavery may perish from the minds of men; and only recently, from the Dey of Tunis has proceeded that noble act, by which, " In honor of God, and to distinguish man from the brute creation " — I quote his own words — he decreed its total abolition throughout his dominions. Let Christian America be willing to be taught by these despised Mahomedans. God forbid that our Republic — "heir of all the ages, foremost in the files of time" — should adopt anew the barbarism and cruelty which they have renounced or condemned!

The early conduct of our fathers, at the time of the formation of the Constitution, should be our guide now. On the original suggestion of Jefferson, subsequently sustained and modified by others, a clause was introduced into the fundamental law of the Northwest Territory, by virtue of which Slavery has been forever excluded from that extensive region. This act of wisdom and justice is a source of prosperity and pride to the millions who now live beneath its influence. And shall we be less true to the principles of freedom than the authors of that instrument? Their spirits encourage us to constant and uncompromising devotion to its cause. With the promptings from their example may properly mingle the words of that evangelist of Liberty, Lafayette, who, though born on a foreign soil, by his earnest labors, by his blood shed in our cause, by the friendship of Washington, by the gratitude of every American heart, is enrolled among the patriots and fathers of the land. His opinions of Slavery have only recently been revealed to the world. From the pen of the philanthropist Clarkson, we learn that his amiable nature was specially aroused on this subject. "He was a real gentleman," says Clarkson, "and of soft and gentle manners. I have seen him put out of temper, but never at any time except when Slavery was the subject." To Clarkson, Lafayette said expressly, "*I would never have drawn my sword in the cause of America, if I could have conceived that thereby I was founding a land of slavery.*" Shall we, whom his sword helped to make free, now found a new land of Slavery?

A proposal has been made, that the Missouri compromise shall be applied to any territory to be acquired from Mexico — in other words, that all south of the parallel of 36° 30′ shall be devoted to Slavery. Are you aware, Sir, that this line, so unhappily notorious in our history, is almost precisely the parallel of Algiers, once the chief seat of White Slavery? It is a proper parallel to mark a boundary so disgraceful to our country. It should be called the Algerine line. At the present time there can be no compromises. Compromise with Slavery is treason to Freedom and to Humanity. It is treason to the Constitution also. With every new extension of Slavery, fresh strength is imparted to the political influence, monstrous offspring of Slavery, known as the Slave Power. This influence, beyond any other under our government, has deranged our institutions. To this the great evils which have afflicted the country — the different perils to the Constitution — may all be traced. The Missouri compromise, the annexation of Texas, the war with Mexico, are only a portion of the troubles caused by the Slave Power. It is an ancient fable, that the eruptions of Etna were produced by the restless movements of the giant Enceladus, who was imprisoned beneath. As he turned on his side, or stretched his limbs, or struggled, the conscious mountain belched forth flames, fiery cinders, and red-hot lava, carrying destruction and dismay to all who dwelt upon its fertile slopes. The Slave Power is the imprisoned Giant of our Constitution. It is there confined and bound to the earth. But its constant and strenuous struggles have caused, and ever will cause, eruptions of evil to our happy country, in comparison with which, the flames, the fiery cinders and red-hot lava of the volcano are trivial and transitory. The face of nature may be blasted — the land may be struck with sterility — villages may be swept by floods of flame, and whole families entombed alive in its burning embrace; but all these evils shall be small by the side of the deep, abiding, unutterable curse of an act of national wrong.

Let us, then, pledge ourselves, in the most solemn form, by united exertions, at least to restrain this destructive influence within its original constitutional bounds. Let us at all hazards prevent the extension of Slavery, and the strengthening of the Slave Power. Our opposition must keep right on, and not look back;

> ——— Like to the Pontic sea,
> Whose icy current and compulsive course
> Ne'er feels retiring ebb, but keeps due on
> To the Propontic and the Hellespont.

In this contest, let us borrow from the example of the ancient Greek, who, when his hands were cut off, fought with his stumps, and even with his teeth. Let us borrow from the example of our party in its defence of the Tariff. Let us borrow from the example of the slaveholders themselves, who are united and uncompromising in their unholy cause. Let us struggle for Freedom as earnestly as they struggle for Slavery. Let us rally under our white pavilion, resplendent with the trophies of Justice, Freedom and Humanity, as enthusiastically as they troop together beneath their black flag pictured over with whips, chains and manacles.

And this brings me directly to the important point, How shall we make our opposition felt? How shall it become vital and palpable before the world, and to the Slave Power? On the present occasion we can only declare our course. But this we should do in the form of language most sternly expressive of our *determination.* It will not be enough merely to put forth certain *opinions* in well couched phrase, and to add yet other resolutions to the hollow words which have passed into the limbo of things lost on earth. We must give to our opinions that point and edge which they can derive only from the declared determination to abide by them at all times. We must carry them to the ballot-box, and bring our candidates to their standard. The recent constitution of Louisiana, with the view of discouraging the practice of duelling, has disqualified all persons engaged in a duel from holding any civil office. The Whigs of Massachusetts, so far as in them lies, must pronounce a similar sentence of disqualification against all persons not known to be opposed to the extension of Slavery.

It has been distinctly proclaimed by the Slave Power, that no person can receive its support who is known to be opposed to the extension of Slavery. The issue, which is here offered, let us join. Such a course is due to our character for sincerity. It will show that we are in earnest, and by so doing, help to check the tyrannical spirit of the Slave Power, which has thus far intimidated the politicians — I will not say the people —

of the Free States. It will exclude from all hope of our support for high office any of those who may think to play the part of the Grand Compromiser on a question which admits of no compromise. Our motto must be — "Principles, and those men *only* who will maintain them."

I urge this course upon your attention, at the present moment, from a deep conviction of its importance. And be assured, Sir, whatever may be the final determination of this Convention, there are many here to-day who will never yield their political support to any candidate, whether for the presidency or vice-presidency, who is not known to be against the extension of Slavery, — even although he may have freshly received the sacramental unction of a "regular nomination." We cannot say, with detestable morality, "Our party, *right* or *wrong*." The time has gone by, when gentlemen can expect to introduce among us the discipline of a camp. Loyalty to principle is higher than loyalty to party. The first is a heavenly sentiment, from God: the other is a device of this earth. Far above any flickering light or mere battle-lantern of party is the everlasting sun of Truth, in whose beams are displayed the duties of men.

SPEECH FOR UNION AMONG MEN OF ALL PARTIES AGAINST THE SLAVE POWER, AND THE EXTENSION OF SLAVERY, IN A MASS CONVENTION AT WORCESTER, JUNE 28, 1848.

[Hon. Charles F. Adams, who preceded Mr. Sumner in addressing the Convention, after reviewing the position of the Whig party, concluded as follows: —

"The only thing to be done by all under such circumstances, is what as one, individually, I have made up my mind to do, that is — to have nothing more to do with it. Hereafter, then, I stand free, clear, a freeman, without any pledges, without any promise to any party. I stand, then, ready to go forward as one in this great movement, which shall establish, I hope, forever, the sacred principle of freedom throughout this hemisphere. Forgetting the things that are behind, I propose that we press forward to the high calling of our new occupation; and, fellow-citizens, whatever may be the fate of you or me, all I can now add is, to repeat the words of one with whom I take pride in remembering that I have been connected — 'Sink or swim, live or die, survive or perish;' to go with the liberties of my country, is my fixed determination."

To these words Mr. Sumner alluded at the beginning of his remarks.]

Mr. President and Fellow-Citizens:

At the close of a day, crowded with exciting interest

— full of auguries of triumph — I feel indisposed to add any thing to what you have already heard. What can I say, that can enforce the great cause which has been so successfully commended to you by my friend from Ohio, [Mr. Giddings,] and, lastly, by my friend, [Mr. Adams,] who has just spoken, with the voice of the American Revolution on his lips? One thing, at least, I can do. I can join them in a renunciation of those party relations, which seem now inconsistent with the support of Freedom. They have been Whigs; and I too have been a Whig — though "not an ultra Whig." I was so because I thought this party represented the moral sentiments of the country — that it was the party of Humanity. It has ceased to sustain this character. It does not represent the moral sentiments of the country. It is not the party of Humanity. A party, which renounces its sentiments, must itself expect to be renounced. For myself, in the coming contest, I wish it to be understood, that I belong to the Party of Freedom — to that party, which plants itself on the Declaration of Independence, and the Constitution of the United States.

As I reflect upon the transactions in which we are now engaged, I am reminded of an incident in French history. It was late in the night, at Versailles, that a courtier of Louis XVI., penetrating the bed-chamber of his master, and arousing him from his slumbers, communicated to him the intelligence — big with gigantic destinies — that the people of Paris, smarting under wrong and falsehood, had risen in their might, and, after a severe contest with hireling troops, destroyed the Bastile. The unhappy monarch, turning upon his couch, said, "It is an *insurrection*." "No, Sire," was the reply of the honest courtier, "it is a *revolution*." And such is our Movement to-day. It is a REVOLUTION — not beginning with the destruction of a Bastile, but destined to end only with the overthrow of a tyranny, differing little in hardship and audacity from that which sustained the Bastile of France — I mean the Slave Power of the United States. Let not people start at this similitude. I intend no unkindness to individual slaveholders, many of whom are doubtless humane and honest. And such was Louis XVI.; and yet he sustained the Bastile, with the untold horrors of its dungeons, where human beings were thrust into companionship with toads and rats.

By the Slave Power, I understand that combination of persons, or, perhaps, of politicans, whose animating principle is the perpetuation and extension of Slavery, and the advancement of Slaveholders. That such a combination exists, will be apparent from a review of our history. It shows itself, in the mildest, and perhaps the least offensive form, in the undue proportion of offices under the Federal Constitution, which has been held by Slaveholders. It is still worse apparent in a succession of acts by which the Federal Government has been prostituted to the cause of Slavery. Among the most important of these is the Missouri Compromise, the Annexation of Texas, and the War with Mexico. Mindful of the sanctions, which Slavery derived under the Constitution — from the Missouri Compromise — of the fraud and iniquity of the Annexation of Texas — and of the great crime of waging an unnecessary and unjust war with Mexico — of the mothers, wives, and sisters compelled to mourn sons, husbands, and brothers, untimely slain, — as these things, dark, dismal, atrocious, rise to the mind, may we not brand their author, the Slave Power, as a tyranny hardly less hateful than that which sustained the Bastile?

This combination is unknown to the Constitution; nay, it exists in defiance of the spirit of that instrument, and of the recorded opinions of its founders. The Constitution was the crowning labor of the authors of the Declaration of Independence. It was established to perpetuate, in the form of an organic law, those rights which the Declaration had promulgated, and which the sword of Washington had secured — "We hold these truths to be self-evident — that all men are created equal, that they are endowed with certain inalienable rights, — that *among these are life, liberty and the pursuit of happiness.*" Such are the emphatic words which our country took upon its lips, when it first claimed its place among the nations of the earth. These were its baptismal vows. And the preamble of the Constitution renews them, when it declares its objects to be, among other things, "to establish justice, to promote the general welfare, and *secure the blessings of liberty* to ourselves and our posterity." Mark; it is not to establish *injustice* — not to promote the welfare of a class, or of a few slaveholders, but the *general* welfare; not to foster the curse of slavery, but to secure the blessings of *liberty*. And the declared opinions of the fathers were all in harmony with these instruments. "I can only say," said Washington, "that there is not a man living, who wishes more sincerely than I do to see a plan adopted for the abolition of slavery ; but there is only one proper and effectual mode by which it can be accomplished, and that is, by the legislative authority; and this, as far as my suffrage will go, shall not be wanting." Patrick Henry, while confessing that he was a master of slaves, said, "I will not, I cannot justify it. However culpable my conduct, I will so far pay my devoir to virtue, as to own the excellence and rectitude of her precepts, and lament my want of conformity to them. I believe a time will come, when an opportunity will be offered to abolish this lamentable evil." And Franklin, as President of the earliest Abolition Society of the country, signed a petition to the first Congress, in which he declared that he "considered himself bound to use all justifiable endeavors to loosen the bands of slavery, and promote a general enjoyment of the blessings of freedom." Thus the soldier, the orator, and the philosopher of the Revolution, all unite in homage to Freedom. Washington, so wise in counsel and in battle; Patrick Henry, with his tongue of flame; Franklin, with his heaven-descended sagacity and humanity, all bear testimony to the true spirit of the times in which they lived, and of the institutions which they helped to establish.

It is apparent that our Constitution was formed by the lovers of Human Freedom; that it was animated by their divine spirit; that the institution of Domestic Slavery was regarded by them with aversion, so that, though covertly alluded to, it was not named in the instrument; and that they all looked forward to the day when this evil and shame would be obliterated from the land. Surely, then, it is right to say that the combination, whose object is to perpetuate and extend Slavery, is unknown to the Constitution, and exists in defiance of the spirit of that instrument, and of the recorded opinions of its founders.

Time would fail me to dwell on the growing influence, which it has exerted from the foundation of the government. In the earlier periods of our history it was moderate and reserved. The spirit of the founders still prevailed. But with the advance of time, and as these early champions passed from the scene, it became more audacious, aggressive and tyrannical, till at last it has obtained the control of the government, and caused it to be administered, not in the spirit of Freedom, but in the spirit of Slavery. Yes! the government of the United States is now (let it be said with shame) not what it was at the beginning, a government merely permitting, while it regretted Slavery, but a government openly favoring and vindicating it, visiting also with its displeasure all who oppose it.

It is during late years, that the Slave Power has introduced a new test for office — a test which would have excluded Washington, Jefferson and Franklin. It applies an arrogant and unrelenting ostracism to all who express themselves against Slavery. And now, in the madness of its tyranny, it proposes to extend this curse to new soils not darkened by its presence. It seeks to make the flag of our country the carrier of Slavery into distant lands; to scale the mountain fastnesses of Oregon, and descend with its prey upon the shores of the Pacific; to cross the Rio Grande, and there, in broad territories, recently obtained by robber hands from Mexico, to plant a shameful institution, which that republic has expressly abolished.

In the pursuit of its purposes, the Slave Power has obtained the control of both the great political parties of the country. Their recent nominations have been made with a view to serve its interests, to secure its supremacy, and especially to promote the extension of Slavery. The Whigs and Democrats — I use the old names still — professing to represent conflicting sentiments, yet concur in being the representatives of the Slave Power. General Cass, after openly registering his adhesion to it, was recognized as the candidate of the Democrats. General Taylor, who owns slaves on a large scale, though observing a studious silence on the subject of Slavery, as on all other subjects, is not only a representative of the Slave Power, but an important and constituent part of the Power itself.

I will not dwell upon the manner in which General Taylor has been forced upon the late Whig party. This has already been amply done by others. I cannot forbear alluding, however, to the aid which his nomination derived from a quarter of the country, which should have encountered it with an inexorable opposition, — I refer to New England, and especially to Massachusetts. I speak only what is now too notorious, when I say, that it was the secret influence which went forth from among ourselves, that contributed powerfully to this consummation. Yes! It was brought about by an unhallowed union — conspiracy, rather let it be called — between two remote sections of the country — between the politicians of the South-West and the politicians of the North-East; between the cotton planters and flesh-mongers of Louisiana and Mississippi, and the cotton spinners and traffickers of New England;

between the lords of the lash and the lords of the loom.

And now the question occurs, What is the true line of duty with regard to these two candidates? Mr. Van Buren (and I honor him for his trumpet call to the North) has sounded the true note, when he said he could not vote for either of them. Though nominated by different parties, they represent, as I have said, substantially the same interest — the Slave Power. The election of either would be a triumph of the Slave Power, and entail upon the country, in all probability, the sin of extending slavery. How, then, shall they be encountered? It seems to me, in a very plain way. The lovers of Freedom, of all parties, and irrespective of all party association, must unite, and, by a new combination, congenial with the Constitution, oppose both candidates. This will be the FREEDOM POWER, whose single object shall be to resist the SLAVE POWER. We will put them face to face, and let them grapple. Who can doubt the result?

But I hear the old political saw, that "We must take the least of two evils." My friend, from Ohio, [Mr. Giddings] has already riddled this, so that I might well leave it untouched; but I cannot forbear a brief observation. Then, it is admitted that Cass and Taylor are, both of them, *evils*. Now, for myself, if two evils are presented to me, I will take neither of them. There are occasions of political difference, I admit, when it may become expedient to vote for a person who does not completely represent our sentiments. There are some matters that come legitimately within the range of expediency and compromise. The Tariff and the

Currency are, unquestionably, of this character. If a candidate differs from me, more or less, on these, I may yet be disposed to vote for him. But the question now before the country is of another character. This will not admit of compromise. It is not within the domain of expediency. *To be wrong on this is to be wholly wrong.* It is not merely expedient for us to defend Freedom, when assailed, but our duty so to do, unreservedly and careless of consequences. Who is there in this assembly that would help to fasten a fetter upon Oregon or Mexico? Who is there that would not oppose every effort for this purpose? Nobody. Who is there, then, that can vote for Taylor or Cass?

But it is said that we shall throw away our votes, and that our opposition will fail. Fail, Sir! No honest, earnest effort in a good cause ever fails. It may not be crowned with the applause of men; it may not seem to touch the goal of immediate worldly success, which is the end and aim of so much of life. But still it is not lost. It helps to strengthen the weak with new virtue; to arm the irresolute with proper energy; to animate all with devotion to duty, which in the end conquers all. Fail! Did the martyrs fail, when with their precious blood they sowed the seed of the Church? Did the discomfited champions of Freedom fail, who have left those names in history which can never die? Did the three hundred Spartans fail, when, in the narrow pass, they did not fear to brave the innumerable Persian hosts, whose very arrows darkened the sun? No! Overborne by numbers, crushed to earth, they have left an example which is greater far than any victory. And this is the least we can do. Our example shall be the source of triumph hereafter. It will not be the first time in history that the hosts of Slavery have outnumbered the champions of freedom. But where is it written that Slavery finally prevailed?

But the assurances received here to-day show that we need not postpone our anticipations of success. It seems already at hand. The heart of Ohio beats responsive to the heart of Massachusetts, and all the Free States are animated with the vigorous breath of Freedom. Let us not, then, waste time in vain speculations between the two candidates. Both are bad. Both represent a principle which we cannot sanction.

Whatever may be said by politicians to the contrary, the question of Freedom is the only one now before the American people. The Bank is not the only "obsolete idea" in politics. All those ideas which have been put forward in the controversies of party are now practically obsolete. Peace has come to remove the question of the Mexican War. We shall no longer be obliged to discuss the important point, whether an unnecessary and unconstitutional war shall be maintained by granting supplies. All differences on this will now subside. There is no question with regard to the Sub-Treasury. This is now firmly established. Then there is the cause of Internal Improvements. This is not unimportant, but it is happily removed from the domain of party. The Chicago Convention was composed of persons of various political opinions, and I understand that their recommendations are now sustained by persons of opposite parties.

Of all the past issues, that of the Tariff, probably, excites the most interest. This, it will be remembered, did not find a place in the early history of the country. It is only in comparatively recent times that it has occupied the attention of politicians, and been made the occasion of vehement popular appeals. Regret has been often expressed that it was a subject of party strife. And it will be in the recollection of most persons, that Mr. Webster has made a vigorous effort to take it out of the list of party questions. What he was unable to do in this respect has at length been accidentally accomplished by the Mexican War. The debt of millions, now entailed upon the country, will render it necessary to impose a tariff, which will satisfy the demands of all. Of course the debt must be paid; nor should we lose time in doing it. It must not be postponed to the next generation. The people are not ready to meet it by direct taxation, though, for one, I should be well pleased to see such a corrective applied to war. It can be paid, only through the agency of a tariff, which, for this purpose, if for no other, must be supported by all parties. The tariff question, then, like the others, is no longer a political issue between parties. If not obsolete, it is at least in abeyance.

All these questions being withdrawn, what remains for those, who, in casting their votes, regard *principles* rather than *men*? It is clear, that the only question of any present practical interest is that arising from the usurpations of the Slave Power, and the efforts to extend slavery. This is the vital question of our country at this time. It is *the question of questions*. It was lately said in the Convention of the New York Democracy at Utica, (and I am glad to allude to the doings of that most respectable body of men,) that the movement in which we are now engaged was the most important of any since the American Revolution. Something more might have been said. *It is a continuance of the American Revolution.* It is an effort to carry into effect the principles of the Declaration of Independence, and to revive in the administration of our government, the spirit of Washington, Franklin, and Jefferson; to bring back the Constitution to the principles and practice of its early founders; to the end that it shall promote Freedom and not Slavery, and shall be administered in harmony with the spirit of Freedom, and not with the spirit of Slavery.

There are emphatic words in the last will and testament of Washington, which may be adopted as a motto for the present contest. After providing for the emancipation of his slaves, to take place on the death of his wife, he says, "And I do expressly forbid the sale or transportation out of the said Commonwealth, of any slave I may die possessed of, *under any pretence whatever.*" So at least should the people of the United States expressly forbid the sale or transportation of any slave beyond their ancient borders, under any pretence what ever.

Returning to our forefathers for their principles, let us borrow, also, something of their courage and union. Let us summon to our sides the majestic forms of those civil heroes, whose firmness in council was equalled only by the firmness of Washington in war. Let us listen again to the eloquence of the elder Adams, animating his associates in Congress to independence; let us hang anew upon the sententious wisdom of Franklin; let us be enkindled, as were the men of other days, by the fervid devotion to Freedom, which flamed from the heart of Jefferson.

Deriving instruction from our enemies, let us also be taught by the Slave Power. The two hundred thousand slave holders are always united in purpose. Hence their strength. Like arrows in a quiver, they cannot be broken. The friends of Freedom have thus far been divided. *Union*, then, must be our watchword, — union among men of all parties. By such a union we shall consolidate an opposition which must prevail.

Let me call upon you, then, men of all parties, whigs and democrats, or howsoever named, to come forward and join in a common cause. Let us all leave our old organizations, and come together. In the crisis now before us, it becomes us to forget past differences, and those names which have been the signal of strife. This is no occasion to remember any thing but our duties. When the fire-bell rings at midnight, we do not ask if it be whigs or democrats who join us in efforts to extinguish the flames; nor do we ask this question in selecting our leader on such an emergency. It is then that we defer to the strongest arm and the most generous soul. To him we commit the direction of the engine. His hand grasps the pipe which is to pour the water upon the raging conflagration. So must we do now. Our leader must be that man, who shall make himself the ablest and surest representative of the principles to which we are pledged.

Let Massachusetts — nurse of the men and principles which made our earliest revolution — vow herself anew to her early faith. Let her elevate once more the torch, which she first held aloft. Let us, if need be, pluck some fresh coals from the living altars of France. Let us, too, proclaim "Liberty, Equality, Fraternity," — Liberty to the captive — Equality between the master and his slave — Fraternity with all men, the whole comprehended in that sublime revelation of Christianity, the Brotherhood of Mankind.

In the contemplation of these great interests, the intrigues of party, the machinations of politicians, the combinations of office-seekers, seem all to pass from our sight. Politics and morals, no longer divorced from each other, become one and inseparable in the holy wedlock of Christian sentiment. Such a union elevates politics, while it gives a new sphere to morals. Political discussions have a grandeur which they have never before assumed. Released from those topics, which concern only the selfish strife for gain, and which are perhaps independent of morals, they come home to the hearts and consciences of men. A novel force passes into the contests of party, breathing into them the breath of a new life, of Hope, of Progress, of Justice, of Humanity.

It is easy to see from this demonstration to-day, and from the glad tidings that swell upon us from all the Free States, that this great cause of Freedom, to which we now dedicate ourselves, will sweep the heart-strings of the people! It will smite all the chords with a might to draw forth emotions, such as no political struggle has ever caused before. It will move the young, the middle-aged, and the old. It will find a place in the family circle, and mingle with the flame of the household hearth. It will touch the souls of mothers, wives, sisters, and daughters, until the sympathies of all shall swell in one firm and irresistible voice against the deep damnation, in this age of Christian light, of lending new sanctions to the slavery of our brother-man.

Come forth, then, men of all parties; let us range together. Come forth, all who have thus far stood aloof from parties. Here is an occasion for action. Men of Peace! come forward. All who feel in any way the wrong of Slavery, take your stand! Join us, ye lovers of Truth, of Justice, of Humanity! And let me call especially upon the young. You are the natural guardians of Freedom. In your firm resolves and generous souls, she will find her surest protection. The young man, who is not willing to serve in her cause — to suffer, if need be, for her, — gives little promise of those qualities which secure an honorable age.

SPEECH FOR THE BUFFALO PLATFORM AND CANDIDATES; ON TAKING THE CHAIR AS PRESIDING OFFICER OF A PUBLIC MEETING TO RATIFY THE NOMINATIONS OF THE BUFFALO CONVENTION, AT FANEUIL HALL AUG. 22, 1848.

Fellow-Citizens, Friends of Freedom:

Grateful for this cordial welcome, I cannot consider it as offered to myself, but to the cause, whose humble representative I am. Yes! it is the cause, the good old cause of Freedom, so familiar to the early echoes of this hall, which justly awakens your regards, irrespective of men. We are nothing; the cause is every thing.

And why, in this nineteenth century, are we assembled here in Faneuil Hall, to vow ourselves to this cause? It is because it is now in danger. The principles of our fathers, — of Washington, Franklin, and Jefferson, — nay, the self-evident truths of the Declaration of Independence, — have been assailed. Our Constitution, — which was the work of the lovers of Freedom, — which was watched by its most devoted champions, — which, like the ark of the covenant, was borne on the shoulders of the early patriarchs of our Israel, — has been prostituted to the uses of Slavery. A body of men, whose principle of union was unknown to the authors of the Constitution, have obtained the control of the government, and caused it to be administered, not in the spirit of Freedom, but in the spirit of Slavery. This combination is known as the Slave Power of the United States.

This combination has obtained the sway of both the great political factions of the country. Whatever may be said of the opinions of individuals belonging to these different factions, it would be difficult to say whether the whigs or democrats, in their recent conduct as national parties, had most succumbed to this malign influence. The late Conventions at Baltimore and Philadelphia were controlled by it. At Baltimore, the delegation of the most important State of the Union — known to be opposed to the Wilmot Proviso — was refused admission to the Convention. At Philadelphia, the Wilmot Proviso itself was stifled, according to the report of an Ohio delegate, amidst the cries of "Kick it out!" General Cass was nominated at Baltimore, pledged against the Wilmot Proviso. General Taylor, at Philadelphia, — without any pledge on this all-important question, — was forced upon the Convention by the Slave Power; nor were any principles of any kind put forth by this body of professing whigs. These two candidates, apparently representing opposite parties, both concur in being the representatives of Slavery. They are the leaders of the two contending factions of the Slave Power. I say factions; for, what are factions but combinations of men whose sole cement is a selfish desire for place and power, in disregard of principles? And such were the Conventions at Baltimore and Philadelphia.

In marked contrast with these was the recent Convention at Buffalo, where were represented the good men of all the parties, — whigs, democrats, and liberty men, — forgetting alike all former differences, and uniting in a common opposition to the Slave Power. There, by their delegates, was the formidable and unsubdued Democracy of New York; there also was the devoted, inflexible Liberty party of the country; there also were the true-hearted whigs and democrats of all the Free States, who in this great cause of Freedom have been, among the faithless, faithful found. There also were welcome delegates from the Slave States, — from Maryland and Virginia, — anxious to join in this new and truly holy alliance. In uncounted multitude, — mighty in numbers, mightier still in the harmony and unity of their proceedings, — this Convention consummated the object for which it was called. It has presented to the country a platform of principles, and *candidates who are the exponents of these principles.* In their support the representatives of the parties there assembled, — whigs, democrats, and liberty men, — all united. In the strength and completeness of this union, I am reminded of the Mississippi, Father of Rivers, where the commingling waters of the Missouri and Ohio are lost in one broad, united, irresistible current, in one channel descending to the sea.

The principles which caused this union have already been widely received, and will be responded to by this vast assembly. Look at them. They are frankly and explicitly expressed. They were solemnly and deliberately considered by a large committee, and enthusiastically adopted in the Convention. They not only propose to guard the territories against Slavery, but to relieve the Federal Government from all responsibility therefor, every where within the sphere of its constitutional powers. In short, on the subject of Slavery, they adopt substantially the prayer of Franklin, who by formal petition called upon Congress "to step to the verge of its constitutional power to discourage every species of traffic in human flesh." They propose to bring back the government to the truths of the Declaration of Independence and to the principles of the fathers, to the end that it shall be administered no longer in the spirit of Slavery, but in the spirit of Freedom.

Other important subjects received the attention of the Convention; — cheap postage for the people, retrenchment of the patronage of the Federal Government, the abolition of unnecessary offices, the election by the people of civil officers in all practicable cases, the improvement in rivers and harbors, the free grant to actual settlers of reasonable portions of the public lands, and, lastly, the payment of the national debt by means of a tariff. But these matters are all treated as subordinate to the grand primal principles of opposition to Slavery and the Slave Power. It is no longer banks and tariffs which are to occupy the foremost place in our discussions, and to give their tone, sounding always with the chink of dollars and cents, to the policy of the country. Henceforward, PROTECTION TO MAN shall be the true AMERICAN SYSTEM.

The candidates selected as the exponents of these principles have claims upon your support, in forgetfulness of all former differences of opinion. They were brought forward, not *because* of the *past*, but the *present;* I may add, they were sustained in the Convention, by many persons, *notwithstanding* the past. I name them with pride: Martin Van Buren, the New York democrat, and Charles Francis Adams, the Massachusetts whig. But these designations can no longer denote different principles. Those to whom they are applied, whether democrat or whig, concur in making opposition to Slavery and the Slave Power the paramount principle of political action. The designations may *now* be interchanged. Mr. Adams may be properly hailed as a New York democrat, and Mr. Van Buren as a Massachusetts whig.

There are many here, doubtless, among those once connected with the whig party, who, like myself on former occasions, have voted against Mr. Van Buren, and who regard some portion of his career with any thing but satisfaction. Mr. Adams is a younger man; but there are some, doubtless, among those once connected with the democratic party, who have voted against him. But these differences, and the prejudices they have engendered, are all forgotten, absorbed, and lost in the entire sympathy with their present position. Time changes, and we change with it. He has lived to little purpose, whose mind and character continue, through a lapse of years, untouched by these mutations. It is not for the Van Buren of 1838 that we are to vote; but for the Van Buren of *to-day*, — the veteran statesman, sagacious, determined, experienced, — who, at an age when most men are rejoicing to put off their armor, girds himself anew, and enters the list as the champion of Freedom. Having implicit confidence in the sincerity and earnestness of his devotion to the cause, and in his ability to maintain it to a successful result, I call upon you, as you love Freedom, and value the fair fame of your country, now dishonored, to render him your earnest and enthusiastic support.

Of Mr. Adams I need say nothing in this place, where his honorable and efficient public services, and his private life, are so familiar. Standing as I now do beneath the images of his father and grandfather, it will be sufficient if I say that he is the heir, not only to their name, but to the virtues, the abilities, and the indomitable spirit that rendered that name so illustrious.

Such are our principles, and such our candidates. We present them fearlessly to the country. Upon the people depends the question, whether their certain triumph shall be immediate or postponed; for triumph they must. The old and ill-compacted party organizations are broken, and from their ruins is now formed a new party, *The Party of Freedom.* There are good men who longed for this, and have died without the sight. John Quincy Adams longed for it. William Ellery Channing longed for it. Their spirits hover over us, and urge us to persevere. Let us be true to the moral grandeur of our cause. Have faith in Truth and in God, who giveth the victory.

> O, a fair cause stands firm and will abide;
> Legions of angels fight upon its side!

Fellow-citizens, I am tempted to exclaim, seeing the

spirit which animates your faces, that the work is already done to-night — that the victory is already achieved. But I would not lull you to the repose which springs from too great confidence. I would rather arouse you to renewed and incessant exertions. A great cause is staked upon your constancy; for without you, where among us would Freedom find its defenders?

The sentiment of opposition to the Slave Power, to the extension of Slavery, and to its longer continuance under the Constitution wherever the Federal Government is responsible for it, though recognized by individuals, and adopted also by a small and faithful party, has now for the first time become the leading principle of a broad, formidable, and national organization. It is indeed, as Mr. Webster has lately said, no new idea; it is as old as the Declaration of Independence. But it is an idea now for the first time recognized by a great political party; for if the old parties had been true to it, there would have been no occasion for our organization. It is said our idea is sectional. How is this? Because the slaveholders live at the South? As well might we say that the tariff is sectional, because the manufacturers live at the north.

It is said that we have but one idea. This I deny; but admitting that it is so, are we not, with our one idea, better than a party with no ideas at all? And what is our one idea? It is the idea which combined our fathers on the heights of Bunker Hill. It is the idea which carried Washington through a seven years' war; which inspired Lafayette; which touched with coals of fire, the lips of Adams, Otis, and Patrick

Henry. Ours is an idea which is, at least, noble and elevating; it is an idea which draws in its train, virtue, goodness, and all the charities of life, all that makes earth a home of improvement and happiness.

> Her path where'er the goddess roves,
> Glory pursues, and generous shame,
> The unconquerable mind, and freedom's holy flame.

We found now a new party. Its corner-stone is Freedom. Its broad, all-sustaining arches are Truth, Justice, and Humanity. Like the ancient Roman capitol, at once a Temple and a Citadel, it shall be the fit shrine of the genius of American institutions.

LETTER ON PARTIES, AND THE IMPORTANCE OF A FREE SOIL ORGANIZATION; ADDRESSED TO A COMMITTEE OF THE FREE SOIL PARTY IN BOSTON, OCT. 26, 1848.

BOSTON, Oct. 23, 1848.

CHARLES SUMNER, ESQ.

Dear Sir: At a meeting of the Ward, County and District Convention of the Free Soil party of Suffolk, held on Thursday last, it being proposed to go into a nomination of candidate for Representative to Congress, and nominations being called for, your name, and yours only was placed upon the list.

A member of the Convention, who represented himself as authorized by you for that purpose, urged, in the strongest terms, your disinclination to be a candidate, growing out of an early formed and long cherished resolution never to hold any political office; but notwithstanding all that could be urged, the Convention nominated you, by acclamation, the Free Soil candidate for Congress from District number one, and appointed us a Committee to inform you of the fact.

It seems to us, as it did to the Convention, that a political crisis has come, which calls upon every man to forego his personal wishes, without regard to resolutions formed under circumstances totally different; and considering the extreme importance of a permanent Free Soil organization, firm, enthusiastic and united, we trust we shall have the great pleasure of conveying to the Convention your acceptance of their nomination.

S. G. Howe,
Otis Turner,
Matthew Bolles,
Charles A. Phelps,
Richard Hildreth.

Boston, Oct. 26, 1848.

Gentlemen, —

I have received your communication of Oct. 23d, informing me that I have been nominated by the Ward, County and District Convention of the Free Soil party of Suffolk, as their candidate for Congress, and requesting my acceptance of that nomination.

You state that a member of the Convention, who represented himself as authorized by me for that purpose, urged in the strongest terms my disinclination to be a candidate, growing out of an early formed and long cherished resolution never to hold any political office; but that notwithstanding all that could be urged, I was nominated by acclamation.

The member of the Convention, who undertook to speak for me, at my special request, did not go beyond the truth. I have never held political office of any kind, nor have I ever been a candidate for any such office. It has been my desire and determination to labor in such fields of usefulness as are open to every private citizen, without the honors, the emoluments, or the constraint of office. I would show by my example, (might I so aspire !) that something may be done for the welfare of our race, without the support of public station, or the accident of popular favor. In this course I hoped to be allowed to persevere unto the end.

I was aware of the promptitude with which the world attributed to candidates for office, motives inconsistent with singleness and uprightness of life; I knew the viperous malignity of a party press, ready to shoot its venom upon those who oppose its course; I saw for a succession of years friends, of whose purity of character I was assured, a prey to the vampire ferocity of political partisans. Observing these things, I derived fresh reasons for my determination to keep aloof from office, and from being a candidate therefor.

The active part which I have taken in the recent movement in Massachusetts, resulting in the formation of a separate organization, has exposed me to something of that animosity, which I had supposed was rather reserved for candidates. Desirous to avoid any position which might seem to suggest a desire for office, I have felt an additional motive for adherence to my original purpose. I wished to be allowed to occupy such a place in our contest, as, while it left me free to labor, should put me above suspicion.

You now bid me renounce the cherished idea of my life, early formed, and strengthened by each day's experience, especially by many circumstances at the present moment. In support of this request, you suggest that a political crisis has come which calls upon every man to forego his personal wishes.

Upon serious deliberation, anxious to perform my duty, I feel myself unable to resist this appeal. In my view a crisis has arrived, which requires the best efforts of every citizen; nor should he hesitate with regard to his peculiar post. Happy to serve in the cause, he should shrink from no labor, and no exposure. When the fire-bell rings at midnight — when the ship which bears us, drives furious upon a lee shore, there is no time to select the manner in which we will work. We cannot, without a dereliction of duty, be indifferent to the call which is then addressed to us; nor can we fail to assume the position of responsibility or service, unwelcome though it be, which seems to be cast upon us.

And this is the case now. The principles of Washington, of Jefferson, and of Franklin — the security of our Constitution — the fair fame of our country — the interests of labor — the cause of Freedom, of Humanity, of Right, of Morals, of Religion, of God — all these are now at stake. Holier cause has never appeared in history. Let me offer to it, not my vows only, but my best efforts wherever they can be most effectual.

In thus accepting, as I now do, the nomination as Free Soil candidate for Congress from our District, I might properly close this communication; but I am tempted by a topic in the letter, with which you have honored me, to proceed further. While urging my consent, you suggest "the extreme importance of a permanent Free Soil organization, firm, enthusiastic, and united." Let me consider this question, even at the hazard of wearying your attention.

I agree with the Convention in the importance of the new organization; nor do I think there are many candid persons, recognizing morals as the soul of all true politics, who can hesitate in this conclusion.

The evils of party organization have often been deprecated. Some there are, who, in their visions of possible good, have thought these evils might be entirely removed. They have supposed that men might be left to vote, as they act in other concerns, without the constraint of those giant combinations, by whose struggle the whole land seems to be uptorn. Some have gone so far as to object to all associated action, as interfering with a proper freedom and individuality of conduct. On the other hand, there are many who regard the phalanx and antagonism of party as a necessary agency in the administration of all Free Governments. It is supposed that there must be two sides, whose constant watchfulness of each other shall prevent abuse and misrule. This idea was pointedly expressed by an eminent British statesman, who proposed as a toast, "A strong Administration and a strong Opposition."

Without yielding to any of these extreme views with regard to the mischiefs or the benefits of party, all will agree that the only true and legitimate object of such an association is to uphold, advance, and develop certain principles, regarded by the members of the party as important to the well-being of the State. So far forth as the members honestly concur in these principles, they may properly unite in action. But when they cease to join in their support, or when new principles are called into activity, then the common bond is dissolved, and a new association must be formed.

This law, which will be recognized by all intelligent minds, was developed by Mr. Webster at Faneuil Hall, in 1825. "*New parties*," he said, "may arise, growing out of new events, or new questions; but as to those old parties, which have sprung from controversies now no longer pending, or from feelings which time and other causes have now changed or greatly allayed, I do not believe that they can long remain. Efforts, indeed, made to that end, with zeal and perseverance, may delay their extinction, but, I think, cannot prevent it. There is nothing to keep alive these distinctions in the interests and objects which now engage society. New questions and new objects arise, having no connection with the subjects of past controversies, and present interest overcomes or absorbs the recollection of former controversies. All that are united on these existing questions, and present interests, are not likely to weaken their efforts to promote them by angry reflections on past differences. If there were nothing *in things*, to divide about, I think the people not likely to maintain systematic controversies about *men*. They have no interest in so doing. Associations formed to support *principles*, may be called *parties*, but if they have no bond of union but adherence to particular *men*, they become *factions*."

It is in obedience to this law, that political parties in France and England — the only countries besides our own, whose experience can be of service to us on this occasion — have undergone mutations with time. From the reign of Charles X. to the Republic of February, the former country has witnessed a succession of parties, representing the different principles which were struggling for the sway. It was rare that there were two parties only. In England the lines have been more distinctly drawn, and the early division into two great parties more strictly maintained. But here also it has been found impossible to stand always upon the ancient ways. Much of the old distinction between Whig and Tory has already become traditional; and members of these two great antagonist combinations have recently united in measures which seemed to be demanded by the law of Human Progress. The monopoly of the Corn Laws, first assailed by Radicals, and then condemned by aristocratic Whigs, was finally overthrown by the leader of the Tories, who marshalled in this cause various forces that had never before been associated.

In our own country parties have undergone changes. It would be difficult to find in the modern Democratic party, rejecting the Wilmot Proviso, that early party which recognized as its chief, Jefferson, the original author of the Proviso. It would be equally difficult to find in the modern Whig party, which ignobly trampled upon the Wilmot Proviso, that other early party, which aided in the election of Washington, the emancipator of his slaves, and the advocate of the abolition of Slavery.

The party, lately known as the Whig, is recent in its origin. It cannot plead prescription in its favor. Twenty years have not yet elapsed since its birth. It is still in its minority — without any promise that it can reach the *age of freedom*.

We may be admonished from this survey, not to hesitate in the support of the new organization, from any vain idea of the necessary permanence of the two old parties. Encouragement also may be found from a view of the insufficiency of these parties as the representatives of the existing public sentiment.

It is a humiliating reflection, forced upon us by the history of parties, that the professions of principle are often a mere cover to selfish efforts for place and power. Politics become a game, and principles are the counters which are used. The apparent contests of principle are made subservient to the contests of interest; and the latter is pursued to the neglect of the former. But as this subservience becomes manifest, and as it clearly appears that fidelity to principle is merged in selfish ambition, surrendering all things to the pursuit of a barren "availability," then the party can no longer claim the countenance of honest men. It is a faction — a cabal. It is an engine of mere political brokerage by which preferment is procured. If I used a stronger word, I should only borrow the language of the great poet-patriot, in describing his own Italy, defiled by noxious factions, whose prostitution of sacred principles filled the whole land with the odor of a tavern and a brothel.

Without undertaking to apply this language in all its force to either of the parties convened at Baltimore or Philadelphia, it will be sufficient to say that they do not now embody — if they ever did — those principles which are regarded by large numbers of good men as of vital and paramount importance to the country. The question then arises, Shall these principles continue without any national organ? Shall they find no voice? Shall they be stifled? Clearly not.

And such precisely is our condition. The important sentiment of hostility to the Slave Power, to the extension of Slavery, and to its longer continuance under the Constitution wherever the Federal Government is responsible therefor — though recognized by individuals, and by a small but respectable political organization, has never till now been put forth as the paramount principle of a large, formidable and national party. It is true, indeed, that here is no new idea. It is as old as the Declaration of Independence — as old as Washington, Jefferson and Franklin; but it is an idea, that is not recognized by either of the great parties which have recently swayed the country. Were it recognized by either of these, there would be no occasion for the new party, whose existence has so auspiciously begun.

No person is so hardy as to assert that the present Democratic party embodies this idea. But there are partisans, who, in disregard of well known facts, claim it as the property of the late Whig party, even in its present metamorphosis into the Taylor faction. It is sometimes proclaimed as their "thunder." How is this?

It is well known that the Whigs of Massachusetts, in their local Conventions, and also in formal legislative proceedings, have avowed hostility to the Slave Power, to the extension of Slavery, and to its longer continuance under the Constitution, wherever the Federal Government is responsible therefor; but the *National* Whig party, or what Mr. Webster has called "*The united* Whig party of the United States," have never recognized any such principles. Search its history, and you will find that it has ever been false to them.

As a party, it has never sustained any measure for the abolition of Slavery in the District of Columbia. On the other hand, it has discountenanced all proceedings in this behalf. General Harrison, the only President it has succeeded in electing, in his Inaugural Message covertly took ground against it; and Mr. Clay, the acknowledged representative of the party, uttered himself to the same effect, with a warmth which better became a better cause. Nor did either of these Whig statesmen admit, what Mr. Van Buren more than once distinctly declared, that Congress possessed the constitutional power to abolish Slavery in the District. That part of our principles then, which touches this topic, has formed no portion of the *National* Whig doctrines.

The claim to proprietorship in the principle of opposition to the extension of Slavery is equally vain.

Florida and Arkansas have both been admitted as States with slave-holding Constitutions, without the opposition of the *National* Whig party.

The Annexation of Texas, when first proposed, was opposed by many Whigs of the Slave States; *but on grounds irrespective of the question of Slavery.* It was finally consummated through the agency of John Tyler, President, by the act of the Whig party, and of John C. Calhoun, Secretary of State, by the unanimous vote of the *Whig* and Democratic members of the Senate, *by joint resolutions, moved in the House by Mr. Milton Brown, a Slave-holding Whig from Tennessee, and in the Senate, by Mr. Foster, a Slave-holding Whig from the same State.* Thus even against the Annexation of Texas the Whig party did not present a constant and uniform front.

The question of sanctioning the extension of Slavery was afterwards distinctly presented, on the application of Texas for admission into our Union, with a Constitution, which not only established Slavery, but took from the Legislature all power to abolish it. The spirit of New England was aroused against this act. Remonstrances went up to Congress on the single ground of opposition to the extension of Slavery. John Quincy Adams undertook to present them. But notwithstanding his earnest efforts, the measure was hurried through the House by the vote of every slaveholder present, Whig and Democrat. It went to the Senate, where it was ushered under the sanction in part of Mr. Berrien, a slave-holding Whig from Georgia, and finally triumphed in that body, notwithstanding the opposition of Mr. Webster, by the vote of every slaveholder present, Whig and Democrat. Let it be mentioned to their credit, that Mr. Thomas Clayton, of the Senate, from Delaware, and Mr. J. G. Chapman, of the House of Representatives, from Maryland, united with the friends of Freedom; but I have understood that they were not slaveholders. The associations of the day, on which this deed was done, added to its character as a mockery of Human Rights. It was on the 22d December, 1845, the anniversary of the landing of the Pilgrims at Plymouth rock.

At a later day this great question again entered Congress, overshadowing all others by its magnitude and importance. In 1846, Mr. Wilmot, a Democrat of Pennsylvania, with a view of securing the territories of the country for Freedom, moved his Proviso borrowed from the Ordinance of 1787. His motion was sustained by the Northern Whigs; but opposed by the slaveholders *without distinction of party*. Exertions were made to rally the Free States on this high ground. But the *National* Whig party, anxious to avoid this issue, strove, through the agency of Mr. Berrien and

Mr. Webster, to substitute the question of *No more Territory;* thus avoiding the recognition of the paramount principle, now vaunted as theirs, of opposition to the extension of Slavery.

At the Convention of the Whigs in Philadelphia, two different efforts were made to obtain the recognition of this principle; but it was laid upon the table, or stifled amidst unseemly noises, and cries of "Kick it out."

This same Convention nominated for the Presidency Gen. Taylor, who is justly supposed, by his position, to be adverse to the Wilmot Proviso — and who has re-recently been advocated by Mr. Berrien, a leading slaveholding Whig, remarkable for his hostility to the Proviso, on this ground, thus candidly expressed, that "the Southern man who is furthest from us, is nearer to us than any Northern man can be — that Gen. Taylor is identified with us in feeling and interest — was born in a slaveholding State — is himself a slaveholder — that his slave property constitutes the means of support to himself and family, — *that he cannot desert us*, without sacrificing his interest, his principle, the habits and feelings of his life; and that with him, therefore, our institutions are safe." In sustaining such a candidate, while professing to be a Free Soil party, the Whigs imitate those barbarians, who elevate in their temple a Pagan idol, while professing to serve, in the light of the Gospel, the only true God.

There are leading supporters of General Taylor, not slaveholders, who frankly disclaim the Wilmot Proviso as belonging to the Whig party. Mr. Clayton, of Delaware, is reported as declaring to the Senate, July 5th, 1848 — "No man has a right to say that the Wilmot

Proviso is a Whig principle, or that its opposite is a Whig principle. We repudiate the question altogether as a political question. Neither the one side or the other of the question forms any part of our platform." And my friend, Mr. Choate, the accomplished orator, is reported as saying, in one of his recent speeches, — "On all the great questions of the day BUT JUST SLAVERY, we mean to remain the same party of Whigs, one and indivisible, from Maine to Louisiana — upon this question alone, *we always differ from the Whigs of the South*, and on that one we propose simply to vote them down."

I conclude, then, that the principle of opposition to the extension of Slavery, like that of opposition to its longer continuance under the Constitution, wherever the Federal government is responsible therefor, is not recognized by the national political combination which supports Gen. Taylor. None will say that this combination will oppose the Slave Power, of which their candidate is a component part.

It is to uphold and advance these principles, thus neglected by others, that we have come together, leaving the parties to which we have been respectively attached. Now, in the course of human events, it becomes our duty to dissolve the political bands which bound us to the old organizations, and to assume a separate existence. Our Declaration of Independence was put forth at Buffalo. Let us, in the spirit of our fathers, pledge ourselves to sustain it with our lives, our fortunes, and our sacred honor. Our cause is holier than theirs, inasmuch as it is nobler to struggle for the freedom of others, than for our own. The love of

Right, which is the animating principle of our movement, is higher than the love of Freedom. But both Right and Freedom inspire our cause.

In thus taking our place as a new party, we fulfil the desires of many good men, living and dead, who have longed to see the thraldom of the old organizations broken. It was the earnest hope of John Quincy Adams, expressed more than once, that this should take place. "God grant that it may come!" was his aspiration.

Another person, not a politician, whose opinions are now widely influencing the minds of the present generation, the late William Ellery Channing, has left on record a similar aspiration. In a letter dated Jan. 11, 1840, recently published in his biography, he says: "The Whig interest seems to be too strong to be put down at once. This party has the wealth, and in so rich a State [Massachusetts] has great advantages for perpetuating its power. No party, however, which thinks only of securing wealth, can last long. There must be some higher principle." And in another letter, dated March 1, 1842, the same patriot and philanthropist says: "The political state of the country is exceedingly perplexed. *The Whig party has little unity, and is threatened with dissolution.* * * * * *Would the Democrats break up too, and could we start afresh, the Government would probably be less of an evil than it is.*"

And another eminent person, honored wherever the pulpit and philosophy of our country are known, Rev. Francis Wayland, of the Baptist denomination, has recently put forth sentiments in a similar strain: "But," says he, "it may be said that a course of conduct like this, would destroy all political organizations, and render nugatory the designations in which we have for so very long prided ourselves. If this be all the mischief that is done, the Republic, I think, may very patiently endure it. * * * If a disciple of Christ has learned to value political party more highly than he does truth, and justice, and mercy, it is surely time that his connection with it were broken off. Let him learn to surrender party for moral principle. *Let all good men do this, and they will form a party by themselves acting in the fear of God, and sustained by the arm of Omnipotence.* * * *

"Let virtuous men, then, unite on the ground of *universal moral principle*, and the tyranny of party will be crushed. Were the virtuous men of this country to carry their moral sentiments into practice, and act alone rather than participate in the doing of wrong, all parties would, from necessity, submit to their authority, and the acts of the nation would become a true exponent of the moral character of our people."

Let me add, that I am glad to adduce this high testimony from the pulpit. The Gospel is never more truly or sublimely preached than when the politician is told that he too is bound by its laws; and when communities, whether villages, towns, states, or nations, are summoned, like individuals, to obey its sacred behests.

In such a spirit our organization has been established. It is sometimes said, that it does recognize certain measures of public policy, deemed by some persons of special importance. If this be so, it does what is better, and what the other parties fail to do. It acknowledges those high principles which, like the great central light, vivify all, and without which all is dark and sterile.

Surely the people will not be diverted from these truths by the holding up of the Sub-Treasury and the Tariff. The American people are intelligent and humane; they are not bulls, to be turned aside by shaking in their eyes a bit of red cloth; or whales, to be stopped by a tub. In listening to the recent pertinacious and exclusive advocacy which these questions have received, in disregard of the sacred cause of Freedom, I have been reminded of the scene so vividly portrayed by Mr. Wirt, where the humor and eloquence of Patrick Henry defeated an effort of selfishness in the midst of the troubles of the Revolution. The American army was in great distress, exposed almost naked to the rigor of a winter's sky, and marking the frozen ground over which they marched with the blood of their unshod feet. "Where was the man," said Patrick Henry, "who would not have thrown open his fields, his barns, his cellars, the doors of his house, the portals of his breast, to receive the meanest soldier in that little band of famished patriots? Where is the man? There he stands — but whether the heart of an American beats in his bosom, you are to judge." It was to John Hook that he pointed, who had brought a vexatious suit for two steers taken for the use of the troops. "What notes of discord do I hear?" said the orator. "They are the notes of John Hook, hoarsely brawling through the American camp, *Beef! Beef! Beef!*"

As a separate party, following the example of the

other parties, and recognizing the necessity of such a course, we nominate candidates for the Presidency, Vice-Presidency, and for all State offices. We cannot support Taylor or Cass; nor can we support the supporters of Taylor or Cass. We cannot sustain men who contribute by their votes to place the power and patronage of the highest offices in hands which may exercise them against Freedom. I know there are some who will do this with a regard for Freedom; but her friends should be of sterner stuff. Nor is it easy to put confidence in the moral firmness of those, who, while this great cause is pending, can sustain any party or any individual not unequivocally pledged to its support.

From this review you will perceive, gentlemen, that I join with you in a conviction of the "extreme importance of a permanent Free Soil organization, firm, enthusiastic, and united." In this conviction Ifind an additional motive, now that this organization is commencing its most difficult struggle, to accept the nomination which you have tendered to me. Let us labor, then, together. Confident in the justice of our cause, let us dedicate to it our best powers, careless of the clamors of opposing factions, or the misrepresentations of a mendacious press — sustaining it with enthusiasm and yet with candor, with firmness and yet with moderation. The great law of Human Progress, the all-prevailing might of truth and of God, are on our side.

I have the honor to be, Gentlemen,

Your faithful friend and servant,

CHARLES SUMNER.

S. G. Howe, Otis Turner, Matthew Bolloo,
Charles A. Phelps, Richard Hildreth, Esquires.

REMARKS ON CALLING THE FREE SOIL STATE CONVENTION OF MASSACHUSETTS TO ORDER; AT WORCESTER, SEPT. 12, 1849.

FELLOW CITIZENS OF THE CONVENTION: —

In behalf of the State Central Committee of the Free Soil Party of Massachusetts, it is now my duty to call this body to order.

I do not know that it is my privilege at this stage of your proceedings, to add yet one other word to these words of form which I have now pronounced. But I cannot look at this large and generous assembly of the friends of Freedom, without uttering from my heart one salutation of welcome and encouragement. You have come from widely scattered homes to bear your testimony once more to that great cause with which are identified the truest welfare and honor of our country, and also the highest aspirations of our souls. Others may prefer the old combinations of party, stitched together by the devices of expediency only. You have chosen the better part in thus coming here to mingle in this sacred alliance of principle.

In the labors now before you there will be, I doubt

not, that concord which always prevails among earnest men, devoted to a good work. We all have but one object in view — the success of our cause. Turning neither to the right nor to the left, moving ever onward, we freely adopt into our ranks all who adopt our principles. These we offer freely to all who will come and take them. These we can communicate to others without losing them ourselves. These are gifts, which, without parting with, we can yet bestow; as from the burning candle other candles may be lighted without diminishing the original flame.

It was the sentiment of Benjamin Franklin, that great apostle of Freedom, uttered during the trials of the Revolution, that, "Where Liberty is, there is my country." I doubt not that each member of this Convention will be ready to respond in a similar strain, "Where Liberty is, there is my party."

It now remains, gentlemen of the Convention, that I should call upon you to proceed to the business of the day.

ADDRESS TO THE PEOPLE OF MASSACHUSETTS, EXPLAINING AND VINDICATING THE FREE SOIL MOVEMENT; REPORTED TO THE FREE SOIL STATE CONVENTION, AND ADOPTED BY THAT CONVENTION, AT WORCESTER, SEPT. 12, 1849.

FELLOW-CITIZENS;

Another year has gone round, and you are once more called to bear your testimony at the polls to those truths which you deem of vital importance in the government of the country. By your votes you are to declare, not merely your predilections for men, but your devotion to principles. Men are erring and mortal; principles are steadfast and immortal.

If the occasion is less calculated, than that of a Presidential contest, to arouse the ardors of opponents, it is also less calculated to stimulate their animosities. With less passion, the people will be more under the influence of reason. Truth may be heard over the prejudices of party. Candor, kindly feelings, and conscientious thoughts, may take the place of embittered, unreasoning antagonism, or of timid, unprincipled compliance. If the controversy is without heat, there may be no viper to come forth and fasten upon the hand.

Though of less apparent consequence in its immediate results, the election now approaching is of great importance. We do not choose a President of the United States, or members of Congress, but a Governor, Lieutenant Governor, and other State officers. Still the same question, which entered into the election of national officers, arises now. The Great Issue, which has already convulsed the whole country, presents itself anew in a more local sphere. Omnipresent wherever any political election occurs, it will never cease to challenge your attention, until at least two things are accomplished; *first*, the divorce of the Federal Government from all support or sanction of Slavery; and *secondly*, the conversion of this Government, within its constitutional limits, to the cause of Freedom, so that it shall become Freedom's open, active, and perpetual ally.

Impressed by the magnitude of these interests, — devoted to the triumph of the rightous cause, — solicitous of the true welfare of the country, — animated by the example of the fathers of the Republic, and desirous of breathing their spirit into our Government, the Free Democracy of Massachusetts, in Convention assembled at Worcester, now address their fellow-citizens throughout the Commonwealth. Imperfectly, according to the necessity of the occasion — earnestly, according to the fullness of their convictions — hopefully, according to the confidence of their aspirations, they will proceed to unfold the reasons of their appeal.

They now ask your best attention. They trust, through this, to secure your votes.

Our Party a permanent National Party. — Fellow-citizens; we make our appeal as a *National* party, established to promote principles deemed to be of paramount importance to the country. In assuming our place as a distinct party, we simply give form and direction, in harmony with the usage and the genius of popular governments, to a Movement which stirs the whole country, and does not find an adequate and constant organ in either of the other existing parties. In France, under the royalty of Louis Philippe, the faithful friends of the yet unborn Republic, formed a band together, and by their publications, speeches, and votes, sought to influence the public mind. Few at first in numbers, they became strong by united political action. In England, the most brilliant popular triumph in her history, the repeal of the monopoly of the Corn-Laws, was finally carried, by means of a newly-formed, but wide-spread political organization, which combined men of all the old parties, Whigs, Tories, and Radicals, and recognized opposition to the Corn Laws as a special test. In the spirit of these examples, the friends of Freedom have come together, in well-compacted ranks, to uphold their cherished principles, and, by combined efforts, according to the course of parties, to urge them upon the Government, and upon the country.

All the old organizations have contributed to our numbers, and good citizens have come to us, who have not heretofore mingled in the contests of party. Here are men from the ancient democracy, believing all that any democracy must be a name only, no better than sounding brass or a tinkling cymbal, which does not recognize, on every occasion, the supremacy of Human Rights, and which is not ready to do and to suffer in their behalf. Here also are men, who have come out of the Whig party, weary of its many professions, and of its little performance, and especially revolting at its recent sinister course with regard to the cause of Freedom; believing all that, in any devotion to Human Rights, they cannot err. Here also, in solid legion, is the well-tried band of the Liberty Party, to whom belongs the praise of first placing the cause of Freedom under the guardianship of a special political organization, whose exclusive test was opposition to Slavery.

In thus associating and harmonizing from opposite quarters, in order to promote a common cause, we have learned to forget former differences of opinion, and to appreciate the motives of each other. We have learned how trivial are the matters on which we may disagree, compared with the Great Issue on which we all agree. Old prejudices have vanished. Even the rancors of political antagonism have been changed and dissolved, as in a potent alembic, by the natural irresistible affinities of Freedom. In our union we have ceased to wear the badges of either of the old organizations. We have become a party, distinct, independent, permanent, under the name of the Free Democracy. Thus in our very designation expressing our devotion to Human Rights, and especially to Human Freedom.

Professing honestly the same sentiments, wherever we exist, in all parts of the country, East and West, North and South, we are truly a NATIONAL party. We are not compelled to assume one face at the South and another at the North; to blow hot in one place, and blow cold in another; to speak loudly of Freedom in one region, and vindicate Slavery in another; in short, to present a combination, in which the two extreme wings profess opinions, on the Great Issue before the country, diametrically opposed to each other. We are the same every where. And the reason is, because our party, unlike the other parties, is bound together in support of certain fixed and well defined principles. It is not a combination, fired by partisan zeal, and kept together, as with mechanical force, by considerations of political expediency only; but a sincere, conscientious, inflexible union for the sake of Freedom.

The Old Issues obsolete. — In thus assuming a place, as an independent party, we are cheered, not only by the grandeur of our cause, but by the favorable omens in the existing condition of parties. Devotion to Freedom impels us; Providence itself seems to open the path for our triumphant efforts. The old questions which have divided the minds of men, have lost their importance. One by one they have disappeared from the political field, leaving it free to be occupied by a question more transcendent far. The Bank, the Sub-Treasury, the Public Lands, are all obsolete issues. Even the Tariff is not a question in which opposite political parties take opposite sides. The opinions of Mr. Clay and Mr. Polk, as expressed in 1844, are so nearly identical, that it is difficult to distinguish between them.

CLAY.

Let the amount which is requisite for an economical administration of the government, when we are not engaged in war, be raised exclusively on foreign imports; and in adjusting a tariff for that purpose, let such discriminations be made as will foster and encourage our own domestic industry. All parties ought to be satisfied with a tariff for revenue and discrimination for protection. —*Speech at Raleigh, in National Intelligencer, of June* 29, 1844.

POLK.

I am in favor of a tariff for revenue, such a one as will yield a sufficient amount to the treasury to defray the expenses of the government, economically administered. In adjusting the details of a revenue tariff, I have heretofore sanctioned such moderate discriminating duties as would produce the amount of revenue needed, and at the same time afford reasonable protection to our home industry. I am opposed to a tariff for protection merely, and not for revenue.—*Letter to J. Kane, June* 13, 1844.

The friends and the enemies of the tariff are to be found, more or less, in both the old organizations. From opposite quarters we are admonished that it is not a proper question for the strife of party. Mr. Webster, from the Whigs, and Mr. R. J. Walker, from the Democrats, both plead for its withdrawal from the list of political issues, that the industry of the country may not be entangled in the constantly recurring contests. And why have they thus far pleaded in vain? It is feared no better reason can be given, than that certain political leaders wish to use the Tariff as a battle-horse by which to rally their followers in a desperate warfare for office. But the debt entailed upon the country by the Mexican war comes to aid the admonitions of wisdom, and to disappoint the plots of partisans, by imposing upon the country the necessity of taxation to so large an amount as to make the protection, thus incidentally afforded, satisfactory to all judicious minds.

The Great Issue. — And now, instead of these superseded questions, which were connected for the most part only with the material interests of the country, and which, though not unimportant in their time, all had the odor of the dollar, you are called to consider a cause which is connected with all that is divine in Religion, with all that is pure and noble in Morals, with all that is truly practical in Politics. Unlike the other questions, it is not temporary or local in its character. It belongs to all times, and to all countries. It is an everlasting link in the golden chain of Human Progress. It is a part of the great Movement, under whose strong pulsations, all Christendom now shakes from side to side. It is a cause, which, though long kept in check throughout our country, as also in Europe, now confronts the people and their rulers, demanding to be heard. It can no longer be avoided, or silenced. To every man in the land it now says, with clear penetrating voice, "Are you for Freedom, or are you for Slavery?" And every man in the land must answer this question when he votes.

The devices of party can no longer stave it off. The subterfuges of the politician cannot escape it. The tricks of the office-seeker cannot dodge it. Wherever an election occurs, there this question will arise. Wherever men come together to speak of public affairs, there again it will be. In the city and in the village, in the field and in the workshop, every where will this question be sounded in the ears, "Are you for Freedom, or are you for Slavery?"

The Anti-Slavery Sentiments of the Founders of the

Republic. — A plain recital of facts will show the urgency of this question. At the period of the Declaration of Independence there were upwards of half a million of colored persons held in slavery in the United States. These unhappy people were originally stolen from Africa, or were the children of those who had been so stolen, and, though distributed throughout the whole country, were to be found in the largest numbers in the Southern States. But the spirit of Freedom was then abroad in the land. The fathers of the Republic, leaders in the War of Independence, were struck with the impious inconsistency of an appeal for their own liberties while holding in bondage their fellow-men, "guilty of a skin not colored like their own." In private and in public they did not hesitate to bear their testimony against the atrocity. The following resolution, passed at Darien, in Georgia, in 1775, and preserved in the American Archives, (Vol. 1, 4th series, p. 1134,) speaks, in tones worthy of freemen, the sentiments of the time: "We, therefore, the representatives of the extensive district of Darien, in the Colony of Georgia, having now assembled in Congress, by authority and free choice of the inhabitants of the said District, now freed from their fetters, do *resolve*; — To show the world that we are not influenced by any contracted or interested motives, but by a general philanthropy for all mankind, of whatever climate, language, or complexion, *we hereby declare our disapprobation and abhorrence of the unnatural practice of Slavery in America*, however the uncultivated state of our country, *or other specious arguments may plead for it*; a practice founded in injustice and cruelty, and highly dangerous to our liberties as well as lives, debasing part of our fellow-creatures below men, and corrupting the virtue and morals of the rest, and as laying the basis of that liberty we contend for (and which we pray the Almighty to continue to the latest posterity) upon a very wrong foundation. We, therefore, resolve to use our utmost endeavors for the manumission of our slaves in this colony, upon the most safe and equitable footing for the masters and themselves." Would that such a voice could be heard once more from Georgia!

The soul of Virginia, during this period, found eloquent utterance through Jefferson, who, by his precocious and immortal words against Slavery, has enrolled himself among the earliest Abolitionists of the country. In the Declaration of Independence he embodied sentiments, which, when practically applied, will give Freedom to every Slave throughout the land. "We hold these truths to be self-evident," says our country speaking by his voice, "that all men are created equal — that they are endowed with certain inalienable rights — that among these are life, *liberty*, and the pursuit of happiness." And again, in the Congress of the Confederation, he brought forward, as early as 1784, a resolution to exclude Slavery from all the territory "ceded or to be ceded" by the States to the Federal Government, and including the territory now covered by Tennessee, Mississippi and Alabama. Lost at first by a single vote only, this measure was substantially renewed at a subsequent day, by a son of Massachusetts, and in 1787 was finally confirmed, in the Ordinance of the North-Western Territory, by a unanimous vote of the States and their respective delegates.

Thus early and distinctly do we discern the Anti-Slavery character of the founders of our Republic, and their determination to place the Federal Government openly, actively and perpetually on the side of Freedom.

The Federal Constitution was adopted in 1788. And here we discern the same spirit. Express provision was made for the abolition of the slave trade. The discreditable words *Slave* and *Slavery* were not allowed to find a place in the instrument, while a clause was subsequently added, by way of amendment, and therefore, according to the rules of interpretation, specially revealing the sentiments of the founders, which is calculated, like the Declaration of Independence, if practically applied, to carry Freedom to all within the sphere of its influence. It was specifically declared, that, "No person shall be deprived of life, *liberty*, or property without due process of law."

It is evident, from a perusal of the debates on the Federal Constitution, that Slavery, like the slave trade, was regarded as temporary; and it seems to have been supposed by many that they would both disappear together. Nor do any words employed in our day denounce it with an indignation more burning than that which glowed on the lips of the fathers. Mr. Morris, of Pennsylvania, said in Convention, that "he would never concur in upholding domestic slavery. It is a nefarious institution." In another mood, and with mild juridical phrase, Mr. Madison "thought it wrong to admit in the Constitution the idea of property in man." And Washington, in a letter written near this period, says, with a frankness worthy of imitation, "There is but one proper and effectual mode by which the abolition of slavery can be accomplished, and that is by legislative action, *and this as far as my suffrage will go, shall never be wanting*."

In this spirit was the Federal Constitution adopted. Glance now at the earliest Congress assembled under this Constitution. Among the petitions presented to that body, was one from the Abolition Society of Pennsylvania, signed by Benjamin Franklin, as President. This venerable man, whose active life had been devoted to the welfare of mankind at home and abroad, who both as a philosopher and a statesman had arrested the attention of the world, — who had ravished the lightning from the skies, and the sceptre from a tyrant, — who, as a member of the Continental Congress, had set his name to the Declaration of Independence, and as a member of the Convention, had again set his name to the Federal Constitution, — in whom, more perhaps than in any other person, the true spirit of American institutions, at once practical and humane, was embodied, — than whom no one could be more familiar with the purposes and aspirations of the founders, — this veteran, eighty-four years of age, within a few months only of his death, now appeared by his petition at the bar of that Congress, whose powers he had helped to define and establish. "Your memorialists," he says, and this Convention now repeats the words of Franklin, "particularly engaged in attending to the distresses arising from slavery, believe it to be their indispensable duty to present this subject to your notice. They have observed with real satisfaction that many important and salutary powers are vested in you for promoting the welfare and securing the blessings of liberty to the people of the United States; and as they conceive that these blessings ought rightfully to be administered, *without distinction of color*, to all descriptions of people, *so they indulge themselves in the pleasing expectation, that nothing which can be done for the relief of the unhappy objects of their care, will be either omitted or delayed.*" And the memorialists conclude as follows: "Under these impressions they earnestly entreat your serious attention to the subject of Slavery; *that you will be pleased to countenance the restoration of liberty to those unhappy men, who alone, in this land of Freedom, are degraded into perpetual bondage*, and who, amidst the general joy of surrounding freeman, are groaning in servile subjection; that you will promote mercy and justice towards this distressed race, and *that you will step to the very verge of the power vested in you for DISCOURAGING every species of traffic in the persons of our fellow-men.*"

Fellow-citizens; there are men in our day, who, while professing a certain disinclination to slavery, are careful to add, that they are not Abolitionists. Jefferson, Washington and Franklin shrank from no such designation. It is a part of their lives, which the honest historian will commemorate with pride, that they were unhesitating, open, avowed Abolitionists. By such men, and under the benign influence of such sentiments, was the Federal Government first inaugurated, and dedicated to Freedom.

At this time, no where under the Federal Government did Slavery exist. In the States only, skulking beneath the shelter of local laws, it was allowed to remain.

Change from Anti-slavery to Pro-slavery. — But the generous sentiments, which filled the souls of the early patriots, and which impressed upon the government that they founded, as upon the very coin that they circulated, the image and superscription of LIBERTY, gradually lost their power. The blessings of Freedom being already secured to themselves, the freemen of the land grew indifferent to the Freedom of others. They ceased to think of the slaves. The slave-masters availed themselves of this indifference, and, though few in numbers, compared with the non-slaveholders, even in the Slave States, they have, under the impulse of an imagined self-interest, by the skilful tactics of party, and especially by an unhesitating, persevering union among themselves, — swaying by turns both the great political parties — succeeded, through a long succession of years, in obtaining the control of the Federal Government — bending it to their purposes — compelling it to do their will — and imposing upon it a policy friendly to slavery, offensive to Freedom only, and directly opposed to the sentiments of its founders. Here was a fundamental change in the character of the Federal Government, to which may be referred much of the evil which has perplexed the country.

The Usurpations and Aggressions of the Slave Power. — Look at the extent to which this malign influence has predominated. The Slave States are far inferior to the Free States in population, in wealth, in education, in libraries, in resources of all kinds, and yet they have taken to themselves the lion's share of the offices of honor and profit under the Constitution. They have held the presidency for fifty-seven years, while the Free States have held it for twelve years only. But without pursuing the exposition of this game of political "sweep-stakes," which the Slave Power has perpetually played, let us present what is more important, as indicative of its spirit — the aggressions and usurpations by which it has turned the Federal Government from its original character of Freedom, and prostituted it to Slavery. Here is a brief catalogue :

Early in this century, when the District of Columbia was finally occupied as the national capital, the Slave Power succeeded, in defiance of the spirit of the Constitution, and even of the express letter of one of its amendments, in securing for Slavery, within the District, the countenance of the Federal Government. Until then Slavery had existed nowhere within the exclusive jurisdiction of this Government.

It next secured for Slavery another recognition under the Federal Government, in the broad territory of Louisiana, purchased from France.

It next placed Slavery again under the sanction of the Federal Government, in the territory of Florida, purchased from Spain.

Waxing powerful, it was able, after a severe struggle, to dictate terms to the Federal Government, in the Missouri Compromise, compelling it to receive that State into the Union with a slave-holding Constitution.

It instigated and carried on a most expensive war in Florida, mainly to recover fugitive slaves, thus employing the army of the United States as slave catchers.

It wrested from Mexico the Province of Texas in order to extend Slavery, and triumphing over all opposition, finally secured its admission into the Union with a Constitution making Slavery perpetual.

It next plunged the country in war with Mexico, in order to gain new lands for Slavery.

With the meanness, as well as the insolence of tyranny, it has compelled the Federal Government to abstain from acknowledging the neighbor republic of Hayti, where slaves have become freemen, and established an independent nation.

It has compelled the Federal Government to stoop ignobly and in vain, before the British Queen, to secure compensation for slaves, who, in the exercise of the natural rights of man, had asserted and achieved their Freedom on the Atlantic ocean, and afterwards sought shelter in Bermuda.

It has compelled the Federal Government to seek to negotiate treaties for the surrender of fugitive slaves, thus making it assert property in human flesh.

It has joined in declaring the foreign slave trade *piracy*, but insists upon the coastwise slave trade, with the sanction of the Federal Government.

For several years it rejected the petitions to Congress adverse to Slavery, thus, in order to shield Slavery, practically denying the right of petition.

It denies to the free colored citizens of Massachusetts the privileges secured to them under the Constitution of the United States, by imprisoning them, and sometimes selling them into Slavery.

It insulted and exiled from Charleston, and New Orleans, the honored representatives of Massachusetts, who were sent to those places in order to throw the shield of the Constitution over her colored citizens.

It has, by the pen of Mr. Calhoun, as Secretary of State, in formal dispatches, made the Republic stand before the nations of the earth as the vindicator of Slavery.

It has put forth the hideous effrontery that Slavery can go to all newly acquired territories, and have the protection of the national flag.

Such are some of the usurpations and aggressions of the Slave Power! By such steps the Federal Government has been perverted from its original purposes, its character changed, and its powers subjected to Slavery. It is pitiful to see Freedom suffer at any time from any hands. It is doubly pitiful when she suffers from a Government, whose earliest energies were inspired by her breath, and who learned by her teachings to be strong.

So the struck eagle, stretched upon the plain,
No more through rolling clouds to soar again,
Viewed his own feather on the fatal dart,
And winged the shaft that quivered in his heart.
Keen were his pangs, but keener far to feel,
He nursed the pinion which impelled the steel,
While the same plumage that had warmed his nest
Drank the last life-drop of his bleeding breast.

That we may fully estimate the enormity of this *system of conduct*, we must call to mind the evils of Slavery, where it is allowed to exist. And here language is inadequate to portray the infinite sum of wretchedness, of degradation, of injustice, which are legalized by this unholy relation. There is no offence against religion, against morals, against humanity, which may not stalk, in the license of this institution, "unwhipt of justice." For the husband and wife there is no marriage. For the mother there is no assurance that her infant child will not be torn from her breast. For all who bear the name of Slave, there is nothing which they can call their own. But the bondman is not the only sufferer. He does not sit alone in his degradation. By his side is his master, who, in the debasing influences on his own soul, is compelled to share the degradation to which he dooms his fellow-man. "He must be a prodigy," says Jefferson, "who can retain his manners and morals undepraved by such circumstances." And this is not all. The whole social fabric is disorganized; labor loses its dignity; industry sickens; education finds no schools; religion finds no churches; and all the land of Slavery is impoverished.

Shall Slavery be extended? — And now at last the Slave Power threatens to carry Slavery to the vast regions of New Mexico and California, existing territories of the United States, already purged of this evil by the express legislation of the recent Mexican government. It is the immediate urgency of this question, that has contributed to arouse the country to the successive aggressions of the Slave Power, and to its undue influence over the Federal Government. This is without doubt the most pressing form in which the Great Issue can be presented. Nor can it be exaggerated. These territories, excluding Oregon, embrace upwards of five hundred thousand square miles. The immensity of this tract may be partially comprehended, when we consider that Massachusetts contains only 7,800 miles, all New England only 66,280, and all the original thirteen States, which declared Independence, only 352,000. And the distinct question is presented, whether the Federal Government shall carry to this imperial region the curse of Slavery, with its monstrous brood of ignorance, poverty, and degradation; or Freedom with her attendant train of blessings.

A direct Prohibition by Congress necessary to prevent Extension of Slavery. — An attempt has been made to divert attention from this question, by denying the necessity of legislation by Congress to prevent the extension of Slavery to California, on the ground that the climate and physical condition of the territory furnish natural obstacles to its existence there. This is a weak device of the enemy. It is well known that Slavery did exist there for many years, until excluded by law, — that California lies in the same range of latitude as the Slave States of the Union, and it may be added also, as the Barbary States of Africa, — that the mineral wealth of California creates a demand for slave labor, which would overcome any physical obstacles to its introduction, — that Slavery has existed in every country from which it was not excluded by the laws or religion of the people, — and still further, it is an undeniable fact, that slaves have already been taken into California and publicly sold there at enormous prices, and thousands are now on their way thither from the Southern States and from South America. In support of this last statement numerous authorities might be adduced. It is stated that a member of Congress from Tennessee has recently declared, that, within his own knowledge, there would be taken to California, during the summer just passed, from ten to twelve thousand slaves. And another person states, from reliable evidence, that whole families are moving with their slaves from Tennessee, Arkansas, and Missouri. Mr. Rowe, under date of May 13, at Independence, Mo., on his way to the Pacific, writes to the paper, of which he was recently the editor, the *Belfast Journal*, Maine, — "I have seen as many as a dozen teams going along *with their families of slaves.*" And Mr. Boggs, once Governor of Missouri, now a resident of California, is quoted as writing to a friend at home as follows, — "If your sons will bring out two or three negroes, who can cook and attend at a hotel, your brother will pay cash for them at a good profit, and take it as a great favor."

After these things, to which many more might be added, it will not be denied, that in order to secure Freedom in the territories, there must be a direct and early prohibition of Slavery there, by an act of Congress.

POSITION OF THE FREE SOIL PARTY.

The way is now prepared to consider our precise position with regard to the accumulating aggressions of the Slave Power, the true character of which has been revealed, especially by the recent efforts to extend Slavery.

Wilmot Proviso. — To the end that the country and the age may not witness the foul sin of a Republic dedicated to Freedom, pouring into vast unsettled lands, as into the veins of an infant, the festering poison of

Slavery, destined, as time advances, to show itself only in cancers and leprous disease, we pledge ourselves to unremitting endeavors to procure the passage of the Wilmot Proviso, or some other form of Congressional legislation, prohibiting Slavery in the territories, without equivocation or compromise of any kind.

Opposition to Slavery wherever we are responsible for it. — But we do not content ourselves with opposing this last act of aggression. We go yet further. Not only from a desire to bring the Federal Government back again to the spirit of the Fathers, but also from the deep convictions of morals and religion, is our hostility to Slavery derived. Slavery is wrong; nor can any human legislation elevate into respectability the blasphemy of tyranny, that man can hold property in his fellow-man. Slavery, we repeat, is wrong, and, therefore, we cannot sanction it. From these convictions may be drawn the measure of our duties.

Wherever we are responsible for Slavery, we oppose it. Our opposition is co-extensive with our responsibility. In the States, Slavery is sustained by local laws; and although we may be compelled to share the stigma which its presence inflicts upon the fair fame of the country, yet it receives no direct sanction at our hands. We are not responsible for it there. The Federal Government, in whom we are represented, is not responsible for it there. The evil is not at our own particular doors. But Slavery every where under the Constitution of the United States — every where under the exclusive jurisdiction of the Federal Government — every where under the national flag — is at our own particular doors. The freemen of the North are responsible for it equally with the traffickers in flesh, who haunt the shambles of the South. Nor will this responsibility cease, so long as Slavery continues to exist in the District of Columbia, in any territories of the United States, or any where on the high seas, beneath the protecting flag of the Republic. The fetters of every slave within these jurisdictions are bound and clasped in part by the votes of Massachusetts. Their chains, as they clank, seem to say, "Massachusetts helps commit this outrage."

Divorce of the Federal Government from Slavery.— This must not be so any longer. Let the word go forth, that the Federal Government shall be divorced from all support of slavery, and shall never hereafter sanction it So doing, it will be brought back to the condition and character which it enjoyed on the adoption of the Constitution.

Federal Government must be on the side of Freedom. — In accomplishing these specific changes, a new tone would be given to the Republic. The Slave Power would be broken, and Slavery driven from its present intrenchments under the Federal Government. The influence of such a change would be incalculable. The whole weight of the Government would then be taken from the side of Slavery, where it has been placed by the Slave Power, and put on the side of Freedom, according to the original purposes and aspirations of its founders. This of itself is an end for which we should labor earnestly, in the spirit of the Constitution.

Let it never be forgotten, as the pole-star of our policy, that the Federal Government must be placed openly, actively and perpetually, on the side of Freedom.

It must be openly on the side of Freedom. There must be no equivocation, concealment, or reserve in its opinions. It must not, like the witches in Macbeth, "palter in a double sense." Let it avow itself distinctly and firmly as the enemy of Slavery, and thus give to the friends of Freedom, now struggling throughout the Slave States, the advantage of its countenance.

It must be actively on the side of Freedom. It should not be content with bearing its testimony openly. It must act. Within the constitutional sphere of its influence, it must be felt as the enemy of Slavery. Let it now study to exert itself for Freedom as zealously and effectively as for many years it has exerted itself for slavery.

It must be perpetually on the side of Freedom. It must not be uncertain, vacillating or temporary, in this beneficent policy. Let it be fixed and constant in its hostility to Slavery, so that hereafter it shall know no change.

In our endeavors to give the Government this elevated character, we are cheered by the high examples, whose opinions have already been adduced. We ask only that the Republic should once more be inspired by their spirit, and be guided by their counsels. Let it join with Jefferson, in open, uncompromising hostility to Slavery. Let it join with Franklin in giving its *countenance* to the cause of emancipation, and *in stepping to the very verge of the power vested in it for* DISCOURAGING *every species of traffic in the persons of our fellow-men.* Let all its officers and members join with Washington in declaring, that, in any legislative effort for the abolition of Slavery, THEIR SUFFRAGES SHALL NEVER BE WANTING.

Other National Matters. — Such are the principles of this Convention on the *national* question of Slavery. There are other matters of national interest, on which their opinions have often been expressed, which are of a subordinate character. These concern cheap postage — the abolition of all unnecessary offices and salaries — the election of civil officers, so far as may be practicable, by the people — the retrenchment of the expenses and patronage of the Federal Government — the improvement of rivers and harbors — and the free grant to actual settlers of reasonable portions of the public lands.

The Administration of Gen. Taylor. — In support of these principles, we felt it our duty to oppose the election of General Cass, and General Taylor — both of them being brought forward under the influence of the Slave Power; the first, as openly pledged against the Wilmot Proviso, and the second, as a large slaveholder and recent purchaser of slaves, who was not known, by any acts or declared opinions, to be hostile in any way to Slavery, or even against its extension, and who, from his position, and from the declarations of many of his friends and neighbors, was supposed to be friendly to that institution. General Taylor was elected by the people. And now, while it becomes all to regard his administration with candor, we cannot forget our duty to the cause which has brought us together. His most ardent supporters will not venture the assertion, that his conduct will bear the test of the principles of our party. We look in vain for any token that the Federal Government, while in his hands, will be placed, openly, actively, and perpetually, on the side of Freedom. Indeed, all that his "Free Soil" supporters vouchsafe, in his behalf, is the assurance, that the "Second Washington" will not assume the responsibility, if the Wilmot Proviso should receive the sanction of both branches of Congress, — if it should prevail in the House of Representatives, and then, in that citadel of Slavery, the American Senate — of arresting its final passage by the Presidential Veto! This is all. The first Washington freely declared his affinity with Anti-Slavery Societies, and said, that in support of any legislative measure for the abolition of Slavery, HIS SUFFRAGE SHOULD NEVER BE WANTING.

But the character of the Administration may be inferred from other circumstances. *First.* — The Slave Power continues to hold its lion's share in the cabinet, and in the diplomatic posts abroad, thus ruling the country at home, and representing it in foreign lands. The number of votes cast in the Slave States, exclusive of South Carolina, where the electors are chosen by the Legislature, at the last Presidential election, was 845,050, while the number of votes cast in the Free States was 2,027,006. And yet there are four persons in the cabinet from the Slave States, and three only from the Free States, while a slave-holding President presides over all. The diplomatic representation of the country at Paris, St. Petersburg, Vienna, the Hague, Brussels, Frankfort, Madrid, Lisbon, Naples, Chili, Mexico, is now confided to persons from Slave-holding States; and at Rome, our Republic is represented by the son of the great adversary of the Wilmot Proviso, and in Berlin, by a late Senator, who was rewarded with this high appointment in consideration of his services to Slavery; while the principles of Freedom abroad are confided to the anxious care of the recently appointed Minister to England. But this is not all. *Secondly.* — The administration, through one of its official organs at Washington, has made the President threaten to "frown indignantly" upon the movements of the friends of Freedom at the North, though he has had no word of indignation, and no frown, for the schemes of disunion openly put forth by the friends of Slavery at the South. *Thirdly.* — Mr. Clayton, as Secretary of State, in defiance of justice, and in mockery of the principles of the Declaration of Independence, has refused a national passport to a free-colored citizen, alleging that by a rule of his Department, passports are not granted to colored persons. In marked contrast, are the laws of Massachusetts, recognizing such persons as citizens; and also those words of gratitude and commendation, in which General Jackson, after the battle of New Orleans, addressed the black soldiers who had shared, with a "noble enthusiasm," "the perils and glory of their *white fellow-citizens.*" — *Fourthly.* — The Post-Office Department, in a formal communication with regard to what are called "incendiary publications," has stated that the Postmaster-

General "leaves the whole subject to the discretion of Postmasters under the authority of State Governments." Here is no word of indignation at the idea that the mails of the United States are exposed to lawless interruption from the partisans of Slavery. The Post-Office, intrusted to a son of New England, assumes an abject neutrality, when the letters intrusted to its care are rifled at the instigation of the Slave Power.

Surely we cannot err, in declaring, that an Administration, marked, during a short career, by such instances of submission to the Slave Power, and of infidelity to the great principles of Freedom, cannot be entitled to our support.

Necessity of our Organization. — Such is the national position of the Free Democracy. We are a national party, established for national purposes, such as can be accomplished by a national party only. If the principles, which we have at heart, were supported openly, actively, constantly, by either of the other parties, there would be no occasion for our organization. But whatever may have been, or whatever may now be, the opinions of individual members of these parties, it is undeniable, that, *as national parties*, they have never opposed Slavery in any form. Neither of them has ever sustained any measure for the abolition of Slavery in the District of Columbia, but, on the other hand, discountenanced all such measures. Neither of them has ever opposed, in any form, the coastwise slave trade under the flag of the United States. Neither of them has opposed the extension of Slavery. Neither of them has ever striven to divorce the

Federal Government from Slavery. Neither of them has ever labored to place the Federal Government openly, actively, and perpetually, on the side of Freedom. Nor is there any assurance, satisfactory to persons not biased by their political associations, that either of these organizations will ever, as a *national party*, undertake the cause of Freedom.

There are circumstances in the very constitution of these parties, which render it difficult, if not impossible, for them to act in this behalf. Constructed subtly with a view to political success, they are spread every where throughout the Union, and the principles which they uphold are pruned and modified to meet existing states of sentiment in different parts of the country. Neither can venture, as a party, to place itself on the side of Freedom, because, by such a course, it would disaffect the slave-holding support, which is essential to its political success. The Anti-slavery resolutions, passed by the legislatures of the North, are regarded as the expressions of individual or local opinion only, and are not suffered to control the action of the national party. To such an extent has this been carried, that Whigs of Massachusetts, professing immitigable hostility to Slavery, recently united in support of a candidate for the Presidency, in whose behalf the eminent slave-holding Whig, Mr. Berrien, had "implored his fellow-citizens of Georgia, Whig and Democratic, to forget for a time their party divisions, and to know each other only as Southern men."

Fellow-citizens, — Individuals in each of the old parties strove in vain to produce a change, and to induce them to become the exponents of the growing

Anti-slavery sentiments of the country. At Baltimore and Philadelphia, in the great Conventions of these parties, Slavery triumphed. So strongly were they both arrayed against Freedom, and so unrelenting were they, in ostracism of its generous supporters — of all who had written or spoken in its behalf — that it is not going too far to say, that if Jefferson, or Franklin, or Washington, could have descended from their spheres above, and revisited the country which they had nobly dedicated to Freedom, they could not, with their well known and recorded opinions against Slavery, have received a nomination for the Presidency from either of these Conventions!

To maintain the principles of Freedom, as they have been set forth in this Address, it becomes necessary to borrow a lesson from the old parties — to learn from them the importance of perseverance, union, and especially of a distinct political organization in their support — and, profiting by these instructions, to direct the efforts of the friends of Freedom every where throughout the country into this channel.

OBJECTIONS.

From various quarters proceed objections to the establishment of our party. Some of these are urged in ignorance, some in the sophist spirit, which would make the worse appear the better reason. Glance at them.

Single Idea. — It is often said that it is a party of a single idea. This is a phrase, and nothing more. The moving cause, and the animating soul of our party, is the idea of Freedom. But this idea is manifold in its character and influence. It is the idea of the Declaration of Independence. It is the great idea of the founders of the Republic. In adopting it as the paramount principle of our Movement, we declare our purpose to carry out the Great Idea of our institutions as originally established. In other words, it is our high aim to bring back the administration of the Government to the standard of a Christian Democracy, with a sincere and wide regard for Human Rights — that it may be, in reality as in name, a Republic. With the comprehensive cause of Freedom are associated in our vows, as has already been seen, other questions of importance to the well-being of the people. Nor is there any cause by which mankind may be advanced that is not embraced by our aspirations. "I am a man, and regard nothing human as foreign to me," was the sentiment of the Roman poet, who had once been a slave; and these words might be adopted as the motto of our Movement.

Sectional, or against the South. — Again, it is said that ours is a sectional party, and the charge is sometimes put in another form, that it is a party against the South. The significant words of Washington are quoted to warn the country against "geographical" questions. Now, if we proposed any system of measure calculated to exclude absolutely any "geographical" portion of the country from the benefit of the general laws and the Constitution of the United States, or to operate exclusively and by name upon any "geographical" section — or perhaps, if we proposed to interfere with Slavery in the States — there might be some ground for this charge; but, as we propose to act against Slavery directly, only where it exists under the Federal Government, and where that Government is responsible therefor, it is absurd to say that we are sectional, or against the South. Our aim is in no respect sectional, but in every respect national. It is in no respect against the South, but against the Evil Spirit, whose chief home is at the South, that has obtained the control of the Government. As well might it be said that Jefferson, Franklin and Washington were sectional, and against the South.

It is true that at present a large portion of the party are at the North; but if our cause is sectional on this account, then is the Tariff sectional, because its chief supporters are also in the North.

Unquestionably there is a particular class of individuals against whom we are obliged to act. These are the slave-masters, wherever situated throughout the country, constituting, according to recent calculations, not many more than 100,000 in all. This band has for years acted against the whole country, and subjugated it to Slavery. Surely it does not become them, or their partisans, to complain that an effort is now made to rally the whole country against their tyranny. There are many who forget that the larger portion of the people at the South are non-slaveholders, interested equally with ourselves — nay, more than we are — in the overthrow of that power which has so long dictated its disastrous and discreditable policy to the Government. To these we may ultimately look for support, so soon as our Movement is able to furnish them with the needful hope and strength.

If at the present moment our efforts shall seem in any respect sectional or against the South, it is simply because the chief opponents of our principles are there. But our principles are not sectional — they are applicable to the whole Union — nay more, to all the human race. They are as universal as Man.

Interference with other Parties. — Again it is sometimes said, that we interfere with the other parties. This is true. And it is necessary because the other parties do not represent the principles which we consider of paramount importance. No intelligent person, who is careful and honest in his statements, will undertake to say, that either of them does represent these. Failing to do this, they are unworthy of support. They do not embody the great ideas of the Republic.

And here again it is important to distinguish between individuals, and the parties to which they adhere. There are doubtless many in both the old parties, who subscribe to our principles, but who still hug the belief, that these principles can be best carried into action by the parties to which they are respectively attached. Influenced by the common bias, which indisposes people to distrust the political party with which they have been associated, they continue in the companionship they early adopted, and often learn to combat for an organization, which, *as a whole*, is hostile to the very principles they have at heart. *Most certainly his devotion to Freedom may well be questioned, who adheres to a national party which declines to be the organ of that cause.* He only is in earnest, who places Freedom above party, and does not hesitate to leave his party when it ceases to serve Freedom. Such men we trust to welcome in large numbers from both the old organizations.

Alleged injurious Influences in the Slave States. — Once more, it is said, that the Anti-Slavery Movement at the North, and particularly its political form, have caused unnecessary irritation among slave-owners, and thwarted a more proper movement at the South. It is sometimes declared, that we have not promoted, but rather retarded the cause of Emancipation. To this let it be said, in the first place, that our direct and primary object is not Emancipation in the States, but the establishment of Freedom every where under the Federal Government; and there is reason to believe that we have already done something towards the accomplishment of this object. By the confession of slaveholders themselves, in one of the recent "Addresses" put forth from their conclave at Washington, we may learn that we have not labored in vain. "This agitation and the use of means," says the Address prepared by Mr. Berrien, "have been continued with more or less activity for a series of years, *not without doing much towards effecting the object intended.*" Take courage, fellow-citizens, from these words, and do not doubt that your continued efforts must finally prevail.

But, in the second place, whatever may have been the temporary shock to the cause of Emancipation in the Slave States, it will not be denied by candid minds that the efforts in the North have hastened the great day of Freedom. They have encouraged its friends in Kentucky, Missouri, Virginia, Maryland, and Tennessee, and have contributed to diffuse the information and awaken the generous resolve, which are so much needed. Nor can it be doubted that, if the North had continued silent, Mr. Clay in Kentucky, and Mr. Benton in Missouri, would both have been silent. Without the moral support of the Free States, these powerful statesmen would have shrunk from the unequal battle. Let us, then, continue to speak and to act, believing that no honest earnest word or deed for Freedom can be in vain. And let us be sure to vote, so as best to promote this cause, that we may extort yet other confessions from other conclaves of slave-holders, that we are "*doing much towards effecting the object intended.*"

Why carry the Question of Slavery into State Elections? — Having thus reviewed the objections to our organizaton, as a National Movement, applying its principles as a test in the choice of national officers, it remains only to meet one other objection, founded on its introduction into State elections. To this we might content ourselves by replying, that we are a national party, and, as such, simply follow the example of both the other parties. From the beginning of the government, the necessity of such a course has been uniformly recognized and acted upon by these parties; and it does not become them now to question the propriety of it, when recognized and acted upon by us.

But, independent of the example of parties, we are led to this course by a conviction of its necessity, in the maintenance of our great cause. It is our duty so to cast our votes on all occasions, as most to promote the *principles* which we have at heart. And it would be wrong in us to disregard the experience of political history, both at home and abroad, which teaches that it is, through the constant well directed organization of party, that these can be best maintained. The influence which has already been exerted by our Movement over both the old parties, and over the general sentiment of the country, affords additional encouragement. And still further, assuming what few will be so hardy as to deny, that it is proper for people to combine in parties to promote their cherished convictions, it follows, as an irresistible consequence, that this combination should be so made as to be most effective for the purpose in view. What is worth doing, is worth well doing. If men unite in constructing the powerful and complex machine of a political organization, it must be rendered complete, and thoroughly competent to do its work. This will be admitted by all.

Now it will be apparent to those familiar with political transactions, that such an organization, acting only in national elections, and suspending its exertions in state elections, will not effectually do its work. People who have acted antagonistically in state elections cannot be brought to act harmoniously in national elections. It would be practically impossible to have one permanent party in national affairs, and another in state affairs. Such a course would cause uncertainty in the Movement, and ultimate disorganization.

It is true that peculiar local interests may control certain local elections. But these constitute the exceptions, and not the rule. They may arise, where, within the locality, a greater sum of good might be accomplished by sustaining a certain person, independent of party, than by voting strictly according to party. But it is clear, that such instances cannot be frequent without impairing the efficiency of the Movement.

And it is natural that parties in our country should take their strongest complexion from national affairs, because these affairs are of the most absorbing interest. Justly important as may be the election of municipal and state officers, we feel that they are of less importance than the election of a President of the United States — as the character of the State Government, whose influence is confined to a limited sphere, is of less importance than that of the Federal Government, whose influence embraces all the States, and reaches to foreign lands. It is, therefore, that the organizations of party in the states are properly treated as subordinate, though ancillary to the national organizations. They are branches, or limbs, which repay the strength they derive from the great trunk, by helping to extend in all directions its protecting power. But these branches cannot be lopped off or neglected.

Again, the influence of each individual is of importance in the support of our organization. But the State itself is a compound individual, and just in proportion to its size and character it is important that it should be arrayed as a powerful unit in support of our organization. In this way only can its influence be brought to bear most effectually upon the Federal Government in support of our *principles.*

Fellow-citizens, the question again returns, "Are you for Freedom, or are you for Slavery?" If you are for Freedom, do not hesitate to support the National party dedicated to this cause. Strive in all ways to extend its influence, to enlarge its means of efficiency, and to consolidate its strength. And consider well, that this can be properly accomplished only by casting our votes always for those, who, while avowing our principles, are willing to sacrifice their ancient party ties in order to maintain them. Massachusetts must, by her towns, counties, and districts — by her executive and legislative departments — call upon the Federal Government to change from the policy of Slavery to the policy of Freedom. *Massachusetts must refuse to support any Government which does not hearken to this request.*

Local Matters. — A few brief words remain to be said of Local Matters.

The sentiments which inspire the Party of Freedom in their opposition to Slavery, must naturally control their conduct on all questions of local policy. The friends of Human Rights, they cannot regard with indifference any thing by which these are impaired. Recognizing Justice and Benevolence as the great end and aim of government, they must sympathize with all efforts to extend their sway. Let the Government be ever just. Let it be ever benevolent. Abuses and wrongs will then disappear, and the State will stand forth in the moral dignity of true manhood. If there be any thing in the Commonwealth inconsistent with these sentiments, it must be changed. This should be done, however, in no spirit of political empiricism, but with an honest and intelligent regard to practical results.

Complaint is made in many and even opposite quarters of the large number of Corporations, annually established by our Legislature — of the undue amount of time thus consumed in special legislation — and still further of the influence which these corporations are able to exert over political affairs, dispensing a patronage exceeding that of the Federal Government within the borders of our State. Without considering these things in detail, it is impossible to avoid calling attention to the perverse influence which often proceeds from this source. Of this we can speak with knowledge. *The efforts to place the Federal Government on the side of Freedom* have received little sympathy from corporations, or from persons largely interested in them; but have rather encountered their opposition, sometimes concealed, sometimes open, often bitter and vindictive. It is easy to explain this. In the corporations is embodied the Money Power of the Commonwealth. The instinct of property has proved stronger in Massachusetts than the instinct of Freedom, and the Money Power here has joined hands with the Slave Power. Selfish, grasping, subtle, tyrannical, like its ally, it will not brook opposition. It claims the Commonwealth as its own, and too successfully enlists in its support that needy talent and easy virtue which are required to maintain its sway. Perhaps the true remedy for this evil must be found in a more enlightened public sentiment; but it belongs to us to do what in us lies to restrain this influence — by watchful legislation, if need be; but especially by directing against it the finger-point of a generous indignation.

The natural influence of the Money Power is still further increased by the defects in our present system of representation in the Legislature. The large cities, particularly Boston, electing representatives by a general ticket, are able to return to the Legislature a compact delegation, united in their political opinions, while the country, through the divisions into small towns, is practically subdivided into districts, and chooses representatives differing in opinions. A careful estimate of the influence, which is thus wrought, will show that Boston alone, actually casting 13,000 votes, is able to neutralize the 26,500 votes cast by all Western Massachusetts, including Berkshire, Franklin, Hampshire and Hampden. The large cities, which are the seat of the Money Power, are thus able, though a minority, to control the State. Like the Slave Power they are strong from union. This abuse calls loudly for amendment; and it will be for the friends of our cause to urge such measures as the necessity of the case may require.

Our Candidates. — Thus much it has occurred to us to say at this time, in explanation of our present position. In the fulfilment of our duty to sustain our principles at all times, in all elections, National or State, we have nominated Hon. Stephen C. Phillips, of Salem, as our candidate for the office of Governor. It is with confidence and pride that we ask for him your support. Few in the community have entitled themselves, by a long series of beneficent services, to the same degree of kindly regard. In him we find a liberal education blended with a liberal spirit — the experience and the wealth of the successful merchant turned into the sacred channels of benevolence — and the influence earned by various labors, in various posts of honor and trust, consecrated to Human Improvement. All the great causes, which have done so much to renovate the age — Temperance, Education, Peace, Freedom — have ever found in him a discreet, practical, devoted, self-sacrificing friend. Formerly associated with the Whig party, and a member of Congress, chosen by Whig votes, he set the example of renouncing his party, when it became openly faithless to Freedom, and by his unreserved and noble efforts, has done much to strengthen the Movement in which we are now engaged.

As a candidate for the office of Lieutenant Governor, we nominate Hon. JOHN MILLS, of Springfield, a gentleman of spotless life, with ample experience in manifold spheres of action, formerly an honored member of the Democratic party, who has filled responsible stations under the Governments of the State and the Nation, and who, like Mr. Phillips, has testified his fidelity to Freedom, by renouncing the party to which he belonged.

CONCLUSION.

Fellow-citizens: Such are our principles, and such our candidates. Join us in their support. Join us, all who love Freedom and hate Slavery. Join us, all who cherish the Constitution and the Union. Help us in our endeavors to restore to them their early virtue. Join us, all who reverence the memory of the fathers of the Republic, and would have their spirit once more animate the land. Join us, all who would have the Federal Government administered in the spirit of Freedom, and not in the spirit of Slavery. The occasion is urgent. Active, resolute exertions must be made. It will not become the sons of the Pilgrims, and the sons of the Revolution, to be *neutral* in this contest. Such was not the temper of their fathers. In such a contest neutrality is treason to Human Rights. In questions *merely political*, an honest man may stand neuter; but what true heart can be neuter, when the distinct question is put, which we now address to the people of Massachusetts, "Are you for Freedom, or are you for Slavery?"

Finally, we appeal to the moral and religious sentiments of the Commonwealth. When these are fully moved, there can be no question of the result. We invoke the sympathy of the pulpit in our cause. Let it preach deliverance to the captive. We call upon good men, of all sects and of all parties, to lend us their support. You all agree in our PRINCIPLES. Do not practically oppose them, by continuing your adhesion to a national party that is hostile to them. Join us in proclaiming them through the new Party of Freedom. And may God, whose service is perfect freedom, grant his succor to our cause!

ARGUMENT AGAINST THE CONSTITUTIONALITY OF SEPARATE COLORED SCHOOLS, BEFORE THE SUPREME COURT OF MASSACHUSETTS, IN THE CASE OF SARAH C. ROBERTS *vs.* THE CITY OF BOSTON, DEC. 4, 1849.

MAY IT PLEASE YOUR HONORS: —

Can any discrimination, on account of color or race, be made, under the Constitution and Laws of Massachusetts, among the children entitled to the benefit of our Public Schools? This is the question which the Court is now to hear, to consider, and to decide.

Or, stating the question with more detail, and with a more particular application to the facts of the present case, are the Committee, having the superintendence of the public schools of Boston, intrusted with the *power*, under the Constitution and Laws of Massachusetts, to exclude colored children from these schools, and to compel them to resort for their education to separate schools, set apart for colored children only, at distances from their homes less convenient than those open to white children?

This important question arises in an action by a

colored child, only five years old, who, *by her next friend*, sues the city of Boston for damages, on account of a refusal to receive her into one of the public schools.

It would be difficult to imagine any case which could appeal more strongly to your best judgment, whether you regard the parties or the subject. On the one side is the city of Boston, strong in its wealth, in its influence, in its character; on the other side is a little child, of a degraded color, of humble parents, still within the period of natural infancy, but strong from her very weakness, and from the irrepressible sympathies of good men, which, by a divine compensation, come to succor the weak. This little child asks at your hands her *personal rights*. So doing, she calls upon you to decide a question which concerns the personal rights of other colored children; which concerns the Constitution and Laws of the Commonwealth; which concerns that *peculiar institution* of New England, the Common Schools; which concerns the fundamental principles of human rights; which concerns the Christian character of this community. Such parties, and such interests, so grand and various, may justly challenge your most earnest attention.

Though this discussion is now for the first time brought before a judicial tribunal, it is no stranger to the public. For five years it has been an occasion of discord in the School Committee. No less than four different reports — two majority reports, and two minority reports — forming pamphlets of solid dimensions, devoted to this question, — have been made to this Committee, and afterwards published. The opinions of learned counsel have been enlisted in the cause. The controversy, leaving these regular channels, has overflowed the newspaper press, and numerous articles have appeared, espousing opposite sides. At last it has reached this tribunal. It is in your power to cause it to subside forever.

Forgetting many of the topics, and all of the heats, which have heretofore mingled with the controversy, I shall strive to present the question in its juridical light, as becomes the habits of this tribunal. It is a question of jurisprudence on which you are to give judgment. But I cannot forget that the principles of morals and of natural justice lie at the foundation of all jurisprudence. Nor can any reference to these be inappropriate in a discussion before this Court.

The great principle involved in this case, I shall first exhibit in the Constitution of Massachusetts, next in the legislation, and then in the judicial decisions. I shall then consider the special circumstances of this case, and show the violation of the Constitution and Laws, by the School Committee of Boston — answering, before I close, some of the grounds on which their conduct has been vindicated.

I. I begin with the principle, that, according to the spirit of American institutions, and especially of the Constitution of Massachusetts, *all men, without distinction of color or race, are equal before the law.*

I might, perhaps, leave this proposition without one word of comment. The Equality of men will not be directly denied on this occasion; and yet it has been so often assailed of late, that I trust I shall not seem to occupy your time superfluously in endeavoring to show what is understood by this term, when used in laws, constitutions, or other political instruments. Mr. Calhoun, in the Senate of the United States, and Lord Brougham, in his recent work on *Political Philosophy*, (Part 2. cap. 4,) have characterized Equality as impossible and absurd. If they had chosen to comprehend the true extent and application of the term, as employed on such occasions, something, if not all of the force of their objections, would have been removed. That we may better appreciate its character and its limitations, let me develop with some care the origin and growth of this sentiment, until it finally ripened into a formula of civil and political right.

The *sentiment* of Equality among men was early cherished by generous souls. It showed itself in the dreams of ancient philosophy. It was declared by Seneca; when writing to a friend a letter of consolation on death, he said, *Prima enim pars Equitatis est Equalitas.* (Epist. 30.) The first part of Equity is Equality. But it was enunciated with persuasive force in the truths of the Christian Religion. Here we learn that God is no respecter of persons; that he is the father of all; and that we are all his children, and brethren to each other. When the Saviour taught the Lord's prayer, he taught the sublime doctrine of the Brotherhood of Mankind, infolding the Equality of men.

Slowly did this sentiment enter the *State.* The whole constitution of government in modern times was inconsistent with it. An hereditary monarchy, an order of nobility, and the complex ranks of superiors and inferiors established by the feudal system, all declared, not the Equality, but the inequality of men, and they all conspired to perpetuate this inequality. Every infant of royal blood, every noble, every vassal, was a present example, that, whatever might be the truths of religion, or the sentiments of the heart, men living under these institutions were not born equal.

The boldest political reformers of early times did not venture to proclaim this truth; nor did they truly perceive it. Cromwell beheaded his king, but caused the supreme power to be secured in hereditary succession to his eldest son. It was left to John Milton, in poetic vision, to be entranced —

> With fair Equality, fraternal state.

Sidney, who perished a martyr to liberal sentiments, drew his inspiration from the classic, and not from the Christian fountains. The examples of Greece and Rome fed his soul. The Revolution of 1688, partly by force, and partly by the popular voice, brought a foreigner to the crown of Great Britain, and according to the boast of loyal Englishmen, the establishment of Freedom throughout the land. But the Bill of Rights did not declare, nor did the genius of Somers or Maynard conceive the political axiom, that all men are born equal. It may find acceptance in our day from individuals in England; but it is disowned by English institutions.

It is to France that we must pass for the earliest development of this idea, for its amplest illustration, and for its most complete, accurate, and logical expression. In the middle of the last century appeared the renowned *Encyclopedie*, edited by D'Alembert and

Diderot. This remarkable production, where science, religion, and government were all discussed with a revolutionary freedom, contains an article on Equality, which was published in 1755. Here we find the boldest expression that had then been given to this sentiment. "Natural Equality," says the Encyclopedia, "is that which exists between all men by the constitution of their nature only. This Equality is the principle and the foundation of liberty. Natural or moral equality is then founded upon the constitution of human nature, common to all men, who are born, grow, subsist, and die in the same manner. Since human nature finds itself the same in all men, it is clear, that, according to nature's law, each ought to esteem and treat the others as beings who are naturally equal to himself; that is to say, who are men as well as himself." It is then remarked, that political and civil slavery is in violation of this Equality; and yet there is a recognition of the inequalities of nobility in the state. Alluding to these, it is simply said, that they, who are most elevated above others, ought to treat their inferiors as beings naturally their equals, shunning all outrage, and demanding nothing beyond what is due, and demanding with humanity that which is most incontestably their due.

When we consider the period at which this article was written, we shall be astonished less by its incompleteness and vagueness, than by its bravery and generosity. The dissolute despotism of Louis XV. overshadowed France. Selfish nobles and fawning courtiers filled the royal antechambers. The councils of Government were controlled by royal mistresses.

Only a few years before, in 1751, the King had founded, in defiance of the principles of Equality — but in entire harmony with the conduct of the School Committee in Boston — a military school, *for nobles only*, carrying into education the distinction of Caste. At such a period the Encyclopedia did well in uttering such important and effective truth. The *sentiment* of Equality was here fully declared. Nor should we be disappointed, that, at this early day, even the boldest philosophers did not adequately perceive, or if they perceived, did not dare to utter, our axiom of liberty, that all men are born equal, in civil and political rights.

It is thus with the history of all moral and political ideas. First appearing merely as a sentiment, they animate those who receive them with a noble impulse, filling them with generous sympathies, and encouraging them to congenial efforts. Slowly recognized, they finally pass into a formula to be acted upon, to be applied, to be defended in the concerns of life.

Almost contemporaneously with this article in the Encyclopedia, our attention is arrested by a solitary person, poor, of humble extraction, born at Geneva, in Switzerland, of irregular education and life, a wanderer from his birthplace, enjoying a temporary home in France, a man of audacious genius, who set at naught the received opinions of mankind, — Jean Jacques Rousseau. His earliest appearance before the public, was by an eccentric *Essay on the Origin of Inequality among Men*, in which he sustained the irrational paradox, that men are happier in a state of nature than under the laws of civilization. This was followed by a later work, the *Social Contract*. In both of these productions, the sentiment of Equality was invoked against many of the abuses of society, and language was employed going far beyond Equality in Civil and Political Rights. The conspicuous position, since awarded to the speculations of Rousseau, and the influence they have exerted in diffusing this sentiment, make it proper to refer to them on this occasion; but the absence of precision in his propositions renders him an uncertain guide.

The French Revolution was now at hand. That great movement for enfranchisement was the expression of this sentiment. Here it received a distinct and authoritative enunciation. In the constitutions of government successively adopted, amidst the throes of bloody struggles, the Equality of men was constantly proclaimed. Kings, nobles, and all distinctions of birth, passed away before this mighty and triumphant truth.

Look at these Constitutions, and see at once the grandeur of the principle, and the manner in which it was explained and illustrated. The Constitution of 1791 declares in its first article as follows: "Men are born and continue free and *equal in their rights.*" In its sixth article it says: "The law is the expression of the general will. It ought to be the same for all, whether it protects or punishes. *All citizens being equal in its eyes, are equally admissible to all dignities, places, and public employments, according to their capacity, and without other distinction than their virtues and talents.*" At the close of the Declaration of Rights there is this further explanation of it: "The National Assembly, wishing to establish the French Constitution on principles which it has just acknowledged and declared, *abolishes irrevocably the institutions which bounded liberty and equality of rights.* There is no longer, neither nobility, nor peerage, nor hereditary distinctions, nor distinction of order, nor feudal rule, nor patrimonial justices, nor any titles, denominations and prerogatives, which were thence derived, nor any order of chivalry, nor any corporations or decorations, for which proofs of nobility are required, or which supposed distinctions of birth, nor any other superiority than that of public functionaries in the discharge of their functions. * * * *There is no longer, for any part of the nation, nor for any individual, any privilege or exception to the law, common to all Frenchmen.*" (*Moniteur*, 1791, *No.* 259.)

In fitful mood another Declaration of Rights was brought forward by Condorcet, Feb. 15, 1793. Here also are fresh inculcations of the Equality of men. Article 1st, places Equality among the natural, civil, and political rights of man. Article 7th declares: "*Equality consists in this, that each can enjoy the same rights.*" Article 8th: "*The law ought to be equal for all*, whether it recompense, or punish, or repress." Article 9th: "All citizens are admissible to all public places, employments, and functions. *Free people cannot know other motives of preference than talents and virtues.*" Article 23d: "Instruction is the need of all, and society owes it equally to all its members." Article 32d: "There is oppression when the law violates the natural, civil, and political rights which it ought to guarantee. There is oppression when a law is violated by public functionaries in its application to individual facts." (*Moniteur*, 1793, *No.* 49.)

Next came the Constitution of June, 1793. This announces in its second article, that the natural and imprescriptible rights of men are "*Equality*, liberty, safety, property." And in the next article it shows what is meant by Equality. It says, "All men are equal by nature, *and before the law.*" (*Moniteur*, 1793, *No.* 178.) Here we first meet this form of definition. At a later day, after France had passed through an unprecedented series of political vicissitudes, in some of which the rights of Equality had been trampled under foot, when, at the revolution of 1830, Louis Philippe was called to a "throne surrounded by republican institutions," the charter then promulgated repeated this phrase. In its first article it declared, "that Frenchmen are *equal before the law*, whatever may be their titles or ranks."

While recognizing this peculiar enunciation of the Equality of men, as more specific and satisfactory than the naked statement that all men are born equal, it is impossible not to be reminded that this form of speech finds its prototype in the ancient Greek language. In the history of Herodotus, we are told that "the government of the many has the most beautiful name of ἰσονομία" — or *Equality before the law.* (Book 3, § 80.) Thus this remarkable language, by its comprehensiveness and flexibility, in an age when *Equality before the law* was practically unknown, nevertheless supplied a single word, which is not to be found in modern tongues, to express an idea which has been practically recognized only in modern times. Such a word in our own language, as a substitute for Equality, might have superseded some of the criticism to which this political doctrine has been exposed.

After this review, the way is now prepared to consider the nature of Equality, as secured by the Constitution of Massachusetts. The Declaration of Independence, which was put forth after the French Encyclopedia, and the political writings of Rousseau, places among self-evident truths this proposition, — "*That all men are created equal*, and that they are endowed by the Creator with certain unalienable rights; that among these are life, liberty, and the pursuit of happiness." The Constitution of Massachusetts repeats the same idea in a different form. In the first article it says: "*All men are born free and equal*, and have certain natural, essential and unalienable rights, among which may be reckoned the right of enjoying and defending their lives and liberties." The sixth section further explains the doctrine of Equality. It says: "*No man, nor corporation, or association of men, have any other title to obtain advantages, or particular and exclusive privileges, distinct from those of the community, than what arises from the consideration of services rendered to the public;* and this title being in nature neither hereditary, nor transmissible to children, or descendants, or relations by blood, the idea of a man being born a magistrate, lawgiver, or judge, is absurd and unnatural." The language here employed, in its natural signification, condemns every form of inequality, in civil and political institutions.

Though these declarations preceded, in point of time, the ampler declarations of France, they may, if necessary, be construed in the light of the latter. It is evident that they aim to declare substantially the same things. They are declarations of *Rights*, and the language employed, though general in its character, is obviously to be restrained to those matters which are within the design and sphere of a declaration of *Rights*. It is a childish sophism to adduce in argument against them the physical or mental inequalities by which men are characterized.

It is a palpable truth, that men are not born equal in physical strength, or in mental capacities; in beauty of form or health of body. Diversity or inequality, in these respects, is the law of creation. From this difference springs divine harmony. But this inequality is in no particular inconsistent with a complete civil and political equality.

The equality declared by our fathers in 1776, and made the fundamental law of Massachusetts in 1780, was *Equality before the law*. Its object was to efface all political or civil distinctions, and to abolish all institutions founded upon *birth*. "All men are *created* equal," says the Declaration of Independence. "All men are *born* free and equal," says the Massachusetts Bill of Rights. These are not vain words. Within the sphere of their influence no person can be *created*, no person can be *born*, with civil or political privileges, not enjoyed equally by all his fellow-citizens; nor can any institution be established recognizing any distinctions of birth. Here is the Great Charter of every human being drawing his vital breath upon this soil, whatever may be his condition, and whoever may be his parents. He may be poor, weak, humble, black — he may be of Caucasian, of Jewish, of Indian, or of Ethiopian race — he may be of French, of German, of English, of Irish extraction — but before the Constitution of Massachusetts all these distinctions disappear. He is not poor, or weak, or humble, or black — nor Caucasian, nor Jew, nor Indian, nor Ethiopian — nor French, nor German, nor English, nor Irish; he is a MAN, — the equal of all his fellow-men. He is one of the children of the State, which, like an impartial parent, regards all its offspring with an equal care. To some it may justly allot higher duties, according to their higher capacities, but it welcomes all to its equal, hospitable board. The State, imitating the divine justice, is no respecter of persons.

Here nobility cannot exist, because it is a privilege from birth. But the same anathema, which smites and banishes nobility, must also smite and banish every form of discrimination founded on birth;

Quamvis ille niger, quamvis tu candidus esses.

II. I now pass to the second stage of this argument, and ask attention to a further proposition. The Legislature of Massachusetts, in entire harmony with the Constitution, has made no discrimination of color or race, in the establishment of Public Schools.

If such discrimination were made by the Laws, they would be unconstitutional and void. But the legislature of Massachusetts has been too just and generous, too mindful of the Bill of Rights, to establish any such privilege of *birth*. The language of the statutes is general, and applies equally to all children, of whatever color or race.

The provisions of the law regulating this subject are entitled, *Of the Public Schools.* (Revised Statutes, ch. 23.) To these we must look in order to ascertain what constitutes a Public School. None can be legally such which are not established in conformity with the Law. They may, in point of fact, be more or less public; yet, if they do not come within the terms of the Law, they do not form a part of the beautiful system of our Public Schools; they are not Public Schools.

It is important then to examine these terms. The first section provides, that in "Every town containing fifty families, or householders, there shall be kept in each year, at the charge of the town, by a teacher or teachers of competent ability and good morals, *one school* for the instruction of *children* in Orthography, Reading, Writing, English Grammar, Geography, Arithmetic and Good Behavior, for the term of six months, or two or more such schools for terms of time that shall together be equivalent to six months." The 2d, 3d, and 4th sections provide for the number of *such* schools to be kept in other towns having more than five hundred inhabitants. The language here employed does not recognize any discrimination of color or race. Thus in every town, whether there be one or more schools, they are all to be "schools for the instruction of *children*" generally — not children of any particular class, or color, or race, but children, — meaning the children of the town where the schools are.

The 5th and 6th sections provide for the establishment, in certain cases, of a school, in which additional studies are to be pursued, "which shall be kept *for the benefit of all the inhabitants* of the town." Here the language not only does not recognize any discrimination among the children, but seems directly to exclude it.

In conformity with these sections is the peculiar phraseology of the memorable law of the Colonies in 1647, founding Public Schools, "to the end that learning be not buried in the graves of our forefathers." This law obliged towns having fifty families "forthwith to appoint one" within their limits "to teach *all such children as shall resort to him,* to write and read." (Ancient Charters, 186.)

It is on this legislation that the Public Schools of Massachusetts have been reared. The clause of the Revised Statutes (chap. 23,) and the statute (1838, chap. 154,) appropriating small sums, in the nature of a contribution, out of the school fund for the support of common schools among the Indians, do not interfere with this system. These partake of the anomalous character of all the legislation with regard to the Indians in this Commonwealth. It does not appear, however, that any separate schools are established by law among the Indians, nor that the Indians are in any way excluded from the Public Schools in their neighborhood.

I conclude from this examination, that there is but one kind of Public School established by the laws of Massachusetts. This is the general Public School, free to all the inhabitants. There is nothing in these laws establishing any exclusive or separate school for any particular class, whether rich or poor, whether Catholic or Protestant, whether white or black. In the eye of the law there is but *one class*, in which all interests, opinions, conditions and colors commingle in harmony — excluding none, comprehending all.

From the legislation of the Commonwealth, I pass to the adjudication of the Courts.

III. The Courts of Massachusetts have never recognized any discrimination, founded on color or race, in the administration of the Public Schools; but have recognized the equal rights of all the inhabitants.

There are a few decisions only of our Court bearing on this subject, but they all breathe one spirit. The sentiment of Equality animates them. In the case of *Commonwealth* v. *Davis*, (6 Mass. R. 146,) while declaring the equal rights of all the inhabitants, both in the grammar and district schools, the Court said: "The schools required by the statute are to be maintained for the benefit of the whole town, *as it is the wise policy of the law to give all the inhabitants equal privileges for the education of their children in the Public Schools.* Nor is it in the power of the majority to deprive the minority of this *privilege.* * * * * Every inhabitant of the town has a right to participate in the benefits of both descriptions of schools, and it is not competent for a town to establish a grammar school for the benefit of one part of the town to the exclusion of the other, although the money raised for the support of schools may be in other respects fairly apportioned."

In the case of *Withington* v. *Eveleth*, (7 Pick. 106,) the Court said, they "were all satisfied that the power given to towns to determine and define the limits of school districts, can be executed only by a geographical division of the town for that purpose." A limitation of the district, which was merely *personal*, was held invalid. This same principle was again recognized in *Perry* v. *Doe*, (12 Pick. R. 213,) where the Court say, "Towns, in executing the power to form school districts, are bound so to do it as to include *every inhabi-*

tant in some of the districts. They cannot lawfully omit any, and thus deprive them of *the benefits of our invaluable system of free schools*."

The Constitution, the legislation, and the judicial decisions of Massachusetts, have now been passed in review. We have seen what is contemplated by the Equality secured by the Constitution. We have seen also what is contemplated by the system of Public Schools, as established by the laws of the Commonwealth, and illustrated by the decisions of the Supreme Court. The way is now prepared to consider the peculiarities in the present case, and to apply the principle thus recognized in the Constitution, in the Laws and judicial decisions.

IV. The exclusion of colored children from the Public Schools, open to white children, is a source of practical inconvenience to them and their parents, to which white persons are not exposed, and is, therefore, a violation of Equality. *The black and the white are not equal before the law.*

It appears from the statement of facts, that among the rules of the Primary School Committee, is one to this effect: "*Scholars to go to the school nearest their residence.* Applicants for admission to our schools (with the exception and provision referred to in the preceding rule) are especially entitled to enter the schools nearest to their places of residence." The exception here is "of those for whom special provision has been made" in separate schools; that is, colored children.

In this rule — without the exception — is seen a part of the beauty of our Public School system. It is the boast of England, that justice, through the multitude of courts, is brought to every man's door. It may also be the boast of our Public School system, that education in Boston, through the multitude of schools, is brought to every *white* man's door. But it is not brought to every black man's door. He is obliged to go for it — to travel for it — often a great distance. The facts in the present case are not so strong as those of other cases which have come to my knowledge. But here, the little child, only five years old, was compelled, if she went to the nearest African School, to go a distance of 2100 feet from her dwelling, while the nearest Primary School was only 900 feet, and, in doing this, she would pass near no less than five different Primary Schools, forming part of our Public Schools, and open to white children, all of which were closed to her. Surely this is not *Equality before the law.*

This simple fact is sufficient to determine this case. If it be met by the suggestion, that the inconvenience is trivial, and such as the law will not notice, I reply, that it is precisely of that character which reveals distinctly an existing inequality, and, therefore, the law cannot fail to notice it. There is a maxim of the civilian, Dumoulin, which teaches that even a trivial fact may give occasion to an important application of the law. *Modica enim circumstantia facti inducit magnam juris diversitatem.* Also, from the best examples of our history, we learn that the insignificance of a fact cannot obscure the grandeur of the principle at stake. It was a paltry tax on tea, laid by a Parliament in which they were not represented, that aroused our fathers to the struggles of the Revolution. They did not feel the inconvenience of the tax; but they felt its oppression. They went to war for a principle. Let it not be said, then, that the inconvenience is so slight in the present case as not to justify the appeal I now make, in behalf of the colored children, for *Equality before the law.*

I may go, however, beyond the facts of this case, and show that the inconvenience arising from the exclusion of colored children, is of such a character as seriously to affect the comfort and condition of the African race in Boston. The two primary schools open to these children are in Belknap street and in Sun court. I need not add that the whole city is dotted with schools open to white children. The colored parents, anxious that their children should have the benefit of education, are compelled to live in the neighborhood of the schools, to gather about them — as in Eastern countries people come from a distance to rest near a fountain or a well. They have not, practically, the same liberty of choosing their homes, which belongs to the white man. Inclination, or business, or economy, may call them to another part of the city; but they are restrained for their children's sake. There is no such restraint upon the white man; for he knows that wherever in the city inclination, or business, or economy, may call him, he will find a school open to his children near his door. Surely this is not *Equality before the law.*

Or if a colored person, yielding to the necessities of his position, removes to a distant part of the city, his children may be compelled, at an inconvenience which will not be called trivial, to walk a long distance in order to enjoy the advantages of the school. In our severe winters, this cannot be disregarded by children so tender in years as those of the primary schools. There is a respectable colored person, I am told, who became some time since a resident at East Boston, separated by the water from the main land. There are, of course, proper Public Schools at East Boston, but none that were then open to colored children. This person, therefore, was obliged to send his children, three in number, daily, across the ferry to the distant African school. The tolls for these children amounted to a sum which formed a severe tax upon a poor man.

This is the conduct of a colored parent. He is well deserving of honor for his generous efforts for his children. As they grow in knowledge, they will rise and call him blessed; but at the same time they will brand as accursed the arbitrary discrimination of color, in the Public Schools of Boston, which rendered it necessary for their father, out of his small means, to make such sacrifices for their education.

Such a grievance, even independent of any stigma from color, calls for redress. It is an inequality which the Constitution and Laws of Massachusetts repudiate. But it is not on the ground of inconvenience only that it is odious. And this brings me to the next point.

V. The separation of children in the Public Schools of Boston, on account of color or race, is in the nature of *Caste*, and, on this account, is a violation of Equality.

The facts in this case show expressly that the child was excluded from the school nearest to her dwelling, the number in the school at the time warranting her admission, "on the sole ground of color." The first

Majority Report presented to the School Committee, to which reference is made in the statement of facts, gives, with more fullness, the grounds of this discrimination, saying, "It is one of *races*, not of *color*, merely. The distinction is one which the Almighty has seen fit to establish, and it is founded deep in the physical, mental, and moral natures of the two races. No legislation, no social customs, can efface this distinction." Words more apt than these to describe the heathenish relation of Caste, could not be chosen.

This will be apparent from the very definition of Caste. This term is borrowed from the Portuguese word *casta*, which signifies family, breed, race. It has become generally used to designate any hereditary distinction, particularly of race. In India it is most often applied; and it is there that we must go in order to understand its full force. A recent English writer on the subject, says, that it is "not only a distinction by birth, but is founded on the doctrine of an essentially distinct origin of the different races, which are thus unalterably separated." (Roberts on Caste, p. 134.) This is the very ground of the Boston School Committee.

But this word is not now applied for the first time to the distinction between the white and black races. Alexander von Humboldt, in speaking of the negroes in Mexico, has characterized them as a Caste, and a recent political and juridical writer of France has used the same term to denote, not only the distinctions in India, but those of our own country. (Charles Comte, *Traité de Legislation*, tom. 4, p. 129, 445) In the course of his remarks, he refers to the exclusion of colored children from the Public Schools, as among "the humiliating and brutal distinctions" by which their Caste is characterized. It is, then, on authority and reason, that we apply this term to the hereditary distinction on account of color, which is established in the Public Schools of Boston.

It is when we see this discrimination in this light, that we learn to appreciate its true character. The Brahmins and the Sudras, in India, from generation to generation, were kept apart. If a Sudra presumed to sit upon a Brahmin's carpet, he was punished with banishment. With a similar inhumanity among us, the black child, who goes to sit on the same benches at school with the white child, is banished, not from the country, but from the school. In both cases it is the triumph of Caste. But the offence is greater with us, because, unlike the Hindoos, we acknowledge that *men are born equal.*

So strong is my desire that the Court should feel the enormity of this system, thus legalized, not by the legislature, but by an inferior local board, that I shall here introduce an array of witnesses to the unchristian character of Caste, as it appears in India, where it has been most studied and discussed. As you join in detestation of this foul institution, you will learn, perhaps, to condemn its establishment among children in our Public Schools.

I borrow these authorities from the work to which I have already referred, of Mr. Roberts, *Caste opposed to Christianity*, published in London, 1847.

Bishop Heber, of Calcutta, characterizes Caste as follows:

It is a system which tends, more than any else the devil has yet invented, to destroy the feelings of general benevolence, and to make nine tenths of mankind the hopeless slaves of the remainder.

Bishop Wilson, also of Calcutta, the successor of Heber, says:

The Gospel recognizes no such distinctions as those of castes, imposed by a heathen usage, bearing in some respects a supposed religious obligation, condemning those in the lower ranks to perpetual abasement, placing an immovable barrier against all general advance and improvement in society, cutting asunder the bonds of human fellowship on the one hand, and preventing those of Christian love on the other. Such distinctions, I say, the Gospel does not recognize. On the contrary, it teaches us that God "hath made of one blood all the nations of men."

Bishop Corrie, of Madras, says:

Thus Caste sets itself up as a judge of our Saviour himself. His command is, "Condescend to men of low estate. Esteem others better than yourself." "No," says Caste, "do not commune with low men; consider yourself of high estimation. Touch not, taste not, handle not." Thus Caste condemns the Saviour.

Rev. Mr. Rhenius, a zealous and successful Missionary, says:

I have found Caste, both in theory and practice, to be diametrically opposed to the Gospel, which inculcates love, humility, and union; whereas Caste teaches the contrary. It is a fact, in those entire congregations where Caste is allowed, the spirit of the Gospel does not enter; whereas in those from which it is excluded, we see the fruits of the Gospel spirit.

The Rev. C. Mault, also a Missionary, says:

Caste must be entirely renounced; for it is a noxious plant, by the side of which the graces cannot grow; for facts demonstrate, that where it has been allowed, Christianity has never flourished.

The Rev. John McKenny, a Wesleyan Missionary, says:

I have been upwards of twelve years in India, and have directed much of my attention to the subject of Caste, and am fully of opinion, that it is altogether contrary to the nature and principles of the Gospel of Christ, and therefore ought not to be admitted into the Christian Church.

The Rev. R. S. Hardy, a Wesleyan Missionary, and author of "Notices of the Holy Land," says:

The principle of Caste I consider so much at variance with the spirit of the Gospel, as to render impossible, where its authority is acknowledged, the exercise of many of the most beautiful virtues of our holy religion.

Rev. D. J. Gogerly, of the same Society, says:

I regard the distinction of Caste, both in its principles and operations, as directly opposed to vital godliness, and consequently inadmissible into the Church of Christ.

The Rev. W. Bridgnall, also of the same Society, says:

I perfectly agree with a writer of respectable authority, in considering the institution of Caste as the most formidable engine that was ever invented for perpetuating the subjugation of men; so that, as a friend of humanity only, I should feel myself bound to protest against and oppose it; but in particular as a Christian, I deem it my obvious and imperative duty wholly to discountenance it, conceiving it to be utterly repugnant to all the principles and the whole spirit of Christianity. He, who is prepared to support the system of Caste, is, in my judgment, neither a true friend of man, nor a consistent follower of Christ.

The Rev. S. Allen, of the same Society, says:

During a residence of more than nine years in Ceylon, I have had many opportunities of witnessing the influence of Caste on the minds of the natives; and I firmly believe it is altogether opposed to the spirit of Christianity; and it appears to me, that its utter and speedy extinction cannot but be desired by every minister of Christ.

The Rev. R. Stoup, of the same Society, says:

From my own personal observation, during a four years' residence in Ceylon, I am decidedly of opinion that *Caste* is directly opposed to the spirit of Christianity, and, consequently, ought to be discouraged in every possible way.

The Rev. Joseph Roberts, author of the work on Caste, says:

We must, in every place, witness against it, and show that even government itself is nurturing a tremendous evil, that through its Heathen managers it is beguiled into a course which obstructs the progress of civilization, which keeps in repulsion our kindlier feelings, which creates and nurses distinctions the most alien to all the cordialities of life; and which, more than any other thing, makes the distance so immense betwixt the governed and governors.

This is the testimony of a native of Hindostan, converted to Christianity:

Caste is the stronghold of that principle of pride which makes a man think of himself more highly than he ought to think. Caste infuses itself into, and forms the very essence of pride itself.

Another native speaks as follows:

I therefore regard Caste as opposed to the main scope, principles, and doctrines of Christianity; for, either Caste must be admitted to be true and of divine authority, or Christianity must be so admitted. If you admit Caste to be true, the whole fabric of Christianity must come down; for the nature of Caste and its associations destroy the first principles of Christianity. Caste makes distinctions among creatures where God has made none.

Another native expresses himself as follows:

When God made man, his intention was, not that they should be divided, and hate one another, and show contempt, and think more highly of themselves than others. Caste makes a man think that he is holier than another, and that he has some inherent virtue which another has not. It makes him despise all those that are lower than himself, in regard to Caste, which is not the design of God.

Another native uses this language:

Yes, we regard Caste as part and parcel of idolatry, and of all heathen abominations, because it is in many ways contrary to God's word, and directly contrary to God himself.

In the words of these competent witnesses may be read, as in a mirror, the true character of the discrimination of color, which I now arraign before this Court.

It will be vain to say that this distinction, though seeming to be founded on color, is in reality founded on natural and physical peculiarities, which are independent of color. These peculiarities, whatever they may be, are peculiarities of race, and any discrimination on account of them constitutes the relation of Caste.

Disguise it as you will, it is this hateful institution. But the words Caste and Equality are contradictory. They mutually exclude each other. Where Caste is, there cannot be Equality. Where Equality is, there cannot be Caste.

It is unquestionably true that there is a distinction between the Ethiopian and Caucasian races. Each has received from the hand of God certain characteristics of color and form. The two may not readily intermingle, although we are told by Homer that Jupiter

> —— did not disdain to grace
> The feast of Ethiopia's blameless race.

One may be uninteresting or offensive to the other, precisely as different individuals of the same race and color may be uninteresting or offensive to each other. *But this distinction can furnish no ground for any discrimination before the law.*

We abjure nobility of all kinds; but here is a nobility of the skin. We abjure all hereditary distinctions; but here is an hereditary distinction, founded not on the merit of the ancestor, but on his color. We abjure all privileges derived from birth; but here is a privilege which depends solely on the accident, whether an ancestor is black or white. We abjure all inequality before the law; but here is an inequality which touches not an individual, but a race. We revolt at the relation of Caste; but here is a Caste which is established under a Constitution, declaring that *all men are born equal.*

Condemning Caste and inequality before the law, let us now consider more particularly the powers of the School Committee. Here it will be necessary to enter into some details.

VI. The Committee of Boston, charged with the superintendence of the Public Schools, have no *power* under the Constitution and Laws of Massachusetts, to make any discrimination on account of color or race, among children in the Public Schools.

It has been already seen that this power is inconsistent with the Constitution and Laws of Massachusetts, and with the adjudications of the Supreme Court. The stream cannot rise higher than the fountain-head, and if there be nothing in these elevated sources, from which this power can draw its sanction, it must be considered a nullity. Having already seen that there is nothing, I might here stop. But I wish to show the shallow origin to which this power has been traced.

Its advocates, unable to find it among the express powers conferred upon the School Committee, and forgetful of the Constitution, where "either it must live, or bear no life," place it among the implied or incidental powers. Let us consider this. The Revised Statutes (cap. 23, § 10) provide for the appointment of a School Committee "who shall have a *general charge and superintendence* of all the Public Schools" in their respective towns. Another section (§ 15) provides that the "Committee shall determine the number and qualifications of the scholars to be admitted into the school kept for the use of the whole town." These are all the clauses conferring powers on the Committee.

Surely from these no person will be so rash as to imply a power to defeat a cardinal principle of the Constitution. It is absurd to suppose that the Committee, in their general charge and superintendence of the schools, and in determining the number and qualifications of the scholars, may ingraft upon the schools a principle of inequality, unknown to the Constitution and Laws, and in defiance of their spirit and letter. In the exercise of the general charge and superintendence, they cannot put colored children to personal inconvenience in attending school, greater than that of white children. Still further, they cannot brand a whole race with the stigma of inferiority and degradation, constituting them into a *caste*. They cannot in any way violate that fundamental right of all citizens, *Equality before the law*. To suppose that they can do this, would place the Committee above the Constitution. It would enable them, in the exercise of a brief and local authority, to draw a fatal circle, within which the Constitution cannot enter; nay, where the very Bill of Rights shall become a dead letter.

But the law, in entire harmony with the Constitution, says expressly what the Committee shall do. Besides having the general charge and superintendence, they shall "determine the *number* and the *qualifications* of the scholars to be admitted into the school;" thus, according to a familiar rule of interpretation, excluding other powers: *Mentio unius est exclusio alterius*. The power to determine the *number* is easily executed, and admits of no question. The power to determine the *qualifications*, though less simple, must be restrained to the qualifications of age, sex, and moral and intellectual fitness. The fact that a child is black, or that he is white, cannot of itself be considered a qualification, or a disqualification. It is not to the skin that we can look for the criterion of fitness for our Public Schools.

But it is said that the Committee are intrusted with a discretion, in the exercise of their power, and that, in this discretion, they may distribute, assign, and classify all children belonging to the schools of the city, *according to their best judgment*, making, if they think proper, a discrimination of color or race. Without questioning that they are intrusted with a discretion, it is outrageous to suppose that their discretion can go to this extent. The Committee can have no discretion which is not in harmony with the Constitution and Laws. Surely, they cannot, in their mere discretion, nullify a sacred and dear-bought principle of Human Rights, which is expressly guaranteed by the Constitution.

Still further,— and here I approach a more technical view of the subject,— it is an admitted principle, that the regulations and by-laws of municipal corporations must be *reasonable*, or they are inoperative and void. This has been recognized by this Court in *Commonwealth* v. *Worcester*, (4 Pick. R. 462,) and in *Vardine's Case*, (6 Pick. 187.) And in the *City of Boston* v. *Jesse Shaw*, (1 Met. 130,) it was decided that a by-law of the city of Boston, prescribing a particular form of contribution towards the expenses of making the common sewers, was void for inequality and unreasonableness.

Assuming that this principle is applicable to the School Committee, their regulations and by-laws must be *reasonable*. Their discretion must be exercised in a reasonable manner. And this is not what the Committee, or any other body of men, may think reasonable, but what shall be reasonable in the eye of the law. It must be *legally reasonable*. It must be approved by the *reason* of the Law.

And here we are brought once more, in another form, to the question of the validity of the discrimination on account of color by the School Committee of Boston. Is this *legally reasonable*? Is it reasonable, in the exercise of their discretion, to separate the descendants of the African race from the white children, in consequence of their descent merely? Passing over those principles of the Constitution, and those provisions of the Law, which of themselves would decide the question, constituting as they do *the highest reason*, but which have been already amply considered, look for a moment at the Educational system of Massachusetts, and it will be seen that practically no discrimination of color is made by Law in any part of it. A descendant of the African race may be Governor of the Commonwealth, and as such, with the advice and consent of the Council, may select the *Board of Education*. As Lieutenant Governor, he may be *ex officio*, a member of the Board. He may be the *Secretary* of the Board, with the duty imposed on him by law of seeing "that *all* children in this Commonwealth, who depend upon common schools for instruction, may have the best education which those schools can be made to impart." He may be a member of any School Committee, or a teacher in any public school of the State. As a legal voter, he can vote in the selection of any School Committee.

Thus, in every department connected with our Public Schools, throughout the whole hierarchy of their government, from the very head of the system down to the humblest usher in the humblest primary school, and, to the humblest voter, there is no distinction of color known to the Law. It is when we reach the last stage of all, the children themselves, that the beautiful character of the system is changed to the deformity of Caste ; as, in the picture of the ancient poet, what was a lovely woman above, terminated in a vile, unsightly fish below. And all this is done by the Committee, with more than necromantic power, in the exercise of their mere discretion.

It is clear, that the Committee may classify scholars, according to their age and sex; for the obvious reasons that these distinctions are inoffensive, and especially recognized as *legal* in the law relating to schools. (Revised Statutes, c. 23, § 63.) They may also classify scholars, according to their moral and intellectual qualifications, because such a power is necessary to the government of schools. But the Committee cannot assume, *à priori*, and without individual examination, that an *entire race* possess certain moral or intellectual qualities, which shall render it proper to place them all in a class by themselves. Such an exercise of the discretion with which the Committee are intrusted, must be unreasonable, and therefore illegal.

But it is said that the Committee, in thus classifying the children, have not violated any principle of Equality, inasmuch as they have provided a school, with competent instructors, for the colored children, where they have equal advantages of instruction with those enjoyed by the white children. It is said, that in excluding the colored children from the Public Schools open to white children, they furnish them an equivalent.

To this there are several answers. I shall touch them only briefly, as the discussion, through which we have now travelled, substantially covers the whole ground.

1. The separate school for colored children is not one of the schools established by the law relating to Public Schools. (Revised Statutes, c. 23.) It is not a Public School. As such, it has no legal existence, and, therefore, cannot be a legal equivalent. In addition to what has already been said, bearing on this head, I will call the attention to one other aspect of it. We have already seen that it has been decided, that a town can execute its power to form a School District only by a geographical division of its territory — that there cannot be, what the Court have called a *personal* limitation of the District, and that *certain individuals* cannot be selected and set off by *themselves* into a District. (*Perry* v. *Dover*, 12 Pick. 213.) The admitted effect of these decisions is to render a separate school for colored children illegal and impossible in towns that have been divided into Districts. They are so regarded in Salem, Nantucket, New Bedford, and in other towns of this Commonwealth. The careful opinion of a member of this Court, who is not sitting in this case, given while at the bar, (Hon. Richard Fletcher,) and extensively published, has been considered as practically settling this point.

But there cannot be one law for the country, and one for Boston. It is true, that Boston is not divided strictly into geographical districts. In this respect its position is anomalous. But if separate colored schools are illegal and impossible in the country, they must be illegal and impossible in Boston. It is absurd to suppose that this city, by failing to establish School

Districts, and by regarding all its territory as a single district, should be able legally to establish a *Caste* school, which it otherwise could not do. Boston cannot do indirectly what the other towns cannot do directly.

This is the first answer to the suggestion of equivalents.

2. The second is, that, in point of fact, it is not an equivalent. We have already seen that it is the occasion of inconveniences to the colored children and their parents, to which they would not be exposed, if they had access to the nearest public schools, besides inflicting upon them the stigma of Caste. Still further, and this consideration cannot be neglected, the matters taught in the two schools may be precisely the same; but a school, exclusively devoted to one class, must differ essentially, in its spirit and character, from that Public School known to the law, where all classes meet together in Equality. It is a mockery to call it an equivalent.

3. But there is yet another answer. Admitting that it is an equivalent, still the colored children cannot be compelled to take it. Their rights are *Equality before the law;* nor can they be called upon to renounce one jot of this. They have an equal right with white children to the general Public Schools. A separate school, though well endowed, would not secure to them that precise Equality, which they would enjoy in the general public schools. The Jews in Rome are confined to a particular district, called the Ghetto. In Frankfort they are condemned to a separate quarter, known as the Jewish quarter. It is possible that the

accommodations allotted to them are as good as they would be able to occupy, if left free to choose throughout Rome and Frankfort; but this compulsory segregation from the mass of citizens is of itself an *inequality* which we condemn with our whole souls. It is a vestige of ancient intolerance directed against a despised people. It is of the same character with the separate schools in Boston.

Thus much for the doctrine of equivalents, as a substitute for equality.

In determining that the Committee have no *power* to make a discrimination of color or race, we are strengthened by yet another consideration. If the power exists in the present case, it must exist in many others. It cannot be restrained to this alone. The Committee may distribute all the children into classes — merely according to their discretion. They may establish a separate school for the Irish or the Germans, where each may nurse an exclusive spirit of nationality alien to our institutions. They may separate Catholics from Protestants, or, pursuing their discretion still further, they may separate the different sects of Protestants, and establish one school for Unitarians, another for Presbyterians, another for Baptists, and another for Methodists. They may establish a separate school for the rich, that the delicate taste of this favored class may not be offended by the humble garments of the poor. They may exclude the children of mechanics from the Public Schools, and send them to separate schools by themselves. All this, and much more, can be done by the exercise of the high-handed power which can make a discrimination on account of color or race. The grand fabric of our Public Schools, the pride of Massachusetts — where, at the feet of the teacher, innocent childhood should meet, unconscious of all distinctions of birth — where the Equality of the Constitution and of Christianity should be inculcated by constant precept and example — may be converted into a heathen system of proscription and Caste. We may then have many different schools, the representatives of as many different classes, opinions, and prejudices; but we shall look in vain for the true Public School of Massachusetts. Let it not be said that there is little danger that any Committee will exercise their discretion to this extent. They must not be intrusted with the power. In this is the only safety worthy of a free people.

VII. The Court will declare the by-law of the School Committee of Boston, making a discrimination of color among children of the Public Schools, to be unconstitutional and illegal, although there are no express words of prohibition in the constitution and laws.

It is hardly necessary to say any thing in support of this proposition. Slavery was abolished in Massachusetts, by virtue of the declaration of rights in our Constitution, without any specific words of abolition in that instrument, or in any subsequent legislation. (*Commonwealth* v. *Aves*, 18 Pick. R. 210.) The same words, which are potent to destroy slavery, must be equally potent against any institution founded on inequality or *Caste*. The case of *Boston* v. *Shaw*, (1 Metcalf 130,) to which reference has been already made, where a by-law of the city was set aside as unequal and unreasonable, and therefore void, affords another example of the power which I now invoke the Court to exercise. But authorities are not needed. The words of the Constitution are plain, and it will be the duty of the Court to see that these are applied to the discrimination of color now in question.

In doing this, the Court might justly feel great delicacy, if they were called upon to revise a *law* of the legislature. But it is simply the action of a local committee that they are to overrule. They may also be encouraged by the fact, that it is only to the Schools of Boston that their decision can be applicable. The other towns throughout the Commonwealth have already voluntarily banished Caste. In removing it from the schools of Boston, the Court will bring them into much-desired harmony with the schools of other towns, and with the whole system of Public Schools in Massachusetts. I am unwilling to suppose that there can be any hesitation or doubt in coming to this conclusion. But if any should arise, there is a rule of interpretation which may be our guide. It is according to familiar practice that every interpretation is made always in favor of life or liberty. So here, the Court should incline in favor of Equality, that sacred right which is the companion of these other rights. In proportion to the importance of this right, will the Court be solicitous to vindicate and uphold it. And in proportion to the opposition which it encounters from the prejudices of society, will the Court brace themselves to this task. It has been pointedly remarked by Rousseau, that "It is precisely because the force of things tends always to destroy Equality, that the force of legislation ought always to tend to maintain it." (*Contrat Social*, liv. 2, chap. 11.)

In a similar spirit, and for the same reason, the Court should always tend to maintain it.

There are some other matters not strictly belonging to the juridical aspect of the case, and yet of importance to its clear comprehension, upon which I shall touch briefly before I close.

It is sometimes said, in extenuation of the present system in Boston, that the separation of the white and black children was originally made at the request of the colored parents. This is substantially true. It appears from the interesting letter of Dr. Belknap, in reply to Judge Tucker's queries respecting Slavery in Massachusetts, written at the close of the last century, (4 Mass. Hist. Coll. 207,) that no discrimination on account of color was at that time made in the Public Schools of Boston. "The same provision," he says, "is made by the public for the education of the children of the blacks, as for those of the whites. In this town, the Committee who superintend the free schools, have given in charge to the schoolmasters to receive and instruct black children as well as white." Dr. Belknap adds, however, that he has not heard of more than three or four who have taken advantage of this privilege, though the number of blacks in Boston probably exceeded one thousand. It is to be feared that the inhuman bigotry of Caste — sad relic of the servitude from which they had just escaped! — was at this time too strong to allow colored children a kindly welcome in the free schools, and that, from timidity and ignorance, they shrank from taking their places on the same benches with the white children. Perhaps the prejudice against them was so inveterate that they could not venture to assert their rights. It appears that in 1800, a petition was presented to the School Committee from sixty-six colored persons, praying for the establishment of a school for their benefit. Private munificence came to the aid of the city, and the present system of separate schools was brought into being.

These facts are interesting in the history of the Boston Schools, but they cannot in any way affect the rights of the colored people, or the powers of the Committee. These rights and these powers stand on the Constitution and Laws of the Commonwealth. Without adopting the suggestion of Jefferson, that one generation cannot by legislation bind its successors, all must agree that the assent of a few persons, nearly half a century ago — at a time when their rights were imperfectly understood — to an unconstitutional and illegal course, cannot alter the Constitution and the Laws, and bind their descendants forever in the thrall of Caste. Nor can the Committee derive from this assent, or from any lapse of time, powers in derogation of the Constitution and the Rights of Man.

It is clear that the sentiments of the colored people have now changed. The present case, and the deep interest which they manifest in it, thronging the court to hang on this discussion, attest the change. With increasing knowledge, they have learned to know their rights, and to feel the degradation to which they have been doomed. Their present effort is the token of a manly character which this Court will cherish and respect. The spirit of Paul now revives in them, even as when he said, "I am a Roman citizen."

But it is said that these separate schools are for the mutual benefit of children of both colors, and of the Public Schools. In similar spirit, Slavery is sometimes said to be for the mutual benefit of master and slave, and of the country where it exists. In the one case there is a mistake as great as in the other. This is clear. Nothing unjust, nothing ungenerous, can be for the benefit of any person, or any thing. Short-sighted mortals may, from some seeming selfish superiority, or from a gratified vanity of class, hope to draw a permanent good; but even-handed justice rebukes these efforts, and with certain power redresses the wrong. The whites themselves are injured by the separation. Who can doubt this? With the law as their monitor, they are taught to regard a portion of the human family, children of God, created in his image, co-equals in his love, as a separate and degraded class; they are taught practically to deny that grand revelation of Christianity — the Brotherhood of Mankind. Their hearts, while yet tender with childhood, are necessarily hardened by this conduct, and their subsequent lives, perhaps, bear enduring testimony to this legalized uncharitableness. Nursed in the sentiment of Caste, receiving it with the earliest food of knowledge, they are unable to eradicate it from their natures, and then weakly and impiously charge upon their Heavenly Father the prejudice which they have derived from an unchristian school, and which they continue to embody and perpetuate in their institutions. Their characters are debased, and they become less fit for the magnanimous duties of a good citizen.

The Helots of Sparta were obliged to intoxicate

themselves, that they might teach to the children of their masters the deformity of intemperance. In thus sacrificing one class to the other, both were degraded — the imperious Spartan and the abased Helot. But it is with a similar double-edged injustice that the School Committee of Boston have acted, in sacrificing the colóred children to the prejudice or fancied advantage of the white.

It is fit that a child should be taught to shun wickedness, and, as he is yet plastic to receive impressions, to shun wicked men. Horace was right, when speaking of a person morally wrong, false and unjust, he called him black, saying,

—— hic niger est, hunc tu, Romane, caveto.

The Boston Committee adopt the warning, but apply it, not to those black in heart, but only black in skin. They forget the admonition addressed to the prophet: "But the Lord said unto Samuel, *look not on his countenance*, for the Lord seeth not as man seeth; for man looketh at the outward appearance, *but the Lord looketh at the heart*." (1 Samuel, chap. 16, v. 7.)

Who can say, that this does not injure the blacks? Theirs, in its best estate, is an unhappy lot. Shut out by a still lingering prejudice from many social advantages, — a despised class, — they feel this proscription from the Public Schools as a peculiar brand. Beyond this, it deprives them of those healthful animating influences, which would come from a participation in the studies of their white brethren. It adds to their discouragements. It widens their separation from the rest of the community, and postpones that great day of reconciliation which is sure to come.

The whole system of Public Schools suffers also. It is a narrow perception of their high aim, which teaches that they are merely to furnish to all the scholars an equal amount in knowledge, and that, therefore, provided all be taught, it is of little consequence where, and in what company, it be done. The law contemplates not only that they shall all be taught, but that they shall be taught *all together*. They are not only to receive equal quantities of knowledge, but all are to receive it in the same way. All are to approach together the same common fountain; nor can there be any exclusive source for any individual or any class. The school is the little world in which the child is trained for the larger world of life. It must, therefore, cherish and develop the virtues and the sympathies employed in the larger world. And since, according to our institutions, all classes meet, without distinction of color, in the performance of civil duties, so should they all meet, without distinction of color, in the school — beginning there those relations of Equality which our Constitution and Laws promise to all.

As the State receives strength from the unity and solidarity of its citizens, without distinction of class, so the school receives new strength from the unity and solidarity of all classes beneath its roof. In this way, the poor, the humble, and the neglected, share not only the companionship of their more favored brethren, but enjoy also the protection of their presence, in drawing towards the school a more watchful superintendence. A degraded or neglected class, if left to themselves, will become more degraded or neglected. To him that hath shall be given; and the world, true to these words, turns from the poor and outcast to the rich and fortunate. It is the aim of our system of Public Schools, by the blending of all classes, to draw upon the whole school the attention which is too apt to be given only to the favored few, and thus secure to the poor their portion of the fruitful sunshine. But the colored children, placed apart in separate schools, are deprived of this blessing.

Nothing is more clear than that the welfare of classes, as well as of individuals, is promoted by mutual acquaintance. The French and English, for a long time regarded as natural enemies, have at last, from a more intimate communion, found themselves to be natural friends. Prejudice is the child of ignorance. It is sure to prevail where people do not know each other. Society and intercourse are means established by Providence for human improvement. They remove antipathies, promote mutual adaptation and conciliation, and establish relations of reciprocal regard. Whoso sets up barriers to these, thwarts the ways of Providence, crosses the tendencies of human nature, and directly interferes with the laws of God.

May it please your Honors: Such are some of the things which it has occurred to me to say in this important cause. I have occupied much of your time, but I have not yet exhausted the topics. Still, which way soever we turn, we are brought back to one single proposition — *the Equality of men before the law.* This stands as the mighty guardian of the rights of the colored children in this case. It is the constant, ever-present, tutelary genius of this Commonwealth, frowning upon every privilege of birth, upon every distinction of race, upon every institution of Caste. You cannot slight it, or avoid it. You cannot restrain it. God grant that you may welcome it. Do this, and your words will be a "charter and freehold of rejoicing" to a race which, by much suffering, has earned a title to much regard. Your judgment will become a sacred landmark, not in jurisprudence only, but in the history of Freedom, giving precious encouragement to all the weary and heavy-laden wayfarers in this great cause. Massachusetts will then, through you, have a fresh title to regard, and be once more, as in times past, an example to the whole land.

You have already banished Slavery from this Commonwealth. I call upon you now to obliterate the last of its footprints, and to banish the last of the hateful spirits in its train, that can be reached by this Court. The law, interfering to prohibit marriages between blacks and whites, has been abolished by the Legislature. The railroads, which, imitating the Boston schools, placed colored people apart by themselves, have been compelled, under the influence of an awakened public sentiment, to abandon this regulation, and to allow them to mingle with other travellers. Only recently I have read that his Excellency, the present Governor of Massachusetts, took his seat in a train by the side of a negro. It is in the Caste schools of Boston that the prejudice of color has sought its final legal refuge. It is for you to drive it forth. You do well when you rebuke and correct individual offences; but it is a higher office far to rebuke and correct a vicious institution. Each individual is limited in his influence; but an institution has the influence of numbers organized by law. The charity of one man may counteract or remedy the uncharitableness of another; but no individual can counteract or remedy the uncharitableness of an established institution. Against it private benevolence is powerless. It is a monster which must be hunted down by the public, and by the constituted authorities. And such is the institution of Caste in the Public Schools of Boston, which now awaits its just condemnation from a just Court.

The civilization of the age joins in this appeal. It is well known that this prejudice of color is peculiar to our country. You have not forgotten that two youths of African blood only recently gained the highest honors in the college at Paris, and dined on the same day with the King of France, the descendant of St. Louis, at the Palace of the Tuileries. And let me add, if I may refer to my own experience, that in Paris, I have sat for weeks, at the School of Law, on the same benches with colored persons, listening, like myself, to the learned lectures of Degerando and of Rossi — the last is the eminent minister who has unhappily fallen beneath the dagger of a Roman assassin; nor do I remember observing in the throng of sensitive young men by whom they were surrounded, any feeling towards them except of companionship and respect. In Italy, at the Convent of Pallazuola, on the shores of the Alban Lake, and on the site of the ancient Alba Longa, I have seen, for several days, a native of Abyssinia, only recently conducted from his torrid home, and ignorant of the language that was spoken about him, yet mingling with the Franciscan friars, whose guest and scholar he was, in delightful and affectionate familiarity. In these examples may be discerned the Christian spirit.

And, finally, this spirit I invoke. Where this prevails, there is neither Jew nor Gentile, Greek nor barbarian, bond nor free; but all are alike. From this we derive new and solemn assurances of the Equality of mankind, as an ordinance of God. The bodies of men may be unequal in beauty or strength; these mortal cloaks of flesh may differ, as do these worldly garments; these intellectual faculties may vary, as do the opportunities of action and the advantages of position; but amidst all unessential differences there is an essential agreement and equality. Dives and Lazarus were equal in the sight of God. They must be equal in the sight of all just institutions.

But this is not all. The vaunted superiority of the white race imposes upon it corresponding duties. The faculties with which they are endowed, and the advantages which they possess, are to be exercised for the good of all. If the colored people are ignorant, degraded, and unhappy, then should they be the especial objects of your care. From the abundance of your possessions you must seek to remedy their lot. And this Court, which is as a parent to all the unfortunate children of the Commonwealth, will show itself most truly parental, when it reaches down, and, with the strong arm of the law, elevates, encourages, and protects its colored fellow-citizens.

REPORT ON THE LAW SCHOOL OF HARVARD UNIVERSITY; MADE IN BEHALF OF THE COMMITTEE OF THE OVERSEERS, FEB. 7, 1850.

In Board of Overseers, February 1, 1849.

Voted, That Hon. PELEG SPRAGUE, Hon. SIMON GREENLEAF, CHARLES SUMNER, Esq., Hon. ALBERT H. NELSON, and PELEG W. CHANDLER, Esq. be a Committee to visit the Law School during the ensuing year. [Hon. WILLIAM KENT was afterwards substituted for Mr. GREENLEAF, who declined.]

In Board of Overseers, February 7, 1850.

Ordered, That the Report of the Committee appointed to visit the Law School be printed.

Attest,

ALEXANDER YOUNG, *Secretary.*

THE Committee, appointed by the Overseers of Harvard University to visit the Law School, performed that service, Nov. 7, 1849. Among their number present on the occasion was Hon. WILLIAM KENT, of New York, who gratified his associates very much by coming a long distance to join in this duty.

The attention of the Committee was first directed to the actual condition of the School, and its advantages as a place of legal education. Here there was occasion for lively satisfaction. The number of students was one hundred, assembled from all parts of the Union, and constituting a representation of the whole country. Their attendance upon the lectures and other exercises, though entirely voluntary, had been full and regular; while their industry, good conduct, and intelligent reception of instruction, had been a source of peculiar pleasure to their professors.

Lectures had been given, during the current term, by Professor Parker, upon Equity Pleadings, Bailments, and Practice; by Professor Parsons, upon Blackstone's Commentaries, the Admiralty Jurisdiction, Shipping, Bills and Notes; and by Professor Allen, upon Real Law and Domestic Relations. In treating most of these branches, the professors adopted certain text-books, of acknowledged authority, — to which the attention of the students was especially directed, — as the basis of their remarks. They also examined the students in these books, and in the leading cases illustrating the subject.

This system of instruction, which, with substantial uniformity, has been continued in the School since its earliest nofndation, has shown itself well adapted to the end in view. It is essential that the student should be directed to certain text-books. These he must study carefully, devotedly; nor can he properly omit to go behind these, and verify them by the decided cases — letting no day pass without its fulfilled task. In this way he will be prepared for the examinations, and will be enabled to appreciate the explanations and illustrations of the lecture-room, throwing light upon the text, and showing its application to practical cases. The labors of the student will qualify him to comprehend the labors of the instructor. Still further, examinations in the text-books, accompanied by explanations and illustrations, help to interest the student in the subject, and to bring his mind directly in contact with the mind of his instructor.

These same purposes are also promoted by the favorite exercise of moot-courts, which are held twice a week, by the different professors in succession. A case, involving some unsettled question of law, is argued by four students, who have been designated so long previously as to allow time for careful preparation; and at the close of the arguments, an opinion is pronounced by the presiding professor, commenting upon the doctrines maintained on each side, and deciding between them. These occasions are found to enlist the best attention, not only of those immediately engaged in them, but of the whole school; while some of the efforts they call forth are said to show distinguished research and ability. Here, on this mimic field, are trained those forensic powers which are destined to be the pride and ornament of the bar.

We should not neglect to notice the advantages for study afforded by the extensive library of the Law School. This is separate from the Public Library of the University, and contains about fourteen thousand volumes. Here are found all the American Reports, and the Statutes of the United States, as well as those of all the States, a regular series of all the English Reports, including the Year-books, and also the English Statutes, as well as the principal treatises in American and English law; also a large body of works in the Scotch, French, German, Dutch, Spanish, Italian, and other foreign law; and an ample collection of the best editions of the Roman or Civil Law, with the works of the most celebrated commentators upon that ancient law. This library is one of the largest and most valuable, relating to law, to be found in the country. As an aid to study, it cannot be estimated too highly. Here the student may range at will through all the demesnes of jurisprudence. Here he may acquire a knowledge of the books of his profession, — learning their true character and value, — which will be of incalculable service to him in his future labors. Whoso knows how to use a library possesses the very keys of knowledge. Next to knowing the law, is knowing where the law is to be found.

There is another advantage of a peculiar character, afforded by the Law School, in the opportunity of kindly and instructive social relations among the students, and also between the students and their instructors. Young men, engaged in similar pursuits, are professors to each other. The daily conversation concerns their common studies, and contributes some new impulse. Mind meets mind, and each derives strength from the contact. But the instructor is also at hand. In the lecture-room, and also in private, he is ready to afford counsel and help. The students are not alone in their labors. They find an assistant at every step of their journey, ready to conduct them through its devious and toilsome passes, and to remove the difficulties which throng the way. This twofold companionship of the students with each other, and of the students with their instructors, is full of beneficent influences, not only in the cordial intercourse which it begets, but in the positive knowledge which it diffuses, and in its stimulating effect upon the minds of all who enjoy it.

In dwelling on the advantages of the Law School, as a seat of legal education, the Committee place side by side with the lectures and exercises of the professors, the profitable opportunities afforded by the library, and by the fellowship of persons engaged in the same pursuits; all echoing to the heart of the pupil, as from the genius of the place, constant words of succor, encouragement, and hope.

From the present prosperity of the School, the Committee have been led to look back to its early beginning, to observe its growth, and to commemorate with gratitude its benefactors.

It need hardly be added, that a Law School was not embraced by our forefathers in the original design of the College, and that it was ingrafted upon the ancient stock at quite a late period. The College was first planted at a time when the law was not treated, even in England, as a part of academic instruction. The first settlers of our country could not be expected to establish professorships unknown in the land from which they had parted; nor, indeed, in those early days, and for some time later, does there appear to have been occasion for instruction in the law. Indeed, the law, as a science, as a profession, or as a practical instrument of government, was scarcely observed. Lawyers were not known as a class, nor was their business respected. Mr. Lechford, of Clement's Inn, who had emigrated not long after the foundation of the College, — hoping to gain a livelihood as an attorney, — being cautioned at a quarter court "not to meddle with controversies," — returned again to England. But, as the Colony grew, it gradually laid hold of the common law, and, for some time before the Revolution, claimed this law as a birthright of the inhabitants.

The history of the Library of the University exposes the poverty of the means afforded in those early days for the study of the law. In its Catalogue, published in 1727, we find but *seven* volumes of the common law. These are Spelman's Glossary, Pulton's Collection of Statutes, Keble's Statutes, Coke's First and Second Institutes, and a couple of odd volumes of the Year-books. These were the means afforded for the study of our law by the library which Cotton Mather described, some time before the publication of this catalogue, as the "best furnished that could be shown any where in all the American regions." Since books are the very instruments of learning, it must follow, if these were wanting at Harvard College, that the study of the law could make little advance. Happily all this is now changed.

The first professorship of law in the University was established in 1815, upon a foundation partly supplied by an ancient devise of Isaac Royall, Esq.; — a munificent gentlemen of ample fortune, who, being connected by blood and marriage, as well as by political opinions, with the principal royalists of Massachusetts, forsook the country with them at the commencement of the Revolution, and died at Kensington in England, about the year 1781. Though an exile, he did not forget the land he had left. Thither "his heart untravelled fondly turned," before his death. By his will, recorded at the Probate Office in Boston, he devised to the town of Medford in Massachusetts, where he had resided, certain lands in Granby, for the support of schools. The residue of his estate in that town, and certain other lands in the county of Worcester, he devised to the Overseers and Corporation of Harvard College, "to be appropriated towards the endowing *a Professor of Laws in the said College*, or a Professor of Physic and Anatomy, whichever the said Overseers and Corporation shall judge to be best for the benefit of the said College." The capital, with its accumulation resulting from the property thus devised, is $7,943·63, yielding an annual income of about four hundred dollars. It is believed that the University and the lovers of the law are indebted to the late Hon. JOHN LOWELL, while a member of the Corporation of the University, for calling these funds — as yet unappropriated to either object of the devise — from their sleep in the treasury, by procuring the establishment of a professorship of law in 1815, which was ordered, for the present, to bear the name of *Royall*, in honor of him whose will was now first executed in this regard. The residue of the funds for its support have been hitherto supplied by the University, mainly from the fees paid by students of law. The Hon. ISAAC PARKER, late Chief Justice of this Commonwealth, was appointed the first professor.

In 1817, the Hon. ASAHEL STEARNS was placed upon another foundation, established by the University. The statutes of this professorship required him to open and keep a School in Cambridge, for the instruction of the graduates of the University, and of others prosecuting the study of the law; and, besides prescribing to his pupils a course of study, to examine and confer with them upon the subjects of their studies, to read to them a course of lectures, and generally to act the part of a tutor, so as to improve their minds, and assist their acquisitions. From this time may be dated the establishment of the Law School in the University.

Chief Justice Parker never resided at Cambridge, but in the performance of his duties as professor, was in the habit of reading a course of lectures every summer to the students of the Law School, and to the senior class of under-graduates. These were of an elementary nature, adapted to the youthful minds of his audience — the larger part of which belonged to the under-graduates — and were characterized by that free and flowing style which so eminently marks the judicial opinions of this Judge. They comprised a view of the Constitutions of the United States and of Massachusetts, with a particular notice of the early juridical history of New England, explaining the origin of its laws and institutions. Professor Stearns, who resided in Cambridge, was occupied more immediately with the duties of instruction in law. He was accustomed to hear recitations from the students of the School in the more important text-books, to preside in moot-courts, and to read lectures on various interesting titles of law. The valuable work on Real Actions, so well known by the lawyers of the country, was prepared by him in the discharge of his duties as professor, and read to his pupils in a course of lectures. The first edition was dedicated by the author "To the students of Harvard University, as a testimonial of his earnest desire to aid them in the honorable and laborious study of American jurisprudence."

The number who resorted to the Law School at this period was comparatively small. From 1817 to 1830, the largest class for any single year was eighteen, and the average annual number was not more than eight. The first important step, however, was taken. The law was admitted within the circle of University studies; while, by the learning and reputation of its professors, the cause of legal education was commended, and the idea of a Law School was shown to be practicable.

In 1829, Chief Justice Parker and Professor Stearns resigned their places, and a new epoch in the history of the School began. The Hon. NATHAN DANE, emulating the example of Viner in England, from the profits of his extensive Abridgment and Digest of American Law, established a new professorship, still called from his name; to which, according to his request, the late JOSEPH STORY, at that time a resident of Salem, and an Associate Justice of the Supreme Court, was appointed. In his communication to the University, appropriating the funds for this endowment, the venerable founder marked out the duties of the new station as follows: "It shall be the duty of the professor to prepare and deliver, and to revise for publication, a course of lectures on the five following branches of law and equity, equally in force in all parts of our Federal Republic, — namely, the law of nature, the law of nations, commercial and maritime law, federal law, and federal equity, — in such wide extent as the same branches now are, and from time to time, shall be, administered in the Courts of the

United States, but in such compressed form as the professor shall deem proper; and so to prepare, deliver, and revise lectures thereon, as often as the said Corporation shall think proper." The funds originally given by Mr. Dane amounted to $10,000, to which were added $5,000 on his death, making the sum total of his donation $15,000. Mr. Justice Story removed to Cambridge, and commenced his new career, as Dane Professor of Law, in August, 1829, with an inaugural discourse, in which the honorable nature of legal studies, the arduous labors required in their pursuit, and the duties upon which he was about to enter, were reviewed with singular power and beauty. At the same time, John Hooker Ashmun, Esq., a lawyer of remarkable acuteness and maturity, who, though young, had shown already the capacity of a great jurist, was associated with him as Royall Professor of Law.

The Law School, from the exertions of the new professors, received a fresh impulse. The number of students increased, and the fame of the institution was extended. Professor Story, though necessarily absent much in the discharge of his judicial labors, yet found time to take an active part in the duties of teaching. He presided in the moot-courts and lecture-rooms, and, by his earnest encouragements and profuse instructions, not less than by his illustrious example, warmed the classes with ardor in their studies. He continued in this sphere, giving and receiving happiness from his labors, for a period of sixteen years; when, desirous as age advanced to lay down some of his cares, he proposed to resign his seat on the bench, and dedicate the remainder of his days to his professorship. As he was about to make this change, he was arrested by death, Sept. 10, 1845.

Professor Ashmun had already fallen, much regretted, by his side, in 1833, at the early age of thirty-three. Besides the moot-courts, the examinations in the text-books, and oral expositions of the law, this learned teacher had occasionally read written lectures. Among these was a valuable course on Medical Jurisprudence, Equity, and the Action of Assumpsit. His place was supplied by an eminent jurist, Professor GREENLEAF, who labored for a long period with rare success, beloved by a large circle of grateful pupils, and by his associates in instruction, till 1848, when he was compelled by ill health to resign his connection with the Law School. Among his distinguished labors, in the discharge of his duties as professor, is a work on the Law of Evidence, which is now a manual in the courts of our country, and one of the classics of the common law.

Professor Greenleaf, on the death of Professor Story, was made Dane Professor. Hon. WILLIAM KENT, of New York, occupied for a year the place of Royall Professor, when he felt constrained by circumstances beyond his control, to return to New York. Since then, Hon. THEOPHILUS PARSONS has been Dane Professor; and Hon. JOEL PARKER, late Chief Justice of New Hampshire, Royall Professor. Hon. FRANKLIN DEXTER, for a brief period, has lectured on the Constitution of the United States, and the Law of Nations; and the Hon. LUTHER S. CUSHING, on Parliamentary Law and Criminal Law. Hon. FREDERICK H. ALLEN, late a Judge in Maine, as University Professor, without any permanent foundation, is at present coöperating with Professor Parsons and Professor Parker in the general duties of the School.

In reviewing the history of the School, the Committee, while remembering with grateful regard all its instructors, pause with veneration before the long and important labors of STORY. In the meridian of his fame as a Judge, he became a practical teacher of jurisprudence, and lent to the University the lustre of his name. The *Dane Professorship*, through him, has acquired a renown which places it on the same elevation with the *Vinerian Professorship* at Oxford, to which we are indebted for the Commentaries of Sir William Blackstone. These "twin stars" shine each in different hemispheres, but with rival glories. Nor is this the only parallel; for Viner, like our Dane, endowed the professorship, which bears his name, from the profits of his immense Abridgment of the Law. In the performance of his duties, Professor Story prepared and published the most important series of juridical works which have appeared in the English language in our age, embracing a comprehensive treatise on the Constitution of the United States, a masterly exposition of that portion of International Law known as the Conflict of Laws, and Commentaries on Equity Jurisprudence, Equity Pleading, and various branches of Commercial Law.

The character of his labors, and their influence upon the School, will appear from an interesting passage in his last will and testament, bearing date Jan. 2, 1842. After bequeathing to the University several valuable pictures, busts, and books, he proceeds as follows: "I ask the President and Fellows of Harvard College to accept them as memorials of my reverence and respect for that venerable institution at which I received my education. I hope it may not be improper for me here to add, that I have devoted myself as Dane Professor for the last thirteen years * to the labors and duties of instruction in the Law School, and have always performed equal duties and to an equal amount with my excellent colleagues, Mr. Professor Ashmun and Mr. Professor Greenleaf, in the Law School. When I came to Cambridge, and undertook the duties of my professorship, there had not been a single law student there for the preceding year. There was no law library, but a few old and imperfect books being there. The students have since increased to a large number, and, for six years last past, have exceeded one hundred a year. The Law Library now contains about six thousand volumes, whose value cannot be deemed less than twenty-five thousand dollars. My own salary has constantly remained limited to one thousand dollars, — a little more than the interest of Mr. Dane's donations. I have never asked or desired an increase thereof, as I was receiving a suitable salary as a Judge of the Supreme Court of the United States; while my colleagues have very properly received a much larger sum, and of late years more than double my own. Under these circumstances, I cannot but feel that I have contributed towards the advancement of the Law School a sum out of my earnings, which, with my

* At the time of his death it was sixteen years.

moderate means, will be thought to absolve me from making, what otherwise I certainly should do, a pecuniary legacy to Harvard College, for the general advancement of literature and learning therein."

It appears from the books of the Treasurer, that the sums received from students in the Law School, during the sixteen years of his professorship, amounted to $105,000. Of this sum, only $47,200 were spent in salaries, and other current expenses of the School. The balance, amounting to $57,200, is represented by the following items, viz.: —

Books purchased for the Library and for students, including about $1,950 for binding, and deducting the amount received for books sold	$29,000
For the enlargement of the Hall, containing the library and lecture-rooms, in 1844-45	12,700
The Fund remaining to the credit of the School in August, 1845	15,500
	$57,200

Thus it appears that the Law School, at the time of Professor Story's death, actually possessed, independent of the somewhat scanty donations of Mr. Royall and Mr. Dane, funds and other property, including a large library and a commodious edifice, amounting to upwards of *fifty-seven thousand dollars*, all of which had been earned during Professor Story's term of service. As he declined, during this time, to receive a larger annual salary than $1000, and as his high character and the attraction of his name doubtless contributed to swell the income of the School, it will be evident that a considerable portion of this large sum may justly be regarded as the fruit of his bountiful labors contributed to the University.

The Committee, while calling attention to the extent of the pecuniary benefaction which the Law School has received from Professor Story, have felt it their duty to urge upon the Government of the University the propriety of recognizing the benefaction in some suitable form. The name of Royall, attached to one of the professorships, keeps alive the memory of his early beneficence. The name of Dane, attached to the professorship on which Story taught, and sometimes to the edifice, containing the library and lecture-rooms, and also to the Law School itself, attests, with triple academic voice, a well-rewarded donation. But the contributions of Royall and Dane combined — important as they have been, and justly worthy of honorable mention — do not equal what has been contributed by Story. At the present moment, Story must be regarded as the largest pecuniary benefactor of the Law School, and one of the largest pecuniary benefactors of the University. In this respect, he stands before Hollis, Alford, Boylston, Hersey, Bowdoin, Erving, Eliot, Smith, M'Lean, Perkins and Fisher. His contributions have this additional peculiarity, that they were munificently afforded, — from his daily earnings,— not after death, but during his own life; so that he became, as it were, the executor of his own will. In justice to the dead, as an example to the living, and in conformity with established usage, the University should enroll his name among its founders, and inscribe it, in some fit manner, upon the School which he has helped to rear.

Three different courses have occurred to the Committee. The edifice containing the library and lecture-rooms may be called after him, *Story Hall.* Or the branch of the University devoted to law may be called the *Story Law School;* as the other branch of the University devoted to science is called, in gratitude to a distinguished benefactor, *Lawrence Scientific School.* Or, still further, a new and permanent professorship in the Law School may be created, bearing his name.

If the latter suggestion should find acceptance, the Committee recommend that the professorship be of *Commercial Law and the Law of Nations.* It is well known to have been the earnest desire of Professor Story, often expressed, in view of the increasing means of the Law School, and of the necessity of meeting the increasing demands for education in the law, that professorships of both these branches should be established. He regarded that of Commercial law as most needed. His own preëminence in this department is shown in his works, and especially in his numerous judicial opinions. And only a few days before his death, in conversation with one of this Committee, hearing that it had been proposed by some of the merchants of Boston, on his resignation of the seat which he had held on the bench for thirty-four years, to cause his statue in marble to be erected, he said, "If the merchants of Boston wish to do me honor in any way on my leaving the bench, let it not be by a statue, but by founding in the Law School a professorship of commercial law." With these generous words he embraced in his vows at once his favorite law, and his favorite University.

The subject of commercial law is of great and growing practical importance. Every new tie of commerce, in the multiplying relations of mankind, gives new occasion for its application. Besides the general principles of the law of Contracts, it comprehends the law of Bailments, Agency, Partnership, Bills of Exchange and Promissory Notes, Shipping and Insurance; — branches of inexpressible interest to the lawyer, the merchant, and indeed to every citizen. The main features of this law are common to all commercial nations: they are recognized with substantial uniformity, whether at Boston, London, or Calcutta; at Hamburg, Marseilles, or Leghorn. In this respect, they may be regarded as a part of the *private* Law of Nations. They would be associated naturally with the Public Law of Nations; embracing, of course, the Law of Admiralty, and that other branch which, it is hoped, will remain for ever, a dead letter, — the Law of Prize.

The Committee believe that all who hear this statement will agree, that something ought to be done to commemorate the obligation of the University to one of its most eminent professors and largest pecuniary benefactors. They have ventured to make suggestions with regard to the manner in which this may be accomplished, not with any pertinacious confidence in their own views, but simply as a mode of opening the subject, and bringing it to your best attention. In dwelling on the propriety of creating a new and permanent professorship, they do not wish to be understood as expressing a preference for this form of acknowledgment. It may well be a question, whether the services of Professor Story, — important in every respect, — shedding upon the Law School a lasting fame, and securing to it pecuniary competence, an extensive library, and a commodious hall,— can be commemorated with more appropriate academic honors, than by giving his name to that department in the University of which he has been the truest founder. The world, in advance of any formal action of the University, has already placed the Law School in the illumination of his name. It is by the name of STORY that this seat of legal education has become known wherever jurisprudence is cultivated as a science. By his name it has been crowned abroad.

For the Committee,

CHARLES SUMNER.

To the Overseers of Harvard University.

SPEECH ON OUR PRESENT ANTI-SLAVERY DUTIES, AT THE FREE SOIL STATE CONVENTION IN BOSTON, OCT. 3, 1850.

Mr. President:

I had hoped to-day to mingle in the business of the Convention, and to listen to others, without occupying your time by any words of mine. Indeed, when I left our meeting at its adjournment this forenoon, I did not count upon being here this afternoon; but let me say frankly, I was uneasy away — I felt that I ought to be with you — I yielded to the attractions of the cause, which has drawn us together, and here I am, answering to your call, and most grateful for this kind reception.

Let me, without delay, touch upon some topics which seem important to be borne in mind. The session of Congress, so long drawn out, has at last closed; and its members are now hurrying to their homes, to taste a brief respite from legislative labors. It becomes us to consider what has been done, and to endeavor, by an inquiry into the existing state of things, to discern our present duties. "Watchman, what of the night?" And well may the question be asked, "What of the night?" For things have occurred, and measures have passed into laws, which, to my mind, fill the day itself with blackness.

And yet there are streaks of light — an unwonted dawn — in the distant West, out of which a full-orbed sun is beginning to ascend, rejoicing like a strong man to run his race. *Video solem orientem in occidente.* By an Act of the recent Congress, California, with a Constitution forbidding Slavery, adopted in the exercise of its sovereignty as a State, has been admitted into the Union. For a measure like this, required not only by the simplest justice, but by the uniform practice of the country, and the constitutional principles of the slave-holders themselves, we may well be ashamed to confess our gratitude; and yet I cannot but rejoice in this great good accomplished. A hateful institution, which thus far, without check, had travelled with the power of the Republic, westward, is bidden to stop, and a new and rising State guarded from its contamination. Freedom — in whose hands is the divining rod, of magical power, pointing the way, not only to wealth untold, but to every possession of virtue and intelligence — whose presence is better far than any mine of gold — is now at last established in an extensive region on the distant Pacific, between the very parallels of latitude so long claimed by Slavery as its peculiar home.

Here is a moral and political victory; a moral victory, inasmuch as Freedom has secured a new foothold, where to exert her far-reaching influence; a political victory also, inasmuch as by the admission of

California, the Free States have obtained a majority of votes in the Senate, and the *balance of power*, between Freedom and Slavery — so preposterously claimed by the Slave States, in forgetfulness of the true spirit of the Constitution, and in mockery of Human Rights — has been overturned. May free California, and her Senators in Congress, never fail hereafter, amidst the trials before us, in loyalty to Freedom! God forbid that the daughter should turn, with ingratitude or neglect, from the mother that bore her!

Besides this Act, there are two others of this long session, which may be regarded with satisfaction, and which I mention at once, before considering the reverse of the picture. The Slave trade has been abolished in the District of Columbia. This measure, though small in the sight of Justice, is most important. It banishes from the National Capital an odious traffic. But this is its least office. It practically affixes to the whole traffic, wherever it exists — not merely in Washington, within the immediate sphere of the legislative act — but every where throughout the Slave States, whether at Richmond, or Charleston, or New Orleans, the brand of Congressional reprobation. Yes! The people of the United States, by the voice of Congress, have solemnly declared the domestic traffic in slaves to be offensive in their sight. The Nation has judged this traffic. The Nation has said to it, "Get thee behind me, Satan." It is true that Congress has not, as in the case of the foreign slave trade, stamped it as *piracy*, and awarded to its perpetrators the doom of *pirates;* but it condemns the trade, and gives to general scorn those who partake of it. To this extent the

Federal Government has spoken for Freedom. And, in doing this, it has asserted, under the Constitution of the United States, legislative jurisdiction over the subject of Slavery in the District; thus preparing the way for that complete act of Abolition, which is necessary to purge the National Capital of its still remaining curse and shame.

The other measure, which I must hail with thankfulness, is the Abolition of Flogging in the Navy. Beyond the direct reform thus accomplished — after much effort, finally crowned by encouraging success — is the indirect influence of this law, especially in rebuking the use of the lash, wheresoever and by whomsoever employed!

Thus two props and stays of Slavery, wherever it exists in our country, have been weakened and undermined by Congressional legislation. Without the *slave-trade* and the *lash*, Slavery must fall to the earth. By these, the whole hideous monstrosity is upheld. If I seem to exaggerate the consequence of these measures of Abolition, let it be referred to my sincere conviction of their powerful, though subtle and indirect influence, and also to my desire to find something of good in a Congress which has furnished occasion for so much of disappointment. There are other measures, which must be regarded, not only with regret, but with indignation and disgust.

Two broad territories, New Mexico and Utah, under the exclusive jurisdiction of Congress, have been organized without any prohibition of Slavery. In laying the foundation of their governments, destined hereafter to control the happiness of innumerable multitudes, Congress has omitted the Great Ordinance of Freedom, first suggested by Jefferson, and consecrated by the experience of the North-Western Territory; it has neglected to recognize those principles of Human Liberty, which are enunciated in our Declaration of Independence, — which are essential to every Bill of Rights — and without which a Republic is a name, and nothing more.

Still further, a vast territory, supposed to be upwards of seventy thousand square miles in extent, larger than all New England, has been taken from New Mexico, and with ten million dollars besides, given to slaveholding Texas; thus, under the plea of settling the Western boundary of Texas, securing to this State a large sum of money, and consigning to certain Slavery an important territory.

And still further, as if to do a deed, which should "make heaven weep, all earth amazed," this same Congress, in disregard of all the cherished safeguards of Freedom, has passed a most cruel, unchristian, devilish law to secure the return into Slavery of those fortunate bondmen, who have found shelter by our firesides. This is the Fugitive Slave Bill — a bill which despoils the party claimed as a slave — whether he be in reality a slave or a freeman — of the sacred right of Trial by Jury, and commits the question of Human Freedom — the highest question known by the law — to the unaided judgment of a single magistrate, on *ex parte* evidence it may be, by affidavits, without the sanction of cross-examination. Under this detestable, heaven-defying bill, not the slave only, but the colored freeman of the

North, may be swept into ruthless captivity; and there is no white citizen, born among us, bred in our schools, partaking in our affairs, voting in our elections, whose Liberty is not assailed also. Without any discrimination of color, the Bill surrenders all, who may be claimed as "owing service or labor," to the same tyrannical judgment. And mark once more its heathenism. By unrelenting provisions it visits, with bitter penalties of fine and imprisonment, the faithful men and women, who may render to the fugitive that countenance, succor and shelter, which Christianity expressly requires! Thus, from beginning to end, it sets at naught the best principles of the Constitution, and the very laws of God!

I might occupy your time by exposing the unconstitutionality of this act. In denying the Trial by Jury, it is three times unconstitutional; first, as the Constitution declares "The right of the people to be secure in their persons against *unreasonable seizures;*" secondly, as it further declares, that "No person shall be deprived of life, *liberty*, or property *without due process of law;*" and, thirdly, because it expressly declares, that "In suits at common law, where the value in controversy shall exceed twenty dollars, *the right of trial by jury shall be preserved.*" By this triple cord did the framers of the Constitution secure the Trial by Jury in every question of Human Freedom. That man can be little imbued with the true spirit of American institutions — he can have little sympathy with Bills of Rights — he must be lukewarm for Freedom, who can hesitate to construe the Constitution so as to secure this safeguard.

The act is again unconstitutional in the unprecedented and tyrannical powers which it confers upon Commissioners. These officers are appointed, not by the President with the advice of the Senate, but by the Courts of Law; they hold their places, not during good behavior, but at the will of the Court; and they receive for their services, not a regular salary, but fees in each individual case. And yet in these officers, — thus appointed and compensated, and holding their places by the most uncertain tenure — is vested a portion of that "judicial power," which, according to the express words of the Constitution, can be in "Judges" only, who hold their offices "during good behavior," who, "at stated times, receive for their services a compensation, which shall not be diminished during their continuance in office," and, it would seem also, who are appointed by the President and confirmed by the Senate. And, adding meanness to the violation of the Constitution, the Commissioner is bribed by a double fee, to pronounce against Freedom. If he dooms a man to slavery, he receives ten dollars; but if he saves him, his fee is five dollars.

But I will not pursue these details. The soul sickens in the contemplation of this legalized outrage. In the dreary annals of the Past, there are many acts of shame — there are ordinances of monarchs, and laws, which have become a bye-word and a hissing to the nations. But, *when we consider the country and the age*, I ask fearlessly, What act of shame, what ordinance of monarch, what law can compare in atrocity, with this enactment of an American Congress? I do not forget Appius Claudius, the tyrant decemvir of ancient Rome, condemning Virginia as a slave; nor Louis XIV. of France, letting slip the dogs of religious persecution by the revocation of the edict of Nantes; nor Charles I. of England, arousing the patriot rage of Hampden, by the extortion of Ship-money; nor the British Parliament, provoking, in our own country, spirits kindred to Hampden, by the tyranny of the Stamp Act and Tea Tax. I would not exaggerate; I wish to keep within bounds; but I think no person can doubt that the condemnation now affixed to all these transactions, and to their authors, must be the lot hereafter of the Fugitive Slave Bill, and of every one, according to the measure of his influence, who gave it his support. Into the immortal catalogue of national crimes this has now passed, drawing with it, by an inexorable necessity, its authors also, and chiefly him, who, as President of the United States, set his name to the Bill, and breathed into it that final breath, without which it would have no life. Other Presidents may be forgotten; but the name signed to the Fugitive Slave Bill can never be forgotten. There are depths of infamy, as there are heights of fame. I regret to say what I must; but truth compels me. Better far for him had he never been born; better far for his memory, and for the good name of his children, had he never been President!

I have already likened this Bill to the Stamp Act, and I trust that the parallel may be continued yet further by a burst of popular feeling against all action under it, similar to that which glowed in the breasts of our fathers. Listen to the words of John Adams, as written in his Diary for the time: —

The year 1765 has been the most remarkable year of my life. That enormous engine, fabricated by the British Parliament, for battering down all the rights and liberties of America, — I mean the Stamp Act, — has raised and spread through the whole continent a spirit that will be recorded to our honor with all future generations. In every colony, from Georgia to New Hampshire inclusively, the stamp distributors and inspectors have been compelled by the unconquerable rage of the people to renounce their offices. Such and so universal has been the resentment of the people, that every man who has dared to speak in favor of the stamps, or to soften the detestation in which they are held, how great soever his abilities and virtues had been esteemed before, or whatever his fortune, connections, and influence had been, has been seen to sink into universal contempt and ignominy.

Surely the love of Freedom cannot have so far cooled among us, the descendants of those who opposed the Stamp Act, that we are insensible to the Fugitive Slave Bill. The unconquerable rage of the people, in those other days, compelled the stamp distributors and inspectors to renounce their offices, and held up to detestation all who dared to speak in favor of the stamps. And shall we be more tolerant of those who volunteer in favor of this Bill — more tolerant of the Slave-Hunter, who, under its safeguard, pursues his prey upon our soil? The Stamp Act could not be executed here. Can the Fugitive Slave Bill?

And here, Sir, let me say, that it becomes me to speak with peculiar caution. It happens to me to sustain an important relation to this Bill. Early in professional life I was designated by the late Mr. Justice Story one of the Commissioners of the Courts of the United States, and, though I have not very often exercised the functions of this post, yet my name is still upon the lists. As such I am one of those before whom, under the recent Act of Congress, the panting fugitive may be brought for the decision of the question, whether he is a freeman or a slave. But while it becomes me to speak with caution, I shall not hesitate to speak with plainness. I cannot forget that I am a *man*, although I am a *Commissioner*.

Did the same spirit which inspired the fathers inspire our community now, the marshals — and every *magistrate* who regarded this law as having any constitutional obligation — would resign rather than presume to execute it. This, however, is too much to expect from all at present. But I will not judge them. To their own consciences I leave them. Surely, no person of humane feelings, and with any true sense of justice — living in a land "where bells have knolled to church" — whatever may be the apology of public station, could fail to recoil from such service. For myself let me say, that I can imagine no office, no salary, no consideration, which I would not gladly forego, rather than become in any way an agent in enslaving my brother-man. Where for me would be comfort and solace, after such a work! In dreams and in waking hours, in solitude and in the street, in the meditations of the closet, and in the affairs of men, wherever I turned, there my victim would stare me in the face; from the distant rice-fields and sugar plantations of the South, his cries beneath the vindictive lash, his moans at the thought of Liberty once his, now alas! ravished from him, would pursue me, repeating the tale of his fearful doom, and sounding, forever sounding, in my ears, "Thou art the man!"

The magistrate who pronounces the decree of slavery, and the marshal who enforces it, act in obedience to law. This is their apology; and it is also the apology of the masters of the Inquisition, as they ply the torture amidst the shrieks of their victim. But can this weaken our accountability for an act of wrong? Disguise it, excuse it as you will, the fact must glare before the world and penetrate the conscience too, that the fetters and chains, by which the unhappy fugitive is bound, are riveted by their tribunal — that his second life of wretchedness dates from their agency — that his second birth as a slave proceeds from *them.* The magistrate and marshal of the United States do for him here, in a country, which vaunts a Christian civilization, what the naked, barbarous Pagan chiefs, beyond the sea, did for his grandfather in Congo; *they transfer him to the Slave-Hunter*, and for this service receive the very price paid for his grandfather in Congo — *ten dollars!*

Gracious Heaven! Can such things be on our Free Soil! Shall the evasion of Pontius Pilate be enacted anew, and a Judge vainly attempt, by washing his hands, to excuse himself for condemning one in whom he can "find no fault!" Should any Court, sitting here in Massachusetts, for the first time in her history, become the agent of a Slave-Hunter, the very images of our fathers would frown from the walls; their voices would cry from the ground; their spirits would hover in the air, pleading, remonstrating, protesting, against the cruel judgment. There is a legend of Venice, consecrated by the pencil of one of her greatest artists, that the Apostle St. Mark suddenly descended into the public square, and broke the manacles of a slave, even before the Judge who had decreed his doom. Should Massachusetts be ever desecrated by such a judgment, may the good Apostle, with valiant arm, once more descend to break the manacles of the Slave!

Sir, I will not dishonor this home of the Pilgrims, and of the Revolution, by admitting — nay, *I cannot believe — that this Bill will be executed here.* Individuals among us, as elsewhere, may forget humanity in a fancied loyalty to law; but the public conscience will not allow a man, who has trodden our streets as a freeman, to be dragged away as a slave. By his escape from bondage, he has shown that true manhood, which must grapple to him every honest heart. He may be ignorant, and rude, as he is poor, but he is of a true nobility. The Fugitive Slaves of the United States are among the heroes of our age. In sacrificing them to this foul enactment of Congress, we should violate every sentiment of hospitality, every whispering of the heart, every dictate of religion.

There are many who will never shrink at any cost, and, notwithstanding all the atrocious penalties of this Bill, from efforts to save a wandering fellow-man from bondage; they will offer him the shelter of their houses, and, if need be, will protect his liberty by force. But let me be understood; I counsel no violence. There is another power — stronger than any individual arm — which I invoke; I mean that invincible Public Opinion, inspired by love of God and man, which, without violence or noise, gently as the operations of nature, makes and unmakes laws. Let this opinion be felt in its Christian might, and the Fugitive

Slave Bill will become every where upon our soil a dead letter. No lawyer will aid it by counsel; no citizen will become its agent; it will die of inanition — like a spider beneath an exhausted receiver. Oh! it were well the tidings should spread throughout the land, that here in Massachusetts this accursed Bill has found no *servants.* "Sire, I have found in Bayonne honest citizens and brave soldiers only; *but not one executioner*," was the reply of the governor of that place, to the royal mandate from Charles IX. of France, ordering the Massacre of St. Bartholomew.

But it rests with you, my fellow-citizens, by your words and your example, by your calm determinations, and your devoted lives, to do this work. From a humane, just, and religious people, shall spring a Public Opinion, to keep perpetual guard over the liberties of all within our borders. Nay, more, like the flaming sword of the cherubim at the gates of Paradise, turning on every side, it shall prevent any SLAVE-HUNTER from ever setting foot in this Commonwealth. Elsewhere, he may pursue his human prey; he may employ his congenial bloodhounds, and exult in his successful game. But into Massachusetts he must not come. And yet again I say, I counsel no violence. I would not touch his person. Not with whips and thongs would I scourge him from the land. The contempt, the indignation, the abhorrence of the community shall be our weapons of offence. Wherever he moves, he shall find no house to receive him — no table spread to nourish him — no welcome to cheer him. The dismal lot of the Roman exile shall be his. He shall be a wanderer, without *roof, fire, or water.*

Men shall point at him in the streets, and on the highways;

> Sleep, shall neither night nor day,
> Hang upon his pent-house lid;
> He shall live a man forbid.
> Weary seven nights, nine times nine,
> Shall he dwindle, peak and pine.

The villages, towns and cities shall refuse to receive the monster; they shall vomit him forth, never again to disturb the repose of our community.

The feelings, with which we regard the Slave-Hunter, will soon be extended also to all the mercenary agents, and heartless minions, who, without any positive obligation of law, became a part of his pack. They are *volunteers*, and, as such, should share the ignominy of the chief Hunter.

I have dwelt thus long upon the Fugitive Slave Bill, chiefly in the hope of contributing something to the creation of that Public Opinion, which in the Free States is destined to be the truest defence of the slave. I now advance to our more general duties.

We have seen what Congress has done. And yet in the face of these enormities of legislation — of this organization of the territories without the prohibition of Slavery; of the surrender of a large province to Texas and Slavery; and of this execrable Fugitive Slave Bill; in the face also of Slavery still sanctioned in the District of Columbia; of the Slave-trade between domestic ports under the flag of the Union; and in the face of the Slave Power still dominant over the Government of the country, we are told that the Slavery Question is settled. Yes: settled — settled — that is the word. *Nothing, Sir, can be settled, which is not right.* Nothing can be settled, which is adverse to Freedom. Nothing can be settled, which is contrary to the precepts of Christianity. God, nature, and all the holy sentiments of the heart, repudiate any such false seeming settlement.

Amidst the shifts and changes of party our DUTIES remain, pointing the way to action. By no subtle compromise or adjustment can men suspend the commandments of God. By no trick of managers, no hocus-pocus of politicians, no " mush of concession " can we be released from this obedience. It is, then, in the light of our duties, that we are to find true peace, at once for our country, and ourselves. Nor can any settlement promise peace, which is not in harmony with those divine principles from which our duties spring.

In unfolding these I shall be brief. Slavery is wrong. It is the source of unnumbered woes; not the least of which is its influence on the Slave-holder himself, in rendering him insensible to its outrage. It overflows with injustice and inhumanity. Language toils in vain to picture the wretchedness and wickedness, which it sanctions and perpetuates. Reason revolts at the impious assumption, that man can hold property in man. As it is our perpetual duty to oppose wrong, so must we oppose Slavery; nor can we ever relax in this opposition so long as the giant evil continues any where within the sphere of our influence. *Especially must we oppose it, wherever we are responsible for its existence, or are in any way parties to it.*

And now mark the distinction. The testimony which we bear against Slavery, as against all other wrong is, in different ways, according to our position. The Slavery, which exists under other governments — as in Russia or Turkey; or in other States of our Union — as in Virginia and Carolina — we can oppose only through the influence of morals and religion, without in any may invoking the Political Power. Nor do we propose to act otherwise. But Slavery, wherever we are responsible for it, wherever we are parties to it, must be opposed, not only by all the influences of morals and religion, but directly by every instrument of Political Power. As it is sustained by law, it can only be overthrown by law; and the legislature, in which is lodged the jurisdiction over it, must be moved to undertake the work. I am sorry to confess that this can be done, only through the machinery of politics. The politician, then, must be summoned. The moralist, the philanthropist must become for this purpose a politician; not forgetting his morals or his philanthropy, but seeking to apply them practically in the laws of the land.

It is a mistake to say, as is often charged, that we seek to interfere, through Congress, with Slavery in the States, or in any way to direct the legislation of Congress upon subjects not within its jurisdiction. Our *political* aims, as well as our *political* duties, are coextensive with our *political* responsibilities. And since we at the North are responsible for Slavery, wherever it exists under the jurisdiction of Congress, it is unpardonable in us not to exert every power we possess to enlist Congress against it.

Looking at details; —

We demand, first and foremost, the instant Repeal of the Fugitive Slave Bill.

We demand the Abolition of Slavery in the District of Columbia.

We demand the exercise by Congress, in all Territories, of its time-honored power to prohibit Slavery.

We demand of Congress to refuse to receive into the Union, any new Slave State.

We demand the Abolition of the domestic slave-trade, so far as it can be constitutionally reached; but particularly on the high seas under the National Flag.

And, generally, we demand from the Federal Government the exercise of all its constitutional power to relieve itself from responsibility for Slavery.

And yet one thing further must be done. The Slave Power must be overturned; so that the Federal Government may be put openly, actively and perpetually on the side of Freedom.

In demanding the overthrow of the Slave Power, we but seek to exclude from the operations of the Federal Government a *political* influence, — having its origin in Slavery, — which has been more potent, sinister, and mischievous, than any other in our history. This Power, though unknown to the Constitution, and existing in defiance of its true spirit, now predominates over Congress, gives the tone to its proceedings, seeks to control all our public affairs, and humbles both the great political parties to its will. It is that combination of Slave-Masters, whose bond of union is a common interest in Slavery. Time would fail me in exposing the extent to which its influence has been felt — the undue share of offices which it has enjoyed, — and the succession of its evil deeds. Suffice it to say, that, for a long period, the real principle of this union was not observed by the Free States. In the game of office and legislation, the South has always won. It has played with loaded dice — *loaded with Slavery*. Like the Automaton Chess-Player, it has never failed to be conqueror. Let the Free States make a move on the board, and the South has said "Check." Let them strive for Free Trade, as they did once, and the cry has been "Check." Let them jump towards Protection, and it is again "Check." Let them move towards Internal Improvements, and the cry is still "Check." Whether forwards or backwards, to the right or left, wherever they moved, the Free States have been pursued by an inexorable "Check." But the secret is now discovered. Amidst the well-arranged machinery, which seemed to give motion to the victorious chess-player, there was concealed a *motive force*, which has not been estimated — the Slave Power. It is the Slave Power, which has been the perpetual victor, saying always "Check" to the Free States. As this influence is now disclosed, it only remains that it should be openly encountered in the field of *politics*.

Such is our cause. It is not sectional; for it simply aims to establish under the Federal Government the great principles of Justice and Humanity, which are as broad and universal as man. It is not aggressive, for it does not seek in any way to interfere, through Congress, with Slavery in the States. It is not contrary to the Constitution; for it recognizes this instrument, and, in the administration of the Government, invokes the spirit of its founders. It is not hostile to the quiet of the country; for it proposes the only course by which agitation can be allayed, and quiet be permanently established. And yet the attempt is made to suppress this cause, and to stifle its discussion.

Vain and wretched attempt! The important subject, which more than all other subjects needs careful, conscientious and kind consideration in the national counsels — which will not admit of postponement or hesitation — which is connected with most of the great interests of the country — which controls the tariff, and causes war — which concerns alike all parts of the land, the North and the South, the East and the West — which affects the good name of the United States in the family of civilized nations — the *subject of subjects* — has been now at last, after many struggles, admitted within the pale of legislative discussion. From this time forward it will be entertained by Congress. It will be, as it were, one of the orders of the day. It cannot be passed over or forgotten. It cannot be blinked out of sight. The combinations of party cannot remove it. The intrigues of politicians cannot jostle it aside. There it is, in its colossal proportions, in the very Halls of the Capitol, overshadowing and darkening all other subjects. There it will continue, till driven into oblivion by the irresistible Genius of Freedom.

I am not blind to the adverse signs. The wave of reaction, which, during the last year swept over Europe, has reached our shores. The very barriers of Human Rights have been broken down. Statesmen, writers, scholars, speakers, once their uncompromising professors, have became the professors of compromise. All this must be changed. Reaction must be stayed. The country must be aroused. The cause must again be pressed — with the avowed purpose never to moderate our efforts until crowned by success. The Federal Government, every where within its proper constitutional sphere, must be placed on the side of Freedom. The policy of Slavery which has so long prevailed, must give place to the policy of Freedom. The Slave-Power, the fruitful parent of national ills, must be driven from its supremacy. Until all this is done, the friends of the Constitution and of Human Rights cannot cease from their labors; nor can the country hope for any repose, but the repose of submission.

Let men of all parties and pursuits, who wish well to their country, and would preserve its good name, join in these labors. Welcome here to the Conservative and to the Reformer; for our cause stands on the truest Conservatism and the truest Reform. In seeking the reform of existing evils, we seek also the conservation of the principles of our fathers. Welcome especially to the young. To you I appeal with confidence. Trust to your generous impulses, and to that reasoning of the heart, which is often truer, as it is less selfish, than the calculations of the brain. Do not exchange your aspirations for the skepticism of age. Yours is the better part. In the Scriptures it is said, that "the young men shall see visions, and the old men shall dream dreams;" on which Lord Bacon has aptly remarked, that the palm is given to the young men, inasmuch as it is higher to see visions than to dream dreams.

It is not uncommon to hear persons declare that they are against Slavery, and are willing to unite in any *practical* efforts to make this opposition felt. At the same time they pharisaically visit with condemnation, with reproach, or contempt, all the earnest souls that for years have striven in this struggle. To such I would say, if you are sincere in what you declare; if your words are not merely lip-service; if in your heart you are entirely willing to join in any practical efforts against Slavery, then, by your lives, by your conversation, by your influence, by your votes — disregarding "the ancient forms of party strife" — seek to carry the principles of Freedom into the Federal Government, wherever its jurisdiction is acknowledged, and its power can be felt. Thus, without any interference with the States, which are beyond this jurisdiction, may you help to erase the blot of Slavery from our National brow.

Do this, and you will most truly promote that harmony, which you so much desire. You will establish tranquillity throughout the country. Then at last the Slavery Question will be settled. Banished from its usurped foothold under the Federal Government, Slavery will no longer enter, with distracting force, into the national politics — making and unmaking laws, making and unmaking Presidents. Confined to the States, where it was left by the Constitution, it will take its place as a local institution, for which we are in no sense responsible, and against which we cannot justly exert any political power. We shall be relieved from our present painful and irritating connection with it; the existing antagonism between the South and the

North will be softened; crimination and recrimination will cease; the wishes of our fathers will be fulfilled; and this Great Evil will be left to the kindly influences of morals and religion.

To every laborer in a cause like this, there are satisfactions unknown to the common political partisan. Amidst all apparent reverses — notwithstanding the hatred of enemies, or the coldness of friends — he has the consciousness of duty done. Whatever may be existing impediments, his also is the cheering conviction, that every word spoken, every act performed, every vote cast for this cause, helps to swell those quickening influences by which Truth, Justice and Humanity will be established upon earth. He may not live to witness the blessed consummation. But it is none the less certain. Others may dwell on the Past, as secure. Under the laws of a beneficent God, *the Future also is secure* — on the single condition that we labor for its great objects.

The language of jubilee, which, amidst reverses and discouragements, burst from the soul of Milton, at the thought of sacrifices for the Church, will be echoed by every one who toils and suffers for Freedom. "Now by this little diligence," says the great patriot of the English Commonwealth, "mark what a privilege with good men and saints, to claim my right of lamenting the tribulations of the Church, if it should suffer, *when others, that have ventured nothing for her sake, have not the honor to be admitted mourners.* But if she lift up her drooping head and prosper, among those that have something more than wished her well, I have my charter and freehold of rejoicing to me and my heirs."

I have spoken of votes. Living in a community where political power is lodged with the people, and where each citizen is an elector, the vote is an important expression of our opinions. The vote is the cutting edge. It is well to have correct opinions; but the vote must follow. The vote is the seed planted; without it there can be no sure fruit. The winds of heaven may in their beneficence scatter the seed in the furrow; but it is not from such accidents that our fields wave with the golden harvest. He is a foolish husbandman who neglects to sow his seed; and he is an unwise citizen, who, desiring the spread of certain principles, neglects to deposit his vote for the candidates who are the representatives of those principles.

Admonished by experience of the timidity, the irresolution, the want of firmness in our public men, particularly at Washington, amidst the temptations of ambition and power, the friends of Freedom cannot lightly bestow their confidence. They can put trust in men only of tried character and inflexible will. Three things at least they must require; the first is *back-bone;* the second is *back-bone;* and the third is *back-bone.* My language is homely; I hardly pardon myself for using it; but it expresses an idea which I would not have forgotten. When I see a person of upright character and pure soul, yielding to a temporizing policy, I cannot but say, *he wants a back-bone.* When I see a person, talking loudly in private against Slavery, but hesitating in public, and failing in the time of trial, I say *he wants a back-bone.* When I see a person, who coöperated with Anti-Slavery men, and then deserted them, I say *he wants a back-bone.* When I see a person, leaning implicitly upon the action of a political party, and never venturing to think for himself, I say *he wants a back-bone.* When I see a person, careful always to be on the side of the majority, and unwilling to appear in a small minority, or, if need be, to stand alone, I say also, *he wants a back-bone.* Wanting this, they all want that courage, constancy, firmness, which are essential to the support of PRINCIPLE. Let no such men be trusted.

For myself, fellow-citizens, my own course is determined. The first political convention which I ever attended was in the spring of 1845, against the annexation of Texas. I was at that time a silent and passive Whig. I had never held any political office, nor been a candidate for any. No question had ever before drawn me to any active political exertions. The strife of politics had seemed ignoble to me. My desire to do what I could against Slavery, led me subsequently to attend two different State Conventions of Whigs, where I coöperated with several eminent citizens in endeavors to arouse the party in Massachusetts to its duties on this subject. A conviction of the disloyalty of the Whig party to Freedom, and an ardent aspiration to contribute something to the advancement of this great cause, led me to leave that party, and to dedicate what of strength and ability I could command to the present Movement.

To vindicate Freedom, and to oppose Slavery, so far as I might constitutionally — with earnestness, and yet, I trust, without any personal unkindness on my part — has been the object near my heart. Would that I could impress upon all who now hear me something of the strength of my own conviction of the importance of this work! Would that my voice, leaving this crowded hall to-night, could traverse the hills and valleys of New England, — that it could run along the rivers and the lakes of my country, — lighting in every humane heart a beacon-flame to arouse the slumberers throughout the land. In this cause I care not for the name by which I may be called. Let it be democrat, or "loco-foco," if you please. No man who is in earnest will hesitate on account of a name. I shall rejoice in any associates from any quarter, and shall ever be found with that party which most truly represents the principles of Freedom. Others may become indifferent to these principles, bartering them for political success, vain and short-lived, or forgetting the visions of youth in the dreams of age. Whenever I shall forget them, whenever I shall become indifferent to them, whenever I shall cease to be constant in maintaining them, through good report and evil report, in any future combinations of party, then may my tongue cleave to the roof of my mouth, may my right hand forget its cunning!

THREE TRIBUTES OF FRIENDSHIP.

HON. JOSEPH STORY.

[FROM THE BOSTON DAILY ADVERTISER, SEPT. 16, 1845.]

I HAVE just returned from the last sad ceremony of the interment of this great and good man. Under that roof, where I have so often seen him in health, buoyant with life, exuberant in kindness, happy in family and friends, I gazed upon his mortal remains, sunk in eternal rest, and hung over those features, to which my regards had been turned so fondly, and from which even the icy touch of death had not effaced all the living beauty. The eye was quenched, and the glow of life extinguished; but the noble brow seemed still to shelter, as under a marble dome, the spirit that had fled. And is he, indeed, dead, I asked myself,—he whose face was never turned to me, except in kindness; who has filled the civilized world with his name; who has drawn to his country the homage of foreign nations; who was of activity and labor that knew no rest; who was connected by duties of such various kinds, by official ties, by sympathy, by friendship and love, with so many circles; who, according to the beautiful expression of Wilberforce, "touched life at so many points," — has he, indeed, passed away? Upon the small plate, on the coffin was inscribed, "Joseph Story, died September 10th, 1845, aged 66 years." These few words might apply to the lowly citizen, as to the illustrious Judge. Thus is the coffin-plate a register of the equality of man.

At the house of the deceased we joined in religious worship. The Rev. Dr. Walker, the present head of the University, in earnest prayer, commended the soul of the departed to God, who gave it, and invoked a consecration of their afflictive bereavement to his family and friends. From this service we followed the body, in mournful procession, to the resting-place which he had selected for himself and his family, amidst the beautiful groves of Mount Auburn. As the procession filed into the cemetery I was touched by the sight of the numerous pupils of the Law School, with uncovered heads and countenances of sorrow, ranged on each side of the road within the gate, testifying by this silent and unexpected homage their last respects to what is mortal in their departed teacher. Around the grave, as he was laid in the embrace of the mother earth, was gathered all in our community that is most distinguished in law, in learning, in literature, in station — the Judges of our Courts, the Professors of the University, surviving class-mates of the deceased, and a thick cluster of friends. He was placed among the children taken from him in early life, whose faces he is now beholding in heaven. "Of such is the kingdom of heaven," are the words he had inscribed over their names, on the simple marble which now commemorates alike the children and their father.

Nor is there a child in heaven, of a more childlike innocence and purity, than he, who, full of years and worldly honors, has gone to mingle with these children. Of such, indeed, is the kingdom of heaven.

There is another sentence, inscribed by him on this family stone, which speaks to us now with a voice of consolation. "Sorrow not as those without hope," are the words which brought a solace to him in his bereavements. From his bed beneath he seems to whisper them among his mourning family and friends; most especially to her, the chosen partner of his life, from whom so much of human comfort is apparently removed. He is indeed gone; but we shall see him once more forever. In this blessed confidence, we may find happiness in dwelling upon his virtues and fame on earth, till the great consoler Time shall come with healing on his wings.

From the grave of the Judge, I walked a few short steps to that of his classmate and friend, the beloved Channing, who died less than three years ago, aged sixty-three. Thus these companions in early studies — each afterwards foremost in the high and important duties which he assumed, pursuing divergent paths, yet always drawn towards each other by the attractions of mutual friendship, — again meet and lie down together in the same sweet earth, in the shadow of kindred trees, through which the same birds shall sing their perpetual requiem.

The afternoon was of unusual brilliancy, and the full-orbed sun gilded with mellow light the funereal stones through which I wound my way, as I sought the grave of another friend of my own, the first associate of the departed Judge in the duties of the Law School, — Professor Ashmun. After a life crowded with usefulness, he laid down the burden of ill health which he had long borne, at the early age of thirty-three. I remember listening, in 1833, to the flowing discourse which Mr. Justice Story pronounced, in the college chapel, over the remains of his associate; nor can I forget his deep emotion, as we stood together at the foot of the grave, while the earth fell, dust to dust, upon the coffin of his friend.

Wandering through this silent city of the dead, I called to mind those words of Beaumont on the tombs in Westminster:

> Here's an acre sown indeed,
> With the richest, royall'st seed
> That the earth did e'er suck in
> Since the first man died of sin,
> Here are sands, ignoble things,
> Dropt from the ruined sides of kings.

The royalty of Mount Auburn is of the soul. The kings that slumber there were anointed by a higher than earthly hand.

Returning again to the grave of the departed Judge, I found no one but the humble laborers, who were then smoothing the sod over the fresh earth. It was late in the afternoon, and the upper branches of the stately trees that wave over the sacred spot, after glistening for a while in the golden rays of the setting sun, were left in the gloom which had already settled on the grass beneath. I hurried away, and as I reached the gate the porter's curfew was tolling, to forgetful musers like myself, the knell of parting day.

As I left the consecrated field, I thought of the pilgrims that would come from afar, through long successions of generations, to look upon the last home of the great Jurist. From all parts of our own country, from all the lands where law is taught as a science, and where justice prevails, they shall come to seek the grave of their master. Let us guard, then, this precious dust. Let us be happy, that though his works and his example belong to the world, his sacred remains are placed in our peculiar care. To us, also, who saw him face to face, in the performance of all his various duties, and who sustain a loss so irreparable in our own circle, is the melancholy pleasure of dwelling with household affection upon his transcendent excellencies.

His death makes a chasm which I shrink from contemplating. He was the senior Judge of the highest Court of the country, an active Professor of Law, and a Fellow in the Corporation of Harvard University. He was in himself a whole triumvirate; and these three distinguished posts, now vacant, will be filled, in all probability, each by a distinct successor. It is, however, as the exalted Jurist, that he is to take his place in the history of the world, high in the same firmament whence beam the mild glories of Tribonian, of Cujas, of Hale, and of Mansfield. It was his fortune, unlike many who have cultivated the law with signal success on the European continent, to be called as a Judge practically to administer and apply it in the actual business of life. It thus became to him not merely a science, whose depths and intricacies he explored in his closet, but a great and god-like instrument, to be employed in that highest of earthly functions, the determination of justice among men. While the duties of the magistrate were thus illumined by the studies of the Jurist, the latter were tempered to a finer edge by the experience of the bench.

In attempting any fitting estimate of his character as a Jurist, he should be regarded in *three* different aspects; as a Judge, an Author, and a Teacher of jurisprudence, exercising in each of these characters a peculiar influence. His lot is rare who achieves fame in a single department of human action; rarer still is his who becomes foremost in many. The first impression is of astonishment that a single mind, in a single life, should be able to accomplish so much. Independent of the incalculable labors, of which there is no trace, except in the knowledge, happiness, and justice which they helped to secure, the bare amount of his written and printed works is enormous beyond all precedent in the annals of the common law. His written judgments on his own circuit, and his various commentaries, occupy *twenty-seven* volumes, while his judgments in the Supreme Court of the United States form an important part of no less than *thirty-four* volumes more. The vast professional labors of Coke and Eldon, which seem to clothe the walls of our libraries, must yield in extent to his. He is the Lope de Vega, or the Walter Scott of the common law.

We are struck next by the universality of his juridical attainments. It was said by Dryden of one of the greatest lawyers in English history, Heneage Finch,

Our law, that did a boundless ocean seem,
Were coasted all and fathomed all by him.

But the boundless ocean of that age was a *mare clausum* compared with that on which the adventurer embarks in our day. We read, in Howell's Familiar Letters, the saying of only a few short years before the period of Finch, that the books of the common law might all be carried in a wheelbarrow! To coast such an ocean were a less task than a moiety of his labors whom we now mourn. Called to administer all the different branches of law, which are kept separate in England, he showed a mastery of all. His was Universal Empire; and wherever he set his foot, in the wide and various realms of jurisprudence, it was as a sovereign; whether in the ancient and subtle learning of real law; in the criminal law; in the niceties of special pleading; in the more refined doctrines of contracts; in the more rational systems of the commercial and maritime law; in the peculiar and interesting principles and practice of Courts of admiralty and prize; in the immense range of chancery; in the modern but important jurisdiction over patents; or in that higher region, the great themes of public and constitutional law. There are judgments by him in each of these branches, which will not yield in value to those of any other Judge in England or the United States, even though his studies and duties may have been directed to only one particular department.

His judgments are remarkable for their exhaustive treatment of the subjects to which they relate. The common law, as is known to his cost by every student, is to be found only in innumerable "sand-grains" of authorities. Not one of these is overlooked in his learned expositions, while all are combined with care, and the golden cord of reason is woven across the ample tissue. Besides, there is in them a clearness, which flings over the subject a perfect day; a severe logic, which, by its closeness and precision, makes us feel the truth of the saying of Leibnitz, that nothing approached so near the certainty of geometry, as the reasoning of the law; a careful attention to the discussions at the bar, that the Court may not appear to neglect any of the considerations urged; with a copious and persuasive eloquence which invests the whole. Many of his judgments will be land-marks in the law; they will be columns, like those of Hercules, to mark the progress in jurisprudence of our age. I know of no single Judge who has established so many. I think it may be said, without fear of question, that the Reports show a larger number of judicial opinions, from Mr. Justice Story, which posterity will not willingly let die, than from any other Judge in the history of English and American law.

But there is much of his character, as a Judge, which cannot be preserved, except in the faithful memories and records of those whose happiness it was to enjoy his judicial presence. I refer particularly to his mode of conducting business. Even the passing stranger bears witness to his suavity of manner on the bench, while all the practitioners in the Courts, over which he presided so long, attest the marvellous quickness with which he habitually seized the points of a case, often anticipating the slower movements of the counsel, and leaping, or, I might almost say, flying to the conclusions sought to be established. Napoleon's perception in military tactics was not more rapid. Nor can I forget the scrupulous care with which he assigned reasons for every portion of his opinions, showing that it was not *he* who thus spoke with the voice of authority, but the *law*, whose organ he was.

In the history of the English bench, there are but two names with combined eminence as a Judge and as an Author — Coke and Hale; — unless, indeed, the Orders in Chancery, from the Verulamian pen, should entitle Lord Bacon to this distinction; and the judgments of Lord Brougham should vindicate the same for him. Blackstone's character as a Judge is lost in the fame of the Commentaries. To Mr. Justice Story belongs this double glory. Early in life, he compiled an important professional work; but it was only at a comparatively recent period, after his mind had been disciplined by the labors of the bench, that he prepared those elaborate Commentaries, which have made his name a familiar word in foreign countries. They, who who knew him best, observed the lively interest which he took in this extension of his well earned renown. And truly he might; for the voice of distant foreign nations seems to come as from a living posterity. His works have been reviewed with praise in the journals of England, Scotland, Ireland, France, and Germany. They have been cited as authorities in all the Courts of Westminister Hall; and one of the ablest and most learned lawyers of the age, whose honorable career at the bar has conducted him to the peerage, Lord Campbell, in the course of debate in the House of Lords, characterized their author as "The first of living writers on the law."

To complete this hasty survey of his character as a Jurist, I should allude to his excellencies as a *Teacher* of law, that other relation which he sustained to jurisprudence. The numerous pupils reared at his feet, and now scattered throughout the whole country, diffusing, each in his circle, the light which he obtained at Cambridge, as they hear that their beloved master has fallen, will feel that they individually have lost a friend. He had the faculty, rare as it is exquisite, of interesting the young, and winning their affections. I have often seen him surrounded by a group, — the ancient Romans would have aptly called it a *corona* of youths, — all intent upon his earnest conversation, and freely interrogating him on any matters of doubt. In his lectures, and other forms of instruction, he was prodigal of explanation and illustration ; his manner, according to the classical image of Zeno, was like the open palm, never like the closed hand. His learning was always overflowing, as from the horn of abundance. He was earnest and unrelaxing in his efforts, patient and gentle, while he listened with inspiring attention to all that the pupil said. Like Chaucer's Clerk,

> And gladly wolde he lerne, and gladly teche.

Above all, he was a living example of a love for the law, — supposed by many to be unlovely and repulsive — which seemed to grow warmer under the snows of accumulating winters ; and such an example could not fail, with magnetic power, to touch the hearts of the young. Nor should I forget the lofty standard of professional morals, which he inculcated, filling his discourse with the charm of goodness. Under such auspices, and those of his learned associate, Professor Greenleaf, large classes of students of law, larger than any in England or America, have been annually gathered in Cambridge. The Law School is the golden mistletoe ingrafted on the ancient oak of the University;

> Talis erat species auri frondentis opaca
> Ilice.

The deceased was proud of his character as Professor. In his earlier works he is called on the title-page, "Dane Professor of Law." It was only on the suggestion of the English publisher, that he was prevailed upon to append the other title, "Justice of the Supreme Court of the United States." He looked forward with peculiar delight to the time which seemed at hand, when he should lay down the honors and cares of the bench, and devote himself singly to the duties of his chair.

I have merely glanced at his character in his *three* different relations to jurisprudence. Great in each of these, it is on this unprecedented combination that his peculiar fame will be reared, as upon an immortal tripod. In what I have written, I do not think I am biased by the partialities of private friendship. I have endeavored to regard him, as posterity will regard him; as they must regard him now, who know him in his various works. Imagine for one moment the irreparable loss, if all that he has done were blotted out forever. As I think of the incalculable facilities afforded by his labors, I cannot but say with Racine, when speaking of Descartes: *Nous courons; mais, sans lui, nous ne marcherions pas.* Besides, it is he who has inspired in many foreign bosoms, reluctant to perceive aught that is good in our country, a sincere homage to the American name. He has turned the stream of the law refluent upon the ancient fountains of Westminster Hall; and, stranger still, he has forced the waters above their sources, up the unaccustomed heights of countries, alien to the common law. It is he also who has directed, from the copious well-springs of the Roman law, and from the fresher currents of the modern continental law, a pure and grateful stream, to enrich and fertilize our domestic jurisprudence. In his judgments, in his books, and in his teachings always, he drew from other systems to illustrate the doctrines of the common law.

The mind naturally seeks to compare him with the eminent Jurists, servants of Themis, who share with him the wide spaces of fame. In genius for the law, in the exceeding usefulness of his career, in the blended character of Judge and Author, he cannot yield to our time-honored master, Lord Coke; in suavity of manner, and in silver-tongued eloquence, he may compare with Lord Mansfield, while in depth, accuracy and variety of juridical learning, he surpassed him far; if he yields to Lord Stowell in elegance of diction, he excels even his excellence in the curious exploration of the foundations of that jurisdiction which they administered in common, and in the development of those great principles of public law, whose just determination helps to preserve the peace of nations; and, even in the peculiar field illustrated by the long career of Eldon, we find him a familiar worker, with Eldon's profusion of learning, and without the perplexities of his doubts. There are many who regard the judicial character of the late

Chief Justice Marshall as at an unapproachable height. I revere his name, and have ever read his judgments, which seem like "pure reason," with admiration and gratitude; but I cannot disguise, that even these noble memorials must yield in high juridical character, in learning, in acuteness, in fervor, in the variety of topics which they concern, as they are far inferior in amount, to those of our friend. There is still spared to us a renowned Judge, at this moment the unquestioned living head of American jurisprudence, with no rival near the throne, — Mr. Chancellor Kent, — whose judgments and whose works always inspired the warmest eulogies of the departed, and whose character as a Jurist furnishes the fittest parallel to his own in the annals of our law.

It were idle, perhaps, to weave further these vain comparisons; particularly to invoke the living. But busy fancy recalls the past, and persons and scenes renew themselves in my memory. I call to mind the recent Chancellor of England, the model of a clear, grave, learned and conscientious magistrate,— Lord Cottenham. I call to mind the ornaments of Westminster Hall, on the bench and at the bar, where sits Denman, in manner, in conduct, and character "every inch" the Judge; where pleaded only a few short months ago the consummate lawyer Follet, whose voice is now hushed in the grave; their judgments, their arguments, their conversation, I cannot forget; but thinking of these, I feel new pride in the great Magistrate, the lofty Judge, the consummate Lawyer, whom we now mourn.

It has been my fortune to know or to see the chief Jurists of our times, in the classical countries of jurisprudence, France and Germany. I remember well the pointed and effective style of Dupin, in the delivery of one of his masterly opinions in the highest Court of France; I recall the pleasant converse of Pardessus — to whom commercial and maritime law is under a larger debt, perhaps, than to any other mind — while he descanted on his favorite theme. I wander in fancy to the gentle presence of him with flowing silver locks, who was so dear to Germany — Thibaut, the expounder of the Roman law, and the earnest and successful advocate of a just scheme for the reduction of the unwritten law to the certainty of a written text. From Heidelberg I fly to Berlin, where I listen to the grave lecture, and mingle in the social circle of Savigny, so stately in person and peculiar in countenance, whom all the continent of Europe delights to honor; but my heart and my judgment untravelled fondly turn with new love and admiration to my Cambridge teacher and friend. Jurisprudence has many arrows in her golden quiver, but where is one to compare with that which is now spent in the earth?

The fame of the Jurist is enhanced by the various attainments superinduced upon his learning in the law. His "Miscellaneous Writings" show a thoughtful mind, imbued with elegant literature, warm with kindly sentiments, commanding a style of rich and varied eloquence. There are many passages from these which have become the common-places of our schools. In early life he yielded to the fascinations of the poetic muse; and here the great lawyer may find companionship with Selden, who is introduced by Suckling into the "Session of Poets," as "close by the chair"; with Blackstone, whose "Farewell to the Muse" shows his fondness for poetic pastures, even while his eye was directed to the heights of the law; and also with Mansfield, of whom Pope has lamented in familiar words,

> How sweet an Ovid was in Murray lost!

I have now before me, in his own hand-writing, some verses written by him in 1833, entitled, "Advice to a Young Lawyer." As they cannot fail to be read with interest, I introduce them here.

Whene'er you speak, remember every cause
Stands not on eloquence, but stands on laws —
Pregnant in matter, in expression brief,
Let every sentence stand with bold relief;
On trifling points, nor time, nor talents waste,
A sad offence to learning, and to taste;
Nor deal with pompous phrase; nor e'er suppose
Poetic flights belong to reasoning prose.
Loose declamation may deceive the crowd,
And seem more striking, as it grows more loud;
But sober sense rejects it with disdain,
As naught but empty noise, and weak as vain.
The froth of words, the schoolboy's vain parade
Of books and cases — all his stock in trade —
The pert conceits, the cunning tricks and play
Of low attorneys, strung in long array,
The unseemly jest, the petulant reply,
That chatters on, and cares not how, nor why,
Studious, avoid — unworthy themes to scan,
They sink the Speaker and disgrace the Man.
Like the false lights, by flying shadows cast,
Scarce seen when present, and forgot when past.

Begin with dignity; expound with grace
Each ground of reasoning in its time and place;
Let order reign throughout — each topic touch,
Nor urge its power too little, or too much.
Give each strong thought its most attractive view,
In diction clear, and yet severely true.

And, as the arguments in splendor grow,
Let each reflect its light on all below.
When to the close arrived, make no delays,
By petty flourishes, or verbal plays,
But sum the whole in one deep, solemn strain,
Like a strong current hastening to the main.

But the Jurist, rich with the spoils of time, the exalted magistrate, the orator, the writer, all vanish when I think of the friend. Much as the world may admire his memory, all who knew him shall love it more. Who can forget his bounding step, his contagious laugh, his exhilarating voice, his beaming smile, his countenance that shone like a benediction? What pen can describe these — what artist can preserve them on canvas or in marble? He was always the friend of the young, who never tired in listening to his flowing and mellifluous discourse. Nor did they ever leave his presence without feeling a warmer glow of virtue, a more inspiring love of knowledge and truth, more generous impulses of action. I remember him in my childhood; but I first knew him after he came to Cambridge, as Professor, while I was yet an undergraduate, and remember freshly, as if the words were of yesterday, the eloquence and animation, with which, at that time, to a youthful circle, he enforced the beautiful truth, that no man stands in the way of another. The world is wide enough for all, he said, and no success, which may crown our neighbor, can affect our own career. In this spirit he run his race on earth, without jealousy, without envy; nay more, overflowing with appreciation and praise of labors which compare humbly with his own. In conversation, he dwelt with fervor upon all the topics which interest man; not only upon law, but upon literature, history, the characters of men, the affairs of every day; above all, upon the great duties of life, the relations of men to each other, to their country, to God. High in his mind, above all human opinions and practices, were the everlasting rules of *Right;* nor did he ever rise to a truer eloquence, than when condemning, as I have more than once heard him recently, that evil sentiment,—"Our country, *be she right or wrong,*"—which, in whatsoever form of language it may disguise itself, assails the very foundations of justice and virtue.

He has been happy in his life; happy also in his death. It was his hope, expressed in health, that he should not be allowed to linger superfluous on the stage, nor waste under the slow progress of disease. He was always ready to meet his God. His wishes were answered. Two days before his last illness, he delivered in Court an elaborate judgment on a complicated case in equity. Since his death, another judgment in a case already argued before him, has been found among his papers, ready to be pronounced.

I saw him for a single moment on the evening preceding his illness. It was an accidental meeting away from his own house—the last time that the open air of heaven fanned his cheeks. His words of familiar, household greeting, on that occasion, still linger in my ears, like an enchanted melody. The morning sun saw him on the bed from which he never again rose. Thus closèd, after an illness of eight days, in the bosom of his family, without pain, surrounded by friends, a life, which, through various vicissitudes of disease, had been spared beyond the grand climacteric, that Cape of Storms in the sea of human existence:

> Multis ille bonis flebilis occidit,
> Nulli flebilior quam mihi.

He is gone, and we shall see him no more on earth, except in his works, and in the memory of his virtues. The scales of justice, which he had so long held, have fallen from his hands. The untiring pen of the Author rests at last. The voice of the Teacher is mute. The fountain, which was ever flowing and ever full, is now stopped. The lips, on which the bees of Hybla might have rested, have ceased to distil the honeyed sweets of kindness. The manly form, warm with all the affections of life, with love for family and friends, for truth and virtue, is now cold in death. The justice of nations is eclipsed; the life of the law is suspended. But let us listen to the words, which, though dead, he utters from the grave: "Sorrow not as those without hope." The righteous judge, the wise teacher, the faithful friend, the loving father, has ascended to his Judge, his Teacher, his Friend, his Father in Heaven.

HON. JOHN PICKERING.

[FROM THE LAW REPORTER OF JUNE, 1846.]

It was the remark of Lord Brougham, illustrated by his own crowded life, that the complete performance of all the duties of an active member of the British parliament might be joined with a full practice at the bar. The career of the late Mr. Pickering illustrates a more grateful truth: that the mastery of the law as a science, and the constant performance of all the duties of a practitioner, are not incompatible with the studies of the most various scholarship, — that the lawyer and the scholar may be *one*. He dignified the law by the successful cultivation of letters, and strengthened the influence of these elegant pursuits by becoming their representative in the concerns of daily life, and in the common-places of his profession. And now, that this living example of excellence is withdrawn from our personal regard, we feel a sorrow which words can only faintly express. Let us devote a few moments to the contemplation of what he did, and what he was. The language of exaggeration is forbidden by the modesty of his nature, as it is rendered unnecessary by the multitude of his virtues.

JOHN PICKERING, whose recent death we now deplore, was born in Salem, February 17th, 1777, at the period of the darkest despondency of the revolution. His father, Col. Pickering, was a man of distinguished character, and an eminent actor in public affairs, whose name is one of the household words of our history. Of his large family of ten children, John was the eldest.* His diligence at school was a source of early gratification to his friends, and gave augury of future accomplishments. An authentic token of this character, higher than any tradition of partial friends, is afforded by a little book, entitled "Letters to a Student in the University of Cambridge, Mass., by John Clarke, Minister of a Church in Boston," printed in 1796; and which in reality were addressed to him. The first letter begins with an honorable allusion to his early improvement. "Your superior qualifications for admission into the University give you singular advantages for the prosecution of your studies. . . . You are now placed in a situation to become, what you have often assured me is your ambition, *a youth of learning and virtue.*" The last letter of the volume concludes with benedictions, which did not fall as barren words upon the heart of the youthful pupil. "May you," says Dr. Clarke, "be one of those sons who do honor to their literary parent. The union of *virtue* and *science*

* The reporter, *Octavius* Pickering, was the *eighth* child, which was the reason of his name.

will give you distinction at the present age, and will tend to give celebrity to the name of Harvard. You will not disappoint the friends who anticipate your improvement." They who remember his college days still dwell with fondness upon his exemplary character, and his remarkable scholarship, at that period. He received his degree of Bachelor of Arts at Cambridge in 1796.

On leaving the university, he went to Philadelphia, at that time the seat of government, where his father resided as Secretary of State. Here he commenced the study of the law under Mr. Tilghman, afterwards the distinguished Chief Justice of Pennsylvania, and one of the lights of American jurisprudence. But his professional lucubrations were soon suspended by his appointment, in 1797, as Secretary of Legation, under Mr. Smith, to Portugal. He resided, in this capacity, at Lisbon for two years, during which period he became familiar with the language and literature of the country. Later in life, when his extensive knowledge of foreign tongues opened to him, it might almost be said, the literature of the world, he recurred with peculiar pleasure to the language of Camoens and Pombal.

From Lisbon he passed to London, where, at the close of the last century, he became, for about two years, the private secretary of our Minister, Mr. King, residing in the family, and enjoying the society and friendship of this distinguished man. Here he was happy in meeting with his classmate and attached friend, Dr. James Jackson, of Boston, who was then in London, pursuing those professional studies, whose ripened autumnal fruits of usefulness and eminence he still lives to enjoy. In pleasant companionship they walked through the thoroughfares of the great metropolis, enjoying together its shows and attractions; in pleasant companionship they continued ever afterwards, till death severed the ties of a long life.

Mr. Pickering's youth and inexperience in the profession to which he afterwards devoted his days, prevented his taking any special interest, at this period, in the courts or in parliament. But there were several of the Judges who made a strong impression on his mind; nor did he ever cease to remember the vivacious eloquence of Erskine, or the commanding oratory of Pitt.

Meanwhile his father, being no longer in the public service, had returned to Salem; and thither the son followed, in 1801, and resumed the study of the law, under the direction of Mr. Putnam, afterwards a learned and beloved Judge of the Supreme Court of Massachusetts, whose rare fortune it has been to rear two pupils, whose fame will be among the choicest possessions of our country, — Story and Pickering. In due time, he was admitted to the bar, and commenced the practice of the law in Salem.

Here begins the long, unbroken series of his labors in literature and philology, running side by side with the daily untiring business of his profession. It is easy to believe that, notwithstanding his undissembled fondness for jurisprudence as a *science*, he was drawn towards its *practice* by the compulsions of duty rather than by any attractions which it possessed for him. Not removed by fortune from the necessity, to which Dr. Johnson so pathetically alludes, of providing for the day that was passing over him, he could indulge his tastes for study only in hours secured by diligence from the inroads of business, or the seductions of pleasure. Perhaps no lawyer has lived, since the days of the Roman Orator, who could have uttered, with greater truth, those inspiring words, confessing and vindicating the cultivation of letters: "Me autem quid pudeat, qui tot annos ita vivo, judices, ut ab nullius unquam me tempore aut commodo — aut otium meum abstraxerit, aut voluptas avocârit, aut denique somnus retardârit? Quare quis tandem me reprehendat, aut quis jure, succenseat, si, quantum cæteris ad suas res obeundas, quantum ad festos dies ludorum celebrandos, quantum ad alias voluptates, et ad ipsam requiem animi et corporis conceditur temporis; quantum alii tribuunt tempestivis conviviis, quantum denique aleæ, quantum pilæ; tantum mihi egomet ad hæc studia recolenda sumpsero?" *

In his life may be seen two streams, flowing, side by side, as through a long tract of country; one of which is fed by the fresh fountains far in the mountain tops, whose waters leap with delight on their journey to the sea; while the other, having its sources low down in the valleys, among the haunts of men, moves with reluctant, though steady, current onward.

Mr. Pickering's days were passed in the performance of all the duties of a wide and various practice, first at Salem, and afterwards at Boston. He resided at Salem till 1829, when he removed to the latter place, where he was appointed, shortly afterwards, city solicitor; an office, whose arduous labors he continued

* Pro Archia, § 6.

to perform until within a few months of his death. There is little worthy of notice in the ordinary incidents of professional life. What Blackstone aptly calls "the pert debate," renews itself in infinitely varying forms. Some new turn of litigation calls forth some new effort of learning or skill, calculated to serve its temporary purpose, and like the manna, which fell in the wilderness, perishing on the day that beholds it. The unambitious labors of which the world knows nothing, the counsel to clients, the drawing of contracts, the perplexities of conveyancing, furnish still less of interest than the ephemeral displays of the court room.

The cares of his profession, and the cultivation of letters, left but little time for the concerns of politics. And yet, at different periods, he filled offices in the legislature of Massachusetts. He was three times representative from Salem, twice senator from Essex, once senator from Suffolk, and once a member of the executive council. In all these places, he commended himself by the same diligence, honesty, learning and ability which marked his course at the bar. The careful student of our legislative history will not fail to perceive his obligations to Mr. Pickering, as the author of several important reports and bills. The first bill, providing for the separation of the District of Maine from Massachusetts, was reported by him to the senate, in 1816. Though this failed to be adopted by the people of Maine, it is characterized by the historian of that State, as "drawn with great ability and skill."* The report

* Williamson's History of Maine, Vol. II. p. 663.

and accompanying bill, in 1818, on the jurisdiction and proceedings of the Courts of Probate, in which the whole system is discussed and remodelled, is from his hand.

In 1833, he was appointed to the vacancy, occasioned by the death of Professor Ashmun, in the commission for revising and arranging the statutes of Massachusetts, being associated in this important work with those eminent lawyers, Mr. Jackson and Mr. Stearns. The first part, or that entitled *Of the Internal Administration of the Government*, corresponding substantially with Blackstone's division *Of Persons*, was executed by him. This alone would entitle him to be gratefully remembered, not only by those who have occasion to refer to the legislation of Massachusetts, but by all who feel an interest in scientific jurisprudence.

His contributions to what may be called the literature of his profession were frequent. The American Jurist was often enriched by articles from his pen. Among these is a Review of the valuable work of Williams on the Law of Executors; and of Curtis's Admiralty Digest, in which he examined the interesting history of this jurisdiction; also an article on the Study of the Roman Law, in which he has presented, within a short compass, a lucid sketch of the history of this system, and of the growth, in Germany, of the historical and didactic schools, "rival houses," as they may be called, in jurisprudence, whose long and unpleasant feud has only recently subsided.

In the Law Reporter for July, 1841, he published an article of singular merit, on *National Rights* and *State Rights*, being a Review of the case of Alexander

McLeod, recently determined in the Supreme Court of Judicature of the State of New York. This was afterwards republished in a pamphlet, and extensively circulated. It is marked by uncommon learning, clearness and ability. The course of the Courts of New York is handled with freedom, and the supremacy of the Federal Government vindicated. Of all the discussions elicited by that interesting question, on which, for a while, seemed to hang the portentous issues of peace and war between the United States and Great Britain, that of Mr. Pickering will be admitted to take the lead, whether we consider its character as an elegant composition, or as a searching review of the juridical aspects of the case. In dealing with the opinion of Mr. Justice Cowen, renowned for black-letter and the bibliography of the law, he shows himself more than a match for this learned Judge, even in these unfrequented fields, while the spirit of the publicist and jurist gives a refined temper to the whole article, which we seek in vain in the other production.

In the North American Review, for October, 1840, is an article by him, illustrative of *Conveyancing in Ancient Egypt*, being an explanation of an Egyptian deed of a piece of land in hundred-gated Thebes, written on papyrus, more than a century before the Christian era, with the impression of a seal or stamp attached to it, and a certificate of registry on its margin, in as regular a manner as the keeper of the registry in the county of Suffolk would certify to a deed of land in the city of Boston, at this day. Here jurisprudence is gilded by scholarship.

There is another production, which, like the latter,

belongs to the department of literature as well as of jurisprudence; his *Lecture on the Alleged Uncertainty of the Law*, delivered before the Boston Society for the Diffusion of Useful Knowledge. Though originally written for the general mind, which it is calculated to interest and instruct in no common degree, it will be read with equal advantage by the profound lawyer. It would not be easy to mention any popular discussion of a juridical character, in our language, deserving of higher regard. It was first published in the American Jurist, at the solicitation of the writer of these lines, who has never been able to refer to it without fresh admiration of the happy illustrations and quiet reasoning by which it vindicates the science of the law.

In considering what Mr. Pickering accomplished out of his profession, we shall be led over wide and various fields of learning, where we can only hope to indicate his footprints, without presuming to examine or explain the ground.

One of his earliest cares was to elevate the character of *classical studies* in our country. His own example did much in this respect. From the time he left the university, he was always regarded as an authority on topics of scholarship. But his labors were devoted especially to this cause. As early as 1805, he published, in conjunction with his friend, the present Judge White, of Salem, an edition of the Histories of Sallust, with Latin Notes, and a copious Index. This is one of the first examples, in our country, of a classic edited with scholarlike skill. The same spirit led him, later in life, to publish in the North American Review, and afterwards in a pamphlet, "Observations on the Importance of Greek Literature, and the Best Method of Studying the Classics," translated from the Latin of Professor Wyttenbach. In the course of the remarks, with which he introduces the translation, he urges with conclusive force the importance of raising the standard of education in our country. "We are too apt," he says, "to consider ourselves as an insulated people, as not belonging to the great community of Europe; but we are, in truth, just as much members of it, by means of a common public, commercial intercourse, literature, a kindred language and habits, as Englishmen or Frenchmen themselves are; and we must procure for ourselves the qualifications necessary to maintain that rank, which we shall claim as equal members of such a community."

His "Remarks on Greek Grammars," which appeared in the American Journal of Education, in 1825, belong to the same field of labor, as does also his admirable paper, published in 1818, in the Memoirs of the American Academy,* on the proper pronunciation of the ancient Greek language. He maintained that it should be pronounced, so far as possible, according to the Romaic or modern Greek, and learnedly and ably exposed the vicious usage which had been introduced by Erasmus. His conclusions, though controverted when they were first presented, are now substantially adopted by scholars. We well remember his honest pleasure

* "*Observations upon Greek Accent*" is the title of an Essay, in the Royal Irish Transactions, Vol. VII., by Dr. Browne, which was suggested, like Mr. Pickering's, by conversation with some modern Greeks, and which touches upon kindred topics. Dr. Browne is the author of the well known and somewhat antediluvian book on the Civil and Admiralty Law.

in a communication received within a few years from President Moore, of Columbia College, in which that gentleman, who had formerly opposed his views, with the candor that becomes his honorable scholarship, volunteered to them the sanction of his approbation.

But the "*Greek and English Lexicon*" is his work of greatest labor in the department of classical learning. This alone would entitle him to regard from all who love liberal studies. With the well thumbed copy of this book, used in our college days, now before us, we feel how much we are debtors to his learned toils. This was planned early in Mr. Pickering's life, and was begun in 1814. The interruptions of his profession induced him to engage the assistance of the late Dr. Daniel Oliver, Professor of Moral and Intellectual Philosophy at Dartmouth College. The work, proceeding slowly, was not announced by a prospectus until 1820, and not finally published until 1826. It was mainly founded on the well known Lexicon of Schrevelius, which had received the emphatic commention of Vicesimus Knox, and was generally regarded as preferable to any other for the use of schools. When Mr. Pickering commenced his labors, there was no Greek Lexicon with explanations in our own tongue. The English student obtained his knowledge of Greek through the intervention of Latin. And it has been supposed by many, who have not sufficiently regarded, as we are inclined to believe, other relations of the subject, that this circuitous and awkward practice is a principal reason why Greek is so much less familiar to us than Latin. In the honorable efforts to remove this difficulty, our countryman took the lead. Shortly before the last sheets of his Lexicon were printed, a copy of a London translation of Schrevelius reached this country, which proved, however, to be "a hurried performance, upon which it would not have been safe to rely."*

Since the publication of his Lexicon, several others in Greek and English have appeared in England. The example of Germany and the learning of her scholars, have contributed to these works. It were to be wished that all of them were free from the suggestion of an unhandsome appropriation of the labors of others. The Lexicon of Dr. Dunbar, Professor of Greek in the University of Edinburgh, published in 1840, contains whole pages, taken bodily — "convey, the wise it call" — from that of Mr. Pickering, while the Preface is content with an acknowledgment in very general terms to the work which is copied. This is bad enough. But the second edition, published in 1844, omits the acknowledgment altogether; and the Lexicon is welcomed by an elaborate article in the Quarterly Review,† as the triumphant labor of Dr. Dunbar, "well known among our northern classics as a clever man and an acute scholar. *In almost every page*," continues the reviewer, "*we meet with something which bespeaks the pen of a scholar;* and we, every now and then, stumble on explanations of words and passages, occasionally fanciful, but always sensible, and sometimes ingenious, which amply repay us for the search. . . . *They prove, moreover, that the Professor is possessed of one quality, which we could wish to see more general; he does not see with the eyes of others* — he

* Preface to Pickering's Lexicon.

† Vol. LXXV. p. 299.

thinks for himself, and he seems well qualified to do so." Did he not see with the eyes of others? The reviewer hardly supposed that his commendation would reach the production of an American lexicographer.

In the general department of *Languages* and *Philology*, his labors have been various. Some of the publications already mentioned might be ranged under this head. But there are others still which remain to be noticed. The earliest of these is the work generally called "*The Vocabulary of Americanisms*," being a collection of words and phrases, supposed to be peculiar to the United States, with an Essay on the State of the English Language in the United States. This was originally published in 1815, in the Memoirs of the American Academy, and was republished in a separate volume in 1816, with corrections and additions. It was the author's intention, had his life been spared, to publish another edition, with the important gleanings of subsequent observation and study. It cannot be doubted that this work has exerted a beneficial influence over the purity of our language. It has promoted careful habits of composition, and, in a certain sense, helped to guard the "wells of English undefiled." Some of the words, found in this Vocabulary, may be traced to ancient sources of authority; but there are many which are, beyond question, provincial and barbarous, although much used in our common speech, *fæx quoque quotidiani sermonis, fœda et pudenda vitia.**

In 1818 appeared in the Memoirs of the American Academy his "*Essay on a Uniform Orthography of the Indian Languages.*" The uncertainty of their

* De Orator. Dialogus, § 32.

orthography arose from the circumstance that the words were collected and reduced to writing by scholars of different nations, who often attached different values to the same letter, and represented the same sound by different letters; so that it was impossible to determine the sound of a written word, without first knowing through what alembic of speech it had passed. Thus the words of the same language or dialect, as written by a German, a Frenchman, or an Englishman, would seem to belong to languages as widely different as those of these different people. With the hope of removing from the path of others the perplexities which had beset his own, Mr. Pickering recommended the adoption of a common orthography, which would enable foreigners to use our books without difficulty, and, on the other hand, make theirs easy of access to us. For this purpose, he devised an alphabet, to be applied practically to the Indian languages, which contained the common letters of our alphabet, so far as it seemed practicable to adopt them, a class of nasals, of diphthongs, and, lastly, a number of compound characters, which, it was supposed, would be of more or less frequent use in different dialects. With regard to this Essay, Mr. Duponceau said, at an early day, "If, as there is great reason to expect, Mr. Pickering's orthography gets into general use among us, America will have had the honor of taking the lead in procuring an important auxiliary to philological science." * Perhaps

* Notes on Eliot's Indian Grammar, Mass. Hist. Coll., Vol. XIX. p. 11. I cannot forbear adding, that, in the correspondence of Leibnitz, there is a proposition for a new alphabet of the Arabic, Æthiopic, Syriac, and other languages, which may remind the reader of that of Mr. Pickering. Leibnitz, Opera, (ed. Dutens,) Vol. VI., p. 88.

no single paper on languages, since the legendary labors of Cadmus, has exercised a more important influence than this communication. Though originally composed with a view to the Indian languages of North America, it has been succesfully followed by the missionaries in the Polynesian Islands. In harmony with the principles of this Essay, the unwritten dialect of the Sandwich Islands, possessing, it is said, a more than Italian softness, was reduced to writing according to a systematic orthography prepared for them by Mr. Pickering, and is now employed in two newspapers published by the natives. Thus he may be regarded as one of the contributors to that civilization, under whose gentle influence those islands, set like richest gems in the bosom of the sea, have been made to glow with the effulgence of Christian truth.

The Collections of the Massachusetts Historical Society contain several important communications from him on the Indian languages; in 1822, (Vol. 19,) an edition of the Indian Grammar of Eliot, the St. Augustine of New England, with Introductory Observations on the Massachusetts Language by the editor, and Notes by Mr. Duponceau, inscribed to his "learned friend, Mr. Pickering, as a just tribute of friendship and respect;" in 1823, (Vol. 20,) an edition of Jonathan Edwards's "Observations on the Mohegan Language," with Introductory Observations, and Copious Notes on the Indian Languages, by the editor, and a Comparative Vocabulary, containing Specimens of some of the Dialects of the Lenape, or Delaware Stock; in 1830, (Vol. 22,) an edition of Cotton's "Vocabulary of the Massachusetts Language." These labors were calculated, in no ordinary degree, to promote a knowledge of the aboriginal idioms of our country, and to shed light on that important and newly attempted branch of knowledge, the comparative science of languages.

Among the Memoirs of the American Academy, published in 1833, (New Series, Vol. 1,) is the "Dictionary of the Abenaki Language, in North America," by Father Sebastian Rasles, with an Introductory Memoir, and Notes, by Mr. Pickering. The original manuscript of this copious Dictionary, commenced by the good and indefatigable Jesuit in 1691, during his solitary residence with the Indians, was found among his papers after the massacre at Norridgewalk, in which he was killed, and, passing through several hands, at last came into the possession of Harvard College. It is considered one of the most interesting and authentic documents in the history of the North American languages. In the Memoir accompanying the Dictionary, Mr. Pickering, with the modesty which marked all his labors, says, that he made inquiries for memorials of these languages, "hoping to render some small service, by collecting and preserving these valuable materials for the use of those persons whose leisure and ability would enable them to employ them more advantageously, than it was in his power to do, for the benefit of philological science."

The elaborate article on the "*Indian Languages of America*," in the Encyclopædia Americana, is from his pen. The subject was considered so interesting, in regard to general and comparative philology, while so little was generally known respecting it, that it was allowed a space more than proportionate to the usual length of philological articles in that work.

The forthcoming volume of the Memoirs of the American Academy contains an interesting paper of a kindred character, one of his latest productions, on the Language and Inhabitants of Lord North's Island, in the Indian Archipelago, with a Vocabulary.

The Address before the American Oriental Society, published in 1843, as the first number of the Journal of that body, is a beautiful contribution to the history of languages, presenting a survey of the peculiar field of labor to which the Society is devoted, in a style which attracts alike the scholar and the less careful reader.

Among his other productions in philology, may be mentioned an interesting article on the *Chinese Language*, which first appeared in the North American Review, and was afterwards *dishonestly reprinted, as an original article*, in the London Monthly Review for December, 1840; also an article on the *Cochin-Chinese Language*, published in the North American Review for April, 1841; another on Adelung's "Survey of Languages," in the same journal, in 1822; a Review of Johnson's Dictionary, in the American Quarterly Review for September, 1828; and two articles in the New York Review for 1826, being a caustic examination of General Cass's article in the North American Review, respecting the Indians of North America. These two articles were not acknowledged by their author at the time they were written. They purport to be by KASS-*ti-ga-tor-skee*, or the *Feathered Arrow*, a fictitious name from the Latin CAS-*tigator*, and an Indian termination *skee* or *ski*.

But even this enumeration does not close the catalogue of Mr. Pickering's labors. There are still others,

— to which, however, we shall refer by their titles only, — that may be classed with contributions to *general literature.* Among these is an Oration delivered at Salem, on the Fourth of July, 1804; an article in the North American Review, (Vol. 28,) on Elementary Instruction; a Lecture on Telegraphic Language, delivered before the Boston Marine Society, and published in 1833; an article on Peirce's History of Harvard University, in the North American Review for April, 1834; an article on Prescott's History of the Reign of Ferdinand and Isabella, in the New York Review for April, 1838; the noble Eulogy on Dr. Bowditch, delivered before the American Academy, May 29, 1838; and Obituary Notices of Mr. Peirce, the Librarian of Harvard College; of Dr. Spurzheim; of Dr. Bowditch; and of his valued friend and correspondent, the partner of his philological labors, Mr. Duponceau; also, an interesting Lecture, still unpublished, on the Origin of the Population of America, and two others on Languages.

The reader will be astonished at these various contributions to learning and literature, which we have thus hastily reviewed, particularly when he regards them as the diversions of a life, filled in amplest measure by other pursuits. Charles Lamb said that his *real works* were not his published writings, but the ponderous folios copied by his own hand, in the India House. In the same spirit, Mr. Pickering might point to the multitudinous transactions of his long professional life, the cases argued in Court, the conferences with clients, and the deeds, contracts, and other papers, in that clear, legible autograph, which is a fit emblem of his transparent character.

His professional life, then, first invites our attention. And here it should be observed, that he was a thorough, hard-working lawyer, for the greater part of his days in *full practice*, constant at his office, attentive to all the concerns of business, and to what may be called the humilities of the profession. He was faithful, conscientious and careful in all that he did; nor did his zeal for the interests committed to his care ever betray him beyond the golden mean of duty. The law, in his hands, was a shield for defence, and never a sword with which to thrust at his adversary. His preparations for arguments in Court were marked by peculiar care; his brief was very elaborate. On questions of law he was learned and profound; but his manner in Court was excelled by his matter. The experience of his long life never enabled him to overcome the native childlike diffidence, which made him shrink from public diplays. He developed his views with clearness, and an invariable regard to their logical sequence; but he did not press them home by energy of manner, or any of the ardors of eloquence.

His mind was rather judicial than forensic in its cast. He was better able to discern the right than to make the wrong appear the better reason. He was not a legal athlete, snuffing new vigor in the hoarse strifes of the bar, and regarding success alone; but a faithful counsellor, solicitous for his client, and for justice too.

It was this character that led him to contemplate the law as a science, and to study its improvement and elevation. He could not look upon it merely as the means of earning money. He gave much of his time to its generous culture. From the walks of practice, he ascended to the heights of jurisprudence, embracing within his observation the systems of other countries. His contributions to this department illustrate the spirit and extent of his inquiries. It was his hope to accomplish some careful work on the law, more elaborate than the memorials he has left. The subject of the *Practice and Procedure of Courts,* or what is called by the civilians *Stylus Curiæ*, had occupied his mind, and he had intended to treat it in the light of the foreign authorities, particularly the German and French, with the view of determining the general principles or natural law, common to all systems, by which it is governed. Such a work, executed in the fine, juridical spirit in which it was conceived, would have been welcomed wherever the law is studied as a science.

It is, then, not only as a lawyer, practising in Courts, but as a jurist, to whom the light of jurisprudence shone gladsome, that we are to esteem our departed friend. As such, his example will command attention, and exert an influence, long after the paper dockets, in blue covers, chronicling the stages of litigation in his cases, shall be consigned to the oblivion of dark closets, and cobwebbed pigeon-holes.

But he has left a place vacant, not only in the halls of jurisprudence, but also in the circle of scholars throughout the world, and it may be said, in the Pantheon of universal learning. In contemplating the variety, the universality, of his attainments, the mind involuntarily exclaims, "The admirable Pickering!" He seems, indeed, to have run the whole round of knowledge. His studies in ancient learning had been profound; nor can we sufficiently admire the facility with which, amidst other cares, he assumed the task of lexicographer. Unless some memorandum should be found among his papers, as was the case with Sir William Jones,* specifying the languages to which he had been devoted, it may be difficult to frame a list with entire accuracy. It is certain that he was familiar with at least *nine*, — the English, French, Portuguese, Italian, Spanish, German, Romaic, Greek, and Latin; of these he spoke the first five. He was less familiar, though well acquainted, with the Dutch, Swedish, Danish, and Hebrew; and had explored, with various degrees of care, the Arabic, Turkish, Syriac, Persian, Coptic, Sanscrit, Chinese, Cochin-Chinese, Russian, Egyptian hieroglyphics, the Maylay in several dialects, and particularly the Indian languages of America and of the Polynesian Islands.

The sarcasm of Hudibras on the "barren ground," supposed to be congenial to "Hebrew roots," is refuted by the richness of his accomplishments. His style is that of a scholar and man of taste. It is simple, unpretending, like its author, clear, accurate, and flows in an even tenor of elegance, which rises at times to a suavity, almost Xenophontean. Though little adorned

---

* Sir William Jones had studied eight languages, critically,— English, Latin, French, Italian, Greek, Arabic, Persian, Sanscrit; eight others less perfectly, but all intelligible, with a dictionary, — Spanish, Portuguese, German. Runic, Hebrew, Bengali, Hindi, Turkish; twelve studied less perfectly, but all attainable, — Tibetian, Pali, Phalari, Deri, Russian, Syriac, Æthiopic, Coptic, Welsh, Swedish, Dutch, Chinese; in all twenty-eight languages. — *Teignmouth's Life of Jones.*

by flowers of rhetoric, it shows the sensibility and refinement of an ear attuned to the harmonies of language. He had cultivated music as a science, and in his younger days performed on the flute with Grecian fondness. Some of the airs, which he had learned in Portugal, were sung to him by his daughter, shortly before his death, bringing with them, doubtless, the pleasant memories of early travel, and the "incense-breathing morn" of life. A lover of music, he was naturally fond of the other fine arts, but always had particular happiness in works of sculpture.

Nor were those other studies, which are sometimes regarded as of a more practical character, alien to his mind. In college days he was noticed for his attainments in mathematics; and later in life, he perused with intelligent care the great work of his friend, Dr. Bowditch, the translation of the *Mécanique Céleste.* He was chairman of the committee which recommended the purchase of a telescope of the first class, to be used in the neighborhood of Boston, and was the author of their interesting report on the uses and importance of such an instrument. He was fond of natural history, particularly of botany, which he himself taught to some of his family. In addition to all this, he possessed a natural aptitude for the mechanic arts, which was improved by observation and care. Early in life he learned to use the turning lathe, and, as he declared, in an unpublished lecture before the Mechanics' Institute of Boston, *made toys and playthings which he bartered among his schoolmates.*

The latter circumstance gives singular point to the parallel, already striking in other respects, between him and the Greek orator, the boast of whose various knowledge is preserved by Cicero. "Nihil esse ulla in arte rerum omnium, quod ipse nesciret; nec solum has artes, quibus liberales doctrinæ atque ingenuæ continerentur, geometriam, musicam, literarum cognitionem, et poetarum, atque illa quæ de naturis rerum, quæ de hominum moribus, quæ de rebuspublicis dicerentur; *sed annulum, quem haberet, se sua manu confecisse.*" *

It is, however, as the friend of classical studies, and as a student of language, or philologist, that he is entitled to be specially remembered. It is impossible to measure the influence which he has exerted upon the scholarship of the country. His writings and his example, from early youth, have pleaded its cause, and will plead it yet, now that his living voice is hushed in the grave. His genius for languages was profound. He saw, with intuitive perception, their structure and affinities, and delighted in the detection of their hidden resemblances and relations. To their history and character he devoted his attention, more than to their literature. It would not be possible for our humble pen to attempt to determine the place which will be allotted to him in the science of philology; but the writer cannot forbear recording the authoritative testimony, which it was his fortune to hear, from the lips of Alexander von Humboldt, to the rare merits of Mr. Pickering in this department. With the brother, William von Humboldt, that great light of modern philology, he maintained a long correspondence, particularly on the Indian languages; and the letters of our countryman will be

* De Oratore, Lib. III. § 32.

found preserved in the royal library at Berlin. Without rashly undertaking, then, to indicate any scale of preëminence or precedence among the cultivators of this department, at home or abroad, it may not be improper to refer to his labors, as evidence in the words of Dr. Johnson, with regard to his own,* "that we may now no longer yield the palm of philology, without a contest, to the nations of the continent."

If it should be asked, by what magic Mr. Pickering was able to accomplish these remarkable results, it must be answered, by the careful husbandry of time. His talisman was industry. He was pleased in referring to those rude inhabitants of Tartary who placed idleness among the torments of the world to come, and often remembered the beautiful proverb in his Oriental studies, that by labor the leaf of the mulberry tree is turned into silk. His life is a perpetual commentary on those words of untranslatable beauty in the great Italian poet: †

——— seggendo in piuma
In fama non si vien, nè sotto coltre:
Sanza la qual, chi sua vita consuma
Cotal vestigio in terra di se lascia,
Qual fumo in aere od in acqua la schiuma.

With a mind, thus deeply imbued with learning, it will be felt that he was formed less for the contentions of the forum than the delights of the academy. And yet, it is understood that he declined several opportunities, which were afforded him, of entering its learned retreats. In 1806, he was elected Hancock Professor

* Preface to Dictionary.
† Dante, Inferno, Canto 25.

of Hebrew, and other Oriental languages, in Harvard University; and, at a later day, he was invited to the chair of Greek literature, in the same place. On the death of Professor Ashmun, many eyes were turned towards him, as a proper person to occupy the professorship of law in Cambridge, since so ably filled by Mr. Greenleaf; and on two different occasions, his name was echoed by the public prints as about to receive the dignity of President of the University. But he continued, as we have seen, in the practice of the law to the last.

He should be claimed by the bar with peculiar pride. If it be true, as has been said, that Sergeant Talfourd has reflected more honor upon his profession, by the successful cultivation of letters, than any of his contemporaries by their forensic triumphs, then should the American bar acknowledge their obligations to the fame of Mr. Pickering. He was one of us. He was a *regular* in our ranks; in other services, only a *volunteer*.

The mind is led, instinctively, to a parallel between him and that illustrious scholar and jurist, one of the ornaments of the English law, and the pioneer of Oriental studies in England, Sir William Jones. Both confessed, in early life, the attractions of classical studies; both were trained in the discipline of the law; both, though engaged in its practice, always delighted to contemplate it as a science; both surrendered themselves, with irrepressible ardor, to the study of languages, while the one broke into the unexplored fields of Eastern philology, and the other devoted himself more especially to the native tongues of his own Western continent. Their names are, perhaps, equally conspicuous for the number of languages which had occupied their attention. As we approach them in private life, the parallel still continues. In both there were the same truth, generosity and gentleness, a cluster of noble virtues; while the greater earnestness of the one, is compensated by the intenser modesty of the other. To our American jurist-scholar, also, may be applied those words of the Greek couplet, borrowed from Aristophanes, and first appropriated to his English prototype: "The Graces, seeking a shrine that would not decay, found the soul of Jones."

While dwelling with admiration upon his triumphs of intellect, and the fame he has won, let us not forget the virtues, higher than intellect or fame, by which his life was adorned. In the jurist and the scholar let us not lose sight of the *man*. So far as is allotted to a mortal to be, he was a spotless character. The rude tides of this world seemed to flow by without soiling his garments. He was pure in thought, word and deed. He was a lover of truth, goodness and humanity. He was the friend of the young, encouraging them in their studies, and aiding them by his wise counsels. He was ever kind, considerate and gentle to all; towards children, and the unfortunate, full of tenderness. He was of modesty "all compact." With learning to which all bowed with reverence, he walked humbly alike before God and man. His pleasures were simple. In the retirement of his study, and in the blandishments of his music-loving family, he found rest from the fatigues of the bar. He never spoke in anger, nor did any hate find a seat in his bosom. His placid life was, like law, in the definition of Aristotle, " Mind without passion."

Through his long career, extending to the extreme limit of that length of days which is allotted to man, he was blessed with unbroken health. He walked on earth with an unailing body and a serene mind. And at last, in the fullness of time, when the garner was overflowing with the golden harvests of a well-spent life, in the bosom of his family, the silver cord was gently loosened. He died at Boston, May 5th, 1846, in the seventieth year of his age, — only a few days after he had prepared for the press the last sheets of a third and enlarged edition of his Greek Lexicon. His wife, to whom he was married in 1805, and three children, survive to mourn their irreparable loss, and to rejoice in his good name on earth, and his immortality in heaven.

The number of societies, both at home and abroad, of which he was an honored member, attest the wide-spread recognition of his merits. He was President of the American Academy of Arts and Sciences; President of the American Oriental Society; Foreign Secretary of the American Antiquarian Society; Fellow of the Massachusetts Historical Society; of the American Ethnological Society; of the American Philosophical Society; Honorary Member of the Historical Societies of New Hampshire, of New York, of Pennsylvania, of Rhode Island, of Michigan, of Maryland, of Georgia; of the National Institution for the Promotion of Science; of the American Statistical Association; of the Northern Academy of Arts and Sciences, Hanover, N. H.; of the Society for the Promotion of Legal Knowledge,

Philadelphia; Corresponding member of the Royal Academy of Sciences at Berlin; of the Oriental Society of Paris; of the Academy of Sciences and Letters at Palermo; of the Antiquarian Society at Athens; of the Royal Northern Antiquarian Society at Copenhagen; and Titular Member of the French Society of Universal Statistics.

For many years he maintained a copious correspondence, on matters of jurisprudence, science and learning, with distinguished names at home and abroad; especially, with Mr. Duponceau, at Philadelphia; with William von Humboldt, at Berlin; with Mittermaier, the jurist, at Heidelberg; with Dr. Pritchard, author of the Physical History of Mankind, at Bristol; and with Lepsius, the hierologist, who wrote to him from the foot of the pyramids in Egypt.

The death of one, thus variously connected, is no common sorrow. Beyond the immediate circle of family and friends, he will be mourned by the bar, amongst whom his daily life was passed; by the municipality of Boston, whose legal adviser he was; by clients, who depended upon his counsels; by all good citizens, who were charmed by the abounding virtues of his private life; by his country, who will cherish his name more than gold or silver; by the distant islands of the Pacific, who will bless his labors in every written word that they read; finally, by the company of jurists and scholars throughout the world. His fame and his works will be fitly commemorated, on formal occasions, hereafter. Meanwhile, one who knew him at the bar and in private life, and who loves his memory, lays this early tribute upon his grave.

HON. HENRY WHEATON.

[FROM THE BOSTON DAILY ADVERTISER, MARCH 16, 1848.]

THE death of a person like Mr. Wheaton naturally arrests the attention, — even at this period of funereal gloom, when the Angel of Death seems to have overshadowed the whole country with his wings. He was long and widely known in various official relations; devoted for many years to the service of his country; studious always of literature and jurisprudence; illustrious as a diplomatist and expounder of the Law of Nations; with a private character so pure as to incline us to forget, in its contemplation, the public virtues by which his life was filled.

He died after a brief illness, accompanied by a disease of the brain, on Saturday evening, March 11th, 1848, at Dorchester. On that day the remains of John Quincy Adams, who, as President of the United States, had first advanced Mr. Wheaton to a diplomatic place in the service of his country — after a long procession through mourning towns and cities from the capitol which had been the scene of his triumphant death —

were laid in their final resting-place in the adjoining town of Quincy. The faithful friend and servant has thus early followed his venerable chief to the fellowship of another world.

The principal circumstances in Mr. Wheaton's life may be briefly told. He was born at Providence on the 27th November, 1785. He was a graduate of Brown University, in that place, in 1802. After his admission to the bar, he visited Europe, particularly the Continent, where his mind thus early became imbued with those tastes which occupied so much of his later years. Some time after his return — finding little inducement to continue the practice of the law at Providence — he removed to New York. This was in 1812. Here he became the editor of an important journal, the *National Advocate* — a paper which, it is believed, was afterwards merged in *The Courier and Inquirer*. His experience in this character closed May 15th, 1815. As a journalist, he is reputed to have been uniformly discreet, decorous and able, at a time when the fearful trials of war, in which the country was engaged, added to the responsibilities of his position.

But his labors as editor did not estrange him from the law. It was about this period that he became for a short time one of the Justices of the Marine Court, a tribunal which is said now to be shorn of something of its early dignity. In 1815, he appeared as an author of a Treatise on Jurisprudence. This was a *Digest of the Law of Maritime Captures and Prizes.* In the judicial inquiries incident to the administration of the *laws of war* — still maintained by the Christian world — such a treatise was naturally of much practical utility. It may also claim the palm of being among the earliest juridical productions of our country. Nor, indeed, has it been without the disinterested praise of foreign nations. Mr. Reddie, of Edinburgh, in his recent work on Maritime International Law, says, "That although it cannot be strictly called a valuable accession to the legal literature of *Britain*, it gives us much pleasure to record our opinion, that, in point of learning and methodical arrangement, it is very superior to any treatise on this department of the law which had previously appeared in the English language." No American contribution to jurisprudence so early as 1815 has received such marked commendation abroad. Kent and Story had not then produced those works which have secured to them their present freehold of European fame.

In 1816 he became the Reporter of the Decisions of the Supreme Court of the United States, which office he held till 1827. His Reports are in twelve volumes, and embody what may be called the *golden judgments* of our National Judicature, from the lips of Marshall, Livingston, Washington, Thompson, and Story.

It appears, however, that Mr. Wheaton's time was not absorbed by these official duties to the exclusion of other labors. He entered much into the practice of his profession. His name appears as counsel in important causes heard at Washington. He was the editor of divers English law books, republished in our country with valuable notes. On several literary occasions he pronounced discourses of signal merit. One of these, in 1820, before the Historical Society of New York, touches upon his favorite theme, — with which his name is now so firmly connected, — the Law of Nations; another in 1824, at the opening of the New York Athenæum, takes a rapid survey of American literature. In 1826, he published his Life of that great lawyer, William Pinkney. It is also understood, that, during all this period, he was a frequent contributor to the North American Review.

Nor did these accumulated literary and juridical labors detain him from yet other services. He was a member of the Legislature of New York; and in 1821 held a seat in the Convention, which remodeled the Constitution of that State. In 1825, he was placed on the commission for revising the statutes of New York. It will be remembered, that this was the first effort by any State professing the common law, to reduce its disconnected and diffusive legislation to the unity of a code. It is thus that Mr. Wheaton's name is connected with one of the most important landmarks in the history of American law.

All these duties and callings he relinquished in the summer of 1827, when he entered upon the diplomatic service, which then opened before him a new career of usefulness. It was then that he was made *Chargé d'Affaires* at Copenhagen, where he continued till 1834, when he was transferred by President Jackson to Berlin, as Minister Resident. In 1837, he was raised by President Van Buren to the rank of Minister Plenipotentiary and Envoy Extraordinary at the same court. On 22d July, 1846, he had his audience of farewell from the King of Prussia, having been recalled by President Polk. This long period of service was passed abroad with the intermission of a brief passage of time in 1834, when he revisited his country on leave of absence.

During this protracted career in foreign countries, charged with responsible negotiations, he was not lost in the toils of office, or in the allurements of courtly life. He was always a student. At Copenhagen he prepared his *History of the Northmen*, or Danes and Normans, from the earliest times to the Conquest of England by William of Normandy. This was published in 1831, both in London and in our country. In 1836, it was much enlarged, and translated into French. At the time of his death he was occupied in preparing another edition for the press in our country. In 1838, he contributed to the Edinburgh Cabinet Library a portion of the volumes entitled *Scandinavia*. By these works he has earned a place among the historical writers of the country. It will be observed that his History of the Northmen preceded, in time, the productions of Bancroft and Prescott, which have since achieved so much renown.

From literature he passed again to jurisprudence, where he has won his surest triumphs. His *Elements of International Law* appeared in London and the United States in 1836; and again in 1846, much enlarged. This was followed by a *History of the Law of Nations in Europe and America, from the Earliest Times to the Treaty of Washington*, which first appeared in French, at Leipzig, in 1844, under the title of *Histoire des Progrès du Droit des Gens en Europe depuis la Paix de Westphalie jusqu'au Congrès de Vienne, avec un précis historique du Droit des Gens Européen avant la Paix de Westphalie*. This was originally written for a prize offered by the French Institute. Though it received what was called "*mention honorable*," it failed to obtain the prize, which was awarded to a young Frenchman, whose production, as I have been informed, has never been published. It is possible that the constraint of a foreign language, in which Mr. Wheaton wrote, may have so far influenced his style as to place his work at a disadvantage before the polished French tribunal. But an enlightened public opinion has already awarded to it the crown of merit. It has been much enlarged by the author, and published in the English language in an octavo volume of eight hundred pages.

Besides these classical treatises, Mr. Wheaton published an able and thorough Inquiry into the Validity of the Right of Visitation and Search, particularly as recently claimed by Great Britain. On this occasion he upheld the views which had been put forth by the American Government. The acknowledged weight of his opinion in the science of law gave to his conclusions a commanding influence.

On his recent return to his country he was welcomed by many manifestations of regard, both public and private, in the principal places which he visited. Wherever he appeared, he was a favored guest. At the last Commencement of Brown University, he delivered the Address before the Phi Beta Kappa Society. His subject was "Germany." The various departments of thought and conduct, which have been successfully occupied by the "many-sided" mind of this country, were sketched with singular ability. His voice was feeble; and, as he spoke, large numbers of the audience drew near to the pulpit, filling the neighboring aisles, and standing in respectful attention, that they might better catch his learned discourse.

Such were the important and diversified labors of Mr. Wheaton's valuable life. Without any of the adventitious aids of fortune, or of special favor, he achieved an eminent place before the civilized world. By virtue of his office, he lived as an equal among nobles and princes, while his rare endowments opened to him, at will, the fraternities of learning and science. And yet his qualities were not those of the courtier. Nor did any heaven-descended eloquence lend its fire to his conversation or his style. Both were simple, grave, reserved, like his manners, attractive rather from their clearness and matter, than their brilliancy or point.

His career as a *Diplomatist* abroad has been one of the longest in our history — longer even than that of Mr. Adams. It was not his fortune to affix his name to any treaty, like that of 1783, which acknowledged our Independence, or that of Ghent in 1815, which restored peace to England and the United States. But his extended term of service was filled by a succession of wise and faithful labors, which have rendered incalculable good to his own country, while they have impressed his character upon the public mind of Europe. His negotiation with Denmark was important. His careful management of the interests of our country, in connection with the German Zoll Verein, was more important still. But besides these conspicuous acts, with which all are familiar, there is his long and constant correspondence with the Department of State at Washington, the true character of which is, probably, known to comparatively few.

It was his habit, contrary to the usage of many Ministers of the United States abroad, by regular authentic communications, to keep our Government at home apprised of the true posture of foreign affairs, as observed by him. It is believed, that all the matters which prominently occupied the Continental nations during his residence abroad — particularly those two disputes, sometimes known as the *Belgian question*, and the *Egyptian question*, which seemed for a while to fill with "portents dire," the firmament of Europe — were discussed in these dispatches with instructive fullness. These may be found in the archives of his legation, and in the Department of State at Washington — "enrolled in the Capitol," — where they will doubtless be studied by the future historian.

His familiarity with the Law of Nations, derived from his position as a Diplomatist, was enhanced by his mature and thorough study of it as a science. For this he had been prepared by his training at the bar, the influence of which may be discerned in some of his discussions. He was master alike of its learning and its dialectics. It happened to him in Berlin to be called to defend the rights of ambassadors against an injurious usage established or recognized by the Prussian Government. His paper on this occasion, I believe, is still unpublished. All who have read it will attest the force and the sharpness of his unanswered argument. Strange that this task should have devolved upon an American Minister! Strange that the privileges of ambassadors should have found their defender in a Cis-Atlantic citizen! His defence drew the regard of the diplomatic body of Europe. Copies of it were transmitted to the different courts, where it was, as I have understood, discussed, and generally if not universally sanctioned.

Justly eminent as a practical diplomatist, his works derived new value from the high place of their author, while even his official position was aided by his works. His was a solitary example in our age — perhaps the only instance since Grotius — of an eminent minister, who was also an expounder of the science of the Law of Nations. His works, therefore, have been received with peculiar respect. They may be said already to have become *authorities*. Such they seem to be regarded by the two British writers on this subject, who have since appeared, Mr. Manning and Mr. Reddie. The former, in his interesting Commentaries, says, "Dr. Wheaton's work is the best elementary treatise on the Law of Nations that has appeared; " while Mr. Reddie declares, in his Treatise on Maritime International Law, that "This work, although not by a British author, was certainly, at the date of its publication, the most able and scientific Treatise on International Law, which had appeared in the English language." It is admitted that the arrangement is superior to that of Martens, Chitty, Schmalz, or Kluber.

It cannot be disguised, however, that both of his works, in this department, are remarkable rather for their careful statement and arrangement of the subject, than for that elegance, or glow, or freedom of discussion, by which the reader is carried captive. It will not be questioned that his *Elements* afford the best view, which has yet been presented, of the Law of Nations, as practically illustrated in the adjudged cases of England and the United States, and in recent diplomacy. But we miss in them the fullness and variety of illustration which characterize some of the earlier writers, and especially that genial sentiment which interests us so warmly in Vattel. The *History*, which first appeared in *French*, is not less important than the *Elements*. Here the field is more clearly his own. This work supplies a place never before filled in the literature of the English language, if it had been in that of any language. To all students of jurisprudence, — nay more, to all students of history, who ascend above the descriptions of wars and battles, to the grand principles, which in a certain sense are at once the parents and the offspring of events — this view of the Progress of the Law of Nations will be an important guide.

Had Mr. Wheaton's life been longer spared, he would have found it his province, in the discharge of his recently assumed office as Lecturer on the Civil [Roman] and International Law at Harvard University, to survey again the wide field of the Law of Nations. What further harvests he might then have gathered, it is impossible now to estimate. He never entered upon these labors. The reaper was removed, before he began to use his sickle.

Such was his life, — passed not without well deserved honor at home and abroad. In those two great departments of labor, history, and the Law of Nations, he is among the American pioneers. Through him, the literature and jurisprudence of our country have been commended in foreign lands;

Fluminaque in fontes cursu reditura supino.

Others may have done better in the high art of history; but no American historian has, like him, achieved European eminence as a writer on the Law of Nations; nor has any other American writer on the last great theme been recognized abroad as an historian. He was a member of the Institute of France; and I cannot forget, that, at the time of his admission, the question — so honorable to the double fame of Mr. Wheaton — was entertained, by the late Baron Degerando, the jurist and philanthropist, whether he should more properly be received into the section of History or of Jurisprudence. To the latter he was finally attached. Prescott and Bancroft belong to the former.

It is, however, as an expounder of the *Public* International Law that his name will be most widely cherished. In the progress of Christian civilization, many of the rules, now sustained by learned subtlety or unquestioning submission — shaping the public relations of States — may pass away. The Institution of War, with its complex code, now sanctioned and legalized by nations, as a proper mode of adjusting their disputes, may yield to some less questionable Arbitrament. But a profound interest will always attach to the writings of those great masters who have striven to explain, to advance, and to refine that system, which, though incomplete, has helped to constrain in the bonds of Peace the wide Christian Commonwealth. Among these, Mr. Wheaton's place is conspicuous. His name is already inscribed on the same table with that of Grotius, Puffendorf, and Vattel.

It were wrong to close this imperfect tribute, without a renewed testimony to the purity of his life. From youth to age his career was marked by integrity, temperance, frugality, modesty, industry. His quiet unostentatious manners were the fit companions of his virtues. His countenance, which is admirably preserved in the portrait by Healy, wore the expression of thoughtfulness and repose. Nor station, nor fame made him proud. He stood with serene simplicity in the presence of kings. In the social circle, when he spoke, all drew near to listen — sure that, what he said would be wise, tolerant, and kind.

END OF VOLUME II.

www.ingramcontent.com/pod-product-compliance
Lightning Source LLC
LaVergne TN
LVHW020918110826
845150LV00004B/708

* 9 7 8 1 4 2 5 5 5 5 0 1 6 *